JOURNEYS OF EM
THE INTERSECTION OF BODY AND CULTURE

Editorial Advisors

JOURNEYS OF EMBODIMENT AT THE INTERSECTION OF BODY AND CULTURE

THE DEVELOPMENTAL THEORY OF EMBODIMENT

NIVA PIRAN
University of Toronto, Toronto, ON, Canada

ELSEVIER

ACADEMIC PRESS
An imprint of Elsevier

Academic Press is an imprint of Elsevier
125 London Wall, London EC2Y 5AS, United Kingdom
525 B Street, Suite 1800, San Diego, CA 92101-4495, United States
50 Hampshire Street, 5th Floor, Cambridge, MA 02139, United States
The Boulevard, Langford Lane, Kidlington, Oxford OX5 1GB, United Kingdom

Library of Congress Cataloging-in-Publication Data
A catalog record for this book is available from the Library of Congress

British Library Cataloguing-in-Publication Data
A catalogue record for this book is available from the British Library

ISBN: 978-0-12-805410-9

Publisher: Nikki Levy
Acquisition Editor: Emily Ekle
Editorial Project Manager: Barbara Makinster
Production Project Manager: Kiruthika Govindaraju
Cover Designer: Mark Rogers

Typeset by TNQ Books and Journals

For Adam and Andre—my inspiration
For Yuval—my twin soul

Contents

Acknowledgments

The women who participated in the embodiment research program described two key motivations for partaking in it: seeking a greater understanding of challenges they have faced in inhabiting their bodies and wishing to contribute to the well-being of others. Participants' interests coalesced with the quests of the research team and program. The research team and I would like to express our wholehearted thanks to all participants in the research program, from 9-year-old girls all the way to 70-year-old women. We have been enriched by their thoughtful reflections about experiences of joy and pain and touched by their generosity of sharing and wanting to help others.

I want to thank research team members; altogether, over a span of 20 years, more than 30 individuals from a multiplicity of backgrounds contributed creatively to the research studies, mostly while pursuing doctoral studies in clinical and counseling psychology. We spent countless hours together in groups, dialoguing about experiences of embodiment and the social environment; each team member contributed to the knowledge shared in this book.

Wendy Carter, Fiona Downie, Robyn Legge, Nina Mafrici, Parnian Pajouhandeh, and Sarah Thompson were the interviewers in the three qualitative studies. Words cannot describe their care and immersion while conducting these interviews. Further, at different times, Robyn Legge, Sachiko Nagasawa, Nina Mafrici, and Lianne Trachtenberg coordinated different research projects. These projects could not have proceeded without their able and dedicated input.

The Developmental Theory of Embodiment emerged over 20 years of ongoing qualitative and quantitative studies. I gratefully acknowledge the support of this research program by the Social Sciences and Humanities Research Council of Canada.

The idea of writing the book ripened, as our ongoing research studies provided further validation of the theory. Presentations of findings in different forums around the globe reflected its relevance to practice, from policy development to health promotion, therapy, and education. The rich interview data not only informed theory development but also provided a wealth of information about the embodied journeys of girls and women across time. Interviews with adult women followed a life history perspective, and the prospective interviews with girls provided a rich description of changes during a 5-year period. The book, then, could provide, in addition to a theoretical understanding of the social factors that shape embodiment, a rich description of the form the different theoretical constructs take during different phases in girls' and women's lives. Through that, processes of socialization into inequity, as well as liberating processes, could be understood.

Toward this goal, I invited Robyn Legge, Sachiko Nagasawa, Tanya Teall, and Sarah Thompson to join me in conducting an initial age-specific analysis of the theoretical constructs. This analysis, focusing mainly on the younger ages, clarified the richness inherent in examining age-related changes on the key constructs of the Developmental Theory of Embodiment and cemented the organization of the book according to participants' age groupings. For their outstanding contributions through this endeavor, Robyn Legge, Sachiko Nagasawa, Tanya Teall, and Sarah Thompson are recognized as Editorial Advisors to this volume.

Special thanks to chapters' readers: Steven Garber, Robyn Legge, Judy Schapira, Judy Silver, Robin Silverstein, and Andrew Wilmot.

I feel so fortunate to have had the opportunity to be inspired by the work of many scholars around the world, more than I could name in this section. Ongoing exchanges with colleagues have informed and enriched the work presented in the book. I am looking forward to continued collaborations.

I am thankful to Emily Ekle, Senior Acquisition Editor, for her support throughout and to Barbara Makinster for the prompt production of the book, both of Elsevier Press.

My family is spread around the world. I am thankful to members of my family for many good experiences that have stayed with me and given me strength.

I have found that, to write a complete volume, especially while holding a faculty position, required intense immersion and dedication. I am grateful to Runi Børresen, Ann Frisén, Dianne Neumark-Sztainer, and Susan Paxton for their invaluable support. From the inception of this book project, I have felt embraced by a circle of close family and friends whose constant encouragement charged me again and again with the inspiration to complete the project. I am indebted to Adam, Andre, and Steven Garber; Laurel Currie, Oscar and Gabriel Currie Toledo, and Riccardo Toledo; Leslie Mendelson and Bruce Kelleher; Hayley and Susan Rosenbaum; Judy Schapira; Robin Silverstein; Judy Silver; Tehila Jouchovitzky; Margaret and Patrick Ghielmetti; and Susan Paul. Your love and belief in my work kept me going! Thank you!

Ultimately, this work has been nurtured and informed by many: participants, researchers, colleagues, friends, and family, and for all that—I am grateful.

Introduction

BODIES IN DISTRESS

Scholars and practitioners, as well as women and girls of diverse social locations, identify the meeting place of body and culture as a problematic intersection. Studies repeatedly indicate that a majority of girls, age 14 years and above, live with normative discontent regarding their appearance—a number far greater than boys and men (Tiggemann, 2004). Further, this negative body esteem among girls and women is linked to instances of dieting, eating disorders, depression, and social and sexual difficulties (Piran, McVey, & Levine, 2014; Stice, Marti, & Durant, 2011). In turn, disordered eating patterns are associated with the consumption of licit and illicit substances (Piran & Gadalla, 2007). In terms of prevalence, it is estimated that the spectrum of disordered eating behaviors affects approximately 9%–13% of adolescent girls, suggesting around 1.9–2.7 million affected individuals in the United States within any given year (Piran et al., 2014), although the percentage of girls and women who struggle with negative body esteem is actually as high as 70% (Cain, Epler, Steinley, & Sher, 2010). Rates of disordered eating patterns in multiple countries around the globe currently undergoing westernization and modernization are similar to those found in North America. Researchers also highlight other indicators of distress in the body domain, including girls' involvement in sexual activities without desire or protection (Tolman, 2002) and young women's higher rates of engagement in self-injurious behaviors (Whitlock, Eckenrode, & Silverman, 2006) and plastic surgeries (Swami et al., 2008). Therefore, practitioners are often called to address a range of disruptions in the body domain, either through therapy or prevention interventions.

Studying "feminine embodiment" holds a mirror to culture: "the disciplinary power that inscribes femininity in the female body is everywhere and it is nowhere; the disciplinarian is everyone and yet it is no one in particular" (Bartky, 1988, p. 74). In this, Bartky and other feminist scholars highlight the inextricable relationship between social structures of power and privilege and how diverse girls and women live in their bodies; yet, the study of this "disciplinary power" that shapes women's embodied lives has to also consider the varied inscriptions made on women inhabiting diverse bodies at the intersections of social class, race, ethnicity and immigration, sexual orientation, weight, health and physical ability, and age, as well as recognizing women's agency in response to cultural pressures.

A study of the social forces that discipline the bodies of diverse girls and women is particularly current, as a poignant gap exists between prevalent ideologies of equity and the embodied lives of diverse girls and women. For example, while greater opportunities now exist for women's participation in the public sphere, consistent messages transmitted through various outlets (e.g., film, television, etc.) and social media technologies continue to emphasize the *shrinking* of women's bodies. Similarly, rates of violence against women in North America have not decreased during the past decade, greater barriers are being erected in the United States restricting access to reproductive health services, and in Canada, for example, the gender gap in salaries has actually widened over the past few years. Stressing the gap between strived-for ideals and the quality of embodied lives, Susan Bordo (1989) emphasizes that, "[I]n such an era we desperately need an effective political discourse about the female body, a discourse adequate to an analysis of the insidious, and often paradoxical, pathways of modern social control" (pp. 14–15). A research agenda aimed at studying "insidious" social processes that produce "docile" bodies can therefore contribute to feminist theory, activism, and the well-being of girls and women.

This book, in particular, addresses a series of questions faced by both scholars and practitioners that have not yet been answered by research: What construct can capture the multidimensional quality of embodied life, beyond the singular focus on appearance satisfaction? Can such a construct cover the broad spectrum of experiences, from positive to negative embodiment, and be applied to both girls and women? Can the broad range of social experiences be organized along a few key dimensions illuminating the disciplining of diverse bodies into docile bodies and, through that, socialize girls and women into inequity? Can these key dimensions capture both stories of disruption and healing?

HOLDING A MIRROR TO CULTURE

Journeys of Embodiment at the Intersection of Body and Culture aims to share with practitioners and scholars an innovative, research-based developmental and feminist theory, referred to as the Developmental Theory of Embodiment (DTE). The DTE provides a new perspective on the interactions between the social environments of preadolescent and adolescent girls, younger and older women of different social locations, and their embodied experiences of engagement with the world around them. The DTE builds on the emergent constructs of Experience of Embodiment and the Body Journey, and the key social experiences that shape embodiment throughout an individual's development—from agency, functionality, and passion during early childhood, to restriction, shame, and varied expressions of self-harm in puberty, and to the challenge of recapturing agency throughout adulthood. By addressing not only adverse experiences at the aforementioned intersections but also resilience and facilitative social factors, the DTE outlines constructive pathways toward transformation.

The DTE is anchored in the live experiences of girls and women, including 171 interviews: 87 with girls, ages 9–17 years, and 84 with women, ages 20–70 years. In addition, the DTE is also informed by 116 focus groups with schoolgirls and quantitative surveys with women. The narratives of these girls and women, with respect to their embodied lives and the myriad social factors that shape them, enrich *Journeys of Embodiment at the Intersection of Body and Culture,* providing us with an opportunity to hold a magnifying glass to the shaping of girls and women's body journeys from early childhood through their tweens, and early and late adolescence—a time of intense transitions during which docile, corseted bodies are produced. In similar fashion, following the body journeys of adult women reveals the processes in which some women engage to recapture positive body connection and comfort, embodied agency and passion, and attuned self-care.

This book is organized with the aim of acquainting readers with the theoretical constructs of the DTE and their expressions during the different life stages of girls and women—simultaneously anchoring these expressions in the narratives of research participants. This affords readers the opportunity to examine the intersection of body and culture as a lifelong journey while also focusing on particular stages along the way.

The first chapter, entitled "The Developmental Theory of Embodiment: Discovering Paths in Girls and Women's Uncharted Body Journeys," introduces key constructs of the DTE, anchoring them in the life stories of two young women. It explores the multidimensional Experience of Embodiment construct, which reflects the quality of embodied lives by addressing body connection, agency, desire, attuned self-care, and objectification, before going on to describe the three domains of social experiences that shape the quality of embodied lives: the *physical* domain, covering a myriad of physical experiences; the *mental* domain of social discourses and expectations; and the *social power and relational connections* domain, addressing body-related experiences of equity and disenfranchisement. The DTE contends that both protective and risk factors are organized along these three pathways, with the positive and negative aspects being conceptualized as Physical Freedom (vs. Corseting), Mental Freedom (vs. Corseting), and Social Power (vs. Disempowerment and Disconnection).

The second chapter, "Qualified Freedom on Borrowed Territory," addresses the period of early childhood to age eight. During this time, not only are valued experiences of equity possible but also boy–girl boundaries are relatively permeable in terms of permitting "masculine" activities associated with embodied joy and agency. Girls' narratives from this age range, more than at any other phase, reveal experiences of embodied power and agency when engaging with the world in both the private and public spheres.

The third chapter, "Intense Transitions," describes the changes to girls' social environments as they go through puberty, with initial glimpses into the experience of inhabiting a woman's body. At the intersection of physical constraints and lack of safety, discourses of objectification and deficiency, exposure to prejudicial treatment, and subversion of social power to the embodiment of idealized perfection, tween girls experience their maturing bodies not as sites of comfort, worth, and agency but as sites of vulnerability and restraint.

The fourth chapter, "The Practice of Corseting," addresses the experiences of early adolescents, ages 13–14 years. As expressions of gender inequity deepen during early adolescence, so too do expressions of gender oppression, intersecting with other aspects of social location such as social class, ethnic heritage, and sexual orientation. Furthermore, girls at this age face growing physical restrictions and constraining molds of femininity while simultaneously experiencing rifts in their peer communities. As such, resistant voices are increasingly rare and often subject to magnified social pressures and penalties.

The fifth chapter, "The 'Perfection' of Corseting," examines the experiences of late adolescents, ages 15–18 years, outlining the consolidation of their experiences inhabiting young women's bodies through the "perfection" of corseting and further disruptions to embodied agency. The relative lack of resistance and protest over personal losses at this age reflects not only the feared social costs of noncompliance but also the internalization of social rules related to gender and other systems of privilege. Places of strength and resilience are also highlighted, which in turn can guide constructive transformations in the embodied lives of late-adolescent girls.

The sixth chapter, "Recapturing Qualified Freedom," addresses younger to older adulthood. The diversity of body journeys is addressed in this chapter, as is the intensive engagement of adult women in reconnecting with their bodies, leading to an expansion in the range of embodied experiences most similar to what is seen during the tween period. Processes conducive to obtaining greater freedoms are shown to be complex and involve the interaction of women's agency and critical reflections with alternative social experiences, social structures, and relational communities.

The seventh chapter, "Charting a Different Future: Embodied Possibilities" discusses a range of applications of the DTE toward social justice and equity. In broad terms, the theory can guide ways to assess and promote social transformations. At the practice level, the theory adds new perspectives to therapy with girls and women and to health promotion initiatives with families, schools, and the larger social context. The chapter includes reflections from research participants regarding dialogues they found valuable while engaged in studies on embodiment, supporting possibilities for constructive change.

This book suggests that a critical theory of embodiment, at the intersection of psychology and sociology, can deepen the understanding of social processes that create docile, corseted, "feminine" bodies—barred from agency and equitable participation in the public sphere. Aspects of the DTE have been presented in countries around the world, contributing to academic and health promotion forums, governmental and policy initiatives, educational offices and institutions, and therapy workshops. Beyond mere understanding, this book is an invitation—for scholars, researchers, and students in the disciplines of psychology, gender studies, sociology, anthropology, and social critical theory; teachers; social and educational policy makers; and health and mental health professionals—to critically reflect on the body journeys of diverse girls and women. Holding a mirror to culture, *Journeys of Embodiment at the Intersection of Body and Culture* further challenges stakeholders to reimagine transformative possibilities in the lives of diverse girls and women.

References

Bartky, S. (1988). Foucault, femininity, and the modermization of patriarchal power. In I. Diamond, & L. Quinby (Eds.), *Feminism & Foucault: Reflections on resistance*. Boston, MA: Northeastern University Press.

Bordo, S. (1989). The body and the reproduction of femininity: a feminist appropriation of Foucault. In A. M. Jaggar, & S. R. Bordo (Eds.), *Gender/body/knowledge* (pp. 13–33). New Brunswick, NJ: Rutgers University.

Cain, A. S., Epler, A. J., Steinley, D., & Sher, K. J. (2010). Stability and change in patterns of concerns related to eating, weight, and shape in young adult women: a latent transition analysis. *Journal of Abnormal Psychology*, *119*, 255–267.

Piran, N., & Gadalla, G. (2007). Eating disorders and substance abuse in Canadian women: A national study. *Addiction*, *102*, 105–113.

Piran, N., McVey, G. L., & Levine, M. P. (2014). Eating disorders in adolescence. In (2nd ed.) T. P. Gullotta, & M. Bloom (Eds.), *The encyclopedia of primary prevention and health promotion* (Vol. 3) (pp. 1134–1147). New York, NY: Springer.

Stice, E., Marti, C. N., & Durant, S. (2011). Risk factors for onset of eating disorders: Evidence of multiple risk pathways from an 8-year prospective study. *Behavior Research and Therapy Journal*, *49*(10), 622–627.

Swami, V., Artche, A., Chamorro-Premuzic, T., Furnham, A., Stieger, S., Haubner, T., et al. (2008). Looking good: Factors affecting the likelihood of having cosmetic surgery. *European Journal of Plastic Surgery*, *30*(5), 211–218.

Tiggemann, M. (2004). Body image across the life span: Stability and change. *Body Image*, *1*(1), 29–41.

Tolman, D. L. (2002). *Dilemmas of desire: Teenage girls talk about sexuality*. Cambridge, MA: Harvard University Press.

Whitlock, J., Eckenrode, J., & Silverman, D. (2006). Self-injurious behaviors in a college population. *Pediatrics*, *117*, 1939–1948.

CHAPTER

1

The Developmental Theory of Embodiment: Discovering Paths in the Body Journeys of Girls and Women

This chapter provides a description of the Developmental Theory of Embodiment. It begins with an explanation of the meaning and importance of studying embodiment and a description of a related research program. The second and third parts describe the theoretical results of the research, in particular: the Experience of Embodiment construct and the social factors that shape it according to the Developmental Theory of Embodiment. The chapter concludes with the stories of two young women, research participants, told by weaving the theoretical constructs into their body journeys.

WHY STUDY EMBODIMENT?

> I think of myself as a whole, the mind-body all integrated or something like that... I feel comfortable in my own skin letting go of what a girl should look like. [Jane]

> I hate my body and I want my body to die, to disintegrate, I have to overcome my body. This body is an obstacle... Like I feel disconnection, like feeling separate from your body... When you are fully confident you are comfortable in your own skin. [Crystal]

Jane and Crystal, both in their early 20s and pursuing university education, participated in the Young Women study. Jane grew up in a working-class family from a rural area. She described her ethnic heritage as White

Journeys of Embodiment at the Intersection of Body and Culture
http://dx.doi.org/10.1016/B978-0-12-805410-9.00001-3

West European and her sexual orientation as heterosexual. Likewise, Crystal came from a working-class background, grew up in a rural town, but moved as a teenager to an urban center. She also described herself as heterosexual. The experiences of these two participants are referred to repeatedly in the chapter, to ground the theoretical constructs in lived experiences.

The concept of embodiment owes its philosophical underpinnings to the French phenomenologist Merleau-Ponty (1962) and refers to the lived experience of engagement of the body in the world. According to Merleau-Ponty, mind and body are inseparable, and the body is not only the center of perception, but also of subjectivity: experiencing the world meaningfully. Further, dialogical relationships exist between body and culture, such that, through active engagement with the world, the body performs and enacts cultural norms and practices (Crossley, 1995); in turn, the body can alter cultural practices. The embodiment term therefore refers concurrently to the breadth of lived experiences as one engages with his/her body in the world, and to the shaping of these experiences by cultural forces.

Jane and Crystal describe in their narratives above two very different experiences of embodiment. While Jane describes body–mind integration and comfort, Crystal describes body–mind disconnection and negative feelings toward her body—a burdensome and hated site. The first question driving this inquiry related to seeking an understanding of the quality of girls and women's body-anchored experiences as they engage in the world around them. Such an understanding is crucial not only to examining "peculiar feminine embodiment," but also to delineating *positive* ways of engagement with the world and associated facilitative social conditions—hence guiding social transformations. Such a comprehensive goal requires the study of the *lived* experiences of girls and women across the life span.

Jane and Crystal's experiences of embodiment denote different levels of well-being. Indeed, much research indicates close links between ways of inhabiting the body and well-being. We know, for example, that negative body image among adolescent girls predicts the development of eating disorders (Stice, Marti, & Durant, 2011), smoking (Neumark-Sztainer, Paxton, Hannan, Haines, & Story, 2006), depression (Stice et al., 2011), and negative self-esteem (Tiggemann, 2005) in longitudinal studies. Alexithymia, which assesses disruptions in identifying and communicating about internal states, is linked with substance abuse and eating disorders (Taylor, Bagby, & Parker, 1991). The silencing of feelings and needs, as well as the suppression of outward expressions of anger, is correlated with body dissatisfaction, bulimia, and drive for thinness (Piran & Cormier, 2005). Conversely, the assertive expression of one's own views and opinions is associated positively with self-esteem (Oakley et al., 2013). A comprehensive understanding of the quality of embodied lives can therefore enrich concepts of well-being.

The second reason to study embodiment relates to the shaping of embodied experiences and practices by cultural forces. Critical and feminist theories emphasize that the body is a site of social control. Foucault (1979), in particular, described, "The body is directly involved in a political field; power relations have an immediate hold upon it; they invest it, mark it, train it, torture it, force it to carry out tasks" (p. 25). Through the expectation of compliance with widely accepted societal discourses, Foucault contended, society produces compliant, also termed, "docile" bodies. In feminist theory, the discussion of body and power has been productive in explaining "feminine embodiment," such as women moving in the public sphere while restricting the use of physical space (Bartky, 1988), or adhering to varied, potentially harmful, body alterations (Bordo, 1989). Thus, studying "female embodiment," and the social mechanisms that produce "docile" feminine bodies, enriches feminist theory and comprises a key to feminist activism and social transformations (Bordo, 1988; Fahs, 2015; Piran, 2010).

RESEARCH PROGRAM

This book describes the results of a research program that included 171 interviews with girls and women on the topics of embodiment, and the social conditions that shape it. It is also bolstered by knowledge from 116 focus groups with school-aged girls and quantitative surveys with about 1500 women. All interviews and focus groups were conducted in sites across Canada, and included participants from diverse backgrounds, such as varied ethnocultural groups, as well as first- and second-generation immigrants from around the world.

The 171 interviews with girls and women took place in three studies. The 5-year prospective Girl Study included 87 interviews with 27 girls, aged 9–14 years during the first phase of the study, who were interviewed three to four times over a 5-year period. The Young Women Study involved 30 interviews with 11 women, aged 20–27 years. The Older Women Study included 54 interviews with 31 women, aged 50–68 years (see Appendix 1 for detailed participants' descriptions in these three studies, and Piran, 2016a for an expanded description of research methodology).

Feminist, hermeneutic, and constructivist lenses informed all aspects of the inquiry, including the interviews. In line with the feminist lens, interviews emphasized participants' expertise in reflecting about their lived experiences, diversity among participants, and the critical examination of the social context. While the Girl Study utilized a prospective methodology, the Young and Older Women Studies utilized a life history methodology to qualitative interviewing (Cole & Knowles, 2001). This approach aims to examine the intersection between individuals' experiences and their social contexts, emphasizing points of transition throughout their life span. The program of research employed the constructivist grounded theory approach to data analysis, as this approach leads to the construction of a conceptual understanding of the phenomenon under study (Charmaz, 2006).

EXPERIENCE OF EMBODIMENT

The first phase of the research program aimed to explore the key dimensions of embodiment among pre- and post-pubertal girls, as well as that of younger and older women. This analysis involved coding narratives where girls and women described their experiences in their bodies as they engaged with the world around them.

The core construct that emerged from this analysis, which we have labeled as the Experience of Embodiment (EE), provides a new perspective on ways girls and women inhabit their bodies across their life span. In particular, the EE construct addresses a breadth of experiences that, up until this point, have not been captured by other constructs. The broad range of experiences included in the EE is clustered into five related dimensions, reflected along a continuum from positive to negative:

- Body Connection and Comfort
- Agency and Functionality
- Experience and Expression of Desire
- Attuned Self-Care
- Inhabiting the Body as a Subjective Site, Resisting Objectification

Participants differed in their EE depending on the quality of their experiences in the five dimensions. We observed a tendency for the dimensions to align on either the positive or negative side of the continuum. Also, participants' quality of EE changed over time in relation to their social environment. (Refer to Table 1.1 for a definition of the two poles of each dimension).

Importantly, the relationship between these different dimensions led to a new research-based definition of positive embodiment. Accordingly, the definition of Positive Embodiment is Positive Body Connection and Comfort, Embodied Agency and Passion, and Attuned Self-Care. Conversely, the definition of Negative Embodiment is Disrupted Body Connection and Discomfort, Restricted Agency and Passion, and Self-Neglect or Harm.

To contextualize these definitions, let us consider the five dimensions of the EE from Jane and Crystal's unique perspectives and how they align along the positive to negative continuum.

TABLE 1.1 Dimensions of the Experience of Embodiment Construct

	Positive	Negative
Dimensions	Body Connection and Comfort	Disrupted Body Connection and Discomfort
	Agency and Functionality	Restricted Agency and Restraint
	Experience and Expression of Desire	Disrupted Connection to Desire
	Attuned Self-care	Disrupted Attunement, Self-harm, and Neglect
	Inhabiting the Body as a Subjective Site	Inhabiting the Body as an Objectified Site

Dimension 1: Body Connection and Comfort versus Body Disconnection and Discomfort

Jane exhibits Body Connection and Comfort. As reflected in the narrative below, in addition to describing having a positive connection with her body and finding comfort in inhabiting it, Jane also recounts engaging in self-talk that bolstered her acceptance of her natural body shape and her financial constraints in buying clothes—both barriers to embodying an idealized female image.

> I think of myself as a whole, the mind body all integrated or something like that... I feel comfortable in my own skin and letting go, letting go of that, you know, prescribed notions of what a girl should look like. I cannot look like a six-foot-two, 125-pound woman. Okay, let's pass that. Should I be more concerned about clothes? Well, I can't afford those clothes... So there's not much point in stressing over them.

In contrast, Crystal exhibits Body Disconnection and Discomfort. In addition to expressing a strong disconnection from her body and a wish for her body to "disintegrate," Crystal also shares a host of negative feelings toward her woman's body, feeling that a woman's body is "wrong."

> I hate my body and I want my body to die, to disintegrate, I have to overcome my body. This body is an obstacle... Like I feel disconnection, like feeling separate from your body. I realize that growing up in a woman's body you get the idea that your body is wrong... I was never comfortable being a girl. I always wanted to be a boy... I hated having breasts.

As the quotations reflect, the dimension Body Connection and Comfort versus Body Disconnection and Discomfort addresses the quality of girls and women's connection with their bodies, and their experience of their bodies as either comfortable or problematic sites from which to engage with the world. Both girls and adult women often made statements regarding experiences of comfort or discomfort in their bodies. In contrast, only older adolescents and adult women, but not pre-adolescent girls, made explicit statements about the quality of their connection to their bodies.

At the positive end of this dimension, entitled Body Connection and Comfort, girls and women describe having experiences of "comfort" and other positive feelings in their bodies while engaging with the world. Older adolescents and women also describe "feeling at one" or "at home" in their bodies, and engage in positive self-talk that counters adverse social influences, such as exposure to idealized appearance norms or other prejudices related to gender, social class, race, age, or sexual orientation.

At the negative end of this dimension, Body Disconnection and Discomfort, girls and women experience their bodies as problematic sites from which to engage with the world, and associate the body with a host of negative feelings such as shame, hate, fear, and anger. They express the need to control, repair, and monitor their bodies, sometimes even wishing their bodies would "disappear." Adolescent girls and women also often describe being disconnected from their bodies, living "from the head up," or experiencing the body as a separate, "other" territory.

Dimension 2: Agency and Functionality versus Blocked Agency and Restraint

Jane exhibits Agency and Functionality in her interactions with the world, both physically and through the power of her voice. Her narratives allude to a shift from physical agency at pre-puberty, to restriction at puberty, and back to physical agency in early adulthood; however, she has maintained a strong sense of agency through voice during all phases of her life journey.

> [Re: physical agency] I was the fastest girl in my class… I was usually the first person picked to be on the baseball team… playing active games and I really enjoyed that… When we turned about 12, I started menstruating and that's when I started hanging out more with the girls and just doing the walking, sitting, chatting, and watching… I have been getting back into yoga now, which is great for body awareness. I exercise during the week, I have a pretty good cardio, and I'm pretty good with weights.

> [Re: voice] I was never withdrawn. I was always fairly aggressive-assertive. So I would state my ground. I'm fairly comfortable with feeling angry… It has a fairly negative connotation in society for

> women but I think we should get rid of that. You can get so much further in life having your opinion heard, especially in a room full of men... saying, 'let me tell you why that is wrong. And let me propose something that is right.'

Crystal exhibits Blocked Agency and Restraint. She describes stopping to practice Karate at age of 12 years as a devastating loss, never to be re-captured. For her, it was a passionate experience of physical agency. She has also experienced blocked agency in asserting her voice. Further, like other women, she has learned to associate pursuing her own meaningful activities with "selfishness" and other demeaning labels.

> [Re: blocked physical agency] I was taking karate too, up to the age of 12, and I thought I was so macho... I was in control. But when I was 12 I was becoming so uncomfortable in karate being a girl because, it's puberty... everybody staring at me. I stopped doing karate... I was so disappointed 'cause I really loved karate... Now I go to the gym and like I run on the treadmill but it's not something I do, like with pleasure. I gotta do my cardio, because today I have been eating quite a lot.

> [Re: blocked agency through voice] I would feel more empowered if I could assert myself more, by saying no. I can't continue to say yes to so many people, and say no to myself. As soon as you wanna do that, people will tell you you're selfish.

On the positive side of this dimension, entitled Agency and Functionality, girls and women describe experiences of agency and functionality in the body domain. The physical sphere is an important domain of agency for girls, often only until puberty due to multiple restrictions that socialize girls to inhabit docile women's bodies (Piran & Teall, 2012). Adolescent girls and adult women who are able to maintain agency in the physical environment during and following puberty, and even those who re-capture physical agency following the crisis of adolescence, report having more positive embodied experiences. Voice is a second domain of agency for girls and women and involves expressing oneself through singing, expressing views one is passionate about, and guiding and leading others through voice.

On the negative side of this dimension, referred to as Blocked Agency and Restraint, girls and women describe experiences of blocked agency and reduced functionality or competence. Regarding physical agency, restrictions in the physical sphere are associated with the experience of loss—either of never having had the opportunity to develop physical agency or, most commonly, losing the valued experience of physical agency during puberty. Post-puberty, joyful immersion and agency in physical activities are commonly replaced by compulsive, often joyless physical activities aimed at body alterations—such as weight loss or body sculpting—anchored in experiences of deficiency rather than agency. Similar to experiences of disrupted connection to physical agency, girls and women also experience barriers to agency through voice, related to the intentional silencing by others as well as to the demeaning of their powerful voices.

Dimension 3: Experience and Expression of Desire versus Disowning Desire

Jane is comfortable with the Experience and Expression of Desire. She has in her family a model of how to hold on to both appetite and sexual desire, and describes having joy in eating and a positive connection to sexuality.

> [Re: appetite] Well, in terms of hunger appetite, I got it. I love food. I love variety... and I've always had this thing about food.

> [Re: sexual desire] I describe myself as a very sexual person because I was always very much in touch with the sexual feelings that my body had... feeling sexual was a very positive thing. I was curious, so I explored my own body, yeah, there was no shame to it. I have healthy attitudes about sex. I thought, well maybe I am attracted to women and I think that it's more of a continuum... things kind of went on hold when I met [husband] and fell in love with him... I do feel sex was a very good thing for my body.

In contrast, Crystal reflected Disowning Desire.

> [Re: appetite] When I was 14, I had anorexia. I was starving myself so I would eat, like, apples throughout the day, and then a little piece of cheese... [young adulthood] Lately I have been eating quite a lot, a lot of junk... I certainly feel bad about myself. And it's just like a roller coaster.

> [Re: sexual desire] I haven't been sexually active for a while because I can't, and having real issues with intimacy... I just became disgusted having compulsive sex trying to make myself feel better. I went through a very, like, promiscuous phase. I found it very hard to enjoy. I could never, like, orgasm with them... Now with this guy but I'm not gonna let it go down that road. I don't even have to have sex.

On the positive side of this dimension, entitled Experience and Expression of Desire, positive connection to desire involves both experiencing desires and responding to these desires in attuned and self-caring ways. While girls and women commonly report disruptions to their experiences of desire during and following puberty, those who encounter fewer disruptive events, and have the support of positive models toward owning their desire, are able to hold on to attuned connection with, and expression of their desires. In turn, this connection to experiencing and expressing desire relates to having embodied agency in the world. The narratives include participants' descriptions related to both appetite and sexuality.

On the negative side of this dimension, Disowning Desire, girls and women describe disruptions in experiencing or acting in an attuned way toward their own desires. They also describe experiencing either no association between desire and pleasure, or associating desire with negative emotions. Women's disconnection from desire limits their experiences of agency, comfort, and pleasure in engaging with the world. Disrupted connections to appetite most commonly occur at the onset of puberty, when girls start to inhabit women's bodies. Similarly, during puberty girls encounter multiple adverse sexual experiences, which disrupt their connection to sexual desire.

Dimension 4: Attuned Self-care versus Disrupted Attunement, Neglect, and Self-harm

Jane's narratives reflect attuned self-care; in addition to bodily, emotional, and relational needs, Attuned Self-Care includes engagement in meaningful pursuits.

> [Re: bodily needs] I was talking about my body sending me signals... so I'm more in tune to what's going on. It's a heightened sensitivity... [eating] When I am home, I cook and I have time to eat... my body tends to know what it wants, if it wants salt I give it salt, then it's happy... [fatigue] So I've always known, my body is really tired today and my body just wants to sleep today and I'm hearing the signals... You will not make me work 60 hours a week... I want balance... [health practices] so it's a focus on being fit and being active and being healthy... [re: Sexuality] I'm glad that I didn't force myself into a sexual relationship with somebody... I mean the opportunity was there but I was, 'no I don't really feel the need.' Because I felt it was important to be in a comfortable relationship.

> [Re: emotional needs] You have to attend to emotional needs. Until you know what you're feeling, it's hard to take that next step towards how to deal with it. Or, you'll forever be eating M&M's and Coke... better if you can get angry as opposed to suppressing your anger.

> [Re: relational needs] I like the concept of sisterhood. Having friends that share your values that you can talk with, that you can share experiences with.

> [Re: meaningful pursuits] My mother does not understand how much I enjoy my career and how much I'm committed to my career, so I plan to work when I have children... Growing up Catholic, I had

strong opinions for the longest time and so I had to identify with how I felt vs. how the church told me to feel.

At the other end of the spectrum, Crystal describes a lifelong pattern of dis-regulation and self-neglect. At times her behaviors put her at physical risk. These experiences reflect disrupted attunement, neglect, and self-harm.

> [Re: bodily needs] [re: eating] My willpower sucks. Sometimes I eat vegan, sometimes I had put on so much weight because I was eating all this junk.
>
> [Re: sexuality] Always having compulsive sex… from the Internet, one-night stand.
>
> [Re: emotional and relational needs, and the need for meaningful engagements] Sometimes I feel happy and other times it is very hard… I am feeling without direction, I don't wanna offend anybody. I gotta take care of number one, myself, but we've been taught to put other people first. I'm not being true to myself.

Attuned Self-Care is another dimension that shapes the quality of one's embodiment. It reflects the level of attunement to one's internal needs and cues as one engages with the external environment. Internal needs can include bodily, emotional, and relational needs, as well as the need to engage in meaningful pursuits. Further, Attuned Self-Care involves not only awareness of internal needs but also the practice of self-care in light of these needs.

At the positive end of this dimension, Attuned Self-Care, girls and women are aware of, and guided by, internal cues. These internal cues include bodily needs such as hunger, fatigue, varied health practices, or sexual desire; emotional needs such sharing emotional experiences with others or practicing self-soothing strategies; and relational needs such as finding validating relational forums, as well as the need to engage in meaningful, passionate, or spiritual activities.

At the negative end of this dimension, entitled Disrupted Attunement, Neglect, and Self-Harm, girls and women's narratives reflect a disrupted awareness of internal cues. Often girls and women describe a lifelong pattern of neglect shaped by social and relational experiences, or a change in practicing Attuned Self-Care following adverse experiences, such as sexual violations.

Dimension 5: Inhabiting the Body as a Subjective Site versus as an Objectified Site

Displaying the experience of Inhabiting the Body as a Subjective Site, Jane is very clear about respecting her comfort and health. Further, she is critical of the preoccupation with external appearance:

> I'm much happier with the goal of being physically healthy than with the goal of being physically attractive... And I need to be prepared for like child bearing. I've also been getting back into yoga and that's very helpful for the body awareness, and particularly the mind body interactions. But, I don't need to be a particular weight and I don't need to look a certain way. There is over stereotyping in overly simplistic views of what a woman should look like. I am not a petite person and I never will be, allowing your body to be its natural size... Some people were very obsessed with their clothes and they wanted to go to the mall and go shopping, that is how they wanted to spend their time and I found that fairly dull. Yeah, I rather talk about books that I read or go see a movie and chatter about it.

In contrast, through Inhabiting the Body as an Objectified Site, Crystal engages in ongoing monitoring of her weight, and shares how putting on some weight affects her feelings not only about her body, but about all aspects of herself.

> And of course, like, if I put on weight because I haven't been doing my cardio I certainly feel bad about myself. Like, you start feeling bad about your body, and then you start feeling bad about other things, all aspects of yourself.

On the positive side of this dimension, Inhabiting the Body as a Subjective Site, girls and women focus on subjective embodied experiences. Their narratives often include expressions of protest, resistance, and defiance toward "normative" pressures to adopt an external gaze and alter it to abide by appearance or other objectifying expectations.

In contrast, when Inhabiting the Body as an Objectified Site, girls and women live in their body from the outside in, aiming to fit objectified expectations. This preoccupation overrides comfort, safety, and also pleasure, since experiences of deficiency and of requiring ongoing repair adversely affect mood, confidence, relationships, and one's outlook on life.

Understanding Positive and Negative Embodiment: Innovative Aspects of the Experience of Embodiment Construct

The program of research suggests that core dimensions of EE are shared between positive and negative embodiment, and between girls and younger and older women—a continuity not previously studied or reported. Such continuity allows for tracing changes across time in girls and women's experiences in relation to a range of social processes, in particular, identifying disruptive or constructive events in the lives of girls and women.

Moreover, the EE construct clarifies that the quality of one's experience of engaging with the world encompasses a number of key dimensions, conceptualized and studied separately to date. Experiencing the body as a comfortable site from which to engage with the world with embodied agency, connection to desires, attuned care, and engagement in meaningful pursuits while resisting an objectified lens are all part of positive embodiment. This description resonates with Simone de Beauvoir's description of the body as having "...a direct and normal connection with the world" (1989, p. xxi). While she ascribed this experience to that of a (privileged) man, it relates to having power in the world rather than to the construction of masculinity.

When disruption occurs to EE, such as the changes seen in adolescence among all research participants, this multi-dimensional construct captures the complex nature of this loss, beyond the previously reported change in body esteem (Mendelson, Mendelson, & White, 2001). In this process of disruption, the body becomes an uncomfortable "other" site—agency is dampened, ownership of desires is challenged, and compromises to self-attunement are frequent. Moreover, the carefree lack of self-consciousness found in early childhood—"I did not care about what I wore or what I looked like"—is lost as well. These compounded losses, associated with inhabiting a docile, feminine body, markedly change the way adolescent girls engage with the world. Further, examining social processes that shape embodiment during adolescence clarifies that in creating docile bodies, all domains of the EE are concurrently targeted. As girls are initiated into owning and inhabiting women's bodies, their bodies become less safe, their embodied agency gets penalized and negatively labeled, their appetites problematized, and acting in attunement with their needs is questioned. Simultaneously, the body becomes an objectified site. The delineation of the multi-dimensional nature of EE therefore clarifies the co-occurring social processes that disrupt girls' embodied power in the world throughout puberty.

The present research program suggests that the five dimensions of the EE, studied and conceptualized thus far as discrete phenomena, can be viewed, and their understanding enriched, through the broader lens of embodiment. For example, research on eating disorders as a separate phenomenon from the broader EE has led to a major research focus on media-generated pressures for thinness. In contrast, feminist theories have highlighted the impact of inequity and violence in the body domain, linking them to a range of disruptions in embodiment including, but not limited to, disordered eating. Hence, the lens of embodiment may broaden social theories of phenomena in the body domain (Katzman & Lee, 1997; Piran, 2010, 2016a; Piran & Teall, 2012; Smolak & Piran, 2012). Katzman and Lee (1997) exemplified this perspective in their work with rural Chinese women who presented with disordered eating. The authors highlighted that among these women "feelings of powerlessness, oppression, and experience of sexual abuse are reported, but fat phobia is not" (Katzman & Lee, 1997, p. 390). They concluded that,

> "(...) by construing anorexia nervosa as a body image disorder or Western culture bound syndrome, extant models miss the broader contexts and varied meanings of food refusal. The implications of cross-disciplinary perspectives for theory building and treatment are discussed, acknowledging not only the gendered nature of eating disorders but their embodiment of power differentials as well" (p. 385).

In a similar vein, examining eating disorders within the broader frame of disruption in the EE may help link challenges to owning both appetite and sexual desire due to their negative constructions among women (Piran, 2016a; Piran & Teall, 2012; Bordo, 1993). Further, we find in our research program a close relationship between the dimensions of embodied agency and acting assertively in response to one's desires. Hence, the EE provides a broader lens through which to study phenomena, such as eating disorders, that have, thus far, been explored as distinct. Furthermore, a narrow focus on discrete expressions of disrupted embodiment, such as eating disorders or self-harm, might obscure the complex relationships between social structures of power and women's embodiment.

Among girls and women, positive conceptualizations of inhabiting the body are few and far between. Vast amounts of literature address negative conceptualizations, such as body dissatisfaction, self-objectification, and self-sexualization. This study offers the first research-based definition of positive embodiment anchored in girls and women's experiences (Piran, 2016a). Its multidimensional nature can provide a guide toward embodied possibilities for the life journeys of girls and women, and a goal for health promotion interventions (Piran, 2015) and therapy (Piran, 2016b). During the past decade, new conceptualizations of positive body image have been studied. Most of these constructs address women's positive relationships with their bodies, captured by the first dimension of the EE—Body Connection and Comfort. These constructs include, for example, Body Appreciation (Tylka & Wood-Barcalow, 2015) and Body Flexibility (Webb, Butler-Ajibade, & Robinson, 2014). Other positive conceptualizations focus on attunement to one's needs (Cook-Cottone, 2015; Daubenmier, 2005), which relate to the Attuned Self-Care dimension of the EE construct.

Perhaps it is not accidental that, to date, the dimensions most obviously absent from the conceptualization of positive body image are those that involve acting in and on the world with agency and functionality, as well as with passion. These dimensions are related to the Agency and Functionality, and Experience and Expression of Desire dimensions of the EE. Among girls and women, agency as well as ownership of desires and appetites have been consistently negatively constructed, labeled, and penalized. Examples abound in different domains of life, such as political fields or the arts. Hillary Clinton has been labeled a "bitch" in the media for her agency and competence, qualities admired in men but seen as contradicting feminine images (Cottle, 2016). Sarah Palin has been presented in the media as a sexualized and ditzy object while her successful record of working, as a Republican, with Democrats in Alaska, to control the oil companies and subject them to higher taxes, has rarely been mentioned (Green, 2011). Cleopatra, a ruler of Egypt and leader of their army, is most often portrayed solely as a sexualized object. Further, her sexual desire has been often magnified and vilified in the media (Tyldesley, 2008). Georgia O'Keeffe's tremendous talents as an artist were clouded for many years by sexualized interpretations of her work, partly shaped by her partner's—Stieglitz—early exhibition of her nude photos without her consent (Saltz, 2009). Cultural values discouraging agency and passion among women may therefore shape theoretical developments.

Objectification Theory and the constructs of Self-Objectification and Objectified Body Consciousness have addressed the fifth dimension of the EE, Inhabiting the Body as a Subjective Site versus as an Objectified Site. However, since this theory and constructs have relied on the experiences of women, they emphasize the adverse impact of objectification; meanwhile, the Embodiment research program has been additionally informed by girls' narratives about acting in and on the world with immersion, joy, and minimal self-surveillance. The qualitative study with girls has therefore enriched the understanding of the positive pole of this dimension.

The EE construct adds to the existing literature by addressing important dimensions of engaging with the body in the world, reflecting the experiences of girls and women across their life span, all the way from severe disruption to positive and active engagement with the world. It further expands on positive ways of inhabiting the body, a topic infrequently addressed in the literature, by delineating possibilities of engagement in the world and suggesting goals for related interventions.

Establishing the EE construct allows for the close examination of adverse and facilitative social conditions to girls and women's embodiment, the topic of the second part of this chapter.

KEY SOCIAL DOMAINS THAT SHAPE EMBODIMENT: THE DEVELOPMENTAL THEORY OF EMBODIMENT

Developing a social theory that examines the relationship between social processes and girls and women's embodied experiences, anchored in the narratives of girls and younger and older women, was the second primary goal of this research program. No such theory exists to date.

Toward achieving this goal, all descriptions of girls and women's social experiences affecting how they felt in their bodies as they engaged with the world—included in the 171 interviews—were coded utilizing the constructivist grounded theory approach. The analysis progressed in three stages: the theory emerged first in the analysis of the narratives from the Young Women study, was verified and elaborated on during the prospective Girl study, and was further cross-validated during the Older Women's study. A series of quantitative studies have provided cross-method cross-validation (Piran & Cormier, 2005; Piran & Teall, 2012; Piran & Thompson, 2008; Teall, 2015; Teall & Piran, 2015). The Developmental Theory of Embodiment (DTE) provides a critical look at social structures and mores, and brings to light challenges and strengths that exist in the lives of girls and women, which can then guide social, health promotion, and therapy interventions.

The following provides an introduction to the key constructs of the DTE that emerged during the research program (see Table 1.2). These constructs are used throughout this book to describe the embodied journeys of girls and women in relation to varied aspects of their social location such as: age, social class, race and ethnicity, sites of residence, immigration, health, and sexual orientation. The brief summaries of the embodied journeys of Jane and Crystal aim to exemplify the ways in which the DTE can help explain marked differences in the EE of these two women.

The DTE proposes that the multitude of social experiences described by girls and women shape their body experiences via three core pathways: experiences in the *physical* domain, experiences in the *mental* domain, and experiences related directly to *social power*. The theory contends that both protective and risk factors are organized along these three pathways, with the positive and negative aspects being conceptualized as Physical Freedom (vs. Corseting), Mental Freedom (vs. Corseting), and Social Power and Relational Connections (vs. Disempowerment and Disconnection). Table 1.2 describes the key dimensions of the DTE.

The Physical Domain: Physical Freedom versus Physical Corseting

Experiences in the physical domain are centrally important to the EE. The DTE describes experiences of Physical Freedom that enhance positive embodiment, and contrasts them with experiences of Physical Corseting that lead to disrupted embodiment (Piran, 2002; Piran & Teall, 2012). Experiences of Physical Freedom cluster into four main categories: Freedom in Physical Engagement and Movement, Safety for the Body Territory, Care of the Body, and Freedom of Desire. In contrast, experiences of Physical Corseting cluster into four parallel categories: Corseted

TABLE 1.2 Domains of Social Experiences According to the Developmental Theory of Embodiment

PHYSICAL DOMAIN	**PHYSICAL FREEDOM** A. **Freedom in Physical Engagement and Movement** 1. Freedom in Physical Engagement 2. Freedom of Movement and Taking Physical Space B. **Safety for the Body Territory** 1. Safety from Violations 2. Safety from Coercive Body Alterations and Practices C. **Care of the Body** D. **Freedom of desire**	**PHYSICAL CORSETING** A. **Corseted and Blocked Physical Engagement and Movement** 1. Blocked Physical Engagement 2. Constriction of Movement and Physical Space B. **Violations to the Body Territory** 1. Exposure to Violations 2. Engagement in Coercive Body Alterations and Practices C. **Neglect of Body Care** D. **Restriction of Desire**
MENTAL DOMAIN	**MENTAL FREEDOM** **A Critical Stance toward Social Discourses**	**MENTAL CORSETING**[a] A. **Appearance-related Discourses: Body as a Deficient Object** 1. Body as an Object of Gaze 2. Woman's Body as Deficient B. **Comportment-related Discourses: Woman as Docile** 1. Engagement in 'Feminine' Activities 2. Woman as Submissive/Demure 3. Woman as Desired but Desireless 4. Patriarchal Shaping of Relational Patterns C. **Regulating Dichotomies and Labels**
SOCIAL POWER AND RELATIONAL CONNECTIONS DOMAIN	**SOCIAL POWER AND RELATIONAL CONNECTIONS** A. **Freedom from Prejudice and Harassment** 1. Access to Resources 2. Freedom from Body-based Prejudice and Harassment B. **Freedom from Appearance-based Social Power** C. **Empowering Relationships** D. **Membership in Equitable Communities**	**SOCIAL DISEMPOWERMENT AND DISCONNECTION** A. **Exposure to Prejudice and Harassment** 1. Restricted Access to Resources 2. Exposure to Body-based Harassment B. **Appearance-based Social Power** C. **Disempowering Relational Connections** D. **Membership in Inequitable Communities** (or no access to desired communities)

[a] *The discourses in this table relate to "femininity discourses." Discourses exist in relation to all aspects of social location.*

and Blocked Physical Engagement and Movement, Violations to the Body Territory, Neglect of Body Care, and Restriction of Desire. The four categories of Physical Freedom and Corseting are described in detail below, and are listed in Table 1.2.

Freedom in Physical Engagement and Movement (vs. Corseted and Blocked Physical Engagement and Movement)

Girls and women repeatedly describe the ways in which the freedom to act in the physical environment, rather than on their bodies, provides them with a sense of embodied agency, comfort, joy, and well-being. In contrast, restrictions or barriers to physical engagement with the world, and to free movement, lead to embodied powerlessness, compromised physical competence, and to living in the body with discomfort and low self-esteem. Two types of experiences fall under Freedom in Physical Engagement and Movement:

Freedom in Physical Engagement (vs. Blocked Physical Engagement)

Immersion in joyful, non-objectifying, non-sexualizing, non-appearance– or weight-related physical activities is found to enhance body functionality, physical agency, and body awareness and connection. Such activities include playing physical games, engaging in team sports, hiking, biking, yoga, gardening, and other physical activities. In contrast, Corseted and Blocked Physical Engagement and Movement lead to disrupted embodiment. Girls and women's narratives allude to multiple barriers to joyful physical engagement. These include direct prohibitions or restrictions placed on girls and women's engagement in varied physical activities; limited resource allocation for girls and women's engagement in sports compared to that of boys and men's; lack of girl teams or access to co-ed teams; compromised safety or sexualization during physical activities; restrictive and exposing clothing, or sports uniforms that limit physical movement; feminine discourses that construct physical competence as masculine; and inequitable burden in carrying domestic chores. These sorts of barriers communicate to girls that their right to engage in the world with physical prowess and competence is not supported by their social environment.

In the transition from girlhood to womanhood, we commonly find that women lose the experience of physical agency in the world. As described in the following chapters, upon the onset of puberty, the introduction of barriers to engagement in physical activities intensifies and, with that, girls' access to sites of physical engagement becomes more regulated and constricted. Shared neighborhood-based physical activities cease, and access to physical activities programs for pubertal girls becomes restricted by factors like fees and the cost of uniforms, transportation to activity sites, ethnocultural or religious norms, and other factors.

Freedom of Movement and of Taking Physical Space (vs. Constriction of Movement and of Physical Space)

Moving freely and safely in the private and public spheres, in urban landscapes or nature, is another embodying component in the lives of girls and women that is centrally related to embodied agency and positive connection with one's body. Similarly, feeling free to take physical space through body size, movement, or comportment enhances positive embodiment. In contrast, restrictions on movement in the public sphere or in the freedom to take physical space, disrupt embodiment.

The program of research on embodiment took place in North America, where there are no laws that prohibit women's freedom of movement in the public sphere. Participants in the study emigrated from countries where strict norms limit women's movement in varied public sites. However, we find that even in countries where the laws do not prohibit freedom of movement by women, barriers abound. It is a sober reminder that, Hart House, the students' recreational center at the University of Toronto, where the embodiment research office is located, has allowed women to become full members and participate in its activities, since 1972. Prior to that, women were only permitted to enter the building as dates escorted by men during special events.

Additionally, violence commonly limits freedom of movement of children and women, and sometimes the movement of men in particular neighborhoods. Further, violence serves as a strong reminder about social privilege: who has and who does not have the privilege of safety in the public sphere. As this book describes, other processes restrict access to public spaces. For example, there is a preferential allocation of physical sites to boys or men's activities, such as the typical allocation of large parts of school yards to boys' sports, while girls gather at the sidelines, or the greater allocation of public facilities to boys' or men's sports, such as in hockey arenas. In addition, the inequitable assignment of duties at home keeps girls and women more often in the domestic sphere. Further, we often find that boys and men become the "gatekeepers" of public territories. For example, only if invited to join a boys' game in the schoolyard will a girl have access to free movement within that territory.

Clothing can also limit movement in the public sphere. The current trends toward sexualized, tight, and exposing clothing, as well as unstable high-heeled shoes, limit girls and women's movement in the public sphere. In this way, current norms of attire for girls and women in Western countries have a kinship with corsets of the Victorian era. Consider the Australian game of netball as an example of the way clothing can disrupt movement in the public sphere. In 2007, when the uniform for netball, the fourth most-popular organized sport for girls and women in Australia, changed from shorts and a t-shirt to a Lycra bodysuit, there was a country-wide reduction of 35,000 in the number of girls and women who engaged in the sport (Dubecki, 2007). They complained that the bodysuits made them feel self-conscious about their bodies when compared with the shorts and t-shirts of their previous uniforms.

Parallel with the freedom to move freely in the public sphere, girls and women in the embodiment research program describe experiencing challenges with respect to occupying physical space. Participants often describe their wish to be altogether "smaller." In the Girls study, we invited girls to draw both themselves and their vision of the "ideal girl." Consistently, girls would draw the ideal girl as being strikingly smaller than themselves in both height and width. A common comment, "you just feel better because you're smaller," reflects their discomfort in occupying physical space (Piran, 2014). Compounding this desired restriction in size is the clothing used to clad the ideal girls in the drawings—tight and exposing, prohibiting physical movement. The drawings and associated narratives, therefore, strongly convey the restriction alluded to in "ideal femininity" by authors such as Bartky (1988) and de Beauvoir (1989). Bartky (1988) described that women "are far more restricted than man in their manner of movement and in their spatiality" (p. 66), and de Beauvoir (1989) noted that "[A] woman is rendered more desirable to the extent that nature is more highly developed in her and more rigorously confined" (p. 159).

Safety for the Body Territory (vs. Violations to the Body Territory)

The second category of the Physical Freedom domain centers on the Safety for the Body Territory. For girls and women, safety was central to the EE. The experience of safety enhanced the experiences of worth, power and agency, positive connection with the body, and attunement with one's needs and passions. Violations to the body territory disrupted all aspects of embodiment and made the body a difficult territory to inhabit. We found two types of experiences related to Safety for the Body Territory: Safety from Violations and Safety from Coercive Body Alterations.

Safety from Violations (vs. Exposure to Violations)

Safety from violations perpetrated against the body territory included safety from sexual and physical abuse, rape and any sexual violation or coercion, sexual harassment involving unwanted sexual touching, attention or sexualized verbal comments, physical violations or threats of violations, and witnessing any of these experiences. The program of research made it exceedingly clear that even common experiences, such as sexual harassment, are not benign and may leave individuals with, as this book will reveal, lifelong adverse impacts on embodiment. In particular, such experiences disrupt the respectful ownership of one's body and lead to the association of the body with a host of negative emotions, such as fear and shame. Further, occurring within the context of inequity of power and privilege, violations are not only embodied expressions of such inequity but remain a silent domain of personal shame and powerlessness.

Safety from Coercive Body Alterations and Practices (vs. Coercive Body Alterations and Practices)

Girls and women live in a culture where there are external expectations that their bodies will be altered and will be subjected to a range of practices that can be painful, depriving, time-consuming, or uncomfortable and may cause permanent damage. In the study girls often questioned the safety of these intrusive practices, which compromise the experience of respectful ownership of the body and establish the body as a deficient, shameful domain, disrupting embodiment. As this book describes, the intrusive impact of these practices is felt most poignantly during the tweens and early adolescence, when coercive pressures for compliance mount. During late adolescence and adulthood women often engage in these practices, becoming detached from the emotions of fear and protest that typified their earlier introduction.

Care of the Body (vs. Neglect of Body Care)

The third category of the Physical Freedom domain centers on Care of the Body. Attuned Care of the Body relates to positive connection with the body as a worthy site, support for its desires, and the internalization of a stance of body attunement throughout one's life journey. In the embodiment research program, we find that patterns of body neglect are sometimes established from girlhood and are commonly reinforced throughout women's lifelong journeys. Girls' labor is enlisted early for domestic chores and the care of others, often inequitably in comparison to their male siblings, even at a cost to their needs for rest, physical activities, or engagement in meaningful pursuits such as education. Several women reported growing up in homes where boys received preferential food options, which the women in turn replicated with their own children. There is a marked lack of support of women during the childbearing and childrearing ages, with inequitable and short parental leaves, and inequitable remuneration of labor at home and outside of the house, forcing overexertion and compromised physical health. Further, we would like to highlight the glaring absence of socially sanctioned discourses that buffer the common "care of others" expectations of girls and women.

Freedom of Desire (vs. Restriction of Desire)

The fourth and final category of the Physical Freedom domain is entitled Freedom of Desire. Experiences that support and validate desire, as well as encourage attuned, assertive, and joyful responses to desire enhance positive connection with the body, embodied agency, and attunement to bodily needs. In contrast, denying or prohibiting the expression of desire not only disrupts attuned connection and response to desire, but also diminishes attunement to other bodily needs, disrupts connection to the body, and diminishes embodied agency. In our research, we found that narratives indicating an excited connection to appetite, without the need to control or contain it, almost always existed exclusively in childhood. Only rarely did girls have healthy adult or peer role models in this area.

Similarly, expressions of positive connection to sexual desire during early puberty most often become encumbered soon after by fears of violence, rampant coercive practices during dating, exposure to pornography sites, and negative labeling of female sexuality. An additional social factor in this is the almost complete lack of validation of female desire in all facets of the social environment, including, for example, significant adults in the life of children or sex education in school (Fine, 1988; Senn, Gee, & Thake, 2011; Tolman, 2002). This lack of validation, especially within the context of multiple negative factors, poses often-insurmountable barriers to a girl or woman's connection to, or assertive communication of, her sexual wishes. In turn, it may make girls and women even more susceptible to violations and unwanted pregnancies.

To conclude, experiences in the Physical Freedom domain are related to one's freedom of physical engagement with the world, and of the freedom to move freely in it; safety from violations and coercive body alteration practices; attuned care practices; and embodied agency and support in owning desire. In turn, these experiences are central to positive embodiment. Nonetheless, girls commonly experience disruption in all these domains in the transition from girlhood to womanhood.

The Mental Domain: Mental Freedom versus Mental Corseting

Mental Freedom relates to engaging with the world meaningfully and passionately, as well as holding a critical stance toward, and experiencing freedom from, constraining social discourses that regulate embodied lives of individuals of different social locations. These social discourses aim to maintain the social status quo, and therefore act as Mental Corsets to embodied possibilities for girls and women, members of different racial and ethnic groups, individuals holding a spectrum of gender identities, individuals living with mental or physical disabilities, and individuals living in poverty. Mental Corseting relates to embodied compliance with constraining socially created molds related to one's social location, and that aim to maintain the social status quo. Like Physical Corseting, Mental Corseting limits one's possibilities of engaging meaningfully and passionately with the world, restricting agency and self-attunement, and hence compromising the EE.

In terms of femininity discourses, the DTE highlights two clusters of discourses that constrain the ways in which girls and women inhabit their bodies and engage with the world: Appearance-related Discourses—Body as a Deficient Object—and Comportment-related Discourses—Woman as Docile (see Table 1.2). It also highlights a related set of dichotomous social constructions, such as tomboy/girly girl, and common social labels such as "selfish," "hysterical," or "narcissistic." These discourses and labels disrupt the experience of the body as a powerful and worthy site from which to engage with the world. These Mental Corsets become dominant in girls' narratives during their tweens years, around and even just prior to the onset of puberty.

Appearance-Related Discourses: The Body as a Deficient Object

The Body as a Deficient Object cluster includes two discourses: Body as an Object of Gaze and Woman's Body as Deficient. The Body as an Object of Gaze establishes girls and women's bodies as an object of male gaze, reflected by the dominance of the patriarchal lens in most societies around the world. The dominance of the patriarchal lens can be easily discerned when one looks at social products, such as historical documents, museum exhibitions, and disseminated media (see also Fredrickson & Roberts, 1997; McKinley & Hyde, 1996). The Woman's Body as Deficient discourse portrays the woman's body as a deficient site, whereby all aspects of the body require ongoing, yet ultimately never successful, repairs. Therefore, a war with the body unfolds rather than with oppressive social ideologies nurtured by power inequity.

Comportment-Related Discourses: Woman as Docile

The Woman as Docile cluster includes four discourses (see Table 1.2). The first discourse, entitled, Woman as Submissive/Demure, reflects the expectation that girls and women act meekly and nice, and not be too vocal, too loud, too dominant, too assertive, too needy, or simply too much. It also reflects the expectation to be submissive and subvert own needs, wishes, and meaningful pursuits to that of boys and men. The second discourse, entitled Engagement in Feminine Activities, guides girls and women to engage in "feminine" activities to gain social approval and acceptance and avoid penalties. By the time girls enter puberty, this discourse includes the expectation that girls replace their engagement in passionate physical activities with sedentary activities, such as self-beautifying and shopping. The Engagement in Feminine Activities discourse also promotes choosing "feminine" academic pursuits and occupations, taking on responsibility for passionless domestic chores, and importantly, taking care of others at the expense of oneself. This discourse is so powerful that girls and women most often describe engagement in feminine activities as "natural" expressions of themselves.

A third Comportment-related Discourse, Woman as Desired but Desireless, reflects the social sanctioning of male desire and the negative social construction of female desire. Sexualized images of girls and women are presented through the male-objectifying gaze, and their sexual responses are commonly presented as reflecting male potency. Women are viewed as responsible for containing male desire and blamed when "male hormones" are out of hand, leading to violations. The "acceptable" level of desire is also regulated by the patriarchal lens: a lack of sexual response or, alternatively, female sexual desire beyond what is possible for their male partners are both penalized (e.g., through assigning demeaning labels such as "frigid" and "prude," or alternatively, "nymphomanic" and "slut," respectively). Controlling women's desire, and with that women's agency in the world, serves to keep the reigns of power with patriarchy.

The Patriarchal Shaping of Relational Patterns discourse reflects an expected pattern of relationships among pubertal girls and women whereby they maintain only sexualized relationships with heterosexual men, prioritize these relationships over other relational connections, and practice competition and policing among themselves (also described by Brown, 2003). This discourse leads to disruptions during early puberty and thereafter to girls' friendship networks, as well as to friendships between girls and boys. Consequently, adolescent girls and women might lose important relational support, and with that, important sources of validation and power.

The research program on embodiment highlights missing discourses related to women's embodied worth, power, passions, or their right for safety. Through this absence, girls and women of diverse social locations learn about their compromised worth within social structures of power.

Regulating Dichotomies and Labels

In line with the constraining discourses of femininity, we also find socially sanctioned linguistic dichotomies that regulate the ways girls and women inhabit their bodies, and which disrupt their embodied journeys. The prevalent tomboy/girly girl dichotomy implies that being a powerful girl with the freedom to act with agency in the physical territory involves being boylike, a temporary option for girls until puberty. A similarly common dichotomy, slut/prude, constructs female embodied desire as inherently problematic, being either "too much" or "too little," with the slut label having far-reaching, damning, and sometimes dangerous implications in adolescent and adult social circles. Other dichotomies, such as popular/loser-nerd and nice/bitch-butch, similarly regulate the ways in which girls and women can inhabit their bodies.

Socially constructed linguistic dichotomies present challenges in relation to dimensions of social location other than gender. For example, the socially constructed Black/White dichotomy, privileges one side while devaluing the other—challenging experiences of inhabiting diverse bodies. This is similar to the old/young dichotomy.

Commonly used social labels similarly work to control diverse girls and women's ways of inhabiting their bodies as they engage with the world. Labels such as "selfish" or "narcissistic" target girls and women's engagement in meaningful pursuits, with the implication that they have neglected the care or well-being of others; "bitch" and "aggressive" aim to curtail assertiveness, competitiveness, and achievement among women. The "needy" or "dependent" label trivializes women's needs and their subjugation to limited opportunities in the world. "Superwoman," meanwhile, clarifies that whatever women do in the world, they need to be successful on the home front—an impossible mission, leading to the erosion of women's well-being, and setting them up for failure.

Further, in addition to "femininity" molds, corseting molds that regulate embodied lives exist in relation to race and ethnicity. Girls and women in the embodiment research program described facing stereotypes related to their heritages denoting being primitive or threatening. Further, at the intersection of gender and race, several girls and women described accentuated objectification and sexualization.

The construct of mental corsets resonates with the construct of controlling images coined by Hill Collins (2000) who described the way in which the portrayal of Black women in different stereotypic ways, such as "mammy," "Jezebel," or "mule" (see also Simms, 2001), work to disempower them and limit their possibilities of acting in the world. Further, as she explained, controlling images are "designed to make racism, sexism, poverty, and other forms of social justice appear to be natural, normal and inevitable parts of everyday life" (p. 69). At the intersection of sexist and racist ideologies, bell hooks (1997) problematized the presentation of African-American as "sexual savages." Peter McLaren (1995) similarly criticized the White/Black dichotomy that, like other socially constructed dichotomies, idealizes one pole while devaluing the other. In addition to gender and race, constraining social discourses exist in relation to other aspects of social location, such as social class, sexual orientation, gender identities, and physical or mental ability.

As has been illustrated in this section on the mental domain, different social constructions limit diverse girls and women's possibilities of embodied engagement with the world. These possibilities can be expressed through widely disseminated molds of social expectations, dichotomized constructions, or labels. These mental molds are entrenched in individuals' lives and are therefore mistaken as natural or inevitable. Toward the goal of positive embodiment, the varied forms of Mental Corseting need to be named and contested, to allow for passionate and meaningful engagement with the world.

The Social Power and Relational Connections Domain (vs. Social Disempowerment and Disconnection)

Together with experiences in the physical and mental domains, girls and women's experiences of Social Power and Relational Connections with others, and with desired communities, relate strongly to the EE. The DTE describes experiences of Social Power and Relational Connections that enhance positive embodiment, and contrasts them with experiences of Social Disempowerment and Disconnection that lead to disrupted embodiment (Piran, 2002; Piran & Teall, 2012). Experiences of Social Power and Relational Connections include four categories: Freedom from Prejudice and Harassment, Freedom from Appearance-based Social Power, Empowering Relationships, and Membership in Equitable Communities. Experiences of Social Disempowerment include, in a parallel way, the categories of Exposure to Prejudice and Harassment, Appearance-based Social Power, Disempowering Relational Connections, and No Access to Equitable Communities (see Table 1.2).

Freedom from Prejudice and Harassment

Freedom from prejudice and harassment is central to inhabiting the body as a site of worth, leading to positive embodiment. In this category, the body is seen as social capital (Bourdieu, 1984), either entitling one to access social resources and be free of prejudicial treatment and harassment or, alternatively, depriving such access and exposing one to maltreatment. Such body-based privilege, or disenfranchisement, relates to intersecting dimensions of social location, such as gender, race/ethnicity, physical ability, sexual orientation, gender identity, or social class. Two types of experiences fall under Freedom from Prejudice and Harassment: Equitable Access to Resources and Freedom from Body-based Harassment.

Access to Resources

A central aspect of social power is its relationship to privileged access to valued resources, such as education, health, employment, remuneration for employment, or the construction of media messages. Access to resources is informed by ideologies that privilege individuals who inhabit particular bodies—in Western countries, male, White, cisgender, heterosexual, able-bodied, young, and financially endowed individuals. These ideologies in turn shape all social structures and mores, including political institutions and associated laws and policies, sites of education and employment, and families. Moreover, ideologies shape individuals' beliefs about themselves. Our participants' narratives reflect common experiences whereby access to resources—such as education or other sites of skills development, support for passionate pursuits, or jobs with livable remuneration—were made less accessible to them and other women in their families, when compared with what was available to boys and men. Other intersecting barriers to accessing resources included race, ethnicity, immigration status, or health. While both girls and young women described this differential access to resources, the Older Women study reflected the lifelong impact of such differential access, with some women living in poverty, and many not believing in their abilities, or feeling powerless to change their adverse circumstances. Therefore, both the ideologies that deprive diverse women of access to resources and the consequent effect on their quality of life adversely impact the EE.

Freedom from Body-Based Harassment

Our research clarifies that Freedom from Body-based Harassment is important to embodied worth and positive embodiment, while Exposure to Body-based Harassment leads to disrupted embodiment. Exposure to Body-based Harassment relates to all aspects of social location (e.g., gender, age, socioeconomic standing, ethnocultural heritage/socially constructed racial groups, immigration status, sexual orientation, health, and physical ability) (see also Bucchianeri, Eisenberg, Wall, Piran, & Neumark-Sztainer, 2014; Larkin & Rice, 2005). Research narratives clarify that body-based prejudicial treatment, harassment, or teasing is commonly used to reinforce structures of privilege and disenfranchisement within one's social environment. Further, the drawings of the ideal girl by participants in the Girl study condense in them visual representations of privilege along multiple aspects of social location. Ideal girls are always white skinned with blue eyes and straight hair (ethnocultural/racial factor), presented in hetero-sexualized ways (sexual orientation factor), adorned by brand name clothing and material gadgets (socioeconomic standing factor), and described as symbols of perfection (health or disability factor). Yet, the drawings of the ideal girl also reflect the inequity of gender, as ideal girls occupy smaller spaces compared with girls' drawings of themselves and their bodies are exposed and objectified.

Freedom from Appearance-Based Social Power

Freedom from reliance on appearance as a central strategy for accessing social power maintains girls and women's focus on acting in the world, with associated opportunities for embodied agency and connection to passionate and meaningful pursuits, and to self-attunement—all aspects of positive EE. In contrast, appearance as a main determinant of social power inherently sets the stage for a struggle with the body, and for diverting the focus away from developing and pursuing a range of opportunities to act in the world with agency and self-attunement. Our research clarifies that even when girls or women perceive themselves as abiding by idealized standards of appearance, their experience of social power is tenuous. First, inevitable changes to biological bodies require ongoing repair. Second, while perceived ideal presentations of girls and women procure social rewards, they concurrently draw devalued labels such as "ditzy" or "dumb" and demeaning behavioral descriptions, such as "they screech" or "they need to go to the doctor because they broke a nail." Ultimately, the inferior status of girls and women is maintained through this focus on appearance: the lack of compliance leads to social penalties while perfected compliance leads to devaluation (Piran, 2014; Piran, Carter, Thompson, & Pajouhandeh, 2002).

Empowering Relationships

This category reflects validation of a girl or woman's worth, pursuits, hopes, and critical reflections about the social environment by another person or a community. This validation of one's embodied self in the world is associated with positive embodiment. Often we find that Empowering Relationships involve at least a single significant person in one's social environment who shares important characteristics with the girl or woman in question, takes pride in their shared group membership, provides a loving and supportive relationship, models embodied pride, and stands up to societal prejudices. Having empowering relationships can provide some protection from the adverse effects of exposure to prejudicial and harassing treatment in one's social environment.

Membership in Equitable Communities

Having the experience of being part of at least one social system where equity, such as in relation to gender or ethnic/racial heritage, is practiced, transmits embodied worth. It is common for girls and women to share astute observations about power structures in their environment, such as in schools, at work, or in their families. Girls and women of diverse backgrounds, who have taken part in equitable social systems for at least part of their life journey, often reflect about the powerful impact of that experience. A study by Kawachi, Kennedy, and Prothrow-Stith (1999) powerfully conveys the value of being part of equitable communities. The researchers first developed four composite indices aimed at assessing gender-related embodied equity—women's political participation, economic autonomy, employment and earnings, and reproductive rights—which they assessed in all 50 American states. They then correlated these indices with female and male mortality rates, causes of death, and activity limitations during a specific time period. Higher political participation and smaller wage gaps between women and men were associated with lower female mortality rates and activity limitations. The researchers concluded that living in states with greater gender inequality adversely affects women's health.

To conclude, the Social Power and Relational Connections domain suggests that the embodied lives of diverse girls and women are affected by access to resources, exposure to body-based harassment, reliance on appearance to procure social power, the availability of empowering relationships or communities, and the opportunity to experience being part of equitable communities.

A Social Theory of Embodiment—Innovative Aspects of the Developmental Theory of Embodiment

The DTE comprises a social theory of the development of embodiment, anchored in narratives of girls as well as younger and older women's lived experiences, and cross-validated utilizing quantitative methodology. Holding up a mirror to culture, it delineates both embodied possibilities for girls and women as well as the barrage of adverse social experiences that target the bodies of diverse girls and women; these adverse social factors work in unison to shift their embodied experiences from connection, embodied agency, and attuned care to disrupted connection, blocked agency, and neglect. In turn, this disrupted embodiment compromises girls and women's power to act in and on the world.

The DTE suggests that in examining women's embodied journeys and well-being, a range of experiences must be concurrently examined. While to date research and related theories of negative body image have tended to highlight discrete social forces—in particular pressures for thinness or objectification—the theory suggests that the striking changes to embodiment seen in bodyjourneys that unfold from girlhood to womanhood can be best understood through a broader, integrated theory. Further, the DTE examines both disruptive and facilitative factors that shape embodiment. To date, studies have focused mainly on disruptive social events. The theory therefore has implications for constructive changes at the individual, institutional, and societal levels.

Experiences in the physical domain are central to well-being. During the second wave of feminism in the 1960s and 1970s, inquiry and activism focused on women's physical lives, including the opening of rape crisis centers, uncovering the high rates of child sexual abuse, celebrating women's sexual desire and choice in sexual relations, contesting lower pay for women's labor, and fighting for reproductive rights (Fonow & Cook, 1991; Hooks, 2000; Piran, 2016c). In contrast, during the third wave of feminism, the discussion of inhabiting the body has focused more on social discourses and postmodern analyses of social identities (Fahs, 2015). This has weakened the relationship between the examination of embodied lives and feminist activism, leading to a call by feminist writers to renew research on physical practices in inhabiting the body (Bordo, 1989; Fahs, 2015; Piran, 2010). Similarly, Herman, in her landmark book, *Trauma and*

Recovery (1992), emphasized how targeting the physical body was a way of destroying a victim's sense of autonomy in any form of captivity. In a similar vein, Ta-Nehisi Coates (2015) poignantly described the subjugation of individuals with African heritage by those "who believe they are white" through targeting the physical body:

> As for now, it must be said that the process of washing the disparate tribes white, the elevation of the belief in being white, was not achieved through wine tastings and ice cream socials, but rather through the pillaging of life, liberty, labor, and land; through the flaying of backs; the chaining of limbs; the strangling of dissidents; the destruction of families; the rape of mothers; the sale of children; and various of other acts meant, first and foremost, to deny you and me the right to secure and govern our own bodies. (p. 8)

Our research findings, and accordingly the DTE, place a strong emphasis on experiences in the physical domain, affecting embodied lives and well-being.

In the physical domain alone, the theory highlights a range of factors, reflecting the complexity of physical engagement with the world. Not only is immersion in joyful physical activities important, but also the freedom of movement in the physical sphere and the freedom to take space. Further, these experiences combine with safety from violations of the body territory, body care, and validation of women's desires to shape the EE. In our research we therefore see varied patterns of interactions among the different factors in the physical domain, with both compounding and mitigating effects. We see a compounding effect, for example, when a woman is subjected to adverse experiences in all facets of physical corseting from childhood on, disallowing her from ever connecting with her body positively. Alternatively, girls and women may encounter a varied pattern of freedom and corseting with mitigating effects, such as a girl who engages passionately and joyfully in a non-appearance–related team sport—a positive factor—and yet is concurrently subjected to the adverse impact of sexual harassment and dating violence.

As the book describes, all aspects of social location affect possibilities of physical engagement with the world. For example, socioeconomic standing can affect the safety of neighborhoods and parks, and the ability to pay for community sports programs. Alternatively, particular ethnic and religious heritages may disallow using a mixed-gender public swimming pool. Moreover, in different communities, the physical corseting of girls and women can take different forms. In some communities, freedom of movement might be restricted due to adverse cultural norms. (such as the sanctioning of violence against women). In some countries, the freedom of movement of women in the public sphere might be constrained by law.

Similarly, female desire may be curtailed in some communities by the lack of validation of female desire and the associated social penalties for sexual activities, while in other communities female desire may be targeted through the physical penalty of female circumcision. Therefore, while we see the same dimensions operating in the physical domain, the exact nature of corsets can vary between social groups.

In the mental domain, passion, freedom of thought, and a critical stance toward constraining social constructions or expectations are highlighted. Similarly to the physical domain, the DTE delineates varied co-occurring corseting discourses in producing feminine docile bodies. Inhabiting one's body with an objectified lens, seeing one's body as a deficient site requiring ongoing repair, experiencing the body as a demure domain of submission, engaging in passionless stereotyped feminine activities, controlling and containing desire, and losing valued sisterhood relationships all work in unison to rob women of agency and power. Rather than singling out just one of these discourses, all of them, and the related linguistic labels, need to be named, interrogated, and contested together. These discourses, aimed at producing docile girls and women who reside in docile bodies, indeed affirm the relationship between social discourses and structures of power. In addition to femininity molds, corseting molds that regulate embodied lives relate to all aspects of social location. The DTE emphasizes the intersection of constraining discourses related to different aspects of social location on embodied lives.

In the social power domain, the DTE expands beyond the current emphasis on exposure to body-based harassment and prejudice (Bucchianeri et al., 2014). Examining the body in terms of its social capital, the theory emphasizes the importance of access to resources, such as education, in determining the long-term quality of embodied lives of diverse girls and women. Freedom from body-based harassment and prejudice similarly enhance embodiment. The theory also highlights the importance of empowering relational connections with individuals or communities. Educational settings can be pivotal; validating one's worth and offering a critical understanding of struggles within existing social structures. Role modeling by an individual who shares important personal characteristics with a specific girl or woman (e.g., gender, race/ethnicity) is an important component of empowering relational connections. The validation provided within the context of empowering relational connections resembles the processes of consciousness-raising groups described by MacKinnon (1989): "Consciousness raising, through socializing women's knowing, transforms it, creating a shared reality that clears a space in the world within which women can begin to move" (p. 101). Similarly, Hill Collins (2000) described the way in which, through daily actions, African-American women have created alternative communities that empower them to act in the world.

Another component emphasized by the DTE is membership in at least one community where equity is practiced. Coates (2015), described the power of this experience when referring to attending Howard University,

> "I first witnessed this power out on the Yard [of Howard University], that communal green space in the center of the campus where the students gathered and I saw everything I knew of my black self multiplied out into seemingly endless variation" (p. 40).

The DTE also problematizes the use of appearance as a source of social power. In particular, the theory describes the ways in which girls and women are penalized for either abiding or not abiding by idealized appearance expectations. The theory therefore suggests that social power shapes embodied lives through multiple weaved processes.

Anchored in girls and women's narratives, the DTE describes multiple social processes, grouped into three key domains: the physical, mental, and social power and relational connections that together shape the embodied lives of girls and women. The delineation of these social processes provides both a close look at the tightening corsets girls endure in the transition from girlhood to womanhood, and of constructive possibilities in the life of girls and women. The rest of this book will be dedicated to examining this transition.

The Body Journeys of Jane and Crystal

The Body Journey construct reflects shifts in the EE in relation to changes in the complex social experiences of girls and women throughout their lives. This last section of the chapter provides a short description of the body journeys of Jane and Crystal with the theoretical constructs of the DTE woven in. (Note: The theoretical constructs have been capitalized throughout the volume.) The stories may help clarify the value of considering all aspects of the theory in explaining the marked differences in the quality of Jane and Crystal's embodied lives.

Jane: A Journey of (Mostly) Freedom

Overall, Jane has experienced considerable Physical Freedom, Mental Freedom, and Social Power and Relational Connections. In terms of Physical Freedom, Jane described experiences of Freedom in Physical Engagement and Movement, and Safety from Body Violations, as well as Safety from Coercive Body Alterations and Practices that she enjoyed as a girl. She contrasted her freedom with the Physical Corseting of other girls.

> Having that freedom to go off to the park and playing on the swings and play and get dirty and have fun. I mean, some girls wore dresses every day, little pretty shoes, and their hair was all done up… so they couldn't go out and play soccer-baseball in the mud field and you're not allowed to come home dirty… I'd go out at recess and play with the boys because they were playing active games and I really enjoyed that, and the girls would usually just sit and chat and that sort of thing.

Jane has also experienced Mental Freedom within her close relationships. In particular, freedom of passion, opinion, and voice was encouraged in her family. "Family conversations… on Sunday though, it was the rule. We all sat together as a family and conversation was anything goes, sexuality, drugs…" Jane was clear that she did not abide by the social mold of Engagement in "Feminine" Activities, in particular care-taking. In her example, she challenges psychological essentialism that views care-taking as an inborn exclusive characteristic of women:

> And while the girls who hung out… were playing with their Barbie dolls so they could dress them up. They were doing the more docile activities, the more traditional thing, what psychologists say girls do, the bonding and pairing, the nurturing things. The stray cat would wander on [the field], they'd be, 'oh look. That's a kitty.' We were like, 'get the kitty off the field so the kitty doesn't get hurt.'

Similarly, unlike most girls and women, Jane did not feel confined by the commonly polarized construction of the tomboy/girly girl dichotomy. Hence, in challenging Regulating Dichotomies and Labels, she saw herself as "a very active girl," one who is engaged in and derives pleasure from active play. "I don't think the two are mutually exclusive. I was always aware of being a girl… but I was a very active girl… I was the fastest girl in my class. I'm allowed to be anything in between."

Regarding social power, Jane has experienced gender equity at home, hence an opportunity for Membership in Equitable Communities: "… and [father] was in the home, he had to cook, he had to iron, he had to take care of laundry and that sort of thing." She also had strong empowering social connections with her family members, peers, and community-based church members. Further, she had positive women role models in life, such as her aunt, hence experiencing Engagement in Empowering Relationships. "My aunt was also very much into reading and so when she had more money we would go to the bookstore and she'd buy us a book so I had an extensive book collection."

Jane's main challenges to social power relate to her family's socioeconomic standing, which she described as being at the "lower end of the SES [socioeconomic status] scale." However, Jane emphasized that she did not experience

Restricted Access to Resources. She described that, as long as she worked as a babysitter, she was able to afford all social activities with her peers. "We could do whatever social activities we want, we just had to pay for them with our own money." While her peers at times targeted the clothes she could afford as a basis for Body-based Harassment, she had well-developed resistant strategies. She highlighted her strengths related to having to work—in particular time management skills, resistant self-talk, and publicly standing up to harassment:

> I had to work. You have to make sacrifices but I learned very early how to adjust. Time management was a skill it taught me—if you wanted to go out and have friends, and if you wanted to do the schoolwork and get half decent grades. Also, I didn't see the need to pay 80 dollars for a pair of jeans when I could buy a perfectly good pair of jeans for 20 dollars… I'd call them on it. I would tease them back.

Jane, like all girls and women in our studies, experienced disruptive events—likely the most commonplace of them upon the onset of puberty, at age 10 and throughout early adolescence. Compelled by the physical changes to her body, she joined other girls engaged in sedentary activities at the margins of her school yard and stopped playing outdoors, hence experiencing Physical Corseting: Blocked Physical Engagement and Constriction of Movement in the public sphere. She described,

> Of course playing soccer-baseball became problematic when you started to develop breasts because you can't catch the ball… that's when I started hanging out with the girls and doing the walking around the school or the sitting and chatting.

Further, it is particularly disturbing that, at that time, she also experienced Violation to her Body Territory by a female teacher—an experience that made her feel like "a freak" for developing early. "What was even worse was my female gym teacher was one of the persons that pinged my bra strap. And that was devastating because I was thinking I was some kind of freak or something." Moreover, as is very common at that age, there was peer pressure on Jane to engage in body alterations—mainly the application of makeup—subjecting her to Coercive Body Alterations. "The fact that I was wearing makeup was sort of peer defined."

Jane also experienced Mental Corseting at the age of 10 in one specific domain. Discovering her brothers' "raunchy magazines" at home shifted the way she saw her body, from a subjective to an objectified site:

> Hey, women are sexual and, you know, the female, naked body is… something to be looked at… I started thinking sexual thoughts and wondering about me personally as a sexual object and that sort of thing.

This jarring exposure to the Body as an Object of Gaze discourse of the Appearance-related cluster (see Table 1.2), led to ongoing preoccupation with the appearance of her body and shifted her subjectively felt sexual desire to that of being a sexual object—at a significant cost to her embodied experience.

Another challenge to Jane's Mental Freedom at that time related to having to deal with peer criticism regarding her academic success and vocal participation in class. She was targeted for not complying with the Comportment-related Discourses: the Woman as Docile, and in particular, Woman as Submissive/Demure, "so you learn not to put your hand up as often as you feel." Yet, a student-teacher at the same time noticed her talent in class and encouraged her to pursue her interests in the sciences, discouraging her from following the Engagement in "Feminine" Activities discourse, also an aspect of the Comportment-related Discourses: the Woman as Docile. He specifically challenged the gender bias in the sciences: "You know you are doing well in sciences and you're a girl. And there aren't enough women in sciences. You might want to consider pursuing a career in it." This encouragement to pursue the sciences protected her at the end of high school from a sexist guidance counselor that tried to dissuade her from pursuing a science education in the sciences.

Despite a number of disruptive experiences in the physical and mental domains during early adolescence, Jane managed to maintain a caring connection to her body, and during young adulthood was able to shift back to embodied experiences that resembled her positive childhood EE. Several protective factors in the physical, mental, and social power domains supported Jane's continued positive embodiment. In the physical domain, besides the episode of her teacher's harassment, Jane had experienced Safety for the Body Territory in all her dating experiences or other social experiences.

Another, very important, protective factor in the physical domain is the continued attuned Care of the Body in which Jane engaged with her parents' support. For example, in managing the onset of menstruation: "it was something my mother and I had discussed and it was something that my mother was fairly open with and I knew what pads were." Further, it should be noted that Jane is the only participant in our studies whose mother provided her with validation of sexual desire and guided her in the practice of said desire. Jane's mother was also open to Jane's questioning of her sexual orientation during adolescence, expressing acceptance of any place in the continuum in which Jane would ultimately find herself. Jane therefore experienced Freedom of Desire throughout the challenging period of adolescence and beyond:

> I loved kissing, but I never really felt the need to go beyond, no one ever really pushed. I mean, my mother was honest enough to tell me that the first time is not a very good thing or not usually all that

> wonderful that it takes time for it to be a good event, and so I didn't want to waste it on something where if it's not going to be good, you at least want to like the person… well I am glad I waited and, well, I do feel sex was a very good thing for my body, also because he likes my body.

Feeling comfortable in sexual desire, Jane has helped other adolescents, and later other women connect with their sexual desires. "Why shouldn't women sit around and talk about sex, but if you don't talk about it, then you can't figure out where the issues lie."

Another protective factor in the physical domain, Safety from Coercive Body Alterations and Practices, relates to the freedom Jane experienced at home, both from pressures to engage in body alterations as well as from pressures not to engage in body alterations:

> And I bless my mother for letting me wear all that makeup in junior high. So I didn't feel the need to rebel against anything that she was imposing on me and I could be now… grow up to be the adult I am now and say, no makeup.

In young adulthood, Jane returns to engagement in physical activities for the first time since the age of 10. While she, like most of our research participants, has not been able to recapture the same sense of Physical Freedom of being joyfully immersed in physical activities in the public sphere, and the same experience of body functionality, Jane regularly engages in yoga, which she finds enhances body awareness, and does weight lifting to strengthen her body and prepare it for pregnancy.

In terms of Mental Freedom, Jane's continued discussions regarding the continuum of sexual preferences indicate her maintained stance of Mental Freedom, challenging Regulating Dichotomies and Labels: "it's more of a continuum and looking at people on more of an individualistic sense as opposed to cutting off half the population because they're the wrong sex."

Throughout later adolescence and into early adulthood, Jane has continued to experience Social Power and Relational Connections with others. A few disruptive events related to her gender, which could have resulted in Restricted Access to Resources, included a guidance counselor that questioned her ability to cope with the sciences and being expected to temporarily compromise certain academic goals in order take care of her parents' household. Nonetheless, receiving loans for university education, reflecting Access to Resources, supported the maintenance of Social Power. Her circle of Engagement in Empowering Relationships has widened in university on discovering a quality of sisterhood she had not experienced in high school: "I found female friendships where the people have the same mindset educationally and have the same values and ideals."

The story of Jane reflects the power of protective factors in the physical, mental, and social power domains, despite the disruptions she encountered in adolescence in the physical and mental domains.

Crystal: A Journey with (Multiple) Corsets

Crystal experienced many challenges in the domains of Physical Freedom, Mental Freedom, and Social Power and Relational Connections. In terms of Physical Corseting, Crystal described repeated Violations to the Body Territory at the hands of her father and neighborhood boys:

> Well, when I was a kid, like, [my father] used to beat me up, right... He would come home from work upset and would take it on us. He is abusive and has a temper problem. He would yell at my mother and she would not yell back. She really appeared not to have any opinion in the house. He threatened her many times... My mom sometimes she would try to stand up for us but he would threaten that he would hit her or that he would divorce her and stuff like that... I feared a lot.
>
> I remember when I was in first, second, and third grade, guys had this silly habit of trying to attack girls with snow and beat them up. And like put snow in their face and like ha ha ha ha. I hated that, right.

Crystal's response to what she perceived as the physical vulnerability of girls and women was to seek Physical Freedom, both Freedom in Physical Engagement and Freedom of Movement, in the *disguise of a boy*. She did this all the way from the beginning of grade school until age 14. Together with a boy from the neighborhood, and looking like him, she was free to roam the streets.

> I cut my hair really short and hanged around with the guys and was pretty violent and everything... I was wearing boys' clothes and this big wool hat. I was pretty much covering my features. You couldn't tell I was a female.

Regarding Mental Freedom, during childhood Crystal also developed rigid molds about girls and women versus boys and men. Her exposure to discourses from the Woman as Docile cluster, and in particular to the Woman as Submissive/Demure and Engagement in "Feminine" Activities discourses (see Table 1.2), caused her much distress. She saw girls and women as "sissies" and firmly resisted identifying as a girl.

> I was never comfortable being a girl. I always wanted to be a boy up until the age of 14. I wanted to have control of my life at least more

> than my mom had or other girls, the way like, the way females are supposed to be. Especially, the way they teach us in school the stories that we read. Like, there was no talk of strong female models. Females were a sidekick to some male... Girls were playing the stereotypical girlie activities. Guys were playing hunters and girls were supposedly cooking and preparing food for them. I never liked playing with dolls so I guess, I was identifying with the boys and I wanted to act more like a bad boy kind of thing. I was violent and I thought I was so macho.

Identifying as a boy helped restore Crystal's experience of social power. She had no access to alternative sources of social power as she experienced power inequity at home. She wished as a child that her "mom would take control of her life." She had no Empowering Relationships with girls or women, and no women role models.

The temporary freedom she achieved through living on the borrowed body territory of a boy came to an abrupt stop at puberty, a process that exerted the most devastating and lasting effect on her senses of physical freedom, identity, and social power. "I started growing breasts in grade five... the worst nightmare... horrible, horrible... I cried so much like I was so sad." Since she could no longer easily pass as a boy, Physical Corseting replaced Physical Freedom. She no longer roamed the streets freely and was exposed to forced compliance with restrictive body practices. "[My parents] forced me to wear this tight pink dress and get out of the house in it." Further, her self-consciousness about her developing body led her to stop her martial arts training. Crystal also complained about street harassment: "you do get whistled at, comments, like 'you have big boobs,' on the street or jogging." In addition, she got little guidance in the area of Body Care with respect to how to deal with menstruation and other bodily changes. "I had the impression that it was a one-time thing. You get it once and then that's it. I hated like having breasts and all the feminine features."

When a "crush" she had on a boy at that time was not responded to in kind, and with little support to help her deal with this experience of early physical desire, she was convinced that there was something "wrong" with her body, leading to the development of anorexia: "I wasn't desired by this guy that he didn't care for me. That caused my hate of my body and I became anorexic. I was totally not interested in... guys anymore. I couldn't care less." Her experience of sexual desire was never restored. Instead, she has engaged in heterosexual sexual practices without desire, often due to pressures by her dates and, at times, re-enacting the lack of physical safety she has experienced at home.

In line with the DTE, Crystal has made a clear distinction between Freedom in Physical Engagement that involved immersion in joyful, non-objectifying, non-sexualizing, non-appearance–related or weight-related physical activities and joyless physical activities aimed at body alteration, which she considers an aspect of Physical Corseting. In that way, she contrasted her passionate immersion in karate with her compulsive jogging while suffering from anorexia during adolescence, and with her continued weight preoccupation during adulthood.

> When I had anorexia I would just not eat. And on top of that I was going *jogging* every day and when your body is like, um, not fed properly obviously you're going to lose a lot of weight and it was a very horrible thing. Like constant emptiness in my stomach and it was just terrible, terrible. And I had changed my, personality completely changed. Like, I *wasn't engaging in all the physical activities anymore.*

> I run on the track sometimes, but it's not something I do, like with pleasure you know. I just did it as… I got to do my cardio, because today, this week, I have been eating quite a lot… And of course, like if I put on weight because I haven't been doing my cardio I certainly feel bad about myself… And it's just like a roller coaster, like as soon as that happens, you know, you start feeling bad about your body, and then you start feeling bad about other aspects of yourself.

Crystal continued to experience Mental Corseting throughout adolescence and young adulthood, related to her strong internalization of both Appearance-related and Comportment-related Discourses. This Mental Corseting compounded the experiences of Physical Corseting. In line with the Appearance-related Discourses: The Body as a Deficient Object, she felt that her body was "wrong."

> I realize that growing up in woman's body, you somehow get the idea that your body's wrong, that there are things that are negative about your body… just like the pressure on women to be thin, and like have that model look. The whole media messages that cause us to feel the way we feel about ourselves. And tell us that you know, 'your body's not good.' If a woman felt beautiful about herself, there wouldn't be in such an industry.

Crystal was similarly struggling with Comportment-related Discourses: The Woman as Docile, and, in particular, Woman as Submissive/Demure. Sharing her wishes to pursue her dreams with her mother, she often encountered her mother's use of the term "selfish." Crystal highlighted this area of struggle for women and contrasted this experience to that of men.

> If I take care of myself, my dreams, people consider you selfish… 'Oh you're so selfish.' Like I hear this from my mom constantly, you know, like 'you only think about yourself'… And even though as a

> mother, she may think she's thinking about myself but really, she's just projecting her own desires on me. Trying to live through me in some way… I do feel, like in a way, of course, like society makes us feel like we are being selfish, if we try to assert ourselves or take care of ourselves, you know. It's like it's because we've been taught, take care of other people, or put other people first, you know. Give, give, give… Be giving, be helpful to others and stuff. But, honestly, I cannot do that wholeheartedly unless I think that I'm taking care of myself first. I mean I'm involved in all those things, and I'm willing to help but I, I don't put my heart in it as much as I could. Because simply my number one needs are not being met, my number one desires are not being fulfilled… I don't think a guy who is trying to assert himself, like for example start his own business, or do his own thing, I don't think there would be as much of… being called selfish for it… Like I think that would seem kind of natural.

Related to these constraining discourses, Crystal has found herself facing challenges in pursuing her passions with clarity, assertiveness, and freedom.

The domain of Social Power and Relational Connections remained challenging for Crystal during her adolescence and early adulthood. The relational disconnection from girls and women she felt as a girl continued through this time. Appearance-based Social Power became prevalent among girls in high school and created competition for thinness—"all the girls were dieting." Similarly, her relationships with boys and then men were disrupted by her continued feelings of vulnerability: "the idea of being with one person, I want to have my freedom." The process of moving from a rural to an urban setting, which happened during later adolescence, further exposed her to prejudicial treatment, "Because of my accent, because I didn't have the best clothes, I got made fun of." Additionally, she had no access at the time to Empowering Relationships. Actually, her mother, likely as a projection of her own helplessness, tended to discourage such hopes. "She's got this negative outlook. Every time I would come up with some idea, like working in the health field, she kept putting my dreams down." Crystal also had never experienced being part of an Equitable Community, at home or elsewhere. Her mother continued to be powerless at home. "Well she never stood up for herself, that my dad would yell at her and she would not yell back. She really appeared not to have any opinion in the house, she played his games." Crystal clarified that she also has never had, "a sense of a community in my life, I miss being part of a supportive community."

Crystal's story reflects the challenges faced by a girl or woman who encounters multiple risk factors and few protective factors in her body journey. Her continued seeking of education and occupational goals and of relational connections is inspiring.

CHAPTER SUMMARY

This chapter provided a delineation of the Experience of Embodiment construct, as well as of the key constructs of the Developmental Theory of Embodiment. The body journeys of two research participants aimed to contextualize the theoretical constructs in lived experiences. Familiarity with these research-based constructs equips the reader to examine the embodied transitions from girlhood to older womanhood described in the following chapters.

References

Bartky, S. (1988). Foucault, femininity, and the modernization of patriarchal power. In I. Diamond & L. Quinby (Eds.), *Feminism & Foucault: Reflections on resistance*. Boston, MA: Northeastern University Press.

de Beauvoir, S. (1989). The second sex (H.M. Parshley, Trans.). New York, NY: Random House.

Bordo, S. (1988). Anorexia nervosa: Psychopathology as a crystallization of culture. In I. Diamond & L. Quinby (Eds.), *Feminism & Foucault: Reflections on resistance* (pp. 87–117). Boston: Northern University Press.

Bordo, S. (1989). The body and the reproduction of femininity: A feminist appropriation of Foucault. In A. M. Jaggar & S. R. Bordo (Eds.), *Gender/body/knowledge* (pp. 13–33). New Brunswick, NJ: Rutgers University.

Bordo, S. (1993). *Unbearable weight: Feminism, western culture, and the body*. Berkeley, CA: University of California Press.

Bourdieu, P. (1984). *Distinction: A social critique of the judgment of taste*. Cambridge, MA: Harvard University Press.

Brown, L. M. (2003). *Girlfighting: Betrayal and rejection among girls*. New York, NY: New York University Press.

Bucchianeri, M. M., Eisenberg, M. E., Wall, M. M., Piran, N., & Neumark-Sztainer, D. (2014). Multiple types of harassment: Associations with emotional well-being and unhealthy behaviors in adolescents. *Journal of Adolescent Health, 54*(6), 724–729.

Charmaz, K. (2006). *Constructing grounded theory: A practical guide through qualitative analysis*. Thousand Oaks, CA: Sage.

Coates, T. (2015). *Between the world and me*. New York, NY: Spiegel & Grau.

Cole, A. L., & Knowles, J. G. (2001). *Lives in context; the art of life history research*. Walnut Creek, CA: Altamira Press.

Cook-Cottone, C. P. (2015). Incorporating positive body image into the treatment of eating disorders: A model for attunement and mindful self-care. *Body Image, 14*, 158–167.

Cottle, M. (2016). The era of 'The Bitch' is coming. *The Atlantic* (August Issue). Retrieved from: https://www.theatlantic.com/politics/archive/2016/08/the-era-of-the-bitch-is-coming/496154/.

Crossley, N. (1995). Merleau-Ponty, the elusive body and carnal sociology. *Body and Society, 1*, 43–63.

Daubenmier, J. J. (2005). The relationship between yoga, body awareness, and body responsiveness to self-objectification and disordered eating. *Psychology of Women Quarterly, 29*, 207–219.

Dubecki, L. (February 08, 2007). *Skimpy dress code deals a body blow to netball numbers. The Age*. Melbourne, Australia. Retrieved from: http://www.theage.com.au/news/national/skimpy-dress-code-deals-a-body-blow-to-netball-numbers/2007/02/07/1170524164114.html.

Fahs, B. (2015). The body in revolt: The impact and legacy of second wave corporeal embodiment. *Journal of Social Issues, 71*(2), 386–401.

Fine, M. (1988). Sexuality, schooling, and adolescent females: The missing discourse of desire. *Harvard Educational Review, 58*, 29–53.

Fonow, M. M., & Cook, J. (1991). *Beyond methodology: Feminist scholarship as lived research*. Bloomington, IN: Indiana University Press.

Foucault, M. (1979). *Discipline and punish (Alan Sheridan, Trans)*. New York, NY: Vintage.

Fredrickson, B. L., & Roberts, T. (1997). Objectification theory: Toward understanding women's lived experiences and mental health risks. *Psychology of Women Quarterly, 21*, 173–206.

Green, J. (2011). The tragedy of Sarah Palin. *The Atlantic* (June Issue). Retrieved from: https://www.theatlantic.com/magazine/archive/2011/06/the-tragedy-of-sarah-palin/308492/.

Herman, J. (1992). *Trauma and recovery*. New York, NY: Basic Books.

Hill Collins, P. (2000). *Black feminist thought: Knowledge, consciousness, and the politics of empowerment* (2nd ed.). New York, NY: Routledge.

Hooks, B. (2000). *Feminism is for everybody: Passionate politics*. London: Pluto Press.

Katzman, M. A., & Lee, S. (1997). Beyond body image: The integration of feminist and transcultural theories in the understanding of self starvation. *International Journal of Eating Disorders, 22*, 385–394.

Kawachi, I., Kennedy, B. P., & Prothrow-Stith, D. (1999). Women's status and the health of women and men: A view from the states. *Social Science and Medicine, 48*(1), 21–32.

Larkin, J., & Rice, C. (2005). Beyond "healthy eating" and "healthy weights": Harassment and the health curriculum in middle schools. *Body Image, 2*, 219–232.

MacKinnon, C. A. (1989). *Towards a feminist theory of the state*. Cambridge, MA: Harvard University Press.

McKinley, N. M., & Hyde, J. S. (1996). The objectified body consciousness scale: Development and validation. *Psychology of Women Quarterly, 20*, 181–215.

McLaren, P. (1995). White terror and oppositional agency: Towards a critical multiculturalism. In C. E. Sleeter, & P. McLaren (Eds.), *Multicultural education, critical pedagogy, and the politics of difference*. New York: SUNY press.

Mendelson, B. K., Mendelson, M. J., & White, D. R. (2001). Body esteem scale for adolescents and adults. *Journal of Personality Assessment, 76*(1), 90–106.

Merleau-Ponty, M. (1962). Phenomenology of perception. Trans. Colin Smith. New York: Humanities.

Neumark-Sztainer, D., Paxton, S. J., Hannan, P. J., Haines, J., Story, M. (2006). Does body satisfaction matter? Five-year longitudinal associations between body satisfaction and health behaviors in adolescent females and males. *Journal of Adolescent Health, 39*(2), 244–251.

Oakley, M. A., Addison, S. C., Piran, N., Johnston, G. J., Damianakis, M., Curry, J., Dunbar, C., & Weigeldt, A. (2013). Outcome study of brief relational-cultural therapy in a women's mental health center. *Psychotherapy Research, 23*(2), 137–151.

Piran, N. (2002). Embodiment: A mosaic of inquiries in the area of body weight and shape preoccupation. In S. Abbey (Ed.), *Ways of knowing in and through the body: Diverse perspectives on embodiment* (pp. 211–214). Welland, ON: Soleil Publishing.

Piran, N. (2010). Social critical theory, embodiment and counseling. In *Building bridges for wellness in counselling and psychotherapy* (pp. 77–89). Center for Diversity in Counselling and Psychotherapy Sampura-Montfort (Bangalore, India) and the Center for Diversity in Counselling Ontario Institute of Studies in Education of the University of Toronto.

Piran, N. (July 2014). Embodying the 'ideal girl' appearance in adolescence: The eroding journey to elusive power. In *Paper presented at the appearance matters 6 conference, Bristol, England*.

Piran, N. (2015). New possibilities in the prevention of eating disorders: The introduction of positive body image measures. *Body Image, 14*, 146–157.

Piran, N. (2016a). Embodied possibilities and disruptions: The emergence of the experience of embodiment construct from qualitative studies with girls and women. *Body Image, 18*, 43–60.

Piran, N. (2016b). Embodied paths in aging: Body journeys towards enhanced agency and self-attunement. *Women and Therapy, 39*, 186–201.

Piran, N. (2016c). Embodiment and well being: The embodied journeys of girls and women. In T.-A. Roberts, N. Curtin, L. Cortina, & L. E. Duncan (Eds.), *Best practices in feminist psychological science: Gender beyond difference* (pp. 43–60). New York, NY: Springer.

Piran, N., Carter, W., Thompson, S., & Pajouhandeh, P. (2002). Powerful girls: A contradiction in terms? Young women speak about the experience of growing up in a girl's body. In S. Abbey (Ed.), *Ways of knowing in and through the body: Diverse perspectives on embodiment* (pp. 206–210). Welland, ON: Soleil Publishing.

Piran, N., & Cormier, H. (2005). The social construction of women and disordered eating patterns. *Journal of Counseling Psychology, 52*(4), 549–558.

Piran, N., & Teall, T. L. (2012). The developmental theory of embodiment. In G. McVey, M. P. Levine, N. Piran, & H. B. Ferguson (Eds.), *Preventing eating-related and weight-related disorders: Collaborative research, advocacy, and policy change* (pp. 171–199). Waterloo, ON: Wilfred Laurier Press.

Piran, N., & Thompson, S. (2008). A study of the Adverse Social Experiences model to the development of eating disorders. *International Journal of Health Promotion and Education, 46*(2), 65–71.

Saltz, J. (2009). Out of the erotic ghetto: The Whitney's welcome retrospective rescues Georgia O'Keeffe from sex and flowers. *The New York Times* (Sep 20 Issue). Retrieved from: http://nymag.com/arts/art/reviews/59249/.

Senn, C. Y., Gee, S. S., & Thake, J. (2011). Emancipatory sexuality education and sexual assault resistance: Does the former enhance the latter? *Psychology of Women Quarterly, 35*(1), 72–91.

Simms, R. (2001). Controlling images and the gender construction of enslaved African women. *Gender & Society, 15*(6), 879–897.

Smolak, L., & Piran, N. (2012). Gender and the prevention of eating disorders. In G. McVey, M. P. Levine, N. Piran, & H. B. Ferguson (Eds.), *Preventing eating-related and weight-related disorders: Collaborative research, advocacy, and policy change* (pp. 201–224). Waterloo, ON: Wilfred Laurier Press.

Stice, E., Marti, C. N., & Durant, S. (2011). Risk factors for onset of eating disorders: Evidence of multiple risk pathways from an 8-year prospective study. *Behavior Research and Therapy, 49*(10), 622–627.

Taylor, G. J., Bagby, R. M., & Parker, J. D. A. (1991). The alexithymia construct: A potential paradigm for psychosomatic medicine. *Psychosomatics, 32*, 153–164.

Teall, T. L. (2015). *A quantitative study of the developmental theory of embodiment implications to health and well-being*. Toronto, Canada: University of Toronto. Retrieved from: https://tspace.library.utoronto.ca/handle/1807/69750.

Teall, T. L., & Piran, N. (August 2015). The embodiment scales for women: A psychometric study of the experience of embodiment scale. In *Poster presented at the annual convention of the American Psychological Association, Toronto.*

Tiggemann, M. (2005). Body dissatisfaction and adolescent self-esteem: Prospective findings. *Body Image, 2*(2), 129–135.

Tolman, D. L. (2002). *Dilemmas of desire: Teenage girls talk about sexuality*. Cambridge, MA: Harvard University Press.

Tolman, D. L., Bowman, C. P., & Fahs, B. (2014). Sexuality and embodiment. In D. L. Tolman & L. M. Diamond (Eds.), *APA handbook of sexuality and psychology*. Washington DC: American Psychological Association.

Tylka, T. L., & Wood-Barcalow, N. L. (2015). Body appreciation scale-2: Item refinement and psychometric evaluation. *Body Image, 12*, 53–67.

Tyldesley, J. (2008). *Cleopatra: The last queen of Egypt*. New York: Basic Books.

Webb, J. B., Butler-Ajibade, P., & Robinson, S. A. (2014). Considering an affect regulation framework for examining the association between body dissatisfaction and positive body image in black older adolescent females: Does body mass index matter? *Body Image, 11*, 426–437.

CHAPTER

2

Qualified Freedom on Borrowed Territories: Early Childhood to Age Eight

> My best friend was a boy and I'd always go with him and we'd catch bugs and frogs and stuff. And then I just liked playing outside and playing sports and stuff. I hung out with mostly guys. We played soccer and stuff. There were another couple of girls that I played with but then the other girls would be playing Barbies or they played Teletubby games or stuff and I wasn't interested in that. I don't think I cared at all. It was great! It didn't matter what I was wearing or what I looked like. The focus was on who I was with and on what I was doing... I would be out in the field having fun!

In this quotation, 13-year-old Melissa, a White girl from a middle-class rural background, describes her experiences of positive and joyful connection with her body, passionate immersion in active play, physical agency and functionality, and the lack of appearance-related self-consciousness. Girls' narratives about their early childhoods, from their earliest memories to the age of eight, reveal the most positive experiences of embodiment when compared with girls at any other phase in the transition from girlhood to womanhood. These early positive experiences provide an important—and often missing in research—yardstick to positively inhabiting one's body.

Research on the ways girls live in their bodies has focused to date on the experiences of older girls and young women, as well as on experiences of disrupted rather than positive embodiment (Piran, 2015; Tylka & Wood-Barcalow, 2015). The exploration of girls' embodiment needs to address early childhood in order to capture the range of positive experiences not present later in most girls' lives. For example, an interview study on

Journeys of Embodiment at the Intersection of Body and Culture
http://dx.doi.org/10.1016/B978-0-12-805410-9.00002-5

body image among girls and boys (Tatangelo & Ricciardelli, 2013), aged 8–10 years, found that boys maintained their connection to their physical functionality and agency—one dimension of positive Experience of Embodiment (EE)—while girls already emphasized appearance when discussing body image. The experience of physical functionality, free of appearance considerations, might therefore be a fleeting experience for most girls. Indeed, in our research program girls identified the end of third grade and turning 9 years old as bringing about a shift in their embodied experiences. Further, younger and older women repeatedly mentioned their wish to return to the positive experiences of embodiment they remembered from their early childhood, utilizing terms such as "regaining my innocence," and "opening up and being comfortable in my own skin."

The heightened sense of positive embodiment among girls during early childhood, we find, is strongly connected to experiences of Physical Freedom, Mental Freedom, and Social Power and Connection with Others, the three dimensions of social experiences that shape the EE according to the Developmental Theory of Embodiment (DTE). However, concurrently with the experiences of Physical Freedom, Mental Freedom, and Social Power during their first 8 years, girls also learn about the socially constructed girl/boy dichotomy. They further experience the shaping of interpersonal interactions by societal structures of power and privilege related to gender, race and ethnicity, socioeconomic status, weight, and physical ability. These experiences present *corsets* to the relative freedom of early childhood. The next three sections will examine experiences in the domains of the physical, mental (regarding social stereotypes), and social power and connection with others during early childhood.

MAY I COME IN? PHYSICAL FREEDOM ON BORROWED TERRITORIES

> We would go outside but we stayed outside all the time. We'd go to ponds and stuff and try to catch things like mice and frogs and turtles and stuff like that. We'd catch bugs. I'd always have boys over after school and we'd always go out exploring in the bush and the fields whatever. This boy was in my class and we hung out with his older brothers. They'd always take us to these places that they'd found.

In this paragraph, Melissa continues her description of outdoor play, in particular: her nature explorations during early childhood. Girls living in urban settings similarly describe immersion in pleasurable outdoor activities, as 13-year-old Lauren, a White girl of middle-class background, describes her experiences in the first grade:

> We [brothers, and other boys and girls] play tag, we were always outside... we used to play basketball, hockey on the street too, we ran around. We'd bike down... there's the park between our houses so we'd go down that lane.

Madison, 9 year old, of Aboriginal heritage and a working-class background describes, "We'd go to the park near my dad's house to play tennis. It's like our one-person playground." Hilary, a 9-year-old White girl of a working-class background shares, "If you are acting like a guy you can play guy stuff and they can actually trust you to play with them, like play in the mud and everything."

We find that acting physically in the world is most common for girls during early childhood than at any other period in the transition from girlhood to womanhood, whereby acting on one's body gradually replaces acting in the world. This physical agency relates to girls' experiences at that age involving Physical Freedom and, in particular, Freedom in Physical Engagement and Movement in the Public Sphere, and of the Freedom to Take Physical Space (refer to Table 1.2). At this early phase, girls act in response to their own passions for engaging physically in the world with a sense of subjective attunement and limited external consciousness. Their focus is on doing physical activities with immersion and joy. It is also the only phase in girls or women's lives in which action is free of the goal of body alterations.

Through their engagement with the world, girls enhance both their physical competence and their sense of agency. They also experience joy in action. Adjectives related to strength, pride, and joy, as well as to "just doing" and "not caring" (about looks) appear often in relation to physical activities. Madison, a third-grade student of Aboriginal heritage who turned 9 years just prior to the first interview, and is of a working-class background, describes her experiences during the past year:

> I showed [a boy] I can skip frontwards and then you cross over and do it really good backwards so fast and he's like, 'Wow, you can go backwards.' My real hobby is high jump—I am the only one who can jump like that. I feel I can actually do something. Also basketball, I can run really fast. I like that my legs are really long.

Emma, a 9-year-old White girl from a rural area, who has just finished grade 3, describes being in grades 1–3, "I played football and tag and running and doing more activities with the boys outside. And you're *having fun*. Like playing—you're not just sitting there watching people do it. You can actually play it." When asked about how she feels about her body while immersed in these activities, she replies, "Good, strong, and sporty." Older adolescents, younger and older women, often refer to these special experiences, of engaging in the physical environment with immersion, joy, and no self-consciousness, with great longing. Marie, a White woman in her mid-60s living in a rural setting, who describes feeling very comfortable in her body, says,

> I was thinking about how your upbringing affects you. The sports, being outside, were a big part of our life. It was all about what you could do, not what you wore or what you looked like. What a big part of my childhood it was!

In addition to immersed engagement, as the quotes above suggest, during childhood the girls describe a broad range of frequent sites of physical engagement: neighborhood streets or parks, community centers or pools, or other sites of outdoor explorations. They detail engaging in physical activities with boys all over the schoolyard, including at the center field of action—not just watching them from the margins, as happens later on. Furthermore, similar to this Freedom of Movement, they seemed to also feel comfortable Taking Physical Space (see Table 1.2). In particular, during early childhood girls sometimes describe the functional advantages of being bigger in size, especially of being taller. Just like Madison in the quotation above feels that her long legs give her an advantage in skipping and high jumping, Alice, a 9-year-old girl of Aboriginal heritage and a middle-class family, feels that being bigger has given her an edge in playing soccer, in physical encounters with boys, and in protecting other girls from harassment by boys during the first three grades of school. "I helped chase away boys who were chasing girls. Just standing in front of them and they just looked up at me and ran away."

However, despite these opportunities for physical activities, girls learn that physical pursuits in the public sphere take place on *borrowed territories*, territories belonging to boys and men, hence the title of this section. As girls notice, differential entitlement to physical territories is one aspect of privilege embedded in the socially constructed boy/girl dichotomy, which children learn most about during early childhood. The Physical Corseting related to differential entitlement to immersion in physical activity in the public sphere is one reason several girls and women describe wanting to be a boy during early childhood. Amber, a South Asian woman in her early 20s from a middle-class background, describes it aptly:

> Ever since I was old enough to kind of distinguish between guys and girls, I was like, 'I hate being a girl. I want to be a guy.' It was that bad... I remember in second or third grade I hated wearing dresses

> when we had to go out. That was a total pain for me. I mean, it was just that I enjoyed doing things guys did, playing outside, wrestling. My mom would be like 'Girls shouldn't do that.'

Girls observe that boys and men comprise a gateway to physical activities in the public sphere, and hence to Physical Freedom. Most often, girls immerse themselves in physical activities when they join boys in outdoor games or explorations, as their testimonies in this chapter reflect. Melissa describes accessing the gateway to her cherished nature explorations by saying, "He'd always take us." Lauren, Madison, Emma, and all other girls, and younger and older women, often refer to co-ed forums as being the only way to engage in immersed physical activities in the public sphere. Having brothers, friends who are boys, or being selected by the boys to join their games are essential to having such opportunities. Further, being picked by boys to participate in their active games in the schoolyard or out in the neighborhood carried an added bonus of being evaluated by boys as "equally competent." Being so evaluated during childhood remains an indication of physical prowess, a "gold standard" that adolescent girls and women carry with them as they move away from joyful physical activities. As described by Jane, a White woman in her mid-20s residing in a rural area, and having grown up in a working-class family:

> I was usually the first person picked by the boys. I was the fastest. I'd go out at recess and play with the boys because they were playing active games. I enjoyed that… I'm not anymore by any stretch of the imagination. But, back then I seemed to have this physical ability.

Fathers can also open doors to physical engagement in the public sphere. As Emma describes, "With my dad I play outside, explore and stuff, with my mom I do stuff like my hair." Similar to younger girls, adolescents and adult women have fond memories from childhood of engaging in outdoor activities with their fathers. Kelly, a 14-year-old girl of Latino heritage and a working-class background, recalls her experiences with her dad when in early elementary school, "In the summer I would play a lot of sports with my dad, and we had to walk pretty far to the beach, and we walked everywhere."

More rarely, girls prefer to look like boys to gain the same Physical Freedom as boys. For example, Bronwen a 12-year-old White girl from a rural area who resided temporarily in Europe, describes this experience at age 7,

> Bronwen: There was a ditch behind where we were living and there were some boys who used to go and play. So my hair was really short at that time so everyone thought I was a boy, so I'd just go out and play with them. I didn't really care. We just played around on the ice and we had fun.

Interviewer: Did any other girls participate in the game?
Bronwen: Nope.

Crystal, the White woman in her mid-20s whose body journey was portrayed in Chapter 1, describes the Physical Freedom she achieved by looking like a boy, all the way from age 5 to puberty: "I was wearing boy's clothes and this big wool hat... You couldn't tell I was a female... We were singing together in the street and the buses."

In addition to dealing with gaining admission to boys' territories and active pursuits, girls have to go through another hoop—another Physical Corset—to engage in immersed and joyful physical activities in the public sphere: the dress. They have to say "no" to the dress! The dress, a symbol of inhabiting a girl's body and reflecting adults' projections of gender constructions onto young girls' bodies, appears in the early memories of almost all girls and women as a significant and contentious object. Wearing a dress, young girls learn, is associated with the objectifying lens of "being pretty," and with comportment-related expectations of acting docile: nice and neat. Additionally, it is considered part of being a "normal" girl, as Madison, of Aboriginal heritage, describes:

Madison: In kindergarten I liked skirts and dresses. I thought I was pretty when I was wearing my dresses. I remember going to the [kids'] play and I had this sparkly dress on, and I thought I was really pretty 'cause I had like my hair up in a red little bun thingy and I really thought I looked pretty that time and I had my ears pierced and sliver little hoops.
Interviewer: So on that day, what do you think your body would have said?
Madison: That I am pretty but it matters what I wear 'cause like if I wear all these other things [baggy pants] I'm not very pretty but like if I wear *normal* little dresses or anything, I'm pretty.

Descriptions of wearing a dress are often further elaborated on with detailed descriptions of jewelry and the "taming" of hair, and less frequently with sexualizing elements such as wearing a bra in kindergarten. Hilary, a White grade 3 student raised in a working-class family, describes her experiences when in kindergarten:

I was wearing dresses and these boots. [Mom and I] thought they were in fashion. I wanted to wear something in fashion. Dresses were mostly what I had to wear. Actually I had some nylons on—but my skirts and dresses still flew up... people always laughed at me, and it was funny. Most of the time [my girlfriends and I] just walked around and talked about some stuff... I always wore this bracelet like my best friends and we all had pins in our hair... I've had a

> *bra* since kindergarten from my grandma. Actually I don't really like it because it's hard to keep track of them because the straps [slip down]... I'd have to brush my hair for like an hour to make it go like this. So, after that my mom would take the straightener and straighten it so I had to put it up and everything because it looked like I had a *rat's nest* in every part of my hair.

As girls start to engage with peers more independently in the social and physical environment, around kindergarten and the first grades of elementary school, they seek greater freedom to act physically in the world. They keenly observe the Physical Freedom to act passionately and physically in the world granted to boys. A rebellion against the dress-as-corset commonly ensues (sometimes associated with the rebellious cutting of long hair), claiming the right to move freely in the physical environment.

The shedding of the dress during early childhood most often does not involve systemized social penalties, as gender boundaries are most permeable at this stage. However, girls may encounter some parental resistance as well as shunning by girls who continue to comply with the corseting effect of the dress—creating social rifts between them. Girls commonly associate the shift to Physical Freedom with joy and pride, even when encountering struggles. Hilary, for example, started to wear jeans and t-shirts in grade 2 and, correspondingly, became more involved in sports, "because skirts, it's not really funny when they fly up because I don't got no nylons anymore... Now I play volleyball. We learn how to keep the ball up off the ground. It's great." Emma, a White grade 3 student of a middle-class background and who lives in a rural area, describes a similar process in great detail:

> [During Kindergarten] I played with Barbies and putting make up, playing house, dress up. I think I felt happy... In Grade 2 I guess I didn't like wearing dresses anymore. I thought they were too young for me, and stuff like that. So I decided to wear pants and t-shirts and stuff. I didn't really like wearing dresses. You just couldn't run in them and pants you could do a lot more activities and stuff and you get exercise and you're having *fun*... feel *strong and happy*.

Exploring the outdoors required similar attire to that of boys, as Melissa explains,

> I didn't care. My mom would try and force me to wear a dress but I didn't. I'd fight with her—I'd wear just big shirts and everything. I didn't care what I looked like; I just wanted to do stuff. It was great! One of my best friends was a boy and he didn't wear dresses and I just hated them.

Not wearing the dress also involved the freedom to get "messy"—as 14-year-old Lauren summarizes, "the muddier the better." Jane, reflecting as a young woman on her kindergarten years, similarly shares, "having that freedom to go off to the park and playing on the swings and play and get dirty and have fun."

Girls face other Physical Corsets to immersion in joyful physical activities at the intersection of gender and other dimensions of social location. While girls and women commonly describe being restricted to the domestic sphere due to carrying a greater load of home-based chores when compared with their male siblings or partners, only a few of the women describe experiencing restrictions at age 6 or 7 that precluded engagement in play outside of the house. Living with financial constraints is one dimension of social location that, at times, intersects with gender to disallow girls to engage in physical activities outside of the house. For example, Sam, a White woman in her early 20s of a working-class background, describes how as early as she can remember she had no opportunity to play outside, since she herself carried the responsibility of maintaining two households; her parents were separated and were both financially strained, one of them living with disability. She describes a memory from age 7: "[Dad] requested that I go [to mother's house] for one day every weekend instead of all weekend every second weekend because he needed me at home. He always had me doing some kind of chores." Similarly, Alex, a woman in her mid-20s of Latino heritage who grew up in Central America, describes the following:

> I was brought up in a very poor environment. I kind of stopped going to school in Grade 2. I was looking after two little brothers that I had... sometimes I would just want to run around, play soccer in the street and my mom would be calling me to do one thing or another.

In addition, poorer urban neighborhoods sometimes do not provide a safe context for outside physical activities, as experienced by Madison and other girls.

The intersection of gender and ethnocultural factors also shape opportunities for outdoor engagement. Racism sometimes acts to exclude particular individuals from shared activities in the public sphere. Eva, a woman of Asian heritage, describes the following:

> There was a pool. I was five or six. I didn't really have a body awareness like I'm fat, I'm thin. Well I knew I was a girl. The older boy said, 'You have funny hair, you're Chinese.' It was a form of ridicule the way he said it. I didn't go swimming anymore. I love water but I don't swim.

Alternatively, related to ethnocultural traditions, tighter rules may apply such as prohibiting girls' engagement outside of the house. When these values intersect with financial constraints and the multiple domestic chores associated with a busy family household, girls sometimes have no opportunity to experience physical agency in the public sphere. Reni, an Asian-Canadian woman in her 60s, describes life in her parents' household from early childhood: "I was the oldest daughter. I basically went to school and had to come home and help my mom. I didn't have the chance to go out with friends to play. My brothers were able to play sports." Growing up with physical disability also restricts engagement with the physical sphere. Margaret, a woman in her 60s, living with a physical disability since early childhood, spent much time in the hospital as a child. These restrictions have motivated her to seek hiking and travel as an adult.

The experience of Safety for the Body Territory is the second central dimension of Physical Freedom. Girls who are able to engage in the physical environment with freedom, while being safe, describe unequivocal experiences of joy in such engagement and tend to have positive connections to their bodies. Importantly, most girls had this experience during early childhood. There were only infrequent references to boys' teasing of girls, and they did not involve sexual harassment. Girls tend to respond assertively in these instances. For example, Hilary describes a few boys labeling her and other girls "babies," and responding by "[we walked] by them and we hit their shoulders and then we'd walk off."

However, significant ruptures to safety in early childhood did occur, introducing Physical Corsets to girls' experiences of freedom. Several women—about one of every six in our studies—described experiencing physical abuse during early childhood, perpetrated by fathers or stepfathers, and less frequently by mothers. This is roughly comparable with the reported approximately 18%–20% of physical abuse in larger epidemiological studies in Canada (End Violence Together, 2012) and the United States (Child Maltreatment, 2014). Physical abuse leads to significant disruptions to embodiment at a young age. Chapter 1 describes in detail the challenges Crystal, a White woman in her 20s, experienced in relation to her father's eruptive physical abuse. These challenges to embodiment affected her experience of herself, her desires, and her relational patterns. She describes how she felt vulnerable and feared losing control: "I always want to be in control. I don't want to be a kind of girl that acts as if she wants protection." Gwen, a White woman in her 60s of a working-class background, who also experienced the terror of her father's volatile temper and physical abuse, has engaged in multiple processes to reconnect with her body and heal from the physical abuse and other adverse influences of gender inequity. From this vantage point, she summarizes the effect of physical abuse in a way that clarifies its impact on one's experience of freedom and agency to act in the world, saying "It kept me quiet. It kept me from exploring the world. It kept me feeling not able, not as capable. It affected my self-esteem. It was like a container. It held me down."

Adult women also describe sexual abuse as occurring during early childhood, with one out of eight women reporting such abuse. Additional cases of sexual abuse occurred at ages nine and above. This rate is within the range reported by Finkelhor (1994). These women reported experiencing varied forms of sexual abuse by significant adults in their lives: father, grandfather, uncle, a male house boarder, and a priest. Including older women in this research program, in addition to girls and younger women, provided the opportunity to explore the adverse impact of childhood sexual abuse, which introduces lifelong challenges to self and body experiences and to relational patterns and intimacy (Herman, 1992; Rothschild, 2000). Women who experience childhood sexual abuse as young children also tend to engage in different forms of self-harm, such as disordered eating, skin cutting, or substance use. Abuse tended to occur more often in dysfunctional families, adversely affected by alcoholism or other substance use, or where terror reigned; in such homes, family members, including mothers, felt helpless and depressed. As Jane a White woman in her late 50s raised in a middle-class family, who was abused both physically and sexually from a young age, describes:

> I came from a pretty broken background. [My father] was alcoholic. My mother suffered from depression. I wasn't sure where I was going to be fed or sleeping... I developed an eating disorder at a young age. Later food abuse turned to alcohol and drugs. That all translated to confusion in my body. Not being sure what's normal. I thought it's me. There's something wrong with me.

Safety, therefore, is an important condition for positive EE.

The attuned and empathic physical Care of the Body is the third dimension of Physical Freedom that shapes experiences of embodiment (see Table 1.2). From birth and throughout early childhood, girls learn about trust and attachment through the attuned physical care of their bodies. They further learn about the regulation of, and attunement to, needs, desires, and emotions. Health-related practices, such as healthy nutrition, rest, physical activity, or proper clothing, are both taught and modeled. The internalization of such attunement and regulation is an important task of the first years of a child's life (see also Shore, 2015). Several of the young girls discuss their home environment in a way that reflects comfort and trust when describing their early childhood, such as 9-year-old Alice, of Aboriginal heritage and middle class:

> Like my mom did everything for me. She woke me up, she put me on the couch, she made me breakfast, she did my hair, and she got my clothes… I feel comfortable with my parents because my mom has gone through the same growing stages and I can talk to someone… My parents encourage me to play soccer and keep up my homework… and like eating healthy.

In other homes where challenges in parental and social circumstances prevailed, girls experienced a lack of attunement and physical care. Rachel, age 10 expresses her experiences from, and following, kindergarten:

> I don't like my life. I am an expert in teasing, from kindergarten, I haven't really told them [parents] because maybe it is the thing that you did that's making them bully you… I eat soup [from cans] and I have a stash of candy in my room when I need to.

She also describes having stress-related headaches.

At times the lack of Care of the Body takes the form of child neglect. Child neglect is a form of maltreatment of children that is more common than physical or sexual abuse, and centrally related to children's welfare (van der Kolk, 2005). It has a long-term impact on experiences of embodiment. One of six adult women in the study reported significant neglect during their childhood. Neglect can occur without sexual or physical abuse, also with significant adverse impact on embodiment, as Sam's story indicates. Sam, a White woman in her mid-20s of a working-class background, labored hard to maintain two homes throughout her childhood while her needs for a safe and available connection, attuned care, as well as time for rest or play with peers were denied. A she describes, "[In the morning] I'd just have to tiptoe so quietly because anything would wake [father] up. And as soon as he'd got up, well, I would have to start doing something like vacuum." She reflects, "Well, I didn't have any idea at the time [of how unusual that was] except that I wanted more time with my friends." She was repeatedly left alone in the house as a toddler and as a young girl. Her words in the narrative below reflect the intensity of neglect:

> I must have been two and a half and I have this memory. My dad would leave me in the house alone. He'd go out, maybe for the evening. And I remember, I forgot my name. Forgot my freaking name. So I'm running around the house, 'What's my name? What's my name? What's my name?' But again, I didn't want my dad to know. I felt ashamed. I just have to wonder. Maybe I wasn't called enough?

Neglect can lead to challenges to self-care as well as self-harm, as Sam describes. During childhood, at the age of eight, she started to "constantly pick at scabs [on her arms] that I may have gotten from a cut… I kept doing it because it seemed I couldn't stop… but it made it worse. I think that's how I dealt with negative feelings." As a woman in her mid-20s, Sam is inspiring in her hard work to address the impact of neglect, aiming to learn about self-care and attunement to her needs (including her needs for safety and boundaries),

> I realized in the past with situations like where I felt compelled to give in to any request, that I wasn't clear. So I ended up in a situation that I had no control. This is a new realization for myself. I realized that I didn't have boundaries. I've never established boundaries for certain situations, even basic social situations… I believe in trying to return to an awareness of my own needs and desires, standing up for them, learning about myself and others in the process.

The dimension of Care for the Body, therefore, spans the spectrum from attuned care to neglect. Correspondingly, experiences of embodiment in young girls range from internalized self-attunement and self-care to disconnection from the body and disorganized self-care or self-neglect.

Young girls express the fourth central dimension of Physical Freedom, Freedom of Desire (see Table 1.2), by describing freely their joy of eating their favorite foods and "hating" those foods they deem unpalatable. Their list of palatable foods often included a range of foods, from proteins to vegetables or fruits, grains, and different desserts. Alice's description of her eating patterns during grade 3 reflects this: "I like eating. I like pasta with salmon and broccoli. I like chips. I like apples and oranges… I like pop, especially Pepsi." In describing her favorite foods, there was little mention of restriction of certain foods or calories.

To summarize, girls experience more Physical Freedom in early childhood than at any other time in the transition from girlhood to womanhood. Owing to the relative permeability of the barriers defined by the girl/boy dichotomy, girls experience the freedom to engage physically in the world and the freedom to take physical space. Corsets to this Freedom in Physical Engagement and Movement are related to the gatekeeping of physical territories by boys and men, the girdling effect of "the dress," and other constraints (e.g., financial, physical ability). While most girls in the study report Safety in the Body Territory and positive experiences of Care of the Body, others experience sexual or physical abuse, as well as neglect, with adverse consequences. In the dimension of desire, most girls in early childhood describe support for their healthy connection to appetite. Overall, the experience of relative Physical Freedom in childhood contributes to a positive Experience of Embodiment.

BETWEEN PASSION AND PICTURE DAY: MENTAL FREEDOM IN PERMEABLE BOY/GIRL BOUNDARIES

> I think my parents were okay with [playing sports and catching bugs and dressing in big shirts and not caring about looks]. They pretty much "do whatever," except when it was picture day or something then my mom would dress me up. I would like cry and I would fight with her. It was kind of like she was trying to change me into someone else. Cause she wouldn't let me be what I was like all the time and then when you look back on the picture day it was like I was like that, but *really I wasn't*. It just made me mad but when the day was over, I just kind of forgot about it. But now when I look back at the pictures, it's like ugh!

This quotation by 13-year-old Melissa about her early school years, kindergarten to grade 3, reflects the tension between the Mental Freedom to fully engage with the world, choosing from a broad range of meaningful and passionate pursuits, and the forced compliance with corseting gender stereotypes enforced during picture day. The camera in picture day is a good metaphor for the scrutinizing lens of one's compliance with embodied gender stereotypes, a gaze that girls learn about during childhood. For Melissa, what is remembered through picture-day photos, therefore, is not who she was—a girl who felt free to engage in a range of passionate outdoor pursuits, including nature explorations, sports, and construction projects with her father—but rather, what she was not: a girl who complied with constrictive gender stereotypes. This disavowal of the way she experienced her embodied self, caused by the imposition of gender stereotypes, was, understandably, disruptive to Melissa. In her home, which also upheld patriarchal values, Melissa was able to maintain a connection with both parents until her tweens. "I was always with my dad outside, helped him plant plants or other yard work, and building, I enjoyed that… and my mom she looked after me, when I was sad I'd go to her." Having had the experience of Mental Freedom during early childhood, Melissa was able to maintain some resistance toward corseting gender stereotypes during her tweens, while other girls complied unquestionably with constrictive stereotypes.

Our research suggests that girls learn early, during their childhoods, about the distinction between the ways girls and boys can engage with the world. This is done primarily through exposure to two types of social expectations or discourses. The first social discourse, the Body as an Object of Gaze, is *one of two* Appearance-related discourses that fall under the Body as a Deficient Object cluster (see Table 1.2). The Body as an Object of Gaze relates to girls being under a surveilling gaze, needing to look pretty in feminized attire. Girls learn that, irrespective of what they love, pursue, think, or feel, they also have to look pretty to gain approval or be of worth. Conveyed in childhood, this discourse maintains a powerful hold on girls and women's bodies throughout their lives, whether they work at home or in the public sphere. To be a perfect girl, no action or agency in the world is required, unlike what is expected from boys (Smolak & Piran, 2012; Tatangelo & Ricciardelli, 2013).

The learning about "looking pretty" occurs so early that it is often weaved with girls' earliest memories, ages 3–4 years old. As nine-year-old Madison, of Aboriginal heritage and a working-class background, describes, "[In kindergarten] I thought I was pretty when I was wearing my dresses… like if I wear *normal* little dresses, I'm pretty." Being pretty also involved other decorative elements, such as bows or jewelry, and other feminine elements, such as a bra. Nine-year-old Hilary, White and of a working-class background, details how, "[In kindergarten] I was wearing dresses. I wanted to wear something in fashion… I've had a bra… I'd have to brush my hair for like an hour." Groomed, tamed hair, preferably long, is indeed another aspect of being pretty. Melissa, for example, was pressured not only to wear a dress, but also to grow her hair:

> My hair was short. I liked it this way. It was more boyish, I didn't have to brush it or anything… People who didn't know me would think I was a guy sometimes. It made me laugh. I didn't really care then. But [family member] said: 'You should grow out your hair, you're such a pretty little girl.' I said, 'No, I don't want to.'

While adults transmit the Female Body as an Object of Gaze discourse early in the lives of children, girls at these ages do not incur consistent social penalties for not complying with this expectation in their daily lives, though pressures do intensify on more formal occasions, such as picture day. Young girls cherish this freedom from objectification, as told by 9-year-old Emma, White and of a middle-class background, in describing her first 3 years in elementary school: "I didn't care at all [about the body]. Well, no I didn't. I just wore clothes and I didn't care what they looked like; as long as they weren't a dress. As long as it wasn't girly I guess." Nine-year-old Hilary, describing the same years in elementary school, says, "I didn't think about my body. I didn't really care. I didn't care about like how I look" Lauren, a 14-year-old White girl from an urban and middle-class background, talks with longing about this experience:

> I used to wear mismatching socks. Like I wouldn't care what I looked like, anything like that I was like oh let's play tag, Fun. I didn't care. When you're little, you don't care about boys and girls. It's not different. It's just whatever you're feeling like doing you do.

These quotations reflect the cherished freedom in not caring, freeing girls to be immersed in their chosen activities without the distraction of the external gaze. This relative freedom from objectification ends once girls' bodies start to change during the tweens phase; however, the more a girl experiences such freedom, the more likely she is to resist inhabiting her body as an object of gaze.

The second gender-related social discourse girls learn about in early childhood, Engagement in "Feminine" Activities, involves the expectations that girls engage in feminine activities that are docile, dainty, passive, contained, and domestic. These include playing house, playing with dolls, or with small animals requiring care and grooming—such as toy ponies—drawing, or talking. Engagement in "Feminine" Activities is *one of four* discourses classified under the Comportment-related cluster: Woman as Docile (see Table 1.2). The dichotomous classification of activities for girls and activities for boys is reflected in girls' earliest memories, suggesting its early transmission by family members, media outlets, toy manufacturers, and other social venues (Orenstein, 2011). Madison, for example, describes her first memory in the following way:

> When I was three and I had my birthday I got my first Barbie doll house that I've ever had so I got out all my Barbies and I played with it. I still collect them. I liked to play Barbies 'cause we had a Barbie van and I also liked to play with the magic ponies and do some sewing and draw.

Similarly, Chrissy describes how in kindergarten she liked to "play house and stuff, and make believe" Emma describes playing "dress up and house," and Rachel describes "Playing house. Playing dolls, changing their clothes... and pretend to be different animals... princes and princesses." The princes and princesses game reflected the contrast between girls and boys' activities: while the princess "just stood there and waited," as Rachel put it, the prince's job was to "save the princess out of her tower."

An important process takes place during girls' early childhood. Despite the early transmission of the clearly demarcated distinction between girls and boys' activities, girls often seek out those activities classified as for boys. This choice is increasingly pronounced as girls become more involved with mix-gender peer groups in the early years of elementary school, or in their neighborhoods. Girls describe this choice as being related to the freedom, fun, and passion associated with boys' activities—experiences girls highlight as lacking in activities stereotypically directed at them. Additionally, either implicitly or explicitly, girls often devalue activities seen as stereotypical girl activities. Rachel describes,

> I stopped playing Barbies because it just got kind of boring. [Friend] stopped playing princesses and princes because she did not like to wear dresses. She used to wear a sparkly blue dress and just wait there to be saved.

Similarly, Madison emphasizes the pleasure of playing tag in grade 1, "I feel like I can actually do something." Emma describes the fun of playing with boys, "doing more activities with the boys outside, you're having fun—you're not just sitting there watching people do it, you can actually play it." Melissa, meanwhile, contrasts her passion for nature exploration and playing sports with her lack of interest in playing with dolls: "I just liked playing outside... other girls would be playing Barbies... and I wasn't interested in that. It was great! I would be out in the field having fun." Younger and older women describe similar sentiments when they reflect about their early childhood.

While prior to the onset of puberty, girls are not penalized for following their passions and crossing the border into what are conceived of as boys' activities, this problematic classification conveys early to girls that passion, freedom, fun, and even curious exploration reside within boys' domain. Molding girls' activities into passive, passionless embodied practices trains girls not only to engage in domestic service roles but also to be content, or even happy, with such practices. Furthermore, since reaching leadership or proficiency positions in varied pursuits in the world requires passionate immersion, such early training risks diverting girls away from future leadership possibilities. It is not surprising that women in our studies that pursued and achieved such positions in the world were either encouraged throughout their childhood to surpass restrictive limitations or engaged in processes during their adult years that liberated them from such strictures.

To summarize, during this stage, young girls experience considerable Mental Freedom to engage fully with the world, compared with later stages in development when Mental Corsets aggregate. In particular, girls can choose to engage in a broad range of meaningful and passionate pursuits, including activities often constructed as "masculine" such as varied sports or building projects. Two main corseting social discourses operate in early childhood related to constrictive gender stereotypes. The first, the Body as an Object of Gaze, suggests to girls that irrespective of what they love, pursue, think, or feel, they also have to look pretty to be of worth. Learned in childhood, this discourse maintains a powerful hold on girls' and women's bodies throughout their lives, whether they work at home or in the public sphere. The second learned corseting social discourse, Engagement in "Feminine" Activities, involves the expectation that girls engage in "feminine" activities that are docile, dainty, passive, contained, and domestic. Girls, concurrently, learn to devalue activities seen as stereotypical girl activities, which they sometimes experience as passionless and joyless. Both these social discourses can, in the long term, divert girls away from leadership possibilities in their engagement with the world. However, during early childhood, compliance with these constrictive discourses is not strongly reinforced, and alternatively, resistance to these discourses is not consistently penalized. This provides girls with the Mental Freedom to engage in a fuller-embodied way in the world, contributing to positive overall Experience of Embodiment.

WHEN SAILOR MOON MEETS BARBIE: GLIMPSES OF SOCIAL POWER IN INEQUITABLE PLAYING FIELDS

> [In Grade 1] All I know is that some girls would put water balloons up their shirt to pretend they have breasts or something… They wanted boys to like them, 'cause they see lots of boys who have girlfriends who are older that have breasts, so maybe they think the boys who are older will like them if they have breasts. But, I didn't really care. I was too busy with more important stuff like preparing for the play we were doing. It was fun.

This narrative by 10-year-old Alice, of Aboriginal heritage and middle-class background, reflects young girls' accurate read of one socially sanctioned source of social power for girls and women in a heterosexual, patriarchal world: self-sexualization (Murnen & Smolak, 2013). Self-sexualization, which includes body alterations such as breast implants—or balloons, as Alice describes—can provide access to social resources: the right boy, and later man, who wields social power. Deriving social power through aesthetic ideals for women is often conveyed to girls through the image of the Barbie doll, a common early childhood toy for girls. This doll frequently portrays the ideal woman/girl with enhanced body parts (breasts), specific coloring (white, blonde, blue-eyed), and unrealistic proportions (thinness), concurrently transmitting to girls the inherent deficiency of girls and women's real bodies, therefore presenting the body as a project for alteration. Even action figures in the lives of girls, including heroines such as Sailor Moon and Wonder Woman, who have magical powers used to combat the world's villains, inhabit sexualized, exposed, and unrealistically thin bodies; even when endowed with superpowers, a female heroine acts from a confined, objectified, sexualized, and stereotypically beautified space. Sailor Moon expresses fat-phobic views, recognizes the weight-loss impact of some of her activities, utilizes makeup at times to combat villains, and in her transformation from school girl to heroine, her body is temporarily stripped of clothing.

Within the context of an overall emphasis on appearance providing acceptability and social power for girls and women, it is important to highlight Alice's lack of interest in the balloon game. Instead, she seeks agency through pursuing skills—specifically, her cherished activity of acting. Establishing a sense of power and agency in engaging with the world *relatively* free of feminine aesthetic standards, reflecting what the DTE describes as Freedom from Appearance-based Social Power, is more common during early childhood than at any other phase in the transition from girlhood to womanhood. The longer a girl has such freedom, the more she is able to focus her energy and resources on meaningful pursuits and skill development, without being diverted to acting on the body. She can then achieve agency in acting in the world, without relying on adhering to particular appearance standards.

Clearly, young girls examine issues of power in the different social systems that they encounter. In addition to witnessing the impact of Appearance-based Social Power in their social environment, girls also observe other gender-related social inequities that disrupt their experiences of inhabiting their bodies with agency and worth. According to the DTE, Membership in Equitable Communities shapes one's EE. Girls witness gender-related equities or inequities in their varied social systems, especially their families. Crystal, for example, whose body journey was described in Chapter 1, explains that her decision to take on the disguise of a boy when in the early grades of primary school related to her mother's submission to her father:

> She never stood up for herself... my dad would yell at her and she would not yell back. She appeared not to have any opinion... I was never comfortable being a girl. I always wanted to be a boy.

Fourteen-year-old Kelly, a Latino girl of a working-class background who was already self-conscious about her body shape in the early grades of primary school, was aware of her mother's unhappiness with her weight and the possible connection between her mother's weight and her father leaving the marriage and his six children: "My mom doesn't like the way she looks... like she used to be tiny. But then after having six kids, and my dad leaving when we were babies... she is trying to work harder on herself."

Girls also observe and comment about the greater financial hardships faced by their mothers following parental divorce. Kelly describes how as a young girl she visited her father's house—"My dad and his girlfriend were in their nice house"—while perceiving financial pressures at home—"[mother] worked really hard, but she doesn't always get paid for the things she does." Erica, a White girl, and Madison, an Aboriginal girl, both 9 years old, make similar observations:

> I don't like the [rented] house, it has mice and a lot of dirt... My dad's house is much nicer and he is adding new rooms... My friends' houses are not bigger than my dad's but bigger than my mom's. [Erica]

> At my dad's house I play tennis. 'Cause, they have a tennis court at a park that usually no one goes to... at my mom's I can only play outside with her [due to lack of neighborhood safety]. [Madison]

In addition, starting in the early grades of elementary school, girls also observe and protest the inequitable distribution of domestic chores when compared with their brothers. Erica, for example, describes, "I have chores at my mom's place and my dad's place. My brothers don't have chores. It makes me mad."

The DTE describes not only the adverse impact on embodiment of gender inequity, but also highlights that gender equity is central to embodied connection and agency. Indeed, in reflecting about their life journeys, younger and older women highlight the value of having been part of systems where they were treated equally all the way from early childhood on. Jane, who experienced positive embodiment and a positive body journey as described in Chapter 1, emphasizes that her mother and father carried similar roles at home, depending on who was unemployed at any point in time, as well they held similar positions of power in the house. Laya, a White woman, and Amber, an Asian-Canadian woman, both professionals and in their mid-20s reflect:

> I think for kids in terms of gender roles I was very fortunate I was never told I had to do the dishes over my brothers... [during early primary school years and beyond] We all got up at six o'clock in the morning and had to be on soccer field regardless of whether you were male or female. There was no distinction. I have a really good relationship with my partner, where gender roles are not clearly defined, because I think I had a father that treated me as an equal, who always said: you're going to do it. You're smart, you're capable. The gender really didn't factor in to it. [Laya]

> I was a tomboy and I still am to a large extent. [During early primary school year all the way to age 12] In my building I was playing with the guys like most sports and I was in fact better than most

> of them running. In my community, women and men were treated as equals. If a girl wants to study or have a career, it's understood that you will, also after your marriage and have kids. I am also the eldest child so I take the responsibility for my parents… I went into sciences and I love what I do. [Amber]

Empowering Relationships is another component of the Social Power and Relational Connection Domain that enhances embodied experiences among girls. Experiencing empowering relationships with role models who share important aspects of social location, such as gender, social class, or race, can enhance positive connection and agency in one's body, even within inequitable social systems. During early childhood, such role models usually involve family members within the nuclear family—both parents and siblings—and extended family members, such as grandmothers, aunts, or uncles. For example, 9-year-old Madison, who shares an Aboriginal heritage with her mother and resides with her in a working-class neighborhood, feels that her mother's love and social agency has made her feel more comfortable with herself in the public sphere:

> With my mom I could actually play outside and play in shorts outside when I had shorts on because she always encouraged me and said [to teasers] 'Did you say this [teasing comment] about my daughter?' And he said sorry.

Madison's uncle is another role model, encouraging her physical engagements: "I want to be like my uncle, because he likes sports." For 9-year-old Emma, who found it initially difficult to connect with physical activities in her home, where gender role assignments are disparate and distinct, her sisters' role modeling has been important: "My sisters are my role models, I just like that they play sports, and hang out with their friends outside." Jane, whose body journey is detailed in Chapter 1, describes the special role her aunt played during her early primary grades in encouraging her literacy and scholarly passions, while her parents did not have much access to education.

While the discussion of Social Power and Relational Connections has focused so far on gender in relation to embodiment, it is the intersection of different dimensions of social location that shapes embodiment. Young girls commonly observe that toys like Barbie and action figures like Sailor Moon or Wonder Woman represent characteristics of appearance that are cherished or idealized by the culture at large and that differ from their own. This initiates a process of learning about the multi-dimensional nature of Appearance-based Social Power. In addition to the gender-related objectified, sexualized, thin, and exposed appearance, these toys represent other societal structures of privilege—in particular, the often blue-eyed, blonde with long straight hair, peach-colored skin, and round eyes appearance characteristics representing White privilege. Claire, a woman of Caribbean-Canadian heritage in her mid-20s and of a working-class background, describes her experiences during kindergarten, problematizing both race and gender prejudice:

> But I mean, it's so funny that I didn't care about my body because I didn't let myself get affected by all that stuff, that garbage… my sisters, they were like sucking it in. By playing Barbies you had that reference look at this body. Whereas I didn't like Barbies because there was *no black Barbie*. I was like, this sucks. This does not represent me. I don't want to play with this. This is not what my friends look like either. I didn't understand. This sucks. So I wanted to play with Transformers. They were androgynous.

Claire and other girls and women who participated in the Embodiment studies describe so eloquently the disruption to embodied identity brought about by toys, sold across the globe, that represent idealized White-looking icons. For example, the blonde, blue- and round-eyed, long-haired, white-skinned figure of Sailor Moon—the creation of a Japanese woman—has been popular throughout countries in the Far East, such as Japan, Malaysia, and Indonesia, in addition to countries in the West, expressing continued White colonial ideology (Sohail, Naz, & Malik, 2014).

Young girls also describe gaps between their embodied material lives and the representation of material wealth associated with the Barbie doll—in particular, the price of its varied outfits and material gadgets. For example, Rachel, a White girl of strained financial circumstances, presents the parallel between her challenges in owning fashionable clothing, and having no clothing for her Barbie doll:

> I used to like to play with Barbie, change her clothes… We didn't have very much clothes for her. We used to put her in the bath in fake bathing suits; little fake bathing suits they could change into… I'm not very fond of Barbies, I used to be and I still play with Barbies with my sister sometimes just to make her happy…
> I don't have a very good wardrobe. Pants that go out like this. My pants are too short and they are like old. Then they'll just think you're a geek.

Popular toys therefore convey social privilege along different aspects of social location, disruptive to the embodied experiences of young girls.

In addition to cultural representations of appearance-based privilege through toys, young girls examine first hand the impact of equitable or inequitable relationships along varied aspects of social location in shaping interactions in their social environments. These observations affect girls' own embodied experiences of agency, comfort, and worth. For example, Eva, a woman of Asian-Canadian heritage in her mid-20s, relates a story from her early childhood about owning a Barbie doll:

> In my neighborhood everyone else was White… This brother and sister took my Barbie, like we had the same Barbie. They took mine because mine was not damaged and I ended up with this damaged one and, I don't know, I attributed it to, 'okay, I'm [Asian country] they can take advantage of me.' And I don't know if this was like something that my parents had. Because they didn't go to the parents of that home's family to like, 'hey this happened.' They were like, 'whatever, it's not worth it.' Yeah, so they decided to leave that alone. And I was like, 'my Barbie.' But oh well. They were like, 'you know, bad people.' Like, how could they do that? That is so low. Well I knew that I wasn't like them and I wouldn't do something like that. I guess I had a little bit of a higher esteem for myself, not being the type of person who would even think about doing something like that.

The lack of agency of her parents was disruptive to Eva's own sense of embodied agency. Her parents, nonetheless, tried to boost her self-esteem by positively conveying their own behavior norms.

Just like gender, within the context of racial inequity, relationships with empowering role models are particularly important for younger (and older) girls. Fifteen-year-old Ashley, of African-Canadian heritage, who experienced exclusion in several social situations in younger childhood in her mainly White social environment, says, "It happened sometimes. And that was always really, really sad. Like say they were playing a specific game and I wouldn't be included." Counteracting the impact of social exclusion is Ashley's "strong sense of identity" and embodied confidence inspired by her mother, a social activist who has held powerful roles in community organizations:

> My mother, 'cause she came from Africa and like she really wanted an education and all odds were against her and she fought them and she was just able to be really, really successful and she's just really happy with her life. And so I just want to be like her. I want to be really strong and supportive and caring… She's a really vocal person, she likes to express how she's feeling.

Harassment and teasing are social processes anchored in social systems of privilege. They are utilized as methods of perpetuating such stratification. While direct experiences of gender-based harassment become more accentuated once they start going through puberty, girls describe already experiencing and witnessing harassment and teasing related to race and ethnicity, socioeconomic standing, body fat and weight, and ability and disability, during early childhood. Teasing and harassment are strongly related the EE and body image (Puhl & Latner, 2007).

Harassment and teasing related to race and ethnicity target appearance characteristics as well as embodied practices, such as clothing and food. For example, 15-year-old Ashley, of African-Canadian heritage, describes the targeting of her skin color in early elementary school: "Someone commented on like my color of skin as being related to poo. 'Well, you're like bird's poo.' It made me feel bad. What did I do to deserve this? Like I'm born this way." Such early teasing often has long-lasting impact on one's embodied experiences, as evidenced by Orchid, a woman in her 60s of African-Canadian heritage who lived in England during early childhood:

> The girl rubbed her skin against my skin and said… 'they're that 'dirty that it doesn't come off.' I told my mother that I felt uncomfortable for a long time, because it did not feel good to be in my body.

Orchid stood up to this teasing by purposefully generating fictional stories about her skin color, like saying she got her skin color by bathing in chocolate milk, and, most importantly, by refusing to apologize for these stories, which made her feel "empowered." Nine-year-old Madison, of Aboriginal heritage, felt throughout grade 3 that her dark body hair stood out in relation to the lighter body hair of her peers:

> I don't really like my legs to be showing, because I have hairy legs, like an ape, so people tease me at school. So, I just like to cover my legs and my arms so no one else notice. My friend called me monkey.

Body practices can also be a target of teasing—for example, food eaten in daycare or kindergarten, as Eva, a woman of Asian-Canadian heritage, describes:

> I was [name of Asian country]. In kindergarten, I brought rice and I was embarrassed when rice fell on the carpet because someone would know I was eating rice and not a ham sandwich… I wanted to be White.

Similarly, young girls experience and witness harassment and teasing related to perceived lower financial status, with comments often referring to clothing or hygiene. Rachel, as described above, experienced a shortage of clothing choice for both herself and her Barbie. She complains, "My pants are too short and they are like old. Then they'll think you're a geek. I don't know how much I will be teased. I just looked at my clothes and I don't like them." Several girls, such as Madison, describe not wanting to grow, "because I'll have to get out of my good clothes." Young children from challenged financial circumstances also encountered comments about their compromised hygiene, as Rachel describes, "Sometimes in Grade three [girl] teased [another girl from a very financially challenged family] about not brushing or washing her hair."

Weight is also already a target of teasing in early childhood. Even young girls agree that "the good thing about diets is you get thinner, so you're not fat. If you are fat, people make fun of you," as 9-year-old Hilary who just completed grade 3 describes. Fat is targeted not only in the children themselves but also in their significant others. Fifteen-year-old Ashley, of African-Canadian heritage and a working-class background, describes this experience:

> In my elementary, when I was in Grade I, I was having problems with this one girl, [girl's name]. And like she was really, really mean to me and she was like oh yeah, you're really fat, and you're fat 'cause your mom's fat. It was like so mean, right, like we got so heartbroken… But at the time it really, really hurt my feelings and it was just like it hurts, and if you're going to dis me okay, but you don't need to be making fun of my mom. Like what did my mom ever do to you, kind of thing. So it was just like I never make fun of your mother, so don't make fun of mine. Keep her out of this, kind of thing.

The prejudice against fat in countries where thinness is associated with higher social class is pervasive and powerful (Musher-Eizenman, Holub, Miller, Goldstein, & Edwards-Leeper, 2004) and is clearly transmitted to young children through significant adults in their lives, as well as toys, books, and other media. Thinness is one extreme characteristic of Barbie. Similarly, Sailor Moon is not only elongated and thin, but she expresses fat-phobic attitudes and, at times, engages in heroic activities with the motivation of weight loss.

Young children also experience and witness prejudice related to ability and disability. Developmentally delayed children and children with significant learning disabilities are socially excluded, teased, and harassed at school. Rachel, who has a learning disability, says, "I don't usually speak up in class because most of the stuff I don't understand and I have to ask the Special Ed teacher to help me, that way I'm different." Madison is teased about being friendly with a developmentally delayed boy—"they tease me that I hang out with a boy named [boy's name]."

Our research revealed that the more unprivileged positions girls held, the more likely they were to be teased and harassed, with a more devastating impact on their experiences of embodiment. Rachel's teasing relates to her family's strained financial state and her learning disability. She feels devastated by her teasing, saying, "I don't like my life. I want to start again. I'd like to stop being teased. I am an expert in teasing, already in kindergarten. I want to be different…" Madison, teased in relation to her Aboriginal heritage and financial status, describes her discomfort with her body, which she wishes to fully cover by clothes: "I like this day that I wore this suit, that it covers most of my body." At times, girls who are teased extensively are also exploited in the schoolyard through social threats of exclusion. As Rachel and Madison explain, respectively: "She said, 'You'll never get on my good side'… But one day I had canteen money and I bought a bag of Doritos and she's like 'I'll be your friend now if you just give me a few Doritos'"; "They like me for my snacks… They say, if you don't give me any of your snack I won't be your friend."

In summary, girls in early childhood learn about social privilege and power through all four pathways described by the DTE. While young girls learn about Appearance-based Social Power through significant adults in their lives, as well as toys, books, and other media, it is in early childhood where establishing a sense of power and agency in engaging with the world is relatively free of having to comply with aesthetic standards, more so than in any other phase in the transition from girlhood to womanhood. This enables girls to focus their energy and resources on meaningful pursuits and skill development, without being diverted to acting on their bodies. Regarding Membership in Equitable Communities, younger and older women described the positive impact of experiencing gender equity during childhood. Conversely, young girls who witnessed gender inequity in their families, experienced embodied disruptions. Further, Empowering Relationships, especially with familial role models, enhance positive embodied connection and agency among young girls. During early childhood, girls experience relative freedom from gender harassment.

Gender is only one of a number of intersecting dimensions of social privilege that shape embodiment in early childhood. Young girls learn about societal structures of privilege and disenfranchisement associated with race and ethnicity, financial status, weight, and disability. Toys and other childhood media, for example, reflect the privilege of Whiteness, wealth, thinness, and body perfection. Young girls either witness or experience first-hand inequity and harassment related to all these dimensions of social location. As gender becomes a more powerful factor related to Social Power and Relational Connections during the next phase of development, it is important to recognize that girls have already learned about the impact of race, ethnicity, financial status, weight, and physical ability on social power.

CHAPTER SUMMARY

The embodiment research program involves an extensive qualitative study of the narratives of diverse girls and women regarding their experiences of living in their bodies and the social factors that shape them. This program of research reveals that positive experiences of embodiment are most commonly found in early childhood, up to 8 years of age. During this time, more than at any other time in the transition from girlhood to womanhood, girls feel comfortable in their bodies and with their appetites. They also experience physical functionality, agency, and passion in pursuing physical activities, with minimal disruption. Capturing these positive, multi-dimensional experiences of embodiment provides both a description of positive possibilities in the ways girls and women can inhabit their bodies and an account of the losses incurred to embodiment through the socialization of diverse girls into inequity. For example, the prospective research program reveals that the experience of agency, enhanced by the joy of physical activities, already begins to be eroded by the next phase of development. Similar disruptions occur in other dimensions of embodiment.

The DTE provides a broad, yet detailed lens through which social experiences in girls' lives during early childhood are examined. The study of qualitative narratives utilizing DTE constructs reveals that the special freedoms enjoyed by girls during early childhood relate to the permeability of boundaries in the girl/body dichotomy. Within the physical domain, young girls have access to territories in the public sphere to which boys and men are gatekeepers, and they can resist wearing restrictive "feminine" clothing. These freedoms provide them with the opportunity to enjoy and develop their physical skills, and even cherish taking up larger physical space in the world if it helps their physical functioning and social prowess. In terms of safety, while a few of the girls experience sexual, physical, and/or child neglect in their families or within other social organizations with devastating impact on embodiment, girls do not commonly experience sexual harassment. Further, at this phase, girls' appetites are generally validated and are not a target of containment by varied social systems.

Considering the mental domain of social stereotypes, young girls are not penalized for pursuing a range of meaningful activities and passions, even when such embodied practices do not comply with two social discourses to which they are exposed: inhabiting the body as an object to be gazed at and pursuing "feminine," docile activities. In the social power domain, young girls, for the most part, do not derive social power from embodying particular standards of beauty; there are few instances of gender harassment, and, while there are initial rifts in the girls' peer system, there is no consistent mutual devaluation or policing. As described in this chapter, experiences in the physical, mental, and social domains are also shaped by the intersection of gender with other dimensions of social location related to race and ethnicity, social class, disability and health, and weight. Overall, in the tension between freedom and social encroachment on young girls' ways of inhabiting the body, there are more opportunities for freedom at this phase of development.

References

Child maltreatment: Facts at a glance. (2014). Retrieved from: https://www.cdc.gov/violenceprevention/pdf/childmaltreatment-facts-at-a-glance.pdf.

End violence together: Fact sheet. (2012). Retrieved from: http://endingviolence.org/wpcontent/uploads/2014/02/Child_Abuse_Fact_Sheet.pdf.

Finkelhor, D. (1994). The international epidemiology of child sexual abuse. *Child Abuse and Neglect, 18*(5), 409–417.

Herman, J. (1992). *Trauma and recovery*. New York, NY: Basic Books.

van der Kolk, B. A. (2005). Developmental trauma disorder. *Psychiatric Annals, 35*(5), 401–408.

Murnen, S. K., & Smolak, L. (2013). "I'd rather be a famous fashion model than a famous scientist." The rewards and costs of internalizing sexualization. In E. L. Zurbriggen, & T.-A. Roberts (Eds.), *The sexualization of girls and girlhood: Causes, consequences, and resistance* (pp. 235–256). New York, NY: Oxford University Press.

Musher-Eizenman, D. R., Holub, S. C., Miller, A. B., Goldstein, S. E., & Edwards-Leeper, L. (2004). Body size stigmatization in preschool children: The role of control attributions. *Journal of Pediatric Psychology, 29*(8), 613–620.

Orenstein, P. (2011). *Cinderella ate my daughter: Dispatches from the front line of the new girlie-girl culture*. New York, NY: Harper Collins.

Piran, N. (2015). New possibilities in the prevention of eating disorders: The introduction of positive body image measures. *Body Image, 14*, 146–157.

Puhl, R. M., & Latner, J. D. (2007). Stigma, obesity, and the health of the nation's children. *Psychological Bulletin, 133*, 557–580.

Rothschild, B. (2000). *The body remembers: The psychophysiology of trauma and trauma treatment*. New York, NY: W.W. Norton.

Shore, A. N. (2015). *Affect regulation and the origin of the self: The neurobiology of emotional development*. New York, NY: Routledge.

Smolak, L., & Piran, N. (2012). Gender and the prevention of eating disorders. In G. McVey, M. P. Levine, N. Piran, & H. B. Ferguson (Eds.), *Preventing eating-related and weight-related disorders: Collaborative research, advocacy, and policy change*. Waterloo, ON: Wilfred Laurier Press.

Sohail, R., Naz, R., & Malik, N. A. (2014). A post-colonial study of Barbie phenomena and its implications in Pakistani urban context. *European Academic Research, II*(5), 6949–6978.

Tatangelo, G. L., & Ricciardelli, L. (2013). A qualitative study of preadolescent boys' and girls' body image: Gendered ideals and sociocultural influences. *Body Image, 10*, 591–598.

Tylka, T. L., & Wood-Barcalow, N. L. (2015). What is and what is not positive body image? Conceptual foundations and construct definition. *Body Image, 14*, 118–129.

CHAPTER

3

Intense Transitions: Tweens (Ages 9–12)

> Well, I like movement… I like to do intramurals. My favorite sport is soccer. I feel good playing. My body feels like "you're ruling! Go, keep going. You can do it!" I'm the best on my team. I'm the only one who can block a goal like this. (Alice, age 9)

> Why did you [body] have to change? I kinda feel weird and it's hard, having, like big breasts, 'cause you'd catch, like, guys staring at them. And it's just that now my legs are starting to get hair… I want to be blonde, 'cause you can't see the hair on your legs. People notice it and say, "gee, you have hairy legs. Are you an ape?" (Alice, age 12)

In these two narratives, Alice, a girl of Aboriginal heritage and middle-class background, describes two very different experiences of Body Connection and Comfort, the first dimension of the Experience of Embodiment (EE). The first narrative, from Alice's interview at age nine, reflects being "at one" with her body—a site of comfort, joy, and physical agency. In contrast, the second narrative, from her interview at age 12, suggests disruption in her experience of the body—a burdensome, uncomfortable, negative, and deficient site to inhabit. At age 12, Alice also describes two social causes of disruption: unwanted sexual attention and racial- and gender-based harassment.

As the Embodiment research program reveals, losses in the experience of inhabiting the body during the tweens phase meaningfully alter girls' engagement with the world. Adverse changes to the EE include not only disruption to Body Connection and Comfort, but also to Agency and Functionality, Experience and Expression of Desire, Attuned Self-Care, and Inhabiting the Body as a Subjective Site. For example, Alice's positive experience of physical agency at the age 9—"You're [body] ruling!

Journeys of Embodiment at the Intersection of Body and Culture
http://dx.doi.org/10.1016/B978-0-12-805410-9.00003-7

Go, keep going. You can do it!"—shifts by age 12 to discomfort with her muscularity—"Like when you play sports... If you're as muscular as the guys, then that's kinda creepy. It's just weird having a guy friend with the same muscles." Her agency through voice shifts from assertiveness—"When the boys bother us I tell them to go away. I learned to do it from talking back to my parents"—to restricted agency—"like stuff that a guy will do to a girl... if you say like no, he'll like force himself down on top of you so..." Her positive connection to appetite—"I like eating... I like hamburgers and chips... I'll pass on dieting"—changes to ambivalence about eating—"Normal diet is actually the no eating diet, when you don't eat at all, eating, like, apples and like carrots and stuff." Her self-attunement in relation to clothing, for example, has changed from dressing comfortably to wearing, "low cut tops pretty much and skirts and skinny jeans, that's like the latest fashion at my school."

Inviting girls, as part of the study protocol, to draw themselves and describe their drawings, proved productive to examining their embodied experiences in the world. A comparison of Alice's drawings at the ages of 9 and 12 reveals the drastic changes in her embodied experiences in the world, as well as a shift toward self-objectification. At age nine, Alice draws herself smiling in soccer uniforms with one foot on a soccer ball, saying:

> That's me playing soccer. I play defense, forward and midfield, and I play goal. I am the only one who can jump up high enough to block a goal like this. A shirt and shorts, socks and soccer shoes... Hair is in a ponytail. I am kicking the ball into the net.

At age 12, she draws herself in a revealing dress and high heals, standing passively as an object to be gazed at with her arms behind her back and a sad expression on her face:

> Draw a body or anything? This is just a small drawing of me... dress and high heels, purse... I saw that I looked so plain so like I put lip gloss, eye shadow and mascara, I have 12 lip glosses. I'm more obsessing about my hair and makeup.

Alice's transition in the way she inhabits her body—from positive body connection and comfort, embodied agency and passion, and subjective immersion in action to disrupted body connection and discomfort, restricted agency and passion, and self-objectification (see also Piran, 2016)—typifies the tweens period. The transition in the EE is present in the narratives of girls from diverse ethnocultural heritages, urban or rural sites of residence, and social classes. While the intensity, exact timing, and specific behavioral expressions of this transition vary between girls, the disruption in the experience of embodied agency and self-attunement in engaging with the world during tweens is shared. The girls themselves often allude to the drastic transition in the way they inhabit their bodies. Twelve-year-old Kyra, for example, a White girl who lives with her mother in a single-parent household in a rural community and working-class setting, describes the changes in the following way:

> Pretty much until I was like, in Grade 4, I don't really like remember what I wanted to wear. I just didn't care. I'd put on whatever clothes I wanted. "Leave me alone, I don't care." Just run out and play, doesn't matter what I'm wearing. But like around Grade 5 things change. And now it's a *little different*. Like, you know, you want to wear the makeup, and you do your eyebrows, and you like to have kind of smooth legs and stuff… Well, when we were talking over there. It made me realize, like holy crap, *how much has changed*! *I'm just different*!

Unique to the tweens phase among girls is the broad range of ways one can inhabit the body. While a few girls still hold on to their childhood experiences of embodied immersion in action in the world, most go through a gradual transition toward the restriction of action, disruption in self-attunement, and a concurrent increase in body monitoring. Studying the EE during the tweens phase therefore offers two unique opportunities. First, it provides the "last" opportunity to capture the rich experience of inhabiting the body with agency and attunement among girls. Second, it provides an insight into the magnitude and complexity of loss involved in inhabiting a girl's body at the cusp of puberty. As this book describes, by early adolescence, restrictive transitions are ubiquitous, and the journey back to the embodied possibilities of childhood and early tweens can become a lifelong journey.

These potential losses right at the time when girls are just beginning to engage with the world while owning "in-progress" women's bodies raise important challenges in terms of theory development, research, and health promotion. First, as the embodiment research program reveals, in order to validate girls' experiences and help amplify their resistant voices, theory, research, and health promotion interventions need to be inclusive of the full range of changes in embodiment, beyond, simply, documenting a decrease in body esteem. Second, theory needs to examine, in great detail, the broad spectrum of social experiences that effectively reduce the embodied agency of tween girls. Concurrently, it is important at this age to highlight social experiences that enhance a resistant stance. Expanding on this, the next sections outline the corseting processes that start to encroach on Physical Freedom, Mental Freedom, and Social Power, and their disruptive effect on embodiment. These sections also address possibilities for constructive changes in tween girls' lives.

PINK CORSETS IN THE PHYSICAL TERRITORY

Interviewer: How do you think girls should dress?
Erica: Well, I think they should dress the way they want to and um, I personally say something like pants, shorts, capris or something that doesn't show that much skin so you can do cart wheels, climb high without people looking, yeah and you can go on the monkey bars and you can slide down without having to put your legs together, and you could sit more comfortably.

In this quotation, 9-year-old Erica, a White girl from a working class and urban background, describes the possibilities of Physical Freedom inherent in *resisting* different Physical Corsets that girls encounter during their tweens, including clothing that restricts movement—even sitting comfortably—and violations of body ownership in terms of forced body exposure and the fear of harassing stares. Indeed, when Erica is invited to draw herself and the ideal girl, she describes herself as wearing a t-shirt, pants, and runners. However, the ideal girl is "[wearing] fashionable clothes, a gold halter top and her skin is showing, a short skirt, long hair in ponytails, she is wearing high heels and she is thin... She does not get to do much at recess... she is not comfortable." Aware of the introduction of different Physical Corsets during the tweens phase, Erica, who loves physical activities and movement, struggles to hold on to Physical Freedom, understandably vacillating between resistance to the pressures to wear fashionable yet restrictive clothing and compliance with such expectations. By the time she reaches early adolescence, Erica's physical engagement with the world—a passion for her—is markedly more restricted.

Like Erica, as girls journey through the tweens phase, they encounter Physical Corsets along the path of maturation. As the corsets aggregate, tween girls' connection to their physical engagement with the world wavers and, with it, their sense of agency and power. In particular, this section examines the introduction of corsets to the four dimensions of Physical Freedom: Freedom in Physical Engagement and Movement, Safety for the Body Territory, Care of the Body, and Freedom of Desire. All girls are affected by the introduction of these corsets; however, as physical corsets become normative, girls from working-class households—especially in urban sites—and those from ethnocultural heritages that restrict girls and women's movement in the public sphere, tend to face more challenges in maintaining their physical engagement with the world.

Freedom in Physical Engagement and Movement—the opportunity and right to move freely, competently, and joyfully in the physical environment—starts to be encroached on systematically during the tweens phase. As girls' bodies start to go through puberty, boy/girl boundaries become much less permeable. Consequently, girls face restricted access to sites of physical engagement in the public sphere. In school, inhabiting pubertal bodies often comes with a clear gender hierarchy: boys own most of the physical territory of the schoolyard, where physical activities take place, while girls "own" the margins and mainly talk. Erica describes and problematizes this by using the word "weird":

> [In the schoolyard] we usually talk mostly, and plus, that's really all we do. Some people just start saying something and then we'll just start the total commotion things. Really *weird*... [During lunch hour] we usually talk while we're eating and then we'll go outside and do the exact same thing.

Girls at this phase are no longer routinely invited by boys to participate in their continued physical activities, though on rare occasions a girl may still join in. Usually this is related to her undeterred passion for such activities and boys' appreciation of her skills. As the number of girls who participate in physical activities in the schoolyard or on community teams dwindles, girls find it awkward to continue such pursuits. Further, joining other girls at the physical margins of the schoolyard also prevents exclusion from the girls' peer group. Lauren, White and of a middle-class background, for example, describes such exclusion after joining the boys' active play in grade 6: "I've been left out of a bunch of girls who had this girly club, and I played foot hockey with the boys, and I asked, 'can I be in your club?'—no, and I was excluded." Not only do girls who try to stay active feel often "aberrant" and unwelcome, but they might also feel that the norms of play have shifted in ways that are no longer acceptable to them. Erica states,

> [In a community league] Soccer was fun. I don't know. The team that I'm always on is all boys. Last year there were only two girls... and sometimes, there was this one kid and he grabbed the ball... and they [boys] were saying stuff about each other... I felt not really scared but maybe worried... I don't like it anymore. I don't know. I guess I just got older and I didn't like it.

Without support for their physical pursuits, we see a repeated pattern of girls abandoning their passions, shifting from active engagement to a new normative sedentary state. Importantly, girls often ascribe such shifts to internal processes, rather than to restrictive norms or external conditions. Similar to Erica's comment—"I guess I just got older and I didn't like it"—Melissa, who loved outdoor explorations, describes developing (a perceived gender-appropriate!) fear of spiders, saying, "In Grade 5 we stopped [nature explorations] because I didn't like bugs as much any more and stuff like that. Like I started getting really scared of spiders and I don't know. I spent more time with girls."

While all girls during the tweens phase describe a journey toward constriction in occupying physical territories, journeys do vary. Socioeconomic standing is an important factor in shaping these journeys.Higher socioeconomic standing can "buy" privileged spaces of continued engagement in physical activities within a general context of restriction for girls in varied public sites. Buying spaces of continued physical activities can involve payment for community-based programs or for more expensive activities that require costly equipment or fees such as tennis, skiing, hockey, or horseback riding. These activities also require money for transportation, and parental work flexibility and availability. Privileged spaces of physical activities also include privately owned facilities such as private clubs, pools, cottages on a lake, or summer outdoor camps. Girls of higher socioeconomic standing can therefore continue to develop their athletic skills and confidence, and that, in turn, can help them break further barriers to restricted yet continued physical engagement with the world.

Enhanced skills help girls compete for a limited availability of spots in co-ed sports teams, in less available and supported girls' teams, or to be invited by boys in the schoolyard to join their games. For example, Alice, of Aboriginal heritage from a middle-class urban background, is supported by her parents to continue her swimming and soccer training: "I love soccer. Swimming, I love. I take them all year." Roxy, Middle Eastern and living in a middle-to-high socioeconomic context, similarly describes,

> horseback riding, hockey, and soccer, mainly hockey, I like shooting the puck… we had so many tryouts. I like swimming and tubing at the cottage… I have a good swimsuit, it's comfortable: like a shirt and short bottoms.

In comparison, girls of lower socioeconomic standing have less likelihood of having access to alternate spaces that allow them to maintain connection to immersed joy and competence in physical activities.

As we find when we follow girls with limited means for 5 years or when we examine lifelong body journeys with younger and older women, the tweens phase often represents the last time of joyful and passionate engagement in physical activities (not aimed at body alterations). Fourteen-year-old Kelly, of Latino heritage and living in a single-parent, financially strained household describes, "My [soccer] coach never took me off the field. He considered me really good. But I didn't play since Grade 4, because my family is putting the money towards my brother's wedding… I watch TV, movies." Eleven-year-old Madison, of Aboriginal heritage and living with her mother in a working-class urban neighborhood, cannot afford appropriate shoes that would allow her to use the free outdoor skateboarding place: "I can't stay on the board so I can't play at the [park]." Eleven-year-old Tiger, a White girl living in a home supported by social assistance, could only find a bikini in a reduced-price store in her neighborhood, though she wanted a one-piece bathing suit. Wearing a t-shirt over her bikini, she was forced out of the public pool. "They said: 'take off your shirt.' I said, 'I am not taking my shirt off.' I would feel very nude or very exposed. I left." Twelve-year-old Bronwen, a White girl of a middle-class household, that has faced financial difficulties, skips soccer games at recess and does her homework instead, so she has time to do her chores at home. "Some of my friends play soccer… Sometimes I use recess for homework 'cause I don't do homework at home because there are so many things I need to do there."

Ethnocultural group membership may further shape physical engagement with the world, intersecting with gender and social class. Participation in physical pursuits in the public sphere can be even more challenging for tween girls whose heritage involves norms of attire in the public sphere that are very different from those prevalent in North America, especially after the onset of puberty. For example, Hazel is a girl of Middle Eastern heritage living in an urban and working-class setting with her mom and dad, who are both Muslim. Hazel loves swimming. However, at her school, she has been teased for fully covering her body, and wearing the hijab in public since puberty has disallowed her from engaging in swimming, her favorite physical activity. She cannot resume swimming unless public pools have women's only swim time. Related to her socioeconomic standing, she has no access to a private pool and is therefore, essentially, barred from her only joyful activity:

> I used to be more active. My mom put me in swimming when I was five. I love swimming so much. I did lessons. I was almost a lifeguard… I mean, I haven't gone to swim in a while [since age 11] because I can't really take this [hijab] off in a public pool. I love swimming actually, but I can't now.

Overall then, a broader territory accessible for girls' physical activities during childhood becomes restricted to "islands" of physical activities, accessed in specific facilitative contexts.

Like Victorian era corsets, fashionable clothing for tween girls comprises an additional corset to Freedom in Physical Engagement and Movement, as they are already encumbered by the inequitable access to sites of physical activities. All girls describe fashionable clothing for tween girls as both tight and exposing. Girls' clarity about the ways in which this clothing restricts physical engagement, and of their protests against such restrictions, relates to the relative novelty of the ubiquitous introduction and enforcement of such clothing during this phase. While in childhood there was still a way out—opportunities to engage in the physical environment wearing comfortable clothing—toward the end of the tweens phase there is little such opportunity without there being adverse social consequences. In the following narratives, 9-year-old Erica and 10-year-old Alice elaborate on the problems of moving in feminine-restrictive clothing and articulate their protest to such restrictions. These narratives relate to their discussions of their drawings, one of their self and one of the ideal girl.

> Erica: This girl [ideal girl] dressed in fashionable clothes, a gold halter top and her skin is showing, thin, a short skirt... high heels. She does not get to do much at recess. She is not comfortable and her skin is showing. She can walk around; she can sit on a bench. Maybe she can play hopscotch, but she would have to keep her legs more together; it would be pretty hard. But the girl in the t-shirt and jeans [self drawing] can do gymnastics, she can climb high, go on the monkey bars; she can sit, she can lay down, she can do all that stuff.
> Interviewer: How do you think the girl in t-shirt and jeans feels if somebody told her to dress like the girl in halter top, skirt and high heels?
> Erica: If I were her, which I am, I would say, 'No, I'm comfortable the way I am, but thank you.'

> Alice: The popular girl [ideal girl] wears a skirt and a tight top, long hair, pigtails, and really pretty shoes. Her body is long and thin. Long eyelashes, great smile. This girl doesn't play sport.
> Interviewer: How do you think the girl in the t-shirt and shorts feels?
> Alice: She's happy to be a soccer player and not a cheerleader because she'd actually get to play something, instead of cheering for other people. But all the popular girl can do is cheering for other people and jump around in the sideline going 'yay, yay, yay! Go!'

The resistant stance towards restrictive clothing at the early phases of the tweens period enables girls, such as Erica and Alice, to pursue their passionate engagement in physical activities throughout most of the tweens period while still experiencing embodied agency. However, this resistance often wanes toward the end of the tweens phase and the beginning of early adolescence. Even girls like Erica, who excitedly declares at the age of 11 years, "I like sports a lot... I don't know how people can live without sports. If I couldn't play sports... like what would I do?" or Alice, who passionately states at the age of 12 years, "Soccer, swimming, I love," start to comply with the expected dress code and, accordingly, shift their daily activities in school, especially as the tweens phase progresses.

Trying to inhabit the body with previously experienced freedoms while wearing restrictive clothing, inevitably leads to difficulties, as 11-year-old Madison, Aboriginal and living in an urban center and working-class setting with her mother, explains, "I had a skirt on that was short and I jumped over a fence and the boys started laughing, like: what? They saw my skirt come up, I walked away. There are things girls are not supposed to do." Restrictive clothing for girls applies similarly to freedom of movement in water. The norm for girls, of wearing exposing two-piece bathing suits, makes free swimming difficult, especially as the body starts to develop. Eleven-year-old Alice, an avid swimmer, describes this challenge, saying, "It's kind of hard because you move really fast and then my bathing suit... would always come off. And then my friend would laugh, and she'd go and tell her friends, and everybody knows."

Like Erica describes at the age of 11, tween girls often share a poignant daily decision about whether to wear to school comfortable clothing that will allow them to hold on to joyful immersion in physical activities—"Sometimes me and my friends are wearing pants and we'll go out in the field and do flips and cartwheels and stuff"—or to wear the expected tight and revealing clothing and "just walk around and walk around and play four square and stuff."

As the tweens phase progresses, compliance with restrictive dress codes increases and the option of immersion in joyful schoolyard play almost closes. Without relational and systemic support for girls' wishes to dress comfortably, girls disavow such wishes and ascribe their shift to internally guided preferences. As 11-year-old Erica describes,

> I am getting into skirts now... Now I sometimes wear skirts to school. If you wear a skirt it changes what you can do at recess. 'Cause if you play on the monkey bars, and the boys go running under you and try to see up your dress... But now we don't play much on the play structure anymore. I don't really like it anymore, *I don't know why*, I just lost interest in it.

The encroachment on Freedom in Physical Engagement and Movement during the tweens phase, when girls are just starting to inhabit women's bodies, is a disconcerting social phenomenon. It positions girls to be passive and restricted objects in the physical space, rather than agents of physical prowess and action who are also entitled to take equal space in physical territories. It also sets a clear gender hierarchy.

The physical restraint of girls at the emergence of puberty is practiced and may take on different forms around the world. Among the girls who participated in our research, these constraints related, most commonly, to reduced opportunities and resources, constraining norms of femininity, challenges of physical safety, and the adoption of tight and exposing clothing. While Title IX in the United States is an example of an important systemic intervention that has enhanced the allocation of resources to girls' sports, with a consequent increase in the number of girls who participate in sports, marked gender discrepancies still exist. From a mental health perspective, joyful immersion in physical activities and a positive connection to the functionality of the body are important protective factors against the adverse effects of girls' objectification and other social pressures in the domain of the body (Smolak, Murnen, & Ruble, 2000). Indeed, it is at the tweens phase that we see the lowering of body esteem (Mendelson, Mendelson, & White, 2001). It is therefore important to examine other social influences that operate concurrently during the tweens phase to affect experiences of embodiment, such as Safety for the Body Territory.

Safety for the Body Territory, the second dimension of Physical Freedom, is central to positive connection with the body and to the experience of embodied agency in the world. However, just like the right to move comfortably in and engage actively with the physical environment, the experience of safety among girls starts to be encroached on repeatedly during the tweens phase. Girls in their tweens discover that beginning to inhabit women's bodies at the onset of puberty involves increased exposure to violations of their body territory, and they react with fear, anger, protest, sadness, shame, and loss. Due to these violations, the pubertal body becomes a challenge to own, rather than a site of agency, rights, and new possibilities.

Girls in their tweens are acutely aware of the changes in safety associated with the onset of puberty. Here is how Alice, at the age of 12, describes her early response to harassment she experienced at age 11. While she perceives the shift in the behavior of the social environment, she initially does not understand it. Her mother helps her frame the experience:

> I was 11. I was coming out of the store. And these guys drove by and honked at me. And then it was kind of, like, 'Why did they do that?' and my mom says 'cause they probably thought you're older than

> you looked.' Or like when I, like, see, like, when I walk into a room, and I see older guys, they all just look at me. It'll be, like, they are just looking, like... 'What? Do I have something on my face?' So it was, like, it was just kinda awkward.

The pubertal body is now on display and open to commentary and violations. In a school where I conducted focus groups, girls at ages 10 and 11 described this point of transition as well, with comments such as, "The bathing suit made it look like I had breasts... suddenly I saw how [male gym teacher] was looking at me, I froze... I was scared," "I was wearing my white cotton t-shirt that I love so much, and [female teacher] said to me, 'Take this shirt off! You look like a whore.' I feel embarrassed. Is that because I am starting to have breasts now?" or "I was telling [male teacher] that I was pro-abortion and he got angry and said, 'What do you know about abortions, you don't even have breasts yet'... He was using my body to embarrass me, to shut me up." Tween girls learn quickly about the cost of owning women's bodies.

All girls describe the intensification of sexual harassment in school during the tweens phase, including bra snapping (10-year-old Meghan: "They did that [bra snapping] to me and that's when they found out. It hurt. I just tried to fix it. I was kind of embarrassed"), pantsing (11-year-old Kyra: "It's like a joke. My friend dropped them all the way down to her ankles. She fell down, she's like, 'Holy crap! I've never really got them down that far,' it's part fun, part scary, part embarrassing"), looking up skirts (11-year-old Madison: "People would try to look up your skirt and you're just like, 'get away from me!'"), slapping butts (11-year-old Kyra: "They see an ass they like, they'll smack it"), naming and evaluating body parts (11-year-old Alice: "They whistle and say things, and I am like 'shut up'"), and other harassing behaviors. While common, these experiences are not benign; they make girls feel scared, not safe, as well as embarrassed and angry. Without systemic support, girls most commonly feel that they have to cope with this harassment alone, sometimes presenting harassing behaviors as "jokes," even if initially they were very distressed.

The intensification of violations takes place in school, on the street, in parks, pools, parties, and one's neighborhood, forming an inescapable new reality. Alice's experiences during her tweens exemplify these changes. In her urban environment, she resides and goes to a public school in a middle-class neighborhood; sexual harassment is present in the lives of girls of all social classes. At school, Alice, like several other girls, reports on teacher-initiated harassment:

> He [teacher] made all the boys line up for birthday kisses for my friend [a girl]... and said, 'Give her a birthday kiss.' I felt bad for my friend. She just stood there. She didn't want birthday kisses.

Sexual harassment also happens in the local pool. According to Alice, "this boy grabbed onto my bathing suit and yanked them off, and then they told everybody." Harassment takes place on the street as well—"My friend snuck up on me with a water gun and sprayed me until my shirt became see-through and I felt really bad about myself."

Alice goes on to articulate both the shorter and longer impact of the accumulation of harassment and violations:

> Oh my god, find a place to hide. Find a teacher. Nervous breakdown. Who saw? Really embarrassed. Like it makes a girl nervous, kind of sad, sometimes scared if they'll do it again. When she grows up she may be afraid to go outside. Stay in her house. Like this guy, when he was 15 was hiding from [enemies in the war]. And he stayed there for 75 years.

Alice's insightful reflections about the long-term effects of harassment resonate with a feminist lens, referencing agoraphobia, a phenomenon more common in women than in men, suggesting that everyday experiences of violations make women feel unsafe in the public sphere (McHugh & Cosgrove, 2004).

It is during the tweens phase that we hear for the first time about more serious sexual violations within a peer context. Two of the 11 young women interviewed described being raped during their tween years by a male peer. Claire, a woman of Caribbean-Canadian heritage in her early 20s, describes being raped twice by a male peer 3 years her senior, at the ages of 10 and 12—the second time at knifepoint: "Unfortunately he raped me… I blocked it out… I couldn't tell my mom. She would have blamed me. I just felt dirty. I was like a doormat." Following these rapes, she was labeled a slut and became the target of incessant sexual violations by neighborhood male peers. She did not disclose the rapes. Further, no system in her social environment, including the mental health system that was called in by the school to help with her "behavioral problems," was able to connect with her around the trauma. As she says, "They were asking the wrong questions." Ashley, a White woman in her 20s who was sexually abused at home by a male family member, was at age 12 when she was raped in the park by a peer. "I felt guilty and responsible," she says. "I didn't want to tell my mother. I was afraid he was going to make me out like I came onto him."

The increase in the spectrum of violations of girls' body territories at the cusp of puberty meaningfully shifts their experience in the world; since social power and body safety are related, the violations inform girls about their own—and women's—vulnerable social position in the world. From a health and mental health perspective, girls who are the target of this spectrum of violations, and those who witness it, describe a range of adverse responses, from disrupted self and body experience, to negative emotional responses, to behavioral and overall difficulties in adjustment. The scope of reactions of tween girls is in some ways clearer than those of older girls, who often adapt to their new reality by denying its impact. Alice, for example, facing sexual harassment for the first time during the tweens, describes shock, anger, fear, and sadness with great clarity.

Claire, raped twice during her tweens, details feeling that her body is "dirty," stops protecting her body's boundaries, hides her body in public, feels that her body (rather than the environment) betrayed her, becomes withdrawn and angry, and faces challenges at school:

> I wish my body wasn't changing because I'm being treated differently. I felt dirty, never comfortable; my body wasn't of any worth. I let [boys] do whatever. I was trying to hide my scars and pain, wearing sweaters and pants and boots in the summer. I was angry and getting in trouble at school. No girlfriends. I never felt comfortable.

Ashley develops different phobias, as well as an eating disorder, self-harm behaviors, and social isolation: "I was burnt out. I started cutting myself. I started anorexia. Rebelling against myself. My social abilities were severely affected." It is important to note that as the environment becomes harsher toward girls' bodies, and with minimal systemic protection, validation, or support for their experiences, it is common for girls to feel that their bodies have betrayed them rather than the social system. Interventions are strongly needed at this phase of development, including implemented sexual harassment policies at schools, education for all significant adults in the lives of children, and informed health and mental health services. It is also worth noting that at this phase of development, girls have not lost their active voices in relation to common violations and could be enlisted toward the common goal of enhanced safety, which relates to the third dimension of Physical Freedom, discussed next.

Care of the Body, the third dimension of Physical Freedom, takes on particular meaning during the tween years related to the onset of puberty. Girls go through puberty in a culture that is problematic toward women's bodies, which in turn makes it hard for them to cherish and embrace their changing bodies. As girls mature they move away from idealized images of women, as indicated by the use of underage models in the fashion industry; meanwhile boys grow closer to idealized images of men (Smolak & Piran, 2012).

Therefore, girls' reactions toward the physiological processes of puberty inevitably reflect prevalent negative views of women's curves, fat, weight, and menstruation. Kyra, for example, a White girl from a working-class family, describes her adverse reaction to starting to grow breasts at the age of 10; to her, breasts were vilified fat: "I was embarrassed. I'm like, 'oh my god, I have boobs.' Except for me it wasn't boobs, it was like—fat or something, and like I was freaking out, and I always used to wear sweaters to cover me." Similarly, Bronwen at age 11 details her devastation with normal pubertal weight gain, which was for her the "darkest" time of her life, highlighting the lack of supportive and relevant education for girls at this age:

> In Grade 6 I gained like 15 pounds in a space of like three months or something ridiculous and I totally, totally flipped out… that was probably one of the *darkest moments in my life*… I don't think you get enough, nearly enough education, about the weight factor. The worst year of my life.

The attitude toward menarche is commonly negative as well. Not only does menstruation involve a new physical challenge girls need to learn how to handle, but also menstruating girls or women are stigmatized in many parts of the world. Hazel, for example, explains her experience of menstruating at 12 years of age: "When you have your period you can't pray because you're bleeding and it's not clean blood—it's dirty blood." Indeed in Europe and the Far East different myths suggest that menstruating women can spoil the preparation of food (such as mayonnaise or sushi). Particular sects of different religions, including Buddhism, Christianity, Hinduism, Judaism, and Islam, view women as being "impure" during their periods and some ban menstruating women from entering temples. In different parts of the world, menstruating women are expected to stay in segregated physical sites, exposing them to specific dangers.

Under these negative contextual factors, the risk is that different educational forums for girls may replicate adverse influences. Most commonly, girls describe attending a health class in grade 4 whereby different diagrams of girls and boys' bodies are displayed and in which the physiological changes that occur during puberty are outlined. Girls commonly react negatively to the co-ed forums, which accentuate their greater vulnerability in the domain of the body, as Kyra explains:

> With overhead projector, showing the different parts. It's pitiful, boys and girls together. When they would say something we'd like look at the guys and we'd be like, 'oh, my god.' And for the guys it was like, 'ha, ha.'

For Kyra, this graphic display alongside boys amplifies the objectification she has had to handle throughout grade 4: "Guys like me because of my boobs… I wanted them to think of me as more than just that. Yay, I have boobs, that's great, and then it's just like, 'get away from me,' like 'leave me alone.'"

Adults are challenged with the task of providing tween girls with support and developmentally tailored information that will help them maintain a positive connection to their bodies throughout puberty. This involves helping tween girls to appreciate the complexity of healthy physiological processes involved in maturation, understand the importance of nurturing (rather than disrupting) the body through these natural processes, and trust the outcome of the maturational processes. It is important that adults act as role models and convey the opportunities inherent in occupying full women's bodies in the world (Piran, 1999, 2001). There are few (too few!) examples of such constructive approaches from adults in the lives of our girl research participants. For example, in only one interview (out of 171), we heard about encouraging trust and acceptance of the natural processes of weight gain during puberty. The grandmother of Nina, a White middle-class woman in her 60s, helped her accept her weight gain when she was about 12 years old:

> My grandmother who was a very lovely woman and all of a sudden I was putting this weight on and my breasts were growing and all this sort of thing was happening, and she said, 'You know, don't worry about so many things happening at once because it all settles down by the time you're 20. It's just a phase that you go through.' I accepted that as being the truth that that's what would happen. Sure enough you know I turned 19 and my body sort of settled into where it is now. And I accepted that and I've been pretty happy with it.

In one interview, we heard from 12-year-old Bronwen, a White girl from a middle-class family, about a cherished celebration of menarche:

> Bronwen: The four women took me out to this beautiful waterfall. And they each talked to me about being a woman and they each gave me something that had been given to them by another woman, and talked about the strengths and powers that she had…
>
> Interviewer: what did it mean to you to have that ceremony?
>
> Bronwen: It made me feel really special… It's something I would really like to do for others… In different cultures people do more for that kind of getting your period, kind of growing up whatever for girls, but our culture doesn't really recognize that. And in some ways I think they kind of 'oh it's one more headache,' but I think it's

> really important to recognize that, because it is a big moment… The ceremony made me feel more loved, like people will always be there for me.

Amber's mother was very clear that menstruating should have no effect on staying physically active, a stance that Amber, who grew up in South Asia, appreciates:

> My mom had gone through it all before it happened. She's pretty matter of fact about all these things. Any kind of information I wanted I got from her… I got my period when I was 11. I got used to having a period. Many people believe that when you have your period basically you rest all the time and not run around and play too much. My mom was like, 'nothing. You carry on with life as usual.' So I would be playing in school and my building and everything, like regularly. So the period didn't make a difference to the rest of what I had to do. I mean, everything else went on as normal.

Parents can find other ways to help girls in staying physically active throughout puberty and beyond. For example, 12-year-old Alice finds relief in having a sports bra while playing soccer: "With a sports bra the ball does not hurt my chest that much." Eleven-year-old Roxy shares, "I got a Speedo and it's like a shirt and short bottoms, and it's very comfortable (compared with a bikini)."

Considering the challenging social context within which girls go through puberty, adults can do a great deal to help girls care for their bodies during this process. Supporting girls through puberty is an important component of a health promotion program I implemented in a residential ballet school (Piran, 1999, 2001). It was during that time that I met, not at the school, two adolescent girls whose hopes to become prima ballerinas were dashed. At age 11 and with the support of adults around them (including physicians), both girls started to restrict their food intake and drastically lost weight. Having severely starved themselves, both experienced stunted growth. When they met me at ages 14–15, they had just one piercing question: why were they not previously informed about the risk of stunted growth. Their stunted growth and consequent body proportions precluded them from being candidates for a career in ballet.

Freedom of Desire is the fourth dimension of Physical Freedom challenged during the tweens phase (see Table 1.2). Kyra's statement, *"you just feel better because you're smaller,"* or Alice's description of pressure on girls to be thin, explain how the need to be small and thin starts to disrupt tween girls' experiences of appetite just as they are starting to develop into full women and take more space in the world. From experiencing a connection to appetite as a bodily desire, one that guides the need for nurturance and pleasure during childhood and the early tweens phase, the experience of appetite becomes a bodily need that is "dangerous" and requires control, lest a terrible thing happen to the body: it will become bigger and fatter—in other words, it will go through the normal process of puberty! This disruption most often involves the control and containment of appetite, monitoring of food intake, dividing foods in dichotomous categories of "good" and "bad," and aiming to restrict consumption of bad foods. Adults often support girls in the containment of appetite. Erica's description is common:

> I don't eat a lot of stuff. But I get hungry pretty easily. My mom... she'll try and give me non-fat stuff. She'll make me a bowl of cooked carrots—I really like that or she'll make me pizza... I eat non-fat chips. I won't eat anything that has pure sugar in it. That's disgusting. My body does not let me eat sugar.

Less commonly, tween girls deny the presence of hunger, fast, or severely restrict their diet, leading to significant weight loss at the onset of puberty—a process that may adversely affect growth and other physiological processes as Jackie, a girl of Aboriginal heritage, describes:

> I'm at a point in my life [age 11] where... I'm not eating as much. So I eat less. It took me about four months to go from 110 pounds to 92 [16% of body weight]... I ate less fatty stuff, so I didn't eat as much McDonalds, I didn't eat as much Burger King. I had more stuff like salads and stuff like that McCain Superfries where there is less fat.

Socioeconomic standing also shapes this struggle around appetite and eating common to most girls we interviewed—from very low social class to middle class and up. However, girls from middle-class homes describe greater access not only to exercise facilities but also to perishable, "healthier" food choices. As a result, they commonly express trust that they will be able to "count" on their daily diet to control their weight. Meghan, an 11-year-old White girl of middle-to-high social class, describes this experience:

> My favorite foods are apples and blueberry muffins. I love blueberries. I like the wild ones especially. I don't like pineapple. I like chicken and steak. I don't like peas and corn. When I am older I'll be taller and probably get like bigger breasts. I don't want to get fatter. I eat healthy food all the time so I don't think that will happen.

In contrast, girls from lower socioeconomic standing describe having less access to perishable foods and a greater reliance on fast or non-perishable foods. Therefore, attempts at weight loss more often rely on food restrictions, such as restrictions on quantities of fast food consumed or regular family meals, as Jackie describes above. Indeed, there is a well-established correlation between socioeconomic standing and weight: lower social class is associated with higher weights related to multiple environmental factors, such as the lack of access to healthy food choices, exercise facilities, and neighborhoods safe for walking. Weight prejudice therefore inherently includes social class prejudice.

Social processes that disrupt girls' connection with another bodily desire—sexual desire—follow a different time pattern than those disrupting appetite. While appetite becomes a disrupted desire during tweens and beyond, female sexual desire becomes a target of disruption during early adolescence, as sexual desire and dating become more central aspects of social life. During the tweens, especially at the onset of puberty and of budding, mature sexuality, we still hear passionate positive descriptions of owning desire, which we rarely hear after this phase. Here are Alice and Jackie's descriptions, both at age 12:

> I have a crush on a boy. He's really cute... I think he has a crush on me, too because every time when we're playing he'd stop and stare, particularly at me when I'm playing, and then in choir he just turns and stares at me and then I stare at him then he stares at me... Like, well he's so cute like we make all these plans for marriages and stuff. Oh you just act really, like act really silly. Like you go 'AYeeehh!' (Alice)

> There's this one guy that I like and he likes me, too. We're just good friends. He's got the cutest face and he's adorable. He asked me to dance and like I said to him, 'You do know I like you, right?' and he goes, 'Yeah, you know I like you, right?!' But, like, I really hate hormones, 'cause it makes you feel like you're always, like dreamy. Like whenever he's around, I am always going off into space. (Jackie)

We also hear of girls' resistance to starting to date early, feeling the right to wait despite early pressures to enter the dating scene. According to 12-year-old Bronwen, a White girl from a middle-class and rural background,

> I just like I just don't want to date. Like it just doesn't make sense to me and I'm just not ready for it. I think mostly just like I feel there's

> this kind of rush to go out with someone and do all that kissing and all that kind, but I really don't want to do that. Like I'm 12, like I still don't feel that I'm ready for any of that stuff.

In none of the interviews with tween girls, or those with older girls, do we hear about adults in the lives of tween girls validating girls' sexual desire. This includes parents, other adults in parental roles, teachers, health educators, physicians, and nurses. This makes it more challenging for girls to connect positively and feel comfortable with their own desire, as well as engage with their desire with self-attunement and self-care. Girls unanimously describe sexual education classes as unhelpful in addressing and finding equity in desire. Classes most often focus on pubertal physiological changes, and if addressing desire, it is focused on male ejaculation. Taught pregnancy prevention strategies range from abstinence to the use of contraceptives. As Erica describes, "In health class we don't talk about our bodies, only about being pregnant, not about having sex." Inevitably, health education is shaped by the confines of widely sanctioned ideologies, as Bronwen aptly observes:

> Sex Ed class is so inadequate. I'm just like because they have to remain Catholic you know. They have to be like, don't have sex until you are married. It's like, don't have sex until you are pregnant! Oh yeah that makes a lot of sense!

Not only are positive messages regarding girls' desires lacking at this early phase of the dating scene, but tween girls are also exposed to several disruptive social messages. One of the earliest messages we hear involves the restriction of agency and choice:

> Well sometimes I have a little dance thing at the community center. So it's all dark inside but they have these disco light and they slow dance… the girl always does let the boys choose the girls 'cause sometimes the girls don't really like choosing… they'll dance if they get asked. (Erica)

> I Just want to go up and hug him… Go, go up and tell him that you like him. But then I don't. It's probably going to be like well you should not have done it. No. No. No. I can't do it in front of his friends. A guy's allowed to go up to you in front of your friends and give you a hug and kiss, but if you do that in front of his friends, that's like a big no-no, 'cause it's embarrassing you. His friends, like if you're a girl, they'd just say, awwww. (Alice)

Girls learn that agency in owning female desire is not sanctioned and is sometimes even penalized, and therefore needs to be held in check and contained. At the same time, male heterosexual desire is associated with agency, choice, and freedom to act in the world, actually enhancing boys'experience of agency in the world. Hence, as mature sexuality emerges, it most often becomes yet another domain of restriction for girls. Further, additional disruptive processes begin during this phase, in particular the negative labeling of female desire through demeaning labels, such as sluts, and exposure to sexual harassment. These processes intensify during early adolescence and will be described in the next chapter.

In summary, tween girls encounter the introduction of corsets in all four dimensions of Physical Freedom. Barriers to physical engagement take the form of restricted access to sites of physical engagement, as well as the expectation that girls wear tight and exposing clothes, prohibiting free movement. Concurrently, the experience of safety is compromised through the introduction of sexual harassment and dating violence. Further, the lack of attunement by the social environment to the challenges girls face in negotiating their pubertal bodies enhances their body discomfort. Moreover, social messages of containment and constriction in relation to desire, both appetite and sexual, reduce girls' agency and comfort in the world. This introduction of Physical Corsets contributes to the shift in girls' embodied experiences, from passionate agency at the beginning of the tweens phase to restricted agency and discomfort at the end of that stage.

PRETTY GIRLS DO NOT SWEAT: MENTAL CORSETS WITHIN THE TOMBOY/GIRLY GIRL DICHOTOMY

> A lot of times in gym when we're like doing running, I like to run but I don't like cross country. I worry about sweating 'cause I absolutely hate sweating. I think it is *gross* for girls, but boys are meant to sweat. Like on TV when you see guys playing football or basketball there was like sweating and stuff like that… When I am in gym class I sweat and then I try to avoid it. I try not to run as much and move that much because then it causes me to sweat. If I sweat, I go to the fountain and spray my face… Like, usually in gym, obviously, if you don't work as hard then your grades will drop. So you have to kind of balance between trying not to sweat too much, so you don't wanna work too hard. And then you don't want your grades to go down. Like in magazines if a girl is sweating so badly, they take a

> bad picture of her and then show it in the magazine to everybody. I think boys, they look like they're having so much fun. They don't care what they look like. And then when girls wanna play they look so stiff trying not to try as hard. If I didn't care about sweating, I will have so much more fun!

In this quotation, 12-year-old Erica, a White girl from a working-class background, shares her struggle with being a resistor at the latter part of the tweens phase. As earlier quotations from Erica suggest, at age nine, at the start of the tweens phase, she resisted changing her physical activities and wanted to keep wearing comfortable clothes: "I think they [girls] should dress the way they want to… do cartwheels, climb high…" Erica loves sports passionately, identifies herself as a tomboy, and resists the common shift to sedentary feminine activities that exist among girls in her peer group. Yet, even as a tomboy, an identity still partly accepted during this phase, different constraining femininity discourses—Mental Corsets, according to the Developmental Theory of Embodiment (DTE)—disrupt not only the experience of immersion in her beloved physical activities but her actual body movements as well.

One femininity discourse embedded in Erica's narrative is the Body as an Object of Gaze, which is expressed through her preoccupation with her body appearance while engaged in sports. Importantly, she is also addressing a second Appearance-related Discourse that, we find, emerges during the tweens phase: the Woman's Body as Deficient. The particular "deficiency" Erica describes is the natural and healthy bodily process of sweating, which girls perceive as being "gross." This deficiency discourse slows Erica's physical movement in space and disrupts her intense, frequent, and joyful engagement in sports. Clearly, Mental Corsets shape embodied practices.

The two Appearance-related Discourses specified by the DTE that shape many girls and women's embodied lives—the Body as an Object of Gaze and the Woman's Body as Deficient—are both present during the tweens phase, becoming more oppressive in adolescence (see Table 1.2). Girls have already learned in childhood that compliance with the Body as an Object of Gaze discourse relates to approval and worth. As the tweens phase progresses they learn, first, that there are strict appearance-related rules about being an ideal woman object, and second, that there are social penalties for deviating from these widely sanctioned rules. Diverse tween girls consistently both draw and describe the ideal girl as thin, beautiful, with long, straightened blonde hair and blue eyes, and wearing makeup. She is attired in tight and exposing clothes—often pink—and high heels. The ideal girl is also physically restricted and on display as a passive, perfect object. Girls observe that peers who fit this description are the most popular. For example, 12-year-old Jackie, a girl of Aboriginal heritage and a working-class background, describes the ideal girl in the following way:

> Really skinny, pretty, peach skin or blush, long blonde hair, red lipstick, high heels, pink tight shirt, her stomach is showing, high heels, she cares about fashion and makeup. Like *porcelain*, like I'm a *porcelain doll*, I'm just gonna sit here and be perfect. She just likes to sit around and crosses her legs. But the guys—it's like the cool guys are like, 'oh I'm cool, I sweat'… I tried to be popular. You have to be perfect, you slip up once and you're out. Like you get one strike and you're out. You can't run or anything, you have to walk, you have to wear high heels. You have to keep lip balm with you every second, lipstick, wear lipstick all the time. You just couldn't be athletic and I've always wanted to just get up and run but you couldn't do that, you had to sit around and like talk during recess all [through] grades five and six. But in Grade six you need a boyfriend to be popular and I don't have a boyfriend. Some of the popular girls are really smart and stuff like but they have to act stupid because they think they're gonna attract the guys if they act stupid.

Clearly, as girls' bodies start to change into those of young women—often around ages 11–12 years—they are immediately faced with impossible, harsh, and constraining specifications regarding the ideal object of gaze, an object that, now that they are going through puberty, they are expected to embody. The Body as an Object of Gaze therefore tightens by the end of the tweens phase.

Yet, pressures increase even further during the latter parts of this phase with the emergence of the second, powerful appearance-related discourse: the Woman's Body as Deficient. As tween girls start inhabiting women's bodies, they discover that the discourse of deficiency is part of owning a woman's body. This discourse is ever present in the lives of diverse adult women and in all forms of media. It is rare for girls to find a woman who models comfort, acceptance, and pride in her unaltered appearance. This learned and internalized discourse of deficiency charts a course for most women leading them to a diminished sense of embodied comfort, worth, and agency.

The major loss to girls' (and women's) embodiment associated with the discourse of the Woman's Body as Deficient is particularly poignant during the tweens phase, as its emergence marks a significant shift from common embodied experiences in childhood. The scope of the loss becomes even clearer when the harsh critical comments tween girls make about their own bodies are considered, including adjectives such as "gross," "screwed up," "disgusting," and "ugly." Tween girls' harshness toward their bodies mirrors the way women's bodies are often treated in the culture at large, with all aspects of their bodies criticized. For example: hair, "My hair needs to be tamed in the mornings it's like a forest" (Jackie); facial features, "I think my face is a little chubby on the side" (Madison); skin, "I don't like my freckles. I think they make my face look *old and uglier*" (Meghan), or "My skin is too fair so I need make up" (Bronwen); body hair, "I want to be blonde. Like people notice the hair on my legs a lot and say things like 'God you are hairy. Are you an *ape*'" (Alice), or "I cover my legs and arms because of the black hair" (Jackie); and body shape, "I gained like 15 pounds and I totally *flipped out*... I mean like I really like would be happy if I was flat the way I used to be," (Bronwen), "Kinda hard to be tall because you can't find guys your height. I wish I was shorter" (Alice), or "I am embarrassed because of my stomach, it's like a bump, I am afraid they will call me 'one lump' and start laughing, girls that are bigger get teased" (Madison).

As described earlier in this chapter, most girls react negatively toward the physiological processes of puberty that move them away from idealized images of women—in particular gaining curves, fat, and weight, as well as body hair. As 12-year-old Jackie expresses so succinctly:

> Puberty is a terrible part of life. It is *gross*. You gain a lot of weight. You get more hair where you don't want it, like your legs and underarms. You sweat more. I hate bras, they are so uncomfortable. I am worried about getting my period and also need to be cautious about pregnancy.

During the tweens phase, it becomes a burden to carry a body that starts to be defined as deficient and in need of repair. This deficiency discourse concretizes gender inequity, similar to the way processes of inequity have been institutionalized in relation to race, heritage or ability. The body of the disenfranchised is deemed "faulty." The DTE combines the two Appearance-related Discourses, the Body as Object of Gaze and the Woman's Body as Deficient, under the Body as a Deficient Object. It is the intersection of these two Appearance-related Discourses that likely relates to the observed drop in body esteem among tween girls (Mendelson et al., 2001).

Reinforcing these appearance-related expectations are the four Comportment-related Discourses, described by the DTE (a subset of the Woman as Docile discourse cluster) (see Table 1.2). One of these Comportment-related Discourses, Engagement in "Feminine" Activities, is transmitted to girls in early childhood as an aspect of their socialization. This particular discourse remains active throughout girls and women's lives.

While during early childhood the permeability of boy–girl boundaries provides girls with the opportunity to engage in a fuller embodied way in the world, once puberty starts, the constrictive discourse of Engagement in "Feminine" Activities is more strongly enforced. In particular, at this stage, girls often stop being physically active in the world and, instead, comply with being pretty objects to be gazed at, as Jackie's narrative above details: "like I'm a *porcelain doll*, I'm just gonna sit here and be perfect." When Jackie vies for a popular position in her peer group, she, like other tween girls, is clear that she "cannot run" or "be athletic," but instead will "sit around and like talk." The shift from physical action to sitting or walking and talking is the most striking shift in activities during this phase, and reflects the ways in which Physical Corsets (such as less resources for girls' physical activities) combine with restrictive Mental Corsets to change how girls engage with the world.

A second comportment-related discourse becomes active during the end of the tweens phase: Woman as Demure/Submissive. For most tween girls, the emphasis is on the physical component of being small and dainty, though others also mention not being too vocal or too smart. When we ask tween girls to draw themselves and then draw the ideal girl, the drawings of the ideal girl are considerably smaller all around, both shorter and thinner than those of the drawing of the self, suggesting the attractiveness in being physically demure. Girls elaborate, saying, "small is good" (Kyra, 12 years old). However, most tween girls are clear that it is better not only to be small in size but also dainty and, in particular, not muscular:

> My abs got really big and it was *scary*. It was just like girls aren't supposed to have bigger abs like guys; like you see guys with six packs but you see girls very rarely that have abs at all. (Jackie)

> If you're as muscular as the guys, then that's kinda *creepy*. Just kinda awkward. 'Cause most the girls are friends with guys with muscles, and it's just *weird* having a guy friend with the same muscles. It makes you look just weird. (Alice)

Adjectives such as "scary," "creepy," and "weird" suggest how disturbing being muscular is for these girls. While tween girls are focused mainly on being physically demure, a few express already by age 12 feeling the need to not outsmart boys if one wants to be popular. As Jackie describes:

> Some of the popular girls are really smart and stuff like but they have to act stupid because they think they're gonna attract the guys if they act stupid. Just 'cause you want guys to like you doesn't mean you have to act like you're a dim wit.

A third Comportment-related Discourse that starts to becomes active among some girls during the end of the tweens phase relates to the containment of desires, entitled Woman as Desired but Desire-less. At this stage, a few of the girls start to struggle with appetite and eating, specifically feeling that they need to control their appetites to control weight gain: "I am at a point in my life where I'm not eating as much. I don't eat much of my lunch… I do get hungry and get less athletic" (11-year-old Jackie). While several girls mention experiencing peer pressure to start dating, more commonly girls do not speak at this phase about social expectations regarding the containment of sexual desire.

One of the striking aspects of the Comportment-related Discourses during the tweens phase is the way in which the Patriarchal Shaping of Relational Patterns discourse starts becoming activated once girls go through puberty, leading to rifts between girls and within communities of girls (see also Brown, 2003). During this phase, some girls start to view themselves and their peers in relation to patriarchal relational agendas. This refers to a series of relational patterns, such as prioritizing and securing sexualized male dates, implementing norms of competition between girls, and enforcing compliance with femininity practices. Girls explain that once dating starts, friendships between girls become disrupted. Eleven-year-old Hilary, a White girl from a working-class background, explains:

> When a girl agrees to go out, then they start hanging out more and then if they're like a boyfriend and girlfriend and they have friends, they won't be best friends with them anymore. They won't really spend time much together because the boyfriend will try and be first. So the boyfriend ends up coming first before the best friends. I don't think it's really fair. So that's why I don't want a boyfriend until it kind of changes.

Concurrently, girls describe experiencing competition and policing within girl groups. Peer processes that involve policing of compliance with a patriarchal lens can involve modeling, feedback, shaming, social exclusion, and coercion. Alice articulates the way girl peer groups uphold very specific norms of appearance and monitor compliance:

> I'm wearing like low-cut tops pretty much and skirts and like jeans, that's the latest fashion at my school, the skinny jeans. I have a pair of those, they're black, and they are in fashion. But the only big no-no is if you wear skinny jeans with white runners. I made the *mistake* once and my friends are just like, 'Oh my God. Go change now! It's like you're wearing runners that's totally geeky.' I'm just like, 'Oh my God,' so I had to run back to my locker and put on my boots.

Girls who resist inhabiting their bodies as objects to be gazed at might then become particular targets of coercion. For example, Lauren, a White girl from a middle-class background who at age 11 still holds on to her passion for sports and wearing comfortable clothing, experiences some coercion by peers: "In sleepovers, they'd [girls] be like, okay maybe they'll try and put makeup on me or something and I'd be like, you're crazy but I'd—sometimes I'd go along." We hear the harshest policing and enforcement of compliance by peers from 12-year-old Madison, discussing her friend who, like herself, does not fit in because she does not have the financial means to buy clothing and cosmetics that comply with "girly girl" expectations:

> And then if you want to be, like— if you don't fit in, then you can't wear your own clothes, you have to be different… like my friend, [name], but people are going to give her a makeover. But she doesn't want a makeover. So girls are… they sat her down in a chair and they, like, wrapped her up with rope so she wouldn't move… So they plucked her eyebrows and stuff. And she was, like, screaming and stuff. So I just went up and took the rope and I was like: 'Go, Be free!'… She's just going to go get new clothes and stuff.

While this section on Mental Freedom has focused on femininity discourses, these femininity discourses also intersect with discourses related to other aspects of social location. For example, Alice, of Aboriginal heritage, describes how the racist social construction of her heritage as primitive and possibly dangerous (related to sociopolitical issues in her area regarding land ownership) affects her embodied experience with her White peers, especially once puberty starts and she grows taller,

> I get mad at girls who are threatened by me. Like I stand up and all of a sudden I'm like taller than them. And they'll be like: "Okay. Okay. Okay." And they'll back away and run away from me. I feel like I'm a giant and they're afraid of me. I don't like it.

The tomboy/girly girl dichotomy figures centrally in tween girls' narratives. This dichotomy includes both Appearance- and Comportment-related femininity Discourses. Girls of diverse backgrounds are in consensus about the stereotyped meanings of the tomboy and girly girl labels. Jackie's descriptions at age 12 are a good example of these stereotypes:

> *Girly girls* like tight dresses and high-heel shoes. They like pink. A girly girl has her hair up all the time. The definition of a girly girl is just being perfect. This one girl carries lip-gloss, like 15 things of lip-gloss—in her pencil case, in her pockets, she keeps one in her shoe in her locker, and she has lipstick on all the time. She wants to

> be really skinny. She coordinates her clothes, and she always asks everybody 'Do I look okay?' She just likes to sit around and doesn't like to play sports. Girly girls like to talk. They talk behind people's backs. Tomboys hate girly girls. They find them so annoying with their little purses, carrying it around everywhere with their lip balm and stuff. She wears all the right clothes, have boyfriends you know, all that jazz.

> A *tomboy* is really boyish, you wear baggy pants or shorts all the time. With a tomboy, it's like 'watch out.' Tomboys are really tough and it's like, 'you're gone if you come near me.' A tomboy is really boyish—you always do sports, whatever team you try out for, you're the first one to be picked, you're an athletic rep, everything you do is sports, you wear baggy pants or shorts all the time, you get A's in gym.

Like Jackie, girls consistently describe *girly girls'* constant concern with their appearance, their constriction in space, lack of engagement in physical action, and their relational patterns of sexualization and subsequent betrayal by peers. At the opposite end of this dichotomy, girls highlight *tomboys'* comfortable clothing and freedom to engage with the world immersed in physical activities without persistent appearance concerns. They also emphasize tomboys' assertiveness and direct style of communication (not obstructed by pressures to be nice or demure).

The socially constructed tomboy/girly girl dichotomy, which condenses all Appearance- and Comportment-related Discourses, confines embodied possibilities for girls (Legge, 2011; Reay, 2001). As tween girls' bodies mature and they no longer have access to the freedom they once had to engage in the world like boys, as *tomboys*, they are pushed to embody the polar opposite of this "package deal," becoming a girly girl. Being a girly girl is perceived as the only way to fit in and gain approval as young women within a patriarchal social system, even though girly girls are also often devalued. Tween girls therefore commonly shift their position on the dichotomy by the end of the tweens phase, moving away from the tomboy pole and locating themselves either at the middle position—more typically among girls who resist this shift—or, often, by embracing the girly girl label. Jackie, for example, describes her shift to a girly girl position: "I used to wear stuff that wasn't so showy. Now I wear stuff like halter tops and like spaghetti straps. Now I wear, to show, shorter shorts, I never wore shorts when I was little, now I do."

We hear little from tween girls about relational forums that nurture their resistant voices to tightening social discourses. As reflected in the narratives shared in this chapter, tween girls do make resistant comments toward aggregating Mental Corsets that aim to dictate and constrict how they can be in, and engage with, the world. In response, they sometimes try to free themselves from the oppressive tomboy/girly girl dichotomy by trying to hold a middle position (such as dressing girly but staying involved in sports). Hence, there is an important opportunity to intervene at this age to help amplify resistant voices and set resistant norms in girls' peer groups. This can have a powerful impact as tween girls start their path toward early adolescence and inhabiting post-pubertal bodies.

In summary, during the tweens phase, girls face the task of negotiating their embodied identities in relation to tightening femininity discourses, broadly labeled as Mental Corsets. Not only are they expected now to comply with objectifying appearance expectations, but they are also encumbered by the perception that their maturing bodies are inherently deficient, requiring repair. Further shaping their embodied experiences are expectations that they engage in sedentary activities, act demure, contain their desires, and comply with relational priorities that sustain patriarchy. Altogether, the femininity discourses restrict full, passionate, and active engagement with the world and reduce girls' experiences of embodied comfort, worth, agency, and support.

ON BECOMING AN ALIEN: SOCIAL POWER AS BODY CAPITAL AT PUBERTY

> I got this tummy and I couldn't fit into my favorite pair of pants. I had a dance and it was like, 'oh, my God, I have to fit into these pants.' People talked behind my back and said how fat I was and stuff. [My friend] is really overweight but it does not bother her. She knows she can't be teased because she has a boyfriend and he has blond hair and he is real cute, and he has blue eyes, crystal blue eyes... Girls like a good blue-colored eyes. I know I do and I think most girls do. Girls want to be really skinny and to have a peach skin or blush... I wear long sleeves and skirts to cover the black hair on my arms and legs... I was not in the popular class anymore... I was in the dorks, second class... Usually fat people are not in the popular group... I felt like I was an outsider. I felt like an alien. I was like, 'I have to lose weight or else I'm gonna be living on Mars for the rest of my life.'

At age 11, after the onset of puberty and following an expected weight gain, Jackie restricts her eating and loses about 16% of her body weight. Losing such a high percentage of weight during this pubertal stage can affect growth patterns. Jackie explains this weight loss as being related to her position in her peer group. Let us consider Jackie's decision to lose weight, as her experiences are emblematic of issues related to the privileging or, alternatively, disenfranchising, of particular bodies. First, related to her socioeconomic standing, she could not afford to grow out of her favorite pair of pants, which she intended to wear for a special party. It should also be noted that due to financial circumstances Jackie cannot join sports programs outside of school, creating a more sedentary lifestyle. Due to this lack of physical practice she, in turn, fears taking part in school tryouts: "I'm not on any school teams. I haven't tried out because this is really for athletic girls and I'm scared if I try, I'll be humiliated." Jackie therefore misses out on an important protective factor that can help girls stay positively connected to the physical functionality of their bodies.

Second, Jackie has heard indirectly that her weight has been a target of ridicule—a common experience in her peer group. Indeed, fat prejudice and weight teasing are common adverse social phenomena seen across all peer groups. It is well known that in developed countries higher weight correlates with lower social class and that weight prejudice is at least partly related to classism. Indeed, Jackie acutely observes that weight teasing relates not only to one's weight but also to the constellation of other social factors that can make one protected from, or rather more vulnerable to, such teasing. She comments that dating a White boyfriend can raise one's social worth and is an important protective factor against body-based teasing.

The third social factor Jackie highlights relates to her Aboriginal heritage. She assesses how her appearance characteristics do not match those of the ideal girl: she is not White, blue-eyed, with blond hair.

Fourth, related to gender, Jackie is aware that to be popular, she needs to first be skinny, as girls are not supposed to occupy too much physical space. It is at this intersection of social class, weight, race, and gender, that Jackie feels the only way for her to avoid being an "alien" in her peer group is to raise her body capital, and hence her social power, via drastic weight loss.

Jackie's narrative highlights three important dimensions of the Social Power and Relational Connections domain of the DTE. First, she clarifies the adverse impact on one's embodiment via Exposure to Prejudice and Harassment, and, alternatively, the potential importance of Freedom from Prejudice and Harassment. Second, she coveys the growing impact of Appearance-based Social Power during the tweens phase; as girls' appearance wields greater impact on social power, their specific appearance characteristics are more likely to become a target of prejudice and harassment, or, alternatively, a source of social power. She even alludes to the dimension of Membership in Inequitable Communities. Her narrative describes a hierarchical peer group organization with different classes, and her embodied disruption relates to being considered "second class"—a social status she is trying to escape by losing weight at a critical stage of pubertal development.

Starting with the first dimension of the Social Power and Relational Connections domain, namely, Exposure to Prejudice and Harassment (see Table 1.2), shifts occur in the social environments of tween girls as they mature physically. These shifts accentuate prejudicial treatment along gender lines, as well as other dimensions of social location. First, as their bodies change, tween girls start to incur some of the prejudicial treatment encountered by adult women, with understandable negative reactions. Concurrently, their bodies become a greater target of devaluation.

The experience of 12-year-old Bronwen, a White girl from a middle-class and rural background, helps convey tween girls' exposure to such gender-based prejudices in different domains of their lives: home, school, and other settings—in Bronwen's case, a religious institution. Ultimately, she feels "self-conscious" about her body, as well as "inadequate" and "not confident." In particular, she worries that her body will become a target of teasing similar to the teasing she has witnessed of a girl who is "disabled and thicker and poor."

At home, Bronwen feels maltreated by the inequitable distribution of domestic chores when compared to the responsibilities of her brothers, as well as her father's withdrawal from her since puberty, his objectifying comments about her appearance, and his discouragement of her agency.

> [Home—role] I take responsibility doing most of the stuff at home while the cool big masculine guys are sitting on the couch and watching television. Like when my mom is away I basically do all the things that she would normally do. My mom hates it, like me. I just find it so awful. I don't want that to happen in my own relationship because this is just not the position to be in... In the past year or two my dad is really uncomfortable with me becoming a teenager because he doesn't know how to deal with me, but I'm still the same, and it really hurts me because I feel that he likes my brothers more than me... It irritates me that he [father] would tell me that I should wear makeup because of the color of my skin... Yeah, and actually when I'm with him I'm not as self-confident. I feel inadequate. Like whenever I want to take on a project, I find that he's the one who is like, 'Oh you should be really careful about that kind of thing,' and my mom is like, 'Go for it,' and so that really hurts me. Like I really wanted to start a club but he was the one that kind of like, 'I don't know' and so I think that has really hurt me. I think I have to work with myself to be able to take on projects like that, because he's kind of changed that for me.

At school, she feels sexist attitudes through pressures to sexualize her body and also by being silenced regarding her feminist views and opinions:

> I am 12 and I feel as though that pressure for the body being sexy is a problem. That's what I don't like about our culture. I think there is so much pressure put on like wearing really tight clothes and all that thing, it is sexist... There is a teacher who makes me feel insecure. He's full of himself, as though he knows everything, and he does not like my opinions.

She also observes gender and other discriminations in church:

> I don't like how God is supposedly a man, that kind of irritates me, because that is sexism. I think God isn't man or woman... But everything seems to be rotating around boys. And also since I go to a Catholic school, it's all magnified. Like all priests can only be men and that really irritates me. What's up with that? I also find that gay and lesbian people really are discriminated so badly. I don't like that kind of discrimination.

Beginning to inhabit a woman's body, Bronwen experiences prejudicial treatment in her primary domains of life, which is eroding her embodied agency and experience of worth. In addition, she fears that she may become a target of teasing, a social process she has amply witnessed in her peer group. As we invite girls into women's spheres, they encounter prejudices faced by women of diverse social locations throughout their lives, including the greater targeting of their bodies.

Anecdotally, from my own practice, in one school where I worked on the prevention of eating disorders, an 11-year-old girl, just at the cusp of puberty, described an experience she had in a social studies class where she shared strong pro-choice opinions. The male teacher responded by stating that she could not know anything about abortions since she did not "even have breasts yet." As she insightfully commented in our group meeting with other girls, "he was using my body to embarrass me, to shut me down" (Piran, 2001). While she was both embarrassed and angered by this sexual harassment, she was determined she would not be silenced. Indeed, using women's bodies both to disempower them and justify the unbreakable glass ceiling that operates in political, business, and other public arenas is common (see, for example, Ibarra, Ely, & Kolb, 2013).

It is not surprising then that the ongoing prejudicial treatment of girls causes an erosion of embodied agency, as Bronwen and other girls describe, leading in the long run to challenges in assuming leadership roles in the public sphere. In their article in *Harvard Business Review* entitled "Women rising: The Unseen Barriers," Ibarra et al. (2013) describe, for example, that behaviors related to the lack of embodied agency, such as the lack of "executive presence" or of the capacity to "fill the room," are criticisms voiced to bar women from leadership positions in corporations. There is no question that we need to fortify girls with resistant tools in confronting prejudicial treatment, while concurrently working toward constructive social change. We need to provide girls with relational connections and forums where their voices can be validated and resistance and activism can be nurtured (Brown, 2016; Piran, 2001).

Entering the gender-based prejudicial world of young women, pubertal tween girls find themselves facing for the first time the full force of Appearance-based Social Power, the second dimension of the Social Power and Relational Connections domain of the DTE (see Table 1.2). Older tween girls have learned that social power and social rewards, assessed within the peer group through popularity and getting (heterosexual) dates, relate to meeting very strict appearance and comportment criteria. They also understand that failure to meet these criteria leads to social exclusion and teasing. Objectification theory (Fredrickson & Roberts, 1997; McKinley & Hyde, 1996) and related research strongly document the adverse impact of living in this appearance-based social world, ranging in effect from body shame and appearance anxiety to depression, disordered eating patterns, poor self-esteem, and disrupted academic and physical performance (Moradi & Huang, 2008). Starting at the end of the tweens phase, the Appearance-based Social Power dimension remains a powerful damaging factor throughout girls and women's lives. In their article about women leaders, Ibarra, Ely, and Kolb reference a member of Hillary Clinton's press corps who said, "The story is never what she says, as much as we want it to be. The story is always how she looked when she said it." This disregard for intention and meaning in interpersonal communication by women is demeaning and disempowering.

This chapter includes two longer narratives by Jackie at the age of 12: one in the Mental Freedom section, where she describes the appearance and comportment characteristics of the ideal or popular girl; and the second, in this section, on Social Power, whereby she describes her failure to meet these characteristics, related to intersecting dimensions of her social location. Inviting Jackie and other girls to draw themselves and the ideal girl, as an aspect of the research methodology, helps deepen the understanding of tween girls' embodied experiences. First, the drawings and their related narratives reveal the strong hold these idealized images have on girls' subjective experiences, as well as their scrutinizing assessments of their body capital in relation to these idealized images.

Second, to date, most research has focused on the internalization by girls and women of idealized thinness, with much less work being done on other aspects of appearance such as skin color (Buchanan, Fischer, Tokar, & Yoder, 2008). However, our research highlights the intersection of multiple aspects of social location in the widely sanctioned visual images of the ideal girl, as constructed by tween girls. Consequently, as popularity among peers revolves around inhabiting idealized girl bodies, we find greater social divides related to different aspects of social location following puberty. For example, Jackie felt that she was popular in grade 4 but lost that status in grades 5 and 6, during puberty. Similarly, Alice, who was one of few non-White students in her school, found that post-puberty she was no longer included in her girlfriends' plans to attend university together; instead, they invited her to carry their bags on their journey to university. I also witnessed similar accentuations of embodied inequity during puberty in different schools where I conducted body-image workshops.

The centrality of Appearance-based Social Power brings forth a number of dilemmas for tween girls regarding coveted social power. While, as Jackie and all other girls describe, the ideal girl is popular and gets dates, she is also physically constrained: "She just likes to sit around and cross her legs… you can't run." The popular girl's "frozen" power involves carrying herself around as a restrained and perfect object at all times, devoid of embodied functionality and physical freedom. In addition to this physical restriction, girls' narratives also reflect the "caricaturization" of popular or ideal girls and their pursuit of appearance-based perfection. For example: "I'm a porcelain doll" (Jackie), or "I broke a nail! Call a doctor. Call the nail stylist. Get me a new nail. Now!" (Alice). Furthermore, popular status is forever fragile since restrained perfection is impossible to achieve and maintain. As Jackie explains, "You slip up once and you're out. Like you get one strike and you're out." As girls describe, even "running" (Jackie) or getting "a zit on their face" (Tiger) can be problematic. What is important to highlight here is that, while most research literature emphasizes the social power girls associate with thinness, girls' own experiences of restraint, powerlessness, and vulnerability in occupying the popular position are not as commonly problematized or utilized in programs aimed at enhancing positive body image and preventing eating disorders. Providing tween girls with the relational spaces needed to collectively amplify their critical perspectives regarding appearance-based social power can help counter the eroding search for such power.

The next two dimensions of the Social Power and Relational Connections domain of the DTE can indeed address ways to enhance the social power of tweens (see Table 1.2). First, regarding Empowering Relationships, during the tweens phase these can, in particular, help defy Appearance-based Social Power by modeling alternative ways of obtaining social power.

Eleven-year-old Madison describes such an experience with her mom. Madison, a girl of Aboriginal heritage, lives in challenging financial circumstances and in an unsafe neighborhood. At the age of 11, she decides not to rely on accepted norms of beauty and instead conducts her own survey among boys: "I did a little survey of my own and I went to guys and said, 'what are you looking for in a girl,' and they said blonde hair and blue eyes, and she needs to be skinny." Madison has been a frequent target of body-based teasing related to her weight, financial status, and likely her heritage: "They'd call me fat trash, fat slut, dork, really bad. People take things too far with girls and they don't know how it feels to be a girl… People bully because people used to bully them." Considering the results of her survey and the teasing she has endured, Madison assesses herself as being not close to meeting idealized appearance characteristics. However, she has a very close relationship with her mother, whom she perceives as a social resistor that acts in the world with freedom. "I look up to my mom. She does everything that kind of goes against all the rules." Madison's mother also models standing up to harassment and bullying: "… and she came out and said, 'I hope you are not saying this to my daughter.'" Furthermore, her mom engages with Madison in thinking critically about social conventions—for example, she emphasizes to Madison that it is what is on the inside that counts and acts against racism.

Like her mother, Madison has become an activist and a critical thinker. "It doesn't matter what's on the outside," she states, adding one should "Never change who they are because of other people, even if they say if you do this to yourself you'll be popular too." When in health class good health is equated with thinness, Madison assesses her own health as being solid in relation to thinner girls: "All these thinner girls may be faster than me, but I can run longer." Further, her critical and resistant stance is expressed through activism in her school environment—she has successfully campaigned to reduce paper waste and stop the use of animal specimens in science classes. Importantly, Madison's successful activism is associated with *action* rather than with appearance-related social power. "And people say I'm really popular because of the things *that I do*. I stopped the waste of paper in my school. I stopped the use of animals in science classes." Madison's mother is a strong role model of power through critical thinking and activism.

Membership in Equitable Communities, another relational dimension of the Social Power and Relational Connection domain, exerts important influences on girls' embodied agency and worth. Overall, we find that tween girls experience greater exposure to Inequitable Communities toward the end of the tweens phase, a barrier to embodied comfort, agency, and power. The crystallization of social hierarchies, through the value placed on embodying the ideal girl, disrupts pre-existing equitable peer networks. While vying for power within the context of its ongoing erosion, tween girls compete for social resources (dates) and conduct mutual policing of adherence to patriarchal norms. Further, the sexualization by, and sexual harassment from, boys disrupt pre-existing cross-gender friendships. Therefore, girls at the end of the tweens phase often do not find supportive equitable networks that could provide them with a sense of acceptance, support, and validation—experiences inherent to embodied agency and worth in the world.

Events in tween girls' lives that do provide experiences of validation and acceptance within equitable communities stand out as powerful. For example, the ritual, mentioned earlier in this chapter, in which four women welcomed Bronwen to the women's community upon receiving her first period, was a critical event that favorably shapes her embodied experience: "They welcomed me into womanhood and described the strengths and powers of women. It made me feel really special. It made me feel more loved, that people will always be there for me." This welcoming ritual stands in stark contrast to the alienation she has experienced among her peers, during her later tween years, related to what she feels is forced sexualization and dating.

Despite the destabilization of peer support networks, some tween girls find small, alternative networks in which they find validation. Madison is part of a group of three girls who stick up for one another in the face of rampant peer bullying. "My friends started saying, 'why do you care about what people think of you,' and that made me feel better about myself. It made me more confident about my body." Similarly, Melissa, a White girl from a middle-class and urban background, finds, to her relief, a small group of girls who share her love of sports. This small group of like-minded girls is important to Melissa because, at puberty, she became disconnected from her closest friends, who are boys, as well as from girls who engage exclusively in sedentary activities. "I met more girls that had the same interests [in sports] as me so we started playing."

To summarize experiences in the Social Power and Relational Connections domain, living in pubertal bodies and getting involved in the predominantly heterosexual dating scene, girls in early adolescence experience in their daily, embodied lives the poignant inequity in the way girls and boys' bodies are treated in a sexist culture. Starting with the Exposure to Prejudice and Harassment dimension, girls highlight multiple expressions of the double standard that exists in relation to engagement in sexual activities, containment of desire and harsh standards of appearance. During early adolescence, the strong impact of the second dimension, Appearance-based Social Power, reinforces the disempowerment of girls, with power through objectification being inherently restrictive and demoting. Furthermore, the visual representation of popular girls works to stratify the social standing of diverse girls, such that girls who do not fit within idealized visual representations related to financial standing, ethnocultural/racial heritage, sexual orientation, weight, or visible difference/disability may face social exclusion and harassment. At the same time, girls in early adolescence have limited access to two possible sources of social power: Empowering Relationships and Membership in Equitable Communities. Facilitated groups can invite girls to examine daily experiences in their bodies, analyze them in relation to societal structures of power, and guide girls in shared problem solving. Developing new constructive group norms and repairing relational connections can empower girls as well.

CHAPTER SUMMARY

By studying longitudinally the narratives of tween girls as they progress through this developmental phase, the embodiment research program provides an opportunity to examine the striking changes to girls' social environments as they go through puberty and the consequent dramatic effects on their experiences of embodiment. As losses accrue with respect to tween girls' experiences of body connection and comfort, agency and functionality, and inhabiting the body as a subjective site, diverse tween girls' engagement with the world alters meaningfully at a pace not equaled during other developmental phases.

Utilizing DTE theoretical constructs to examine social experiences in the physical, mental, and social power domains reveals an overall constriction in how, by the end of the tweens phase, girls can inhabit their bodies and engage with the world. In the physical domain, Corsets to Physical Freedom involve the restriction of sites and opportunities in which to engage in physical activities, reduced safety related to sexual harassment and dating violations, challenges to the care of pubertal bodies, and initial messages to control one's appetite. In the mental domain, Corsets to Mental Freedom involve the tightening of femininity expectations present during childhood and the emergence of new femininity Appearance- and Comportment-related Discourses. Tween girls describe not only the expectation that they embody the idealized feminine object, but also start to inhabit their pubertal bodies with a pervasive and harsh discourse of deficiency, one that continues to operate throughout the journeys of girls and women. Further, in terms of Comportment-related Discourses, tween girls describe idealized femininity expectations of being and acting docile—small, demure, and sedentary—while also prioritizing sexualized relationships with boys over other friendship networks. These changes are in line with a shift from the tomboy classification toward that of the girly girl.

Corsets to Social Power and Relational Connections relate to exposure to the prejudicial treatment of women and to deriving social power in the peer group through adhering to strict appearance criteria, a pursuit that concurrently robs tween girls of social power and involves rifts within girls' groups. Further, girls experience accentuating embodied inequity in relation to intersecting dimensions of social location.

At the intersection of physical constraints and lack of safety, discourses of objectification and deficiency, exposure to prejudicial treatment, and subversion of social power to the embodiment of idealized perfection, tween girls experience their maturing bodies not as sites of comfort, worth, and agency but as sites of vulnerability and restraint. It behooves significant adults in the life of children to intervene at this critical phase of development, listen to the critical reflections and protests of tween girls, and collaborate in guiding activism and social change.

References

Brown, L. M. (2003). *Girlfighting: Betrayal and rejection among girls*. New York, NY: New York University Press.

Brown, L. M. (2016). *Powered by girl: A field guide for supporting youth activists*. Boston, MA: Beacon Press.

Buchanan, T. S., Fischer, A. R., Tokar, D. M., & Yoder, J. D. (2008). Testing a culture-specific extension of objectification theory regarding African American women's body image. *The Counseling Psychologist*, *36*, 699–718.

Fredrickson, B. L., & Roberts, T. (1997). Objectification theory: Toward understanding women's lived experiences and mental health risks. *Psychology of Women Quarterly*, *21*, 173–206.

Ibarra, H., Ely, R. J., & Kolb, D. M. (September 2013). Women rising: The unseen barriers. *Harvard Business Review*. Retrieved from: https://hbr.org/2013/09/women-rising-the-unseen-barriers.

Legge, R. (2011). *As the body unfolds: Examining girls' changing experiences with socially constructed labels "tomboy" and "girly girl"*. University of Toronto. Retrieved from: https://tspace.library.utoronto.ca/bitstream/1807/31829/1/Legge_Robyn_B_201111_PhD_thesis.pdf.

McHugh, M. C., & Cosgrove, L. (2004). Feminist research methods: Studying women and gender. In M. A. Paludi (Ed.), *The Praeger guide to the psychology of gender* (pp. 155–181). New York, NY: Praeger.

McKinley, N. M., & Hyde, J. S. (1996). The objectified body consciousness scale: Development and validation. *Psychology of Women Quarterly*, *20*, 181–215.

Mendelson, B. K., Mendelson, M. J., & White, D. R. (2001). Body esteem scale for adolescents and adults. *Journal of Personality Assessment*, *76*(1), 90–106.

Moradi, B., & Huang, Y. (2008). Objectification theory and psychology of women: A decade of advances and future directions. *Psychology of Women Quarterly*, *32*, 377–398.

Piran, N. (1999). The reduction of preoccupation with body weight and shape in schools: A feminist approach. In N. Piran, M. P. Levine, & C. Steiner-Adair (Eds.), *Preventing eating disorders: A handbook of interventions and special challenges* (pp. 148–150). Philadelphia: Brunner/Mazel (Taylor & Francis Group).

Piran, N. (2001). Re-inhabiting the body from the inside out: Girls transform their school environment. In D. L. Tolman, & M. Brydon-Miller (Eds.), *From subjects to subjectivities: A handbook of interpretive and participatory methods* (pp. 218–238). New York: New York University Press.

Piran, N. (2016). Embodied possibilities and disruptions: The emergence of the experience of embodiment construct from qualitative studies with girls and women. *Body Image, 18*, 43–60.

Reay, D. (2001). "Spice girls", "nice girls", "girlies", and "tomboys": Gender discourses, girls' cultures and femininities in the primary classroom. *Gender and Education, 13*(2), 153–166.

Smolak, L., Murnen, S. K., & Ruble, A. E. (2000). Female athletes and eating problems: A meta-analysis. *International Journal of Eating Disorders, 27*, 371–380.

Smolak, L., & Piran, N. (2012). Gender and the prevention of eating disorders. In G. McVey, M. P. Levine, N. Piran, & H. B. Ferguson (Eds.), *Preventing eating-related and weight-related disorders: Collaborative research, advocacy, and policy change* (pp. 201–224). Waterloo, ON: Wilfred Laurier Press.

CHAPTER

4

The Practice of Corseting: Early Adolescence (Ages 13–14)

I feel like I really want to just be confident, but sometimes I just need to protect myself and I slouch. My body feels withered, or maybe feeling kind of withdrawn. It needs love. It needs to be comfortable... I like to look nice. My face is kind of disordered. I wear mascara. I wear makeup, it's kind of demeaning as well but I wear it. I want to look nice. It makes me feel that I am pretty. I really would be happy if I was flat and like the way I always was. Like for me it is better to be athletic than curvy... I hate shopping. It always makes me feel fat. When you go to the change room, oh my God, the mirror always makes you feel ugly, and makes me feel big... I'm not really comfortable with like sexuality, even with dances and stuff. (Bronwen, 13 years old)

I lost a lot of weight in the past year, but I still want to be skinnier. So I just want to keep that up. And I still want my stomach to look perfect. Like the girls at the volleyball thing. It makes me feel much better... Every night before I go to bed I do 60 pull-ups, 60 crunches, 40 leg raises, 40 push-ups, five triceps push-ups. And I have weights. And whenever I'm not doing anything in the morning I'll do them... I don't like hair on my legs. I want my legs to be soft and perfect... I hate having to shave... Like with a guy I really like, I would feel kind of in the corner: I need to be perfect for him! But I am sick and tired of trying to be perfect!... Like in doing sexual things, like for girls, it is still more about the guys. (Kyra, 13 years old)

Bronwen and Kyra's narratives reflect ways in which Experiences of Embodiment (EE) for early adolescents are similar to, and different from, their experiences during the tweens phase. Continuous with the end of the tweens phase are feelings of vulnerability and discomfort in the natural body, concerns about body weight and shape affecting appetite and eating, self-objectification, and compromised embodied agency.

Journeys of Embodiment at the Intersection of Body and Culture
http://dx.doi.org/10.1016/B978-0-12-805410-9.00004-9

New to this phase of early adolescence are three types of embodied experiences. First, girls in early adolescence are immersed in body modifications toward the goal of approximating idealized images of beauty such as: body sculpting, dieting, applying makeup, and hair removal; consequently, they become accustomed to negotiating the world while living in altered bodies. As the girls describe, body alterations concurrently reward one's objectified lens ("It makes me feel that I am pretty"), and disrupt one's self-experience and self-attunement ("It's kind of demeaning"; "I am sick and tired of trying to be perfect!"). Second, while connection to appetite becomes disrupted during the tweens phase, connection to sexual desire becomes a challenging domain for most girls in early adolescence; therefore, it is common to hear about girls engaging in sexual activities without protection and without the experience of desire. Third, girls in early adolescence engage in a range of potentially harmful behaviors, including: disordered eating, smoking, drinking alcohol, consuming illicit substances, and engaging in unprotected sexual activities. We also hear for the first time about skin cutting.

Another hallmark of early adolescence, when compared with the tweens phase, is the narrowing range of ways of inhabiting the body. Specifically, we see a more uniform disruption to girls' EE during early adolescence. While some girls hold on to childhood experiences of embodied immersion in action throughout most of their tweens, during early adolescence most girls show considerable embodied restraint and disruption, regardless of whether they actively participate in the burgeoning dating scene, like Kyra, or opt out and observe, like Bronwen. Bronwen and Kyra are both White and live in (different) rural communities under similar financial circumstances. While Bronwen is a highly critical resistor of girls' sexualization and refuses to participate in the dating scene, Kyra takes part in all peer activities. However, as Bronwen's narrative describes, even *witnessing* adverse peer experiences in the dating scene, as well as being subjected to other social pressures, leads to significant embodied disruption.

This ubiquitous embodied disruption relates to more intensely oppressive social processes during early adolescence. These disruptions exist in the physical, mental, and social power and relational connection domains. The intensification of oppression in all these domains accounts for a common emotional tone of loss and defeat. This is in comparison with the tweens phase, where expressions of anger and protest were more common. For this reason, initiating dialogues with tween girls as they move into early adolescence can help in sustaining resistance (Piran, 2001).

ALTERED BODIES IN A TIGHT PINK PHYSICAL WEB

> Like, you have to walk around in tight skirts and like tight jeans and tight shirts and stuff like that… I wish that I could like dress as I want to dress, but people make fun of you for trying to be yourself… If you buy baggy pants then like people would like call you a tomboy and a loser… I drew Gucci runners for myself [in self drawing]… My hair should be more blonder 'cause I got my friend to put more streaks in it. But my hair's already wrecked 'cause I straighten it every day. Girls wear what other people wear, and not what they want to wear. Like showing that much skin, which is weird for them. (Brady, 14 years old)

As Brady describes, having gone through puberty, being barred from engaging in physical activities in spaces controlled mainly by boys and men, clad in tight and exposing clothing, and adhering to peer-enforced feminine expectations of perfection and restraint, girls in early adolescence have very limited or no opportunity to move freely, competently, and joyfully in their physical environment. Brady is White and lives in an urban, working-class context. Similar to Brady, we hear of many Corsets to Freedom in Physical Engagement and Movement, the first dimension of Physical Freedom. Further, Brady describes the challenge of Care of the Body, another dimension of Physical Freedom, related to continued appearance-driven body alterations—she continues to straighten her hair daily even though it is already "wrecked." The daily activity Brady describes is targeted at altering the body rather than acting in the world. Brady clearly conveys both her wish to live freely in her body, without harsh physical restrictions, and the anticipated social penalty for such a choice. She is not hopeful that she would have such an opportunity.

Physical Corsets that have aggregated throughout the tweens phase in all four dimensions of Physical Freedom–Freedom in Physical Engagement and Movement, Safety for the Body Territory, Care of the Body, and Freedom of Desire—weave a tighter web around the bodies of girls in early adolescence. Finding spaces of Physical Freedom without penalty is difficult and rare, and more likely to be found in socially privileged circumstances.

Girls in early adolescence consistently tell of restrictions to Freedom in Physical Engagement and Movement. Freedom of Physical Engagement is, indeed, limited. Kyra's description of her time in school is common among girls in early adolescence:

> We'd sit there and talk. We like climb up the hill and sit and talk. And then we'd hang out with the guys. The guys would like wrestle and they would fight. And we'd be sitting there and watching them. And we would just sit there and talk. We don't do anything sports related.

Sedentary girls commonly watch the guys engage in physical activities. Girls might stay sedentary even during gym classes, as 14-year-old Kelly, Latino and of a working-class background, describes:

> And like in the co-ed gym class, whereas some of my friends would just stand around and talk during gym class, I would be playing sports. So lots of the girls wouldn't really participate, but I would play and it was a lot of fun.

By early adolescence, the gender-based boundaries of physical territories are rigidly drawn. It is therefore more rare to hear about girls participating in physical activities alongside boys in their neighborhoods or schoolyards compared with the tween phase. For most girls, joyful and immersed physical engagement in the world ceases.

Even among girls who have been passionate about sports, special conditions are needed to facilitate continued engagement, in particular, encouragement by parents or coaches, and financial means. Alice, for example, who lives in a middle-class setting, continues to play soccer, and Brady's father is coach of her hockey team. In contrast, Kelly, who lives in strained financial circumstances, cannot continue with her sport. She explains "I wanted to play soccer again this year, but my brother is getting married, so my mother couldn't afford it this year. I am always at home, sitting around, doing nothing." This is a major loss for Kelly; having been teased repeatedly about her weight and body shape, playing soccer had provided her with the opportunity to connect with her physical functionality, competence, and action-related joy. "When I play soccer, I could not care less about how my body looks. My mind is the game. I'm pretty good at it and it's fun." Indeed, research suggests that participation of adolescent girls in non-objectifying physical activities, that do not require thinness, shows a small yet significant relationship to a reduced rate of eating problems (Smolak, Murnen, & Ruble, 2000).

The immersion in acting physically in the world is often replaced with *acting on one's body*. Similar to acting physically in the world, body alterations require practice, skills, and time. Girls in early adolescence describe learning how to target many physical aspects of their bodies for alteration, detailing the labor associated with such practices. For example, Kyra discusses the near constant attention required to manage her eyebrows:

> You can tell my eyebrows are really screwed. The first time after I was done, I'm like 'oh my god, I can't let them grow in.' Like I hate it when they grow in. So I can't do it and I can't stand it, so I keep doing it. They just get in there and then there and I just look all uneven so I have to keep doing it.

Clearly, the practice of body alterations addresses many more natural body features. The body can become an all-consuming target for alteration, replacing active engagement with the world. Girls in early adolescence share that the daily routine of getting ready for school is considerably lengthened by their body alterations: "I straighten my hair every morning, if I am not lazy, 'cause when it's curly it looks like a mess. I put makeup on. I wake up at seven. I usually finish at like quarter to eight" (Alice).

The norms of body alterations are reinforced by ongoing monitoring and peer reactions toward adherence to, or alternatively failure to engage in, expected body alterations. For example, Brady and several of her peers are teased about the delay in starting to shave their legs:

> Yeah. We were like a big tease group! They would call names like 'monster' and 'hairy beast.' And they'd laugh at us and spread it around places. And then wherever we'd go they'd call us names like that. But then I left that group when I started to shave my legs!

At times, a few of the girls engage in body alterations that involve compulsive physical exercises:

> I work out and I am more toned and I lost a lot of weight. Like when I'm doing the exercises I'm like, 'oh yeah, I'm losing weight. Got to keep going!' It's a *pain in the ass* but I do them anyway. Then I feel better in the morning. Like 'cause you have the whole night the body is toning. I don't know I think I look skinny in the morning. I still probably wouldn't wear a bikini. It is just the way my body is. Like right here [stomach] like *excess skin* there, and it looks like I have *two big bubbles*. And right here in my thighs *I want that gone*. I want a six-pack really bad. I will not feel fine with a guy that I like. (Kyra)

As this narrative indicates, rather than be associated with experiences of immersed joy, physical agency, and freedom, such exercises are often practiced compulsively and maintain the discourse of deficiency in which they are steeped.

Additional Physical Corsets restrict early adolescent girls' Freedom in Physical Engagement and Movement. Similar to the end of the tweens phase, girls' attire during early adolescence restricts their engagement in physical activities; however, in early adolescence clothing is not only tight but also revealing, as Brady's narrative above indicates. Moreover, as Brady describes, girls in early adolescence feel greater pressure to adhere to this dress code, even if it is uncomfortable, fearing immediate social penalties for deviations. Alice describes it similarly:

> I wear skinny jeans and low-cut tops. Guys in my school like low-cut tops, it is weird at our school. It kinda sickens me... Tight clothes. That's how everybody wears in school. So you kinda get used to it.

With a lack of social support for wearing comfortable clothing, even occasionally, girls may altogether avoid wearing particular items of clothing, or eliminate engaging in activities associated with such apparel. As Bronwen describes, "I like shorts, like basketball shorts. I really dislike tight short ones. I would feel really self-conscious because I am not comfortable at all."

The nascent dating scene adds another dimension of constriction to girls' free movement in the physical environment. Girls describe boyfriends' jealousy as restricting their freedom,

> It felt weird because we couldn't go and like, hang out with other guys because our boyfriends would be jealous and want to beat them up. So it was kind of hard because you wouldn't be able to hang around with your guys friends, because they think they're like cheating on you… He would get mad at me. Like I wouldn't really care if he was talking with other girls. It wouldn't bother me. I think it's just the way boys are. (Brady)

Kelly describes being called wherever she went: "I liked him, but as soon as we started dating he was totally different… Like everywhere that I went, somehow he would phone me." Kyra even decided to stop dating because of such restrictions:

> I don't know. I just wanted to be able to like talk with other guys and be able to be friends with them. And like, not having to worry about another guy worrying about me cheating on him and saying stuff like that.

On a different note, girls in early adolescence also feel restricted in the physical space that they take. Girls were commonly clear that inhabiting small bodies was most desirable: "I am the smallest of my friends now" (Kyra), "I like being short and thin" (Chrissy), "I'd rather my boyfriend is taller than me and I'd just feel weirded out if the guy was skinnier than me" (Meghan), or "Popular girls are pretty little girls" (Alice). Brady, who describes herself as "skinny," is, like several other girls, worried about her height: "I am pretty happy with myself because I am skinny. I hope I don't get too tall. People called me 'daddy long legs' to make me feel bad about myself because they knew I wanted to be short." For Brady, long legs are "ugly," "'Cause my legs are long and everybody's shorter. So they are, like, ugly." When asked what would her body say if it could talk, she replied, "*Shrink me*," clarifying that, "it is hard to get a boyfriend because the guys are short."

Girls' drawings of the ideal girl in early adolescence are much smaller in both width and height compared with their drawings of themselves. For the first time, girls link "getting bigger" with depression. According to Alice, "I'm just like worried what my body gonna do [when I get older] and when you're overweight you're gonna be like, 'oh my God, I have to get skinny now,' can make people depressed." The fear of getting bigger clearly extends into the future, even into the next generation, as Brady describes, "I don't want to grow up and be fat because growing up to be a mother it would be harder on my kids because they'd be embarrassed of it." Research suggests that body dissatisfaction during early adolescence predicts the development of dieting and smoking, as well as eating disorders and depression (Neumark-Sztainer, Paxton, Hannan, Haines, & Story, 2006; Stice and Bearman, 2001; Stice, Hayward, Cameron, Killen, & Taylor, 2000). The need to stay small weighs heavily on girls.

Early adolescent girls' experiences of Physical Freedom are further compromised by greater challenges on the second dimension of Physical Freedom: Safety for the Body Territory. Challenges here during early adolescence relate to the sexualization of the social environment. Sexual harassment intensifies during early adolescence when compared with the tweens phase, comprising an issue all girls face. They describe being followed ["Like he keeps following girls" (Bronwen)], grabbed and exposed ["They won't only look up a girl's skirt, they will grab it and pull it up, or they will just pull down the underpants" (Kyra)]. Sexual harassment is endemic in many schools, and girls report not feeling safe walking the corridors:

> Guys get to, like, go around and slap those asses… it's so weird, like you're walking down the hall, and like perverts come out of them and they're slapping really hard and they laugh at you… Like, you don't need to run to your teacher for every single little thing… It's like part of me, I don't want to be here… It's scary for a girl. (Alice)

The streets comprise a similar challenge:

> I am also uncomfortable outside of school, 'cause I look older than I am. And, like, walking down the street like guys would honk at you and guys will try talking to you or they'll hit on you, like at the boobs and you're so uncomfortable about it, and it's kinda 'I'm 13. Go away,' and is just like they come to you again and like, 'yeah, but you're hot.' (Alice)

In reaction, girls report wearing "armor" to protect themselves from sexual harassment; they either add a second layer of clothing or wear tight pants instead of skirts.

> We don't wear skirts anymore. We stopped in Grade 7. When guys get older they worry about sex so like most of the girls change what we wear, because guys like look up our skirts. Like my friend was wearing a skirt and the guy walked up behind her and flipped it up… Like, we have pajama day and the guys go and 'pants' the girls 'cause

> they're easy to pants. Like they pull down their pants in front of everyone, I got pantsed in the middle of the hallway. I was wearing shorts underneath. I didn't care because I knew to wear shorts under so they saw nothing. I also got pantsed in front of my class and I did not have shorts under. It was embarrassing, but they all laughed. (Brady)

Despite the common occurrence of severe sexual harassment, none of the girls' narratives indicate active or efficient involvement by adults in setting safer norms in schools—norms that could relieve them from experiencing their bodies as targets of aggression and violation.

Girls often describe their reactions to sexual harassment as embarrassment and fear, as well as implying their own fault in their victimization: "When a guy lifts her skirt up a girl is embarrassed. It scares her 'cause then it might happen again if she wears a skirt. For a boy it's like an invitation to go and do that again" (Brady). Nonetheless, they are left to their own devices to cope. Alice, for example, who finds her body targeted repeatedly in different ways, including harassment, stops eating in school—"you kinda feel, like, uncomfortable with yourself, like walking down the hallways. It's kind of weird. I wish my body was not noticeable for guys." She usually eats after the school day ends. Legge (2009) described the case of an adolescent who developed clinical-level anorexia nervosa related to sexual harassment she experienced at school, reflecting her wish to "disappear" by becoming ultra thin. In the routine clinical interview conducted at the hospital where she was hospitalized, the occurrence and relevance of pervasive sexual harassment did not surface, which became a barrier to healing. A body journey interview, following the same format of inquiry used in our studies, helped in uncovering the cause of this girl's anorexia.

Lacking the support to protest and the opportunity to counter sexual harassment, as it becomes an entrenched part of everyday school life, some girls deny the meaning of the experience of harassment and its adverse impact on their lives. Consequently, they start to construct it as a joke: "Like when a guy smacks the ass of a girl, it's like funny; it's like a joke. Hilarious. My friend dropped the pants all the way down to her ankles" (Kyra). Furthermore, modeling boy-engendered harassment, girls sometimes start to engage in harassing behaviors themselves, making it an even more common aspect of peer interactions: "Guys just smack girls' asses. And then girls will smack each other's asses. Like we slap each other in the ass. Also pulling each other's bra straps. It's just joking, and then your bra's out, you're like, shit!" (Kyra). This collusion further reduces the experience of body safety among adolescent girls.

The dating scene that occurs during early adolescence comprises yet another domain wherein sexual violations of girls' bodies are frequent—from significant pressure by boys to become sexually involved, to a range of coercive sexual acts, including rape. Girls' narratives reveal little cross-gender consensual dialogue, or girls' own desire, in sexual acts. As Brady describes, "that's something different this year that guys would start talking about sex, because girls don't really care about it. And they'd just go along with it." The following are typical narratives depicting the unilateral pressures experienced by girls to become sexually involved:

> If she is popular, the guys will say, 'I can get some out of her.' If she is not popular then she's going to take a lot. I think some of them would just do it because their boyfriend wanted it. Like they will pressure you into it, and then you just feel like, 'okay, fine.' And some girls go, 'Oh I just did that I can't believe it.' And some of them are like, 'Oh my God, I totally did not want to do that.' Well I suppose for a guy it's looked upon like, 'Oh she will screw me so let's go for her.' But the girl is a 'whore.' Well, it depends on what you do. (Kyra)

> He called my friend and he's like, "Give me head right now, bitch." He's mad at her 'cause she wouldn't give him a head. So it was like she's hurt and he's feeling pressured by his friends. "You can't hang out with me if you don't do this then." It happens all the time. Like she feels pressure because she's like, if I don't do it, what will he tell the school, and girls regret so much all the time. (Alice)

It is important to note that girls, but not boys, are commonly labeled "whores," "sluts," "skanks," or other similarly demeaning labels if it is revealed that they have acted sexually. This is the case even if physical coercion is used:

> My friend [name] was just with this guy in a back alley and he pushed her down. He made her give him a blowjob. She got pronounced a whore and everyone was sort of making fun of her… She did not feel good. She just said to me, 'Shut up and leave me alone.' It was horrible. (Alice)

The increased use of drugs and alcohol during early adolescence further heightens the risk of sexual violations.

> You need a lot more *precautions* in Grade 7 because of alcohol and drugs and sex with boys. You never think about that until you actually get to Grade 7 and it happens to you. A lot of my friends are having sex and had scares of pregnancies. They are giving guys blowjobs, and they get labeled *sluts* and whores at the school and it's just *horrible*. And they go, 'I got so wasted last night. I don't remember anything.' And then this guy goes, 'you gave me head,' and she's like, 'I'm pretty sure I didn't.' And he knows that she doesn't remember anything and he would be like, 'yeah, you did. I remember it.' [Alice]

> Guys and girls use Marijuana, coke, ecstasy, hash, mushrooms. And the guys just manage to get the girls *stoned* and *screw* them. (Kyra)

Related to safety then, during early adolescence, girls either experience directly or witness pervasive sexual harassment and violations within the context of dating, further aggravated by the consumption of substances. It is highly damaging to girls and women's embodiment that, right at the beginning of their journey toward mature sexuality, dating positions the body as a site of coercion, fear, disconnection, and helplessness rather than as a site of dialogue, agency, and joy. Girls' narratives indicate no systemic support in dealing with such violations.

Girls in early adolescence also face multiple challenges in the third dimension of the Physical Freedom domain, namely: Care of the Body. First, as sexuality enters the lives of early adolescents, girls encounter beliefs and practices in the sexual arena that are disruptive to caring for their bodies. These beliefs encourage male sexual aggression and support violence against women. Feminist scholars describe these beliefs as endemic to a rape culture (Buchwald, Fletcher, & Roth, 1993). In a rape culture, violations are constructed as the norm, women are often blamed for their violations and there is no space or respect for women's agency or safety in desire, nor for consensual dialogues about sexual engagement. Girls in early adolescence commonly hold and narrate such beliefs without question. For example, girls believe that boys' desires are stronger than theirs, and therefore boys cannot be expected to contain their desire: "Well it's like boys' hormone are, like, raging right now. So like, you can't help it [sexual harassment]" (Alice), or "Well, it's just usually boys are into sex because girls don't really care about it and they'd just go along with it" (Brady). Further, girls commonly believe that assaulted girls are at fault: "When you're drunk, like some of my friends have no self control, so some guys took advantage of them. I guess it's a little bit normal like what people do" (Alice). Within the context of violations, protective measures such as condoms, are not commonly used: "My friends have not used condoms while giving head" (Kyra). Girls most often do not label violations as sexual assaults or rapes, even when their experiences meet such definitions.

Girls' experiences in the sexuality arena suggest that they are commonly "abandoned" within the rape culture and left to deal with their bodies alone. Lacking are forums with youth where these beliefs are contested and analyzed critically, so that alternative peer norms could be established. Similarly lacking are implemented and enforced sexual harassment policies in schools and other community organizations. Moreover, one wonders, for example, about the impact on early adolescents when men who publicly endorse rape culture beliefs are elected to political or other positions of power.

A second factor that may challenge girls in their care of their bodies relates to engagement in body alterations. It can be particularly damaging at this phase for parents to push for body alterations to fit their own image of what a young woman should look like. For example, Jackie gets a razor from her father for Christmas:

> I have huge hairy legs… my dad tried to get me to shave them because he got me a shaver, like a razor and put it in my stocking. But I want my legs waxed 'cause then you don't have to worry about shaving them every day.

Receiving this "gift," Jackie feels "weird" and compelled to get rid of the hair on her legs. Other parents put their daughters on extreme fad diets, for example, Sarah's mother tells her, "I need you to also go on the Atkins diet." This confirms girls' concerns regarding their supposed deficiencies and forces them to engage in body management practices at odds with their own sensibilities. Other times, girls engage in potentially risky body alterations to satisfy peer norms and pressures: "I did some of my own piercings, like these two on top... with some I had pain for a long time and had to take out" (Sarah). Jane, a young woman in her early 20s, describes having a significant allergic reaction to lipstick during her early adolescence: "We were very much into the makeup, the body image thing. Because that's what you do, but I had allergies. So lipstick breaks out my mouth. And I went through a period where I had huge scabs over my mouth." Make up being a norm among the peer group, Jane continued to use it despite this allergic reaction.

Prioritizing appearance over comfort and safety, girls describe neglecting their well-being to appear attractive. As Kyra describes, "We'd sit there and we'd like freeze. We wouldn't care though, like in the middle of winter. We wouldn't like wear hats. I look terrible in them." Madison describes how her friend neglects her well being to look attractive,

> She wears skin tight shirts, and in the middle of the winter she wears miniskirts to school with bare legs, to impress this guy she likes. She found that he liked her because of what she wore. So she kept wearing the same clothes. Guys think that girls that dress like that are hotter than girls that are their selves.

Freedom of Desire is the fourth dimension of Physical Freedom. One of the hallmarks of the transition to early adolescence is the disruption of connection to *both* bodily desires: appetite and sexual passion.

The disruption in connection to appetite relates to a number of experiences described by girls in early adolescence. First, within the context of extensive engagement in body alterations to fit idealized images of appearance—in particular thinness—early adolescent girls often describe the beginning of what is commonly a lifelong engagement in "watching" what one eats, as well as varied methods of dieting. Eating now relates to the shaping of the body, rather than to desire, health, or joy. The fear of appetite as a bodily desire is palpable in girls' narratives, as Lauren explains:

> Sometimes I think eating cookies, 'wow, I'm going to be huge some day.' I could never be a chef. I would eat everything. It would be bad. I would be sampling everything. It would be bad stuff.

While girls may confound health and the need to sculpt the body, the interviews clarify that, often, the construction of "eating healthy" relates to achieving a particular body shape. The dichotomy between eating healthy and "eating junk" is often present in girls' narratives at this age. According to 14-year-old Kelly, of Latino heritage and a financially constrained working-class background:

> I need to watch what I'm eating. I eat healthy, but I also eat junk... I should eat more vegetables... My favorite food is rice, but it's not very healthy for you all the time... I eat burgers plain. Eating healthy means eating stuff that's not fattening. Like fruit and vegetables. Dieting to me is eating healthier, and not just sitting around all the time... People go on diets to make themselves feel better.

Disrupted connection with appetite and eating can relate to motivations other than the pursuit of thinness. For example, Kyra loses weight through dieting and following an exercise regimen because she wants to be petite and "cute" all around; she is concerned about being too big and strong ("a big tough bitch"). Alice stops eating in school because she, "does not want to be here [in school]," related to being a target of harassment. The disruption to her appetite is a reflection of her discomfort in her body and the wish "not to be" a visible target.

> Usually people think I like starve myself, but I don't... It's like, I can't eat in the mornings. Like, I don't eat lunch. It's like I don't feel like eating. So my body's not wanting the food. I get tired or sad at school.

Varied motivations can, therefore, disrupt connection to appetite, such as wanting the body to be thinner, smaller, or 'disappear'.

The discomfort with bodily desires is accentuated during early adolescence due to the additional disruption of girls' connection to sexual desire. Such disruption at this critical juncture—when girls are taking their initial steps toward adult sexuality—encumbers the journey of many girls and women in relation to sexual desire. From a possible embodied experience of passion—associated with excitement, pleasure, body- and self-attunement, agency, safety, and dialogue—sexual desire commonly becomes associated with disconnection, shame, fear, and restricted agency. At this important developmental stage, sexuality becomes yet another domain where girls experience embodied inequity; the social experiences that disrupt girls' connection to sexual desire are steeped in patriarchal and heteronormative values that, in turn, are also in line with beliefs of a rape culture.

The lack of validation for the sexual desires of girls is a powerful adverse factor (see also Fine, 1988; Tolman, 2002). Not only do girls' narratives reveal no validation of female sexual desire in any social or educational forums (such as Sex Ed classes), they also reflect the lack of *language* to describe female passion. As Brady describes:

> Interviewer: Do girls at your age talk about having sexual feelings?
> Brady: Not really. Like guys, they always want to, they'll come up to us and just be like, 'do you want to flash me? Do you want to give me head?' and things like that. Guys will laugh if a girl talks like that. They'll think it's weird. Hearing it from a girl is weird. Because you mostly hear it from a guy saying, 'oh yeah, I'm *horny,*' and stuff like that, and not from a girl… Most of us girls don't talk about stuff like that, it's mostly the guys. I think it's just the way they are. They just grow older faster.

Within patriarchy, there is no space, nor language, for a girl's subjective experience in relation to sexual desire. Indeed, language is constructed by and for privileged members of society. The term "horny," used to describe sexual excitement, is anchored in the male erection—hardly fitting for the experience of girls and women. Just as adolescent girls walk on borrowed territories when they engage in physical activities in the public sphere, girls are forced to tread on linguistic borrowed territories when addressing experiences of desire. Further, within a patriarchal rape culture that sanctions and equates boys' (and men's) experiences of desire with acting on desire (with or without girls' consent), girls find it difficult to conceive of sexual desire as being separate from sexual activity with boys. Adolescent girls, fearing sexual aggression from boys and subsequent deprecation for having engaged sexually, find it even harder to connect to sexual experiences:

> Interviewer: Are girls having sexual feelings yet?
> Brady: Nope. Like sexual feelings is like sex to me… Usually we don't decide. We just go for whatever the person wants it to go. And

> sometimes the girls go along, but then sometimes they don't let them do that. Because when they constantly ask you to give them head and all that and then you go like say no and stuff and they keep on nagging until you actually do it. And that's when you get like called names like easy or slutty.

As this quotation reveals, the dominant equation of sexual desire, with (coercive) action in the boys' world, leaves girls with no validation for the separation between sexual desire and sexual action. Importantly, there is no room for female desire in what unfolds. As the above also reflects, there is no mention of female desire in the sexual action that takes place nor dialogical consent as informed by desire; girls either "go along" or they do not.

Brownen, a keen observer of social processes, problematizes the situation with great insight,

> I am not comfortable with dating. Girls may go further than they are comfortable with because of pressure, and where I don't know is that intercession, the dialogue between okay this is how I'm feeling in my body and this is what I want to do because either it feels good or it feels safe or it feels ready, versus this isn't what I want to do. Nobody talks about that. I'm pretty sure I talked last year about it, but the Sex Ed class is so inadequate. They are Catholic so like don't have sex until you are married. Like they really don't get into it.

Several of the adult women in our studies described experiencing attraction to other girls during early adolescence—attraction that was shunned in their social environments. Consequently, it sometimes took them years to act in line with their sexual attraction and come out as lesbians or bisexual. Andrea, for example, describes feeling attracted to girls:

> So I would have crushes on girls, or find them attractive, but I just thought all girls felt that way. Or when I saw someone I thought was pretty I just thought that I was drawn to her looks because I wanted to be as pretty as her, so, it was a bit confusing… I remember looking at a photo of a woman, and I said to my mother, 'She looks really beautiful in that dress,' and my mother said, 'You mean that dress is really beautiful, girls don't say that other girls are beautiful.' I think I blushed. I was embarrassed.

Only at older age has Andrea been able to return to her earlier passion. "At this point in my life I find it much more erotic to be with a woman than a man. It's more exciting."

Girls need relational forums that support female sexual desire and pleasure as a chosen aspect of one's life, provide knowledge about the biological basis of female desire, expand the understanding of sexuality beyond intercourse, examine sexuality within the context of navigating intimate relationships, explore the process of affirmative consent, emphasize emotional and physical safety in sexuality, and explore diversity in desire. Such forums also need to incorporate a critical look at the ways social power and cultural values shape social interactions around sexuality, as well as internalized values that need to be contested. Similar relational forums for boys are an important element in changing the social environment. My experience working in schools suggests that conducting separate forums for boys and girls facilitates the development of safe dialogues. Effective gender-cohesive groups that include work on creating constructive peer norms often lead to productive cross-gender dialogues.

To summarize experiences in the physical domain, girls in early adolescence face more challenging Physical Corsets in all dimensions of Physical Freedom, compared with the tweens phase. Girls in early adolescence are more uniformly sedentary related to stricter gender-based boundaries and the sexualization of cross-gender peer relationships. Further, their dress code becomes more sexualized and revealing, limiting free movement; concurrently, girls channel greater resources to altering appearance characteristics. The intensification of sexual harassment, and the frequent occurrence of dating violence, aggravated through the use of drugs and alcohol, compromise body safety. Care of the body is adversely affected by abandoning girls to negotiate, unsupported, sexual dating within a culture that holds rape beliefs, as well as by practices aimed at body alterations. One of the hallmarks of the transition to early adolescence is the disruption of connection to bodily desires of both appetite and sexual passion; rather than enhancing pleasure and agency in the world, these desires become associated with fear, shame, and restricted agency.

I HAVE TO BE PERFECT FOR HIM! WALKING THE MINEFIELD OF MENTAL CORSETS

> I wear like pants and a tight tank top. And you don't have to wear a bra because they're built in. And it shows a bit of the stomach, like, I lost weight. I looked at this body, I'm like, 'holy frig I was *fat*.' Like, I was just bigger than my friends. Like sometimes you're a little embarrassed because like, they're absolutely perfect and you're like a little bigger. But they have amazing skinny tiny bodies… I don't like the hair on my legs. I shave it but I hate shaving. I hate armpit hair. It annoys me. I shave it. I do my eyebrows. And, my God, they're screwed up… I have like excess skin [stomach] and here

> [inner thighs] I want that gone… I like being small but then I don't. Sometimes I want to be like a *big tough bitch* that nobody messes with. By being small it's just like being *smallest*. I don't know, you feel small. You know how small things are *cute*… When you are on PMS then you are just a *bitch*. Normally you wouldn't get mad, and I'll get mad at anything. I can realize myself being a *bitch*… A girl who sleeps around is a *slut* but a guy is called a *player*… Like it can be weird, like this girl, she is like, 'I have a broken nail, oh my God, I have to make an appointment'… I could kill her because she is putting on an act… With my girlfriends, like, I'm fine. I *care most with my guy friends*. Like with a guy I really like, I would feel kind of in the corner: I need to be perfect for him!

This collection of Kyra's experiences, from her interview at age 14, reflects the minefield of femininity-related, heteronormative Mental Corsets that girls in early adolescence negotiate. Kyra is a White girl from a working class and urban background. Her detailed scrutiny of her appearance reflects the Body as an Object of Gaze discourse ("I looked at this body"), while her harsh critique of her different body parts (e.g., "I have like excess skin and here I want that gone") reflects the Woman's Body as Deficient discourse—both Appearance-related Discourses. However, her narratives also address femininity Comportment-related Discourses. In particular, her emphasis on being "small" and "cute," and contrasting it with being "a big tough bitch," is an expression of the Woman as Submissive/Demure discourse, as well as the problematic, socially constructed nice/bitch dichotomy. Further, the deprecation of the girly girl who needs a doctor's appointment for having "a broken nail" reflects the adverse impact of the socially constructed tomboy/girly girl dichotomy: both positions in this dichotomy are ridiculed. Kyra's extensive involvement in body modifying activities reflects her Engagement in "Feminine" Activities. As well her use of the slut label for a girl who sleeps around, as opposed to the player label for a boy who does the same, conveys the Woman as Desired but Desire-less discourse, sanctioning girls' (and women's) availability as sexual objects but requiring them to contain their own agency in desire. Kyra's appearance comparisons and hostile competition with other girls, while attending primarily to the guy holding the objectifying lens, reflects the Patriarchal Shaping of Relational Patterns discourse.

Negotiating these social discourses and socially constructed dichotomies is understandably difficult for girls in early adolescence. If a girl at post-puberty wants to engage with the world meaningfully and with agency, a minefield of social discourses stands in her way. Focusing on herself as a deficient object of gaze detracts from her experience of embodied power and derails her focus. Additionally, by acting assertively in her domains of interest and passion, she will likely be labeled a bitch; should she try to avoid such labeling by acting extra feminine, she will be ridiculed as being "hyper-feminine" or "hysterical." If she wants to act with agency in pursuing her sexual desire, she will be seen as a slut; however, should she choose to contain her desire, she will be a prude. Acting equitably and with loyalty toward other girls, while respecting equitable relationships with boys, may make her an outsider in her peer group. If her objects of desire are not boys, she is likely, in addition, to receive other penalizing labels, such as "butch" or "dyke" (our research suggests that during early adolescence these labels are commonly used in a demeaning way, rather than as chosen labels relating to one's sexual orientation or gender identity). Clearly, the field of feminine and heteronormative discourses that govern appearance and comportment challenges girls in early adolescence and deprives them of embodied comfort, safety, and agency from which to engage with the world.

During early adolescence, the Body as an Object of Gaze discourse becomes very powerful in shaping girls' embodied experiences for two main reasons. First, it represents an ongoing preoccupation that pervades the lives of girls at that phase. Second, the objectifying gaze is no longer merely the objectifying gaze portrayed and reinforced by the media; rather, it is the gaze of privileged boys in girls' immediate social environment who are holding the objectifying lens:

> Most girls are like, 'oh, my God! Your shoes don't match,' just like, 'is my hair growing curly? Oh, my God! My hair is curly. Oh, my God! Let's go to the bathroom quickly at lunch!' It's kinda hard. 'Cause like if the guy doesn't look at you then they'll say, 'oh, my God. He didn't look at me. What am I doing wrong?' When you look okay and he pays no attention to you, so like they'll go and change, then the guy would look at them once they've changed to something... like wear low-cut tops. Every single class you have to go downstairs and look at yourself in the mirror. So many girls. Like, it was so bad that they'd put, like, a whole mirror up in one of the bathrooms, only in the girls' bathroom. (Alice)

Girls in early adolescence are ready to go to great lengths to get a "second look" from guys. Alice wears exposing tops that "sicken" her. Kyra loses a significant amount of weight through diet and a rigid exercise routine. She explains "losing weight means, like, people take a, like a *second look*. And then you just feel better because you're smaller." Brady, similarly, elaborates on the vied-for goal of getting a second look, even at the cost of one's discomfort:

> Girls wear the slutty clothes, strapless tops, shirts that have no writing and then if it gets wet they [the boys] can see through it. Like they want guys to see what's under it and everything. Like, girls go to school wearing shirts that have holes in them. Yeah, they're made

> with holes. And boys like the strapless shirts and the shirts that have like thin straps that show your bra straps and everything. I think these clothes are cool but they show too much, like it looks more like you want guys to see you and what's under. So it's kinda dirty and that. Most of the guys go for the girls that dress slutty like that.

Girls in early adolescence, therefore, live in a more intensely objectifying and sexualizing world, where their value is determined by obtaining a second look from members of the privileged group holding the lens: guys. Girls are ready to compromise their comfort and daily quality of life in order to obtain this second look.

The second Appearance-related Discourse, the Woman's Body as Deficient, further complicates the embodied lives of girls in early adolescence. Expressed during the tweens phase via girls' harsh criticisms of their pubertal bodies, this deficiency discourse underlies their existence in *altered bodies* during early adolescence. Early adolescent girls are busy with body practices targeted at addressing perceived deficiencies identified during their tweens, including: hair straightening or bleaching, body and facial hair removal, varied makeup applications or skin bleaching, dieting and compulsive exercise, and finger and toenail treatments. All girls report at least some engagement in body modifying practices, even those who hold a resistant stance toward objectification and sexualization (such as Bronwen), or those who live with severe financial constraints and who do not use paid services for body alterations (such as Kelly: "Sure, it would be nice to have nice nails like a French manicure, but I don't").

During the tweens phase, when girls describe the ideal girl, they inevitably include body alterations as part of this image. As Alice, of Aboriginal heritage, states:

> Perfect little girls, perfect skin, perfectly skinny, maybe I should look like that. They have sunglasses and carry a purse from Guess, a really expensive store, and a cell phone. One of the rich girls. Bigger boobs. *Higher heels to make her look taller*; some of them are born naturally tall. Skinny. They always say: *'count your calories' to stay slim. Little belly button pierced*. She has a miniskirt on. Blonde hair, 'cause all the models have blonde hair, blue eyes, and *lots of makeup, green eye shadow*.

Living in altered bodies exerts a significant toll on girls in early adolescence and beyond, among older adolescents and adult women as well. First, as described in the section on Physical Corseting, the practice of body alterations shifts girls' focus, time, and energy away from acting in the world to working on their own bodies. Second, anchored in a discourse of deficiency, these body alterations may "repair" one or another body part, but cannot shift the deficiency discourse in which diverse women's bodies are couched. Kyra's complaints about her body, following her weight loss and body sculpting through a rigid exercise regimen, exemplify this point:

> I have like excess skin [stomach] and here [inner thighs] I want that gone… but I hate stretch marks. I don't know why I have them there. My muscle grew and that's what stretched it. I hate that.

Similarly, Brady, who is pleased about being blonde "like Christina Aguilera and Britney Spears," feels that she has to be "more blonder" even though it "wrecks" her hair. Among cisgender individuals, countering the deficiency discourse cannot be found in the repair of specific body parts but in a *critical stance* toward social processes that aim to preserve the social status quo by vilifying (and commodifying) the bodies of diverse women and other disenfranchised members of society.

In a paradoxical way, intensive engagement in body modifications *worsens* the experience of deficiency inherent to the Woman's Body as Deficient discourse among cisgender girls. Laboring to modify natural body characteristics, such as body weight, body hair, or hair texture and color, leads to an inevitable betrayal by the body, waging a war between body and owner: "Oh my god, I can't let eyebrows grow in. Like I hate it when they grow in" (Kyra). The attempt to change one's natural weight leads to disordered eating patterns, which are more common among early adolescents than tweens (Smolak & Piran, 2012). As cisgender girls live longer in altered bodies, they become more intolerant toward their own and others' natural appearance, and the need to hide their unaltered appearance increases.

> I am sick and tired trying to be perfect for guys… My friend let her leg hair grow for three months, I swear to God they were that long, and it was disgusting. It was so gross, she is like, 'I'm embarrassed.' I'm like, 'I would be too.' She wore big huge socks and the hairs grew through it. It was so gross. My aunt would sit there and I would see armpit hair, and I'm like, 'Put your armpit down, that's disgusting!' I hate having to shave. I hate it. But I shave because I like the soft feel. (Kyra)

> Oh, I feel ugly today. I just have days where I feel really, really gross. Makeup gives you a chance to express yourself. People could tell what type of mood you are by the colours you wear… You can never see me without even mascara on because, I don't know, I have really dark eyes, like dark themselves. And it's just really gross and I don't like it. It all started at the beginning of Grade 7. (Sarah)

> Well, my face feels kind of naked without makeup. But like, if I was going to a friend's house, I wouldn't wear it, but like, to go to school

> and to go shopping then I need it, or else I look like weird. I don't know. My eyes look really small without it. (Brady)

Living in altered bodies, therefore, perpetuates continued engagement in alterations.

Nonetheless, it is important to be attuned to girls' concurrent protests and discouragement regarding the practice of body beautification and sexualization. Bronwen finds it "demeaning"; Kyra, "a pain in the ass… I hate it"; Alice, "it sickens me"; Brady, "I wish I could be liked for who I am, not for what I look like." These are voices that, without validating group interventions, are usually silenced. In isolation, it is hard for girls to be attuned to voices of protest and defeat.

The four Comportment-related Discourses of femininity, grouped by the DTE under the Woman as Docile discourse cluster, work similarly to the Appearance-related Discourses to corset the embodied lives of girls in early adolescence (see Table 1.2). The first Comportment-related Discourse, Engagement in "Feminine" Activities, continues to segregate the activities of girls and boys, such that activities fully sanctioned for girls do not involve physical activities in the public sphere and are by nature rather sedentary. In addition to sitting or walking, observing boys as they engage in physical action is an accepted method of cross-gender engagement, and a path to being liked by boys. Additionally, a new "feminine" social activity highlighted during early adolescence is shopping, which is in line with self-objectification, self-sexualization, and body alterations. As Brady, who identifies with being a girly girl, describes, "Girly girls go shopping, hang around with friends." Sarah and Olivia describe this in similar fashion:

> My friends are so much fun to hang out with, sit, and talk about stuff. We were first interested in guys so we'd hang out with the guys. And with the girls, just the shopping and stuff. I am a shopaholic. Shopping for fragrance, lip glosses. (Sarah)

> I think the change just kind of came with ageing. Like I just started liking shopping and stuff, like I never really liked it before. (Olivia)

Shopping adds to time already spent on self-objectification, self-sexualization, and body alterations, away from the pursuit of other meaningful activities: "Some people were going to go shopping and I'm like no thank you. I'd rather spend my time doing something better than shopping. I don't like it" (Bronwen). Shopping is also a time of heightened body comparisons and body consciousness. Brady, for example, would only go shopping while wearing makeup: "to go shopping then I need it." Bronwen avoids shopping with her friends because, "the mirror makes you feel ugly, and makes me feel big." This social activity also excludes girls who cannot afford to shop as a leisure activity, as Kelly describes, "I am different. I don't go shopping at the mall constantly always looking for new clothes and stuff."

The second Comportment-related Discourse, Woman as Submissive/Demure, has a greater Corseting impact in early adolescence compared with that of the tweens phase. While the focus during tweens is on maintaining a dainty appearance, during early adolescence the expectation of a submissive and demure demeanor expands to encompass ways of *being* in the world. In particular, this discourse makes early adolescent girls fear acting in the world with power, passion, and agency. In the physical domain, girls who still find narrow spaces in which to engage in physical activities with immersion and strength, problematize their own engagement as "manly" and try to compensate for their perceived lapse by acting in a hyper-feminine manner:

> Well, it's like they're girl-like outside, but when they get to the gym class or something, I mean, guys like we all become like *jocks*. Like *out of our minds*. Like when you play sports, you get more *competitive*, but when you're, like, not, you're just like, 'oh my God! Like *totally*,' and stuff like that. Most girls are like, 'oh my God! Your shoes don't match. Is my hair growing curly? Oh, my God!' (Alice)

The terms "jock" and being "out of our minds" reflect the perception that for an adolescent girl, playing with strength and immersion means stepping *outside the acceptable range* of embodied actions; hence, Alice follows up her sports activities with girly self-objectification and an exaggerated social response to possible appearance deviations. Girls worry about being "a tough big bitch," contrasted with being "small and cute," as explained by Kyra. Embodying physical strength is indeed so problematic that just owning it is a source of concern, even if it protects a girl from common teasing or violations:

> I don't even know why I *haven't really been teased*, but it *really bugs* me. I don't know, just because I beat up my friends a lot, just for the fun type thing. I'll just start smacking them and stuff… I think everyone's learned that I can be a strong kid, I guess. Don't mess with me type thing. I don't know what it is. It's really weird though. (Kyra?)

A clinical example can serve to reinforce this point. An adolescent girl who presented at my office with rapid weight loss, described being labeled a butch by girls in her peer group. She was an athletic girl, who, for most of her life, until puberty, felt proud about her physical ability. Following puberty, her peers started to ridicule her muscularity, which made her feel like "a horse." Her consequent weight loss aimed at muscle loss, making her daintier. Problematizing the label and cherishing her physical strengths were important aspects of her recovery. As our research and this clinical example reflect, girls in early adolescence find that being physically strong challenges expected norms of femininity, in particular, the Woman as Submissive/Demure discourse.

The conflict about power and strength extends to other facets of experience, such as voice, assertion, and anger. Early adolescence is the first time we commonly hear the terms bitch and butch in reference to acting in the world with strength. For example, Bronwen describes that,

> A *butch speaks her mind*… They are more comfortable with themselves I would think. And I find that girly girls are more kind of like not comfortable to be like whom I think they would really be inside. Butches hang out more with guys… and do sports. I don't hang out with guys or do sports. I'm probably between a butch and normal.

Bronwen was taught to be nice, and in her experience, speaking her mind contrasts with girly expectations, placing her outside the expected normal range for girls, closer to butch. It is her voice that places her in this range; not playing sports or hanging around with boys. Similarly, other early adolescent girls label assertive behavior as being bitchy. As Sarah describes, "I don't know, you have to be kind of bitchy, and like, like, I don't know, you have to stand up for yourself." Furthermore, expressing anger is often equated with being bitchy, and is sometimes excused as related to premenstrual syndrome (PMS): "When you are on PMS then you are just a *bitch*. Normally you wouldn't get mad, and I'll get mad at anything. I can realize myself being a *bitch*" (Kyra). During early adolescence, having undergone puberty, girls therefore face the Woman as Submissive/Demure discourse, as a Corset not only to their physical prowess but also to their voice, assertiveness, and anger.

Similar to the discourse of Woman as Submissive/Demure, the third Comportment-related Discourse, entitled Woman as Desired but Desire-less, has a much greater corseting impact during early adolescence than during the tweens phase. First, with the need to be both small and demure, and within the context of common body alterations, the containing of appetite becomes a mission for many adolescent girls and is expressed, often, through disordered eating patterns ["It's like I am hungry but it's like I don't want to eat" (Alice); "You exercise a lot and you don't eat as much as other people" (Meghan)]. Secondly, with girls having gone through puberty and starting to date, their sexual desire becomes the target of social control. Girls learn that, in line with the discourse of Woman as Desired but Desire-less, agency, pleasure, and freedom of expression of sexual desire reside with boys; it is their role to comply with and contain (and even be attuned to) male desire while, concurrently, trying to protect their safety and social standing—often an impossible task. In addition, beliefs inherent in a rape culture condone the association of male sexuality with violence. Under these conditions, there is no room for girls to be attuned to their own desire, agency, and pleasure. Bodily desires, therefore, become liabilities rather than sources of agency and strength.

The socially constructed slut label, derived from the derogatory and penalizing approach to female desire, is directly related to the Woman as Desired but Desire-less discourse. Labeling female desire negatively comprises yet another way of establishing male ownership and control over women's bodies. It is therefore not surprising that the controlling slut label appears in peer group conversations just as the dating scene is unfolding, disrupting girls' connection to their own desire and bodies, as well as their agency and social power.

Both boys and girls use the slut label; however, reflecting the gender-based double standard regarding sexuality, it is almost exclusively reserved for girls. A girl may be labeled a slut due to the clothing she wears, sometimes determined by a mere one-inch difference in skirt length or belly exposure. The following descriptions from Alice, Brady, and Kelly are common to girls in early adolescence: "You could just be labeled a slut from what you wear. Short skirts and low cut tops" (Alice); "We practically just call girls sluts and whores and that. Dressing really sluttyish. Popular girls wear clothes that are more revealing and more slutty" (Brady); "If they're dressing really open then they automatically get the slut name" (Kelly). Girls therefore tread a fine line: they might wear revealing or "slutty" clothes to get the desired second look from a boy, but at the same time risk being given the slut label. The distinction between a sexualized look and a slutty appearance is finicky at best, leaving many girls feeling unsafe.

Girls might be also called sluts for their involvement in any sexual act, even those including assault, regardless of whether illicit or illegal substances are involved: "A lot of my friends, they're giving guys, like, blowjobs. And they get labeled sluts and whores at our school and it's just horrible" (Alice). Girls observe keenly that sexual involvement on the part of boys is rewarded, with the rare male assignment of the slut label being seen as a compliment: "You're a whore. Get away from me. And he'll be like, 'yeah, I know. Thank you, thank you,' and he'll take it as a compliment" (Alice).

Further, girls may be labeled slut out of retaliation, anger, or competition—as the label is so damming, it is an effective way to disrupt a girl's life. A boy may label a girl a slut for her *refusal* to take part in a sexual act, "Like my friend, like, she got called a slut because she didn't wanna give a guy a blowjob. If he doesn't like her, he'll be like, 'she's a slut'" (Alice). Girls describe the dilemma of complying with a guy to avoid his anger or to not lose him; at the same time, they will also be labeled for compliance, revealing that there is no safe or comfortable place for girls. And once a girl is assigned this label, boys will become more sexually aggressive toward her. Girls also describe calling other girls sluts when they feel competitive or angry with them: "She's going out with my ex. She is a slut" (Kyra). Other times, they use it as a "joke," teasing one another, as the term is so common—"It's part of our language now. It's just like another word on the street now" (Alice).

The broad adoption of the slut label should be problematized as collusion with a misogynistic culture that sanctions patriarchal and rape culture beliefs. Further, its common use by girls to label other girls reflects, in addition, the impact of the fourth Comportment-related Discourse described by the DTE: the Patriarchal Shaping of Relational Patterns. The trend of prioritizing and securing sexualized male dates while holding relational norms of competition and policing among girls, which emerges during the tweens phase, continues during early adolescence. Compared with the tweens phase, competition over male dates intensifies and girls involved in the dating scene describe experiencing betrayals between girls. Alice, for example, describes how her boyfriend cheated on her with one of her girlfriends. Brady's friends disrupt her relationship with her boyfriend by communicating to him that she "cheated on him and that I was kissing other guys, so he was mad." Kyra describes her frustration in discovering that her ex-boyfriend is dating another girl from her school, labeling her as a slut.

Mutual policing by girls during early adolescence involves not only adherence to norms of appearance but also to behavior in the sexual arena. For example, Kyra describes in her interview how an ex-girlfriend of a guy she dated, "started telling tales. These girls came up to me when I was walking through town and they are like… did you screw him?" Though she immediately denies the allegation, the rumor disrupts other relations in her life. Alice, meanwhile, provides a description of the chain of rumors faced by a girl who may have given a "hand job" to a guy:

> [Name] thought she liked the guy and gave him a hand job, and then he dumped her. It was gossip, like going around everywhere. He told his friends at school. And then a girl came up to her and said, 'you gave him a hand job.' And then my friend [name] told my friend [name], who told me, and then I told my friend [name], and she confronted [name] and then she got the name 'slut' put on her and everywhere we talked, '[name] is such a slut, you know what she did to this guy.' But he got congratulated.

Penalizing peer communications often includes deprecating terms related to both norms of appearance and sexuality. Kyra, for example, describes a communication between two girls and another girl who has been accused of "backstabbing":

> You are a fucking jealous slut. You stab your friends in the back, dirty bitch. You're a cripple and you are poor. You only shop at [cheap store] and you're a skank. You're fat and you stuff your bra. Why do you gossip about other people? We hate you. You're a dyke.

Related to norms of appearance, the girl is targeted by being labeled "fat," flat chested and needing to "stuff [her] bra," a "cripple," and "poor," therefore not having the money to clad her body in brand name clothing. In sexualized terms, the communication shows a strong collusion with demeaning patriarchal labels aimed at female embodied sexuality: "slut," "skank," "bitch," and "dyke." Further, the tone of this note reflects how stirred up girls become over ongoing betrayals, often reflecting their lack of safety in relational networks, and their vulnerability to gossip and rumors. Girls treat other girls with harshness similar to the ways they are treated by boys and by the culture at large.

As can be gleaned from this section on Mental Freedom, socially constructed dichotomies continue to impact the experiences of girls in early adolescence, deriving their power from condensing multiple oppressive discourses. While during the tweens phase the tomboy/girly girl dichotomy figures centrally in shaping the subjective experiences of girls, during early adolescence the slut/prude dichotomy gets center stage. Nonetheless, both dichotomies work to maintain the social status quo by constricting girls' freedom, agency, and power.

In early adolescence, girls who have completed the pubertal process and are entering the dating scene no longer identify with the tomboy label as such identification is problematized and penalized. They describe that the now-prohibited label assumes new and problematizing names during early adolescence. For example, Alice describes a tomboy as "a manly girl," indicating that the label "stopped in grade 7," Similarly, 13-year-old Bronwen describes a tomboy as "a butch." Clearly, the tomboy label that has provided temporary freedom to engage in the world with the freedom allotted to boys is no longer available. While girls resistant to the sexualizing and objectifying scene that unfolds in early adolescence still describe themselves as being in the middle position—dressing girly but staying physically active outside of school—most girls describe themselves as girly girls and follow a girly style of dress, comportment, leisure activities, and relational patterns. However, it is important to stay attuned to the subjective struggle this forced binary classification entails. According to Brady,

> I am a girly girl. Girly girls wear tight jeans and not so low cut in the hip and like tight t-shirts but like not revealing so much skin. Girly girls curl their hair and make sure their hair looks perfect and leave it down and always have to have something done with it. Girly girls

> go shopping and hang around with friends. Most of the tomboys are losers. They like watching football and are into video games. Tomboys just like put their hair in a ponytail. They don't care what it looks like. When you're younger people don't care what you dress, how you dress, what you look like and stuff. They care more about your personality. But when you get older people make fun of you because of it. They say, like, '*oh yeah you're a man*.' People make fun of you for *trying to be yourself*. I think I'll stay more girly girl as I get older. When I am girly *I feel good about myself and bad*. 'Cause I'm trying to be like other people. But when I'm just like in sweatpants and sweatshirt, *I feel more myself*.

The social expectations and rewards of being girly girls come with significant restrictions on the freedom of engagement in meaningful passions, and with the subjective experience of loss. Girls sometimes refer to "hiding" parts of their selves: "Girls try to hide it 'cause they want to be one of the boys" (Kyra), and "You're just trying to hide yourself" (Kelly). In addition to losing or hiding aspects of the self by assuming this socially rewarded position, girls are made well aware of the concurrent devaluation of girly girls, who are often presented in caricatured fashion—for example, as acting dumb ["A real girly girl is a dumb stupid girl. She puts on an act. She talks like this with her hands like this. I just want to punch her and say, 'you are so dumb'" (Sarah)], as physically restricted ["Girly girls' nails are way too long and then they can't pick up things. Makes me laugh" (Kelly)], or as slutty ["They dress too 'whorish'" (Brady)]. Unlike during the tweens phase, girls in early adolescence who try to hold a middle position in the dichotomy, related to their passion for physical pursuits or their resistance to the oppressive girly mode, find it not as tenable; they often feel "not normal." Bronwen, for example, describes herself as "not a normal girl," and Olivia shares feeling "not normal sometimes, weird, sometimes acting like a boy but you're a girl." Within the socially constructed tomboy/girly girl dichotomy, there is no embodied place for pubertal girls to act with agency and meaningful passions in the world.

Concurrently, early adolescence sees a proliferation of the slut/prude dichotomy, which controls girls' subjectivities in relation to new fields of experience in their social lives: sexuality and dating. This dichotomy condenses a number of adverse social values, including the vilification of women's sexuality, the prohibition of women's agency in the pursuit of desire and passion, the sanctioning of violations against women, and the reinforcing of men's ownership of women's bodies, among others. Highly prevalent in the social lives of early adolescents, girls aim to negotiate this oppressive dichotomy in relation to their own identity. However, this dichotomy leaves no safe or comfortable place for pubertal girls to act in the world with agency in relation to their sexual desire: "So like for girls if they do something they're bad, they're sluts, and if they don't do anything, they're bad, they're prudes" (Melissa). Girls pay a high price for involvement in any sexual activity, even forced. Nonetheless they are also negatively labeled as being prudes, meaning: not making themselves available for male desire. It is not surprising, and is yet worrisome, that girls are flooded by adverse sexuality discourses at this critical time of development—at the very beginning of their sexual embodied journey. Yet, the prominence of adverse sexuality discourses at this phase reflects the centrality of sexual desire in reinforcing gender inequity.

Just like during the tweens phase, we do not hear from girls in early adolescence about sites of corrective dialogues and experiences that could help them to withstand the oppressive social discourses that tighten around them. Instead, they experience major ruptures in relational connections, thus the tone we hear most often from early adolescents is one of individual struggle and shame, as well as resignation. The creation and fostering of supportive and validating communities, where critical perspectives on oppressive social discourses can be nurtured and amplified within the context of relational safety, could be powerful assets in producing alterative, liberating discourses and more constructive peer norms.

To summarize experiences in the mental domain, girls in early adolescence negotiate a minefield of Mental Corsets comprised of multiple femininity discourses. As the dating scene unfolds and peer relations become sexualized, discourses related to objectification and deficiency intensify under the gaze and evaluations of peers and result in extensive engagement in body practices aimed at beautification. Shopping and observing the physical games of boys, appearing and acting demure, and containing desires, become socially sanctioned ways of avoiding social penalty, especially within the context of rifts within the social network of girls. Both the tomboy/girly girl and the slut/prude dichotomies present challenges to girls' negotiation of their identities and behaviors. Femininity discourses therefore form a tight web around girls in early adolescence, further restricting their experiences of agency and comfort in engaging with the world.

EMBODIED DEMOTION: THE COSTLY PATH TO SOCIAL POWER

> I don't know like some stuff that girls wear and stuff like that is really demoralizing. From my perspective it's kinda like selling yourself and it's sexist as well. Like you know how way back like the feminism movement or whatever I think it's really sad how, you

know, we have got a right to vote, we have got everything, but we don't use it. Like we don't see how many women are in Parliament… I just think it's really, really sad how we could have so many opportunities but what those women fought for we don't even appreciate. I find girls who are almost anorexic and they wear really, really tight clothes. That's just sick. I think they are not staying true to who they are. If you look at little kids, they don't care. But then once you are growing up, what you wear is so important, and body image. I think it's stupid.

In this insightful commentary on body politics, Bronwen contrasts the power women have fought for and achieved in the *political arena* with losses they have continued to incur in the *body domain*. She is justifiably demoralized by her observation that, despite women's political achievements, they still derive power from "selling" themselves via their appearance and what they wear. She clearly identifies how the focus on appearance reflects sexist cultural values and that, in turn, girls and women's continued reliance on appearance as a means of achieving social power abides by the rules of a sexist society. In particular, she problematizes the shrunken "anorexic" body for which girls strive, and their tight and sexualized restrictive clothing. She compares the experience of childhood, when girls do not care about their appearance, with early adolescence, when appearance becomes a focus. It is not surprising that Bronwen is both angry and demoralized. Indeed, her observation is amply validated by the feminist literature that examines the backlash against women's progress toward equity and, in particular, the targeting of their bodies (e.g., Bordo, 1989; Faludi, 2006; Piran, 2016; Wolf, 2002). At the same time, in her different domains of life, Bronwen unfortunately cannot find a validating community that can support, amplify, or nurture this critical perspective, to transform it into a shared resistant stance from which activism might develop. Bronwen recognizes this situation: "I think sexism is awful, like I'm a real feminist, but I'm not an active feminist." Rather, she is quite alone with her shrewd analysis, "I talk a lot about the UN and I am interested in world issues, but my friends aren't really." Furthermore, unlike Bronwen's perspective and related feminist literature, much of the professional literature—such as the literature on anorexia—does not make a link between personal embodied distress and political structures of power (Piran, 2010).

In relation to the Social Power and Relational Connections domain of the DTE, Bronwen addresses its first dimension, Exposure to Prejudice and Harassment, by criticizing the impact of sexism on girls' embodied lives, specifically: limiting girls' acceptable body size, as well as their objectification and sexualization. She also addresses the second dimension, Appearance-based Social Power, by highlighting how reliance on appearance to achieve social power contradicts the goal of gender equity and compromises women's pursuit of meaningful life goals. With respect to the other two dimensions of the Social Power and Relational Connections domain, both Membership in Equitable Communities and Empowering Relationships could have constructively shifted Bronwen, in her own words, from being a "real feminist" to an "active feminist."

Starting with the dimension of Exposure to Prejudice and Harassment, living in pubertal bodies and becoming involved in the predominantly heterosexual dating scene, Bronwen and most girls in early adolescence experience, in their daily embodied lives, the poignant inequity in the ways the bodies of girls and boys are treated in a sexist culture. In particular, they point to a double standard in relation to body practices and appearance.

One problem area commonly identified by girls is the double standard that exists in relation to the sexual activity of girls and boys: girls are penalized with the slut label while boys are rewarded with the player label for engaging in the same activities. Another aspect identified by some of the girls interviewed is the expectation that girls restrict the way they dress or act so as to contain male (rather than their own) desire.

Girls, similarly highlight other concrete expressions of double standards related to appearance. They complain that weight prejudice is harsher with girls: "If a boy and a girl were like the same thin size and they got bigger to the same size, the girl would be noticed first, in a bad way, because people pay more attention to what girls look like" (Meghan). They complain that boys are allowed to wear comfortable clothing while girls are not: "A guy can wear baggy pants… but a girl has to walk in tight pants and skirts" (Brady). They complain that they need to alter their bodies but that males do not: "Girls should not have to be put on a diet or to exercise, do all this, because of what they're supposed to look like" (Sarah). They complain about the existence of a double standard in relation to the centrality of appearance:

> I wish girls didn't have to like dress to impress. Like, there is this one kid in my class, he's really popular but he will wear whatever he can find. He just throws something on. But a girl, even if there's a stain on a girl's shirt, it's like people call them gross. This is weird. (Erica)

During early adolescence, girls and boys in grades 7 and 8 practice for the first time, in their newly matured physical bodies, learned embodied patterns of gender relations. The body, therefore, comprises a central domain in the lives of early adolescents, both informing them about gender relations and power, and, in turn, perpetuating societal values. It is therefore not surprising that the areas early adolescent girls highlight as reflecting gender inequity center on embodied expressions of sexism. The understandable discomfort of inhabiting the body as a site of inequity can take different forms. Commonly, girls seek lost power by altering the body to fit idealized appearance expectations. During early adolescence we see an increase in disordered eating patterns aimed at weight loss, as well as engagement in other body alterations.

Body-based harassment in relation to all aspects of social location is also common during adolescence. Such harassment during early adolescence relates strongly to the second dimension of Social Power and Relational Connections: Appearance-based Social Power. In the intensive heterosexual dating scene that takes place during early adolescence, the body and its appearance take center stage. Importantly, as girls describe, the popular girls, who are at the top of the hierarchical social structure, indeed *embody idealized appearance characteristics*. Girls of diverse backgrounds consistently draw and describe the same appearance characteristics of the ideal girl. To achieve the popular rank in early adolescence, a girl needs to: seek perfection, look "white," be thin and yet have larger breasts, expose her body, wear brand name clothes and shoes, carry costly gadgets, and apply makeup. Holding particular postures that communicate self-objectification and availability to boys, such as standing in the hallway with arms behind the back, as Brady explains, is an added bonus and will help toward getting that second look.

While girls seek the avenue of social power available to them through sexualized self-objectification, this experience is inherently disruptive and demoting; concurrently, it reinforces the social power of boys, who hold the scrutinizing lens. Alice's anecdote clarifies the power inequity inherent in objectification:

> So I'm with this guy, and he was, like kind of mean. He's, like, you're more cute with your hair down, so he'd take my hair out. And if I wasn't wearing any makeup, he wouldn't look at me until I actually did wear makeup. So it was kind of depressing. It did not make me feel good. I never used to care so much about what people thought about me until him. I never had the heart to break up. I gave him a second chance, and after that he cheated on me.

Being a visual object is a disempowering experience. Girls describe the power they experience by having large breasts, successfully gaining the second look from guys; concurrently, however, they question the meaning of this power—for what reason are they liked? As Kyra describes:

> Yay, I have boobs, that's great. You're happy because they're looking at you and not at the other girl. Girls are jealous. But still you're just

> like, get away from me, leave me alone. I wanted them to think of more than that.

Brady, who describes the power advantage of dressing "slutty" and appreciates looking like the ideal girl—like "Christina Aguilera and Britney Spears"—similarly describes wanting guys to like her for who she is and not "for what I look like."

The popular girl with idealized characteristics does not act with agency, and is concurrently demoted. Girls consistently describe the sexualized and objectified girl as acting without agency, initiative, or voice. To get the guy she wants, the objectified girl operates indirectly, through attracting attention. This is in contrast with the way a boy is expected to act:

> A lot of girls they just stand around the guys and then start giggling and being all screaming and that. They hang around the popular guys and get all giggly and loud to get their attention. But I think it's mainly how they dress. Like if a girl's dressing really out there and showing herself off and the way she acts, really flirty, then the guy thinks like, 'oh she's interested in me and she want to get with me.' But the boys that want a girl just go up to her and talk to the girl. (Kelly)

Further, when the self-objectification of popular girls becomes extreme, they are intensely ridiculed. Girls' provide many such descriptions, for example: "[Known celebrity] is the fakest most disgusting thing I have ever seen. All done up, nice and amazing clothes, putting on an act, acting all stupid. The dumbest person in the world" (Kyra); "They squeal and it is kinda irritating" (Bronwen); and "The popular girls are all screeching, like 'oh my God, oh my God,' and they are all wearing bright, bright pink" (Shannon). Further, there is a general understanding by girls that, "girly girls are more kind of like not comfortable to be like who they would really be inside" (Bronwen). Power through objectification is not real power and does not come with the comfort to engage with the world with self-attunement, agency, or voice.

As social power becomes increasingly linked to embodying specific appearance characteristics, few girls may approximate the visual ideal and obtain the coveted position of a popular girl, but many more are excluded from this position. These girls describe sometimes relentless and painful body-based harassment perpetrated by both girls and boys. In the intense body comparisons that take place in early adolescence, every aspect of appearance is scrutinized. In particular, material conditions become more centrally related to appearance than during earlier phases of development—wearing brand name clothes (including one's prom dress!) gains greater importance in early adolescence, as does carrying the right material gadgets (the right purse, phone, etc.). Moreover, body alterations can be costly—for example, the costs of makeup, body hair removal services, professional manicures and pedicures, and hair styling. In early adolescence, we hear increasingly about teasing related to being poor and having to purchase clothes in inexpensive stores: "You are poor and you shop at Salvation Army" (Jackie).

In addition to stratification related to socioeconomic standing, sexualization and sexual objectification intersect with other forms of body-based teasing. Fat prejudice becomes accentuated in relation to idealized images of "perfect little girls," and weightist harassment is prevalent: "When you're fat nobody likes you" (Jackie). Fat harassment is so intense at this age that not growing fat as they age is, sadly, a worry expressed by girls in early adolescence. As Brady explains, "I don't want to grow up fat… Like growing up to be a mother it would be harder on my kids because they'd be embarrassed of it."

Racism can get linked to sexual maltreatment, as experienced by Jackie, a member of the Aboriginal community, when told, "You'll always be a one night stand"; and Roxy, of Middle Eastern descent, who boys label a "burnt package." Additionally, the possibility of having a non-heterosexual orientation is yet another target of body-based harassment: "Dyke, you always look at our boobs, but we don't swing this way" (Alice). Combined with varied aspects of social locations, not fitting sexualized images—for example, not having the right body proportions—can be another source of body-based harassment: "You stuff your bra" (Alice), or "Like if the girls don't have boobs they get made fun of, if girls do have boobs they get made fun of. And girls just can't win" (Kelly). Further still, girls with physical disabilities also get teased: "They harass the girl who is poor and she has a disability… that she is disgusting and dirty" (Bronwen).

Body-based teasing is rampant during early adolescence. Survey studies indeed find that experiences of harassment in early adolescence are highly prevalent and associated with negative body image, poor self-esteem, depression, substance abuse, and self-harm behavior. The greater the number of harassment types experienced by an adolescent (related to weight, gender, social class, sexual orientation, and race) the more disruption they show across all measures of well-being (e.g., Bucchianeri, Eisenberg, Wall, Piran, & Neumark-Sztainer, 2014). Therefore, interventions to address body-based harassment among early adolescents are essential in protecting their well-being.

Within the context of the embodied demotion of early adolescent girls via exposure to prejudicial treatment, body-based harassment, and appearance-based social power, the next two dimensions of the Social Power and Relational Connections domain can further impact the overall experience of social power. Starting with the domain of Empowering Relationships, girls describe few empowering relationships in their lives and many more disempowering ones. In terms of adults in their lives, few girls describe their fathers' involvement in coaching their all-girls or co-ed sports teams as opening the door for them to succeed and be empowered in an arena that otherwise would have been closed to them. For Shannon, this opening is particularly empowering:

> My dad was going to coach a girls' team, but no one showed any interest. So, instead he is coaching a mixed soccer team. And it is now half and half... My dad brought me into sports and I have fun playing it, I feel proud. I made it to the school team. I was nervous... I don't think guys get as nervous 'cause there are more opportunities for them to do sports, but not for girls. That's my place, on the field, my happy place. And it's just like kind of an adrenaline rush for me playing hard... But at school like I am not the most popular, 'cause I like sports and no one else likes sports, I am not chatty or flirty, and one day at recess I went outside and the girls just ran away from me. But I kinda like walked after them, and I confronted them. I think like I run on adrenaline. Like anger to adrenaline. If I didn't play sports, I would have bottled it up inside. I still felt down about myself, but I felt like I had to stand up for myself.

Few girls also describe interactions with boyfriends that have counteracted the impact of disrespect and violations they experienced in their larger peer groups. Of particular importance were relationships that were validating and non-objectifying. For example, Alice describes exposure to demeaning objectification with three prior boyfriends, intense sexual harassment at school, and prevalent fat talk and shaming in her peer group. Consequently, she has stopped eating lunch at school. Her boyfriend reassures her about her worth and encourages her to eat:

> I feel, like, better about myself when I'm with him. Everywhere I go it's like talk talk talk about being fat. He tells me, 'Alice, you're not fat, okay? You're just perfect, all right? You stay the way you are.' Sometimes I even think of myself as like pretty. He says, 'You're beautiful'... I think there is something wrong with me 'cause I never feel like eating in school. The other day I didn't have a lunch and I was starving, but I didn't want anything. So he bought me a muffin and he's like, 'You're eating it!' So, I'm like, 'Look, I'm eating,' and he's like, 'I'm amazed, Alice, I'm so proud of you.'

It is important for Alice that her boyfriend does not pressure her sexually. For Kyra, who still feels that she has to be perfectly modified for the guy she cares about, having a non-sexual friendship with a boy where she "would have all the makeup off and be sitting there in sweat pants and a big shirt" and hear him say that she is "the most beautiful person" he has ever seen lowers her appearance anxiety.

The experience of support and acceptance in close friendships between girls provides safety for girls in acting in the world. However, we commonly hear about experiences of betrayal with minimal resolution, even in the closest relationships. As Bronwen describes:

> Like my friends they don't want to talk [about a fight]. They are like, let's ignore each other, and I'm like you are never going to solve things properly where both of you get what you need. You need to see each other's point of view.

Commonly lacking in adolescent girls' narratives are examples of empowering relationships with adult women who can model ways of inhabiting diverse bodies comfortably and with attunement while acting with agency in the world. Girls in early adolescence repeatedly talk about feeling depressed at the prospect of gaining weight with aging, often mirroring the disappointment expressed by their mothers toward the changing shape of their bodies with time. Aiming to prevent their daughters from undergoing the bodily changes they themselves are not at peace with, several mothers warn their daughters about weight gain during early adolescence, or even put their daughters on a diet. These warnings create fears in their daughters regarding their natural bodies. Meghan's mother, for example, tells her to "stay healthy because she was really thin when she was my age and then she started to eat more and it all caught up with her later." Consequently, Meghan restricts her food intake to a noticeable degree, which concerns her boyfriend as well as her mother.

A few mothers do try to model such acceptance. Rachel's mother (White, working class background with strained financial circumstances), who describes herself as "heavy," talks about genetics and body acceptance, and describes the beauty of movie stars such as Queen Latifah. Rachel, in turn, is quite unconcerned about her body image. Thus, empowering relationships in the lives of early adolescents can make a big difference in supporting how they engage in the world with agency and comfort while inhabiting their natural, unaltered, bodies.

Membership in Equitable Communities, the fourth dimension of the Social Power and Relational Connections dimension of the DTE, can also help buffer experiences of embodied inequity faced by girls in early adolescence. However, within the contexts of gender inequity, sexual harassment and violations, accentuated social stratification, and the intense competition and patterns of betrayals among girls, communities of equity at this phase are far and few between. The lack of such communities greatly disempowers girls in early adolescence. Nonetheless, the few examples of membership in communities of equity reflect the power inherent in such communities. Shannon, for example, feels at times like an outcast among her peer group at school. It is of great importance for her that the mixed-gender sports team, which her father coaches, embraces norms of acceptance and gender equity; further, she describes a similar experience while on her school team:

> I play in the mixed [gender] team. Before, I said that the guys don't pass, but this year we actually have a really good team and the guys are really respectful. And it's not as serious in a way because everyone is a little bit more friendly... I am on the school team and the team is working together. And everyone is needed; everyone is being a part of something... It is my happy place.

Brady has had a similar experience with her hockey team: "I'm friends with most of the girls that I started playing with, and I have fun." However, after 1 year she leaves the team when infighting between girls ensues: "Some girls are mean and I'd rather leave."

Importantly, Meghan describes having a unique constructive experience while taking part in a girls' club at her school

> I was in this girls' club at my school. And you talk about anything: guys, fights, like pretty much all the mutual stuff. The teacher said that everything in the room was not allowed to leave the room. It was good. I could help other girls. It was a surprise. And the teacher was really helpful. Like she had a lot of good advice and it made a difference.

In contrast, the last time Kelly felt she was part of an equitable community at school was in kindergarten, when "Everybody was same, shorter, taller, fatter, skinny. So it was the same for everybody and that felt good. I didn't even think about myself. I was just concentrating on what I was doing and having fun. Everybody was the same." Membership in equitable communities, where one is fully accepted and valued, is important to positive embodiment; this is exactly the sort of community that is so hard for girls in early adolescence to find.

To summarize experiences in the Social Power and Relational Connections domain, living in pubertal bodies and getting involved in the predominantly heterosexual dating scene, girls in early adolescence experience in their daily, embodied lives the poignant inequity in the way girls and boys' bodies are treated in a sexist culture. Starting with the Exposure to Prejudice and Harassment dimension, girls highlight multiple expressions of the double standard that exists in relation to engagement in sexual activities, containment of desire, and harsh standards of appearance. During early adolescence, the strong impact of the second dimension, Appearance-based Social Power, reinforces the disempowerment of girls, with power through objectification being inherently restrictive and demoting. Furthermore, the visual representation of popular girls works to stratify the social standing of diverse girls, such that girls who do not fit within idealized visual representations related to financial standing, ethnocultural/racial heritage, sexual orientation, weight, or visible difference/disability may face social exclusion and harassment. At the same time, girls in early adolescence have limited access to two possible sources of social power: Empowering Relationships and Membership in Equitable Communities.

CHAPTER SUMMARY

The longitudinal study of girls as they transit to early adolescence suggests that this phase poses significant challenges to their experiences of embodiment. Girls, quite uniformly, describe experiencing discomfort in their bodies and disconnection from both appetite and sexual desire. It is at this phase that we more commonly hear about patterns of disordered eating, substance use, sexual activity without desire or protection, and self-harm among girls. The study of the social experiences of girls in early adolescence clarifies the great challenges these girls face. In the physical domain, girls encounter limits on participation in physical activities, intensification of sexual harassment and dating violence, and expectations that they contain their desires. Further, beliefs endemic to a rape culture challenge the practice of self-care. In the mental domain, intense objectification and concerns about appearance deficiencies lead girls to engage in practices aimed at self-beautification, while pressures to abide by "feminine" rules of comportment cause girls to worry about acting powerfully in the world. Concurrently, the slut label becomes a central discourse that shapes girls' engagement in desire; it also contributes to growing relational rifts within peers groups. Compounding these rifts are social pressures that stratify girls' social standing based on approximating idealized appearance standards. During early adolescence, the body is therefore often experienced as a liability, rather than as a source of agency.

References

Bordo, S. (1989). The body and the reproduction of femininity: A feminist appropriation of foucault. In A. M. Jaggar, & S. R. Bordo (Eds.), *Gender/body/knowledge* (pp. 13–33). New Brunswick, NJ: Rutgers University.

Bucchianeri, M. M., Eisenberg, M. E., Wall, M. M., Piran, N., & Neumark-Sztainer, D. (2014). Multiple types of harassment: Associations with emotional well-being and unhealthy behaviors in adolescents. *Journal of Adolescent Health*, *54*(6), 724–729.

Buchwald, E., Fletcher, P. R., & Roth, M. (1993). *Transforming a rape culture*. Minneapolis, MN: Milkweed Editions.

Faludi, S. (2006). *The undeclared war against American women* (15th anniversary ed.). New York: NY: Three Rivers Press.

Fine, M. (1988). Sexuality, schooling, and adolescent females: The missing discourse of desire. *Harvard Educational Review*, *58*, 29–53.

Legge, R. (2009). If I am thin, I am safe: Speaking through the body following trauma. Critical Multicultural Series. In O. Oulanova, I. Stein, A. Rai, M. Hammer, & P. Poulin (Eds.), *Within and beyond borders: Critical multicultural counselling in practice* (pp. 84–92). Toronto, ON: University of Toronto, OISE. Retrieved from: http://www.oise.utoronto.ca/cdcp/.

Neumark-Sztainer, D., Paxton, S. J., Hannan, P. J., Haines, J., & Story, M. (2006). Does body satisfaction matter? Five-year longitudinal associations between body satisfaction and health behaviors in adolescent females and males. *Journal of Adolescent Health*, *39*(2), 244–251.

Piran, N. (2001). Re-inhabiting the body from the inside out: Girls transform their school environment. In D. L. Tolman, & M. Brydon-Miller (Eds.), *From subjects to subjectivities: A handbook of interpretive and participatory methods* (pp. 218–238). New York: New York University Press.

Piran, N. (2010). A feminist perspective on risk factor research and on the prevention of eating disorders. *Eating Disorders: The Journal of Treatment and Prevention*, *18*(3), 183–198.

Piran, N. (2016). Embodiment and well being: The embodied journeys of girls and women. In T.-A. Roberts, N. Curtin, L. Cortina, & L. E. Duncan (Eds.), *Best practices in feminist psychological science: Gender beyond difference* (pp. 43–60). New York, NY: Springer.

Smolak, L., & Piran, N. (2012). Gender and the prevention of eating disorders. In G. McVey, M. P. Levine, N. Piran, & H. B. Ferguson (Eds.), *Preventing eating-related and weight-related disorders: Collaborative research, advocacy, and policy change* (pp. 201–224).

Smolak, L., Murnen, S. K., & Ruble, A. E. (2000). Female athletes and eating problems: A meta-analysis. *International Journal of Eating Disorders*, *27*, 371–380.

Stice, E., Hayward, C., Cameron, R. P., Killen, J. D., & Taylor, C. B. (2000). Body-image and eating disturbances predict onset of depression among female adolescents: A longitudinal study. *Journal of Abnormal Psychology*, *109*(3), 438–444.

Tolman, D. L. (2002). *Dilemmas of desire: Teenage girls talk about sexuality*. Cambridge, MA: Harvard University Press.

Waterloo, ON: Wilfred Laurier Press Stice, E., & Bearman, S. K. (2001). Body image and eating disturbances prospectively predict increases in depressive symptoms in adolescent girls: A growth curve analysis. *Developmental Psychology*, *37*, 597–607.

Wolf, N. (2002). *The beauty myth: How images of beauty are used against women* (2nd ed.). NewYork, NY: Harper Perennial.

CHAPTER

5

The "Perfection" of Corseting: Late Adolescence (Ages 15–17)

> We all wear makeup. I feel terrible about myself when I'm not! I always wear makeup. My friend and I, we fix each other's makeup, and then we look in the mirror and both say, 'I look like crap.' It's a routine. We do it every day. Like women have always been the lower kinda thing, so it's more of our way to actually do something with ourselves, impress everybody… I've been taking these pills of natural herbs. They're not like diet pills, but they make your hunger less sharp. So it kind of just helps me so that I don't eat at lunch. I lost a little bit of weight, and off my stomach, which is good for me because I've always had this like weird shaped stomach. Like you see these girls, even at my school, they wear the midriff shirts and I can't do that. And it bugs me. But there is one thing I'm kind of proud of that I have to admit. I have pretty big boobs. I'm also at the gym so I'm losing weight by working out. I don't want to get fat when I am older and I don't want stretch marks… I can't quit smoking, but I have stopped with [other substances]… [re: dating] As soon as I like somebody or somebody wanting stuff from me, I go into total denial mode. I don't let myself get those feelings anymore. It's gonna take a long time for me to be able to accept that again. I don't want to get hurt again. That [sexual violation] was the worst experience ever. So I get attention from guys but in a better way—I am friends with them! But then guys say, 'she's manlier than I am.'

These narratives from Jackie, a 15-year-old girl of Aboriginal heritage and working-class background, reflect important aspects of the Experience of Embodiment (EE) among girls in late adolescence. First,

Journeys of Embodiment at the Intersection of Body and Culture
http://dx.doi.org/10.1016/B978-0-12-805410-9.00005-0

girls often describe experiencing discomfort in their bodies and avoidance of being seen in public without some alteration of their appearance. Preparing for adulthood, they express concerns about how their bodies will change throughout their life journey. Further, girls refer to experiences of less agency in their bodies, such as Jackie's comment that "women have always been the lower kinda thing, so [makeup] is our way to actually do something." Moreover, girls in late adolescence often depict their struggles with appetite and eating. Similarly, girls commonly share their disrupted connection to sexual desire, shaped by a range of negative social experiences—in Jackie's case, by a previous sexual assault. Consequently, it is challenging for them to live in their bodies in self-attuned and self-caring ways. In addition to engaging often in diets or disordered eating behaviors, as well as substance consumption, girls describe self-harm behaviors among some of their peers, sometimes labeled "Emo." The daily engagement in body practices aimed at achieving idealized appearance standards reflects girls' self-objectifying stance. Overall, girls in late adolescence identify their bodies as sites of struggle. While they may make, at this phase, critical comments about the treatment of women and their bodies, this critical lens does not appear to relieve them of their own embodied struggle.

Important differences exist between experiences of embodiment in early and late adolescence. During late adolescence, girls describe having both a greater level of proficiency in body practices aimed beautification and a new *dependence* on such practices—so much so that they commonly cannot conceive of presenting themselves in public without such alterations. In addition, there are increased fears associated with the body, related to sexual violations and to concerns regarding social exclusion, based on one's appearance or sexual behavior. Commonly feared at this phase in the transition to adulthood are future changes to the body related to aging and life transitions, including weight gain and pregnancy. Emerging as well during late adolescence are references to objectification during sexual intimacy. As compliance with embodied social expectations increases among girls in late adolescence, expressions of protest or loss over experienced embodied constraints become less common, even when girls voice critical commentaries regarding challenges to women's embodiment.

Late adolescence comprises a time where embodied journeys may diverge. For most girls, risk factors in the physical, mental, and social power domains intensify. Other girls may see attenuation of exposure to risk factors, and even the emergence of some protective factors, where embodied healing can occur. We therefore see a broadening of the range of possible experiences of embodiment during late adolescence when compared with early adolescence, where girls described a more uniform disruption.

ACTING IN PHYSICAL CONFINEMENT: BODY ALTERATIONS AND PROTECTION

> I don't need to be reminded. Yeah, I am a fat pig. I'm biking to school. It kind of sucks, but I'm like: 'Well, it's good exercise. Do it.' You know?... I live really far away from school. My legs hurt. This completely sucks. By the end of the month, if I haven't shaved off at least 10 minutes, I'm going to go, like, do laps around the school or something... I work at the gym, I do classes: Body Fight, Body Steam, Body Tackle. I feel like crap. I hate it. Also, no chocolate for a week... I love swimming so much. I mean, I haven't gone to swim in a while because I can't take the hijab off in a public pool... In school, this guy tried to hug me and I was like, 'Back off!' Yeah it was pretty bad... Of course, I'm allowed to talk to boys, although I think this is a normal dad thing, but my dad's like, 'All your problems are because you talk to boys'... But there is this creepy stalker that goes to my school. He like followed me home and it's a good thing my grandma was there. I was like, 'This is really freaky.' We were really scared. She was like, 'Lock the door and close the windows. I don't want him coming looking for us.'

In these narratives, Hazel shares her experiences being a 16-year-old. She is of Middle Eastern heritage and a working-class background. Like all girls we interviewed during late adolescence, she struggles with her body weight and size. Joyful immersion in favorite activities—swimming in her case—has been replaced with workout classes, aptly labeled "Body Fight" and "Body Tackle," depicting the state of battle with the body described by most girls. Like all girls in late adolescence, exposure to sexual harassment accentuates the challenges of inhabiting a young woman's body. While for Hazel wearing the hijab marks a meaningful separation between public and private spheres, for other girls, layers of makeup and tight attire mark this separation.

In the public sphere, girls in late adolescence live within the confines of Corsets to Physical Engagement and Movement. Even though they now hang out in co-ed groups with increasing regularity, these shared activities no longer include physical activities: "Just like, before it was like the girl goes out to play sports with the guys kind of thing or whatever, but now like I will hang out with guys and like talk or watch movies and stuff" (Bronwen). This contrasts with boys' activities: "A lot of the guys I know play hockey or are in bands, which girls aren't, you know. Girls are into shopping, movies, hang out, slumber parties" (Sarah). Within the context of a dwindling number of girls' sports teams and strict norms of docile femininity, including well-kempt feminine appearance, girls often allude to choosing sedentary activities at school. As Jackie describes, "I stopped playing sports or trying for teams, and started getting into drama." After-school activities of choice are similarly sedentary, involving social media, TV or movie watching, and shopping: "Like most of my friends lock themselves inside the room, all we do is really talk on the telephone, unless we are like going shopping, or going to the movies, but still that doesn't happen as often" (Sarah). However, even when girls continue to express their wish to remain passionately involved in sports, the barriers to do so are often too great: "I used to play soccer with the guys, but the coaches are like, 'the guys are too big,' and they made me drop out of the guy's team, and I used to love completely getting into it" (Sarah). As a result, acutely missing in the narratives of girls in late adolescence are narratives about *joyful physical immersion*—in particular, joyful group-based physical activities.

Instead, the practice of body alterations takes center stage, consuming girls' time and energy. Girls in late adolescence describe employing considerable skills and expending much energy in body alterations. Regimented physical activity becomes a component of engagement in body alterations and is often practiced alone, toward weight- and shape-related goals. Brady, a White girl from a working class and urban background, for example, describes her immersion, skills, and even fun she has had with body alterations. In line with the goal of body alterations, Brady views her uncommon opportunity in late adolescence to play hockey on a girls' team merely as a way to stay slim, and not as a source of pride and passion—experiences that were part of her earlier involvement in playing on a boys' team:

> I like being a girl. Like, waking up in the morning and not wanting to leave the house because you look like garbage and you have to stick on all the makeup and all the hair, it's just a lot of fun doing that. Just like when you're bored you can like fool around with your hair and makeup and everything, and like figure out new ways to do things… [Wearing] the tight, tight jeans and the low-cut shirts and more of the like skanky kind of shirts, like showing the stomach and having the belly button pierced and trying to show off the figure and everything…So we can't really play boys' hockey anymore because they are stopping us girls from like hitting and body checking… Our school doesn't have a girl team, so I go to play in another school. I'm just playing now to have an activity so I can stay skinny. I want to try and keep myself in shape and skinny as long as I possibly can. My mom says she was skinny till she was 18 and then she gained weight. I'm a light eater, too. Like I don't eat that

> much and I'm really picky with my food. I just have a small stomach so when I eat something I'll get full. And I'm a big runner. I like to run. I usually run twice a day.

Older adolescent girls most often conduct regimented exercises aimed at weight loss and body sculpting in gyms, sometimes alongside adult family members such as their mothers. It is meaningful that "joining in" with women's ongoing efforts in gyms to "discipline" their bodies can become an adolescent "rite of passage."

Above, Brady emphasizes the "tight, tight jeans and low-cut shirts... showing the stomach... and trying to show off the figure." Fashionable clothing styles continue to function as modern sexualized girdles during late adolescence. Such clothing is only available in small sizes, "I think one of the things about shopping that's making me feel fat is that clothes aren't designed for people who aren't stick thin. It's not right, but people buy into it" (Brady). Roxas, a 16-year-old girl of Caribbean-Canadian heritage and a working class family, similarly, describes,

> And they have all those stores and their mannequins are like all skinny, and you're like, um, this outfit doesn't fit me, why don't they have it in a size bigger? Why?? I'm forced to wear stuff that does not look good on me because the stores don't sell my size! Why?? Life hates me!

Other girls, like Hazel, simply have to shop in the boys' section: "But for me I've always been like, I'm gonna go shop in the boys' section, you know?" Not fitting modern-era fashionable clothing, therefore, sometimes creates a group of "othered" girls who do not fit into fashionable clothing, and who are more likely to receive labels such as "manly" and pay a cost in popularity. Thus it is understandable that the availability of only small-size clothing in fashionable stores creates for many girls a pressure to lose weight: "If I lose 10 pounds I could fit into the bathing suit that I want and I am pissed at the company that makes them" (Sarah). The fear of not fitting into the "in" clothes preoccupies girls in late adolescence. Jackie, for example, shares her concerns about what prom dress she will fit into 2 years from the time of her interview:

> Like you know, all the girls go like this. We all, like, 'I'm scared I won't fit into a prom dress and I'm only in Grade 10.' I'm going to be in Grade 12 in two years and I'm already worried.

Clothing therefore comprises a Physical Corset in the lives of older adolescent girls. Girls often comment about the baggy and comfortable clothing worn by boys.

Reinforcing their constriction in space is a conviction held by all girls interviewed in late adolescence that they cannot be larger than the boys they date. Girls hold this view even if their narratives include critical comments regarding the treatment of women's bodies by society and the media. For example, Bronwen, who is an insightful social critic, still comments, "I don't want the guy to be smaller than me. It's just kind of funny." Sarah, similarly, explains,

> I don't like a guy shorter than me. I like him taller and somewhat built. I think it's weird to be with a guy who is really thin, 'cause when you're together you're like, 'oh, this guy's smaller than me. Weird.'

Girls in late adolescence continue to draw and describe ideal girls as being considerably smaller than themselves and the ideal boys. Altogether then, girls in late adolescence most often experience constriction in the physical space that they may occupy; they also commonly do not engage physically with the world, unless these activities aim at body shape alteration.

Already struggling to inhabit confined bodies, girls in late adolescence, similar to early adolescence, face incessant exposure to a second type of Physical Corset: challenges to Safety for the Body Territory. Sexuality being a dimension of the lived experience of girls in late adolescence, girls from all walks of life describe having been exposed to some form of violation of their bodies, ranging from sexual harassment to rape. Sexual harassment is a daily reality in the lives of girls in late adolescence,

> In school like everyone, your friends would just walk up and slap your butt. To me it's like touching my boobs. I cannot stand when people touch my butt. If someone comes up and like gives me a whack on the butt I totally flip out at them. (Brady)

A new phenomenon in late adolescence is sexual harassment by older men, specifically adult men preying on adolescent girls. Bronwen describes her experience while working in a restaurant:

> This old man the other day, who like came up and talked to me and was telling me how hot I was and I was like, that's not comfortable, I find that really disgusting. This guy who came into the restaurant the other day and you kind of get this idea that someone is checking you out and it was horrible. This guy was married and I can totally tell that like, I am a teenager, I am in high school, you have a wife, do not do this. And my [same age] co-worker said that men come

with their families, but come out afterwards as their families are leaving and they will want to talk and they will tip like huge amounts of money and she is like, 'It's disgusting. Oh, it's scary, it's kind of like creepy'—because it feels like being violated... Like one person made a comment that I have a nice butt. Never mind people looking at it, but making a comment about it.

Brady aims to keep herself safe in the sexual domain—"I want to be safe, a guy could go and bugger off after he done something with a girl and then a girl is stuck with a kid. I am not into this stuff now." Importantly, her boyfriend is respectful of her wishes. However, one can see how experiences within a rape culture, nonetheless, encroach on her safety. For example, the industry of recruiting adolescent girls for modeling jobs is rife with sexual exploitation and violations. During the time of this study, Brady is approached by a "representative" of a modeling agency in a manner that raises questions about safety. Wisely, she rejects his offer.

I really wanted to be a model and so I went for a modeling search and they tell you if they want you or not and I didn't get picked. But afterwards, I was walking and this guy had come up to me and he was actually this guy from modeling for like places around the world and he told me that I actually had a gorgeous body and that he could really use me to go around the world and do modeling shoots. So he gave me a bunch of numbers to call to get hooked up but I didn't want to continue with it because I think I'm only a teenager and they'd only pay for me, *they wouldn't pay for my mom*. And I don't think I'm ready to go to some country by myself and I will miss three months worth of school. So I didn't take that option. But yeah, he was like telling me how gorgeous my body was and how I could really be a good model.

Still aiming to keep herself safe, Brady further endures a frightening experience of being accosted by several drunken young men, while walking home from a bar in her neighborhood with her boyfriend and his friends. As her boyfriend and his friends try to protect her, they get attacked and injured by the drunken men. As Brady describes, "They were trying to chase me. They could have hijacked me and rape me. It now scares me when I am walking home alone."

Living in a culture that does not protect girls and women from sexual violations, girls in older adolescence are often deeply affected by, yet commonly silenced about, sexual harassment. Notice in the next narrative the way in which Laya's experiences of sexual harassment during high school were shrouded in silence. Laya is a White woman in her middle 20s from a middle-class background. In a culture that rarely problematizes sexual harassment, it is not surprising that Laya prefaces this description by stating that she was never violated,

> *You know I was never really violated. I was never sexually abused*... [during high school] Like I'd be on the bus going to school and sitting across from a guy and he'd make really disgusting comments... that really made me feel very insecure and like being paralyzed by that and then never telling anybody about it until like years later but like being ashamed of it. Or like being in a streetcar and having a guy, you know, grab my ass and not doing anything about it. And walking to school like totally upset and distraught and never telling anybody or having a guy in a McDonald's [expose himself] and never addressing those kinds of things with men. Those things were hard. They were traumatic, shocking, uncomfortable, a lot of pain and sadness... I didn't have the skills or the tools to be able to deal with it.

Unless violence against women is embraced as an important social agenda, silenced experiences of sexual harassment will continue to rob girls of safety in their social environment.

Most girls during older adolescence are involved in sexual activities. We hear repeatedly about cases of sexual assault. However, most commonly, adolescent girls do not name non-consensual sexual experiences as assault. Such naming is predicated on the social sanctioning of girls' desire and challenging violence against women. For example, 15-year-old Nancy, a White girl of a working class and urban background, has her first intercourse with a university athlete who is more than 5 years her senior: "He wanted and I don't say no, I just think no." Not only is there no active consent but also the age of consent for intercourse in Canada has been raised from 14 to 16 to protect adolescent girls. As a result, a sexual act between a 15-year-old girl and a man more than 5 years her senior is legally defined as rape. Aware of the legal risk he took, the man quickly leaves the scene when a police cruiser drives by. Lacking adequate protection during intercourse, he guides Nancy to the local hospital the following day to seek, on her own, the morning after pill. "I was scared. He told me about it. But they gave it to me." However, her exposure to sexual violations continues. At the age of 17, she moves out of her family home and, seeking affordable accommodation while holding a service job, she shares a place with two young men where she has to constantly defend herself from sexual violations:

> I have to wear pants at home because they are creepy... I found this guy in my room trying to make out... And they make comments or

> touch me, like grabbing and kissing. Like usually I can handle it. But sometimes I don't get much sleep.

Girls exposed to sexual violations experience disruption in the ways they inhabit their bodies, including poor body esteem, disordered eating, substance use/abuse, and other challenges, such as school truancy or self-harm. As the next chapter indicates, embodied journeys of healing from sexual trauma are demanding and lengthy. The challenges to body ownership faced by girls who have experienced violence not only encumber their embodied journeys, but also conveys to them their disenfranchised social status as girls.

Considering the pressures confronting girls in late adolescence in terms of appearance, confinement to size and movement, and violations to ownership of the body territory, it is not surprising that they also face many Corsets toward Care of the Body, the third dimension of Physical Freedom. Girls in late adolescence are clear about prioritizing appearance over health: "Definitely appearance is more important than health. I think like it shouldn't matter, but it does, no way avoiding it" (Sarah); "Appearance is more important because your health usually evens itself out at this age" (Bronwen). In line with such thinking, girls engage in the pursuit of idealized appearance characteristics even at the cost of their physical and mental well-being. The common pursuit of weight loss can exert a significant toll on girls in late adolescence. All girls interviewed describe either their own struggles with disordered eating patterns and weight fluctuations or having friends with eating disorders. While being at the lower end of the average range on BMI charts for her height and age, Bronwen, for example, insightfully describes the toll taken in establishing an even lower target weight:

> If I could lose 10 more pounds. It's exhausting—like I weigh myself every week. If I go up one pound one week, then that sucks, and I feel bad because why am I doing this to myself. There are the moments when I say to myself, 'you can't go down 10 pounds.' And it's tiring… but at the same time it's there all the time. I spend so much energy on that and I know that it's totally wasted. If I did not spend energy on weight loss, I could enjoy my activities and food so much more. Before, I barely ate anything for like a month and I lost 20 pounds, but it was horrible because I was starving all the time. But since then my weight has gone up and down. I am like, why can't I get down again in weight. That's why I get really hard on myself. I am so obsessive. I count calories and pack my food. But then like I eat 10 cookies and I feel crappy.

Most girls in late adolescence similarly describe the effects of yo-yo dieting and their struggle with weight fluctuations. Other body alterations may exert a similar toll on health. Sarah, for example, has continued to engage in piercings, some of which have caused her significant ongoing pain and discomfort:

> The piercing in my septum was so painful. It was tough. I went through so much pain, and when you tuck it up in your nose it hurt so bad. I tried for a while, I cried, but I had to take it out.

Girls also commonly describe having hair removed from their bodies, including pubic hair: "Shave everything but head; arms, legs, crotch, everything for sure" (Sarah). Health professionals have expressed concerns regarding the health consequences of, especially pubic, hair removal (Desruelles, Cunningham, & Dubois, 2013). Hair dying or straightening can also affect hair health: "My hair already wrecked 'cause I straighten it everyday. It's half dead" (Brady).

Important decisions about body alterations are made without the support of trusted adults, either personal relations or professionals. For example, Bronwen who struggles with her weight, shares how useful such information could have been for her:

> I don't think you get enough education, like, for me even the whole weight factor. Like I haven't had information about what my body needs when I exercise. Like my running coach, she is a teacher and she has done everything in sports, and she doesn't really talk about it at all. I think that coaches worry that if you do talk about that kind of thing that people will become obsessed with it, but they don't realize the fact that we already are obsessed with it. It's nice for me to hear [from interviewer] that all the girls struggle with that. I think for me it would be important to hear that everything turns out okay and that even if you are going through a rough time it does get better.

As important as interventions could be in supporting girls in late adolescence, such interventions need to counteract oppressive social conditions rather than collude with them (Piran, 1999, 2001, 2010, 2015). Sarah, for example, describes taking a health course that focused exclusively on healthy eating and exercise:

> The course wanted you to watch what you ate and exercise and instructed to do this and this to get to a goal. It was saying, like record all your foods and calories, and this is healthy and this isn't healthy. I could not tolerate that… Being told what you're supposed to do and what you're supposed to look like, and different influences

> and stuff. I want that course to no longer be a course... I was so stressed in that course, I hated it.

Sarah has already experienced, in early adolescence, being put on a diet against her will, only to regain the weight quickly following the cessation of the diet. Her goal in late adolescence is to live in her body without such regimens while also being aware of general health principles, "like why worry, just, like, as long as you know what you should do to be healthy, that's all that matters." The course she took replicated the social obsession with body modification, and therefore disrupted body acceptance and attunement—important aspects of compassionate self-care. Interventions aimed at supporting girls in late adolescence should be anchored in these girls' experiences, supporting their liberation from oppressive social pressures regarding body alterations.

Sexuality comprises a second domain of compromised Care of the Body. Girls and women face many challenges with respect to the care of their bodies in the sexual arena. This in large part, as described above, is due to living in a coercive rape culture, experiencing sexual violations, lacking validation of their desires, and not receiving systemic social support to counteract these adverse social conditions. Most girls' narratives include descriptions of teen pregnancies during high school:

> There are a couple of girls that are 15 at the school and they're like six months pregnant. I have a friend who is 15 and she just found out she was pregnant, so she's going to keep the kid. A lot of girls are getting pregnant now. (Brady)

Girls are sometimes denied access to birth control pills and/or devices. Nancy, for example, asks to have access to birth control pills, but her mother refuses. Following her rape experience, it is she who disseminates information to her peers—information the hospital wants to be disseminated, but not her school.

> She said that, no, she wouldn't put me on the pill because I'm too young. But I actually got a pretty bad scare. I went to the hospital and they gave me like the day-after pill for free. So it was, 'oh God'... I can't even visit my doctor because I don't trust him. In our school, we get a lecture from a priest and we have a nun for a counselor, so... My friend just told me, 'I had sex and it was totally unprotected.' When I went to the hospital, they were just like, 'yeah, a lot of girls your age don't really know about the day-after pill, so it's good that you know about it and you should inform your friends.' So I totally did. I'm just like, 'hey guess what I found out, the day-after.'

Health professionals can make a big difference by supporting girls in the sexual domain. Following the support she received at the hospital, which was located in a large urban center, Nancy connects with a new family doctor whom she trusts and with whom she can confide regarding challenges in the sexual domain. Yet, some health professionals continue to operate in a way that does not attend to the complexities and challenges of girls in late adolescence. For example, while Jackie's family doctor does conduct a pregnancy test, he does not inquire about her sexual assault at the age of 14, advise her about contraceptives, inform her about Pap smears and HPV vaccines, or book follow-up appointments. "He [family doctor] did not suggest any contraceptives, and he did not book any follow-up appointments. He said that this was a confidential situation so he didn't want to ask a lot of questions."

However, health professionals can address topics that may otherwise be seen as taboo. Hazel is anxious about the future pain she will experience with sexual intercourse, as she is planning to marry a man; however, this is not an acceptable topic of discussion within her family—"it's one of those things that's very taboo"—so she is not sure where to turn to receive the relevant information. Most girls in late adolescence are active sexually, though frequently in an unfavorable social context. It is vital that they be provided with support in safely navigating this phase while retraining a sense of joy and agency in their bodies. Currently, girls' narratives indicate that they receive little such support.

Freedom of Desire, the fourth dimension of Physical Freedom, is also deeply disrupted in late adolescence. Quite uniformly, girls in late adolescence describe their recognition of appetite as a risky bodily desire that could fail them—not only during late adolescence but also throughout their adult journey. This is a heavy thing for girls to consider at this phase of development. Such recognition relates to idealized representations of women in the media, the proliferation and "normalization" of the diet and body-sculpting industries, and the dichotomous presentation of food (as good vs. bad). In addition, girls in late adolescence often hear testimonies and warnings from adult women about how their own adolescent thinness was followed by weight gain throughout adulthood. Such testimonies always imply a sense of longing and loss, though not all adult women are necessarily weight obsessed. Girls are, therefore, invited into the lifelong culture of "watch what you eat," as well as into women's exercise regimens aimed at body repair.

Exercise routines like Body Attack and harsh references to one's body made by adult women and adolescent girls—"personally it's the thighs and hips that kill me; need to slice them"—hardly allow for a positive connection to appetite. Older adolescents' descriptions of eating are most often joyless, and the experience of appetite is confounded by themes of guilt, control, discipline, containment, and the short- and long-term risk of weight gain. Times of constrained eating reflect being "good," while times of subjectively felt uncontrolled eating reflect being "bad." Among these dichotomous experiences, girls have rare and temporary glimpses of eating in response to internal cues. According to Bronwen,

> I really like sugary stuff. So, I mean, I'll bake stuff and eat a lot, but my body does not like that. I feel gross. I go through those stupid diet things. I want to change my build. So that's a bit of a pain. I count calories, but then I eat like 10 cookies, so I am one of those health people who binges.

Social location can significantly influence the now normative struggle with appetite. In middle-class homes, girls like Bronwen are able to exert control over the types of food they choose to eat, "If I am starting and I eat fruits and vegetables then that's fine for a snack." In contrast, Kelly, who has restricted food options at home, uses ice cubes to control her weight:

> We eat pasta. Whenever we do have to have a hamburger we go to Wendy's 'cause Wendy's big hamburger is half of a McDonald's Big Mac [in terms of] calories... My mother says, 'at least I have food to eat, count your blessings'... [To control weight] I love ice water. I have this odd obsession with ice cubes. So I put four or five ice cubes into a tall glass of water rand then I keep refilling it and then once the ice cubes get really small I eat them. I drink like five tall glasses.

Costlier modes of eating, such as a focus on fruits, vegetables, or lean proteins, put greater pressure on girls trying to manage their appetites where not much choice is available. Financial standing can further intersect with traditions of food preparations. For Hazel, family meals include varied sources of grain and some meat: "We eat bread in every meal. Like, pita bread, crusty bread, with sharba (soup). We eat couscous. Everything we have has tomato base. And spaghetti stuff. Fat meat like lamb." Struggling with body weight and shape, Hazel ultimately emphasizes the value of embracing her family foods and family gatherings during meals.

The use of different substances to curb appetite also starts during late adolescence. Jackie, for example, as described at the beginning of the chapter, uses appetite-suppressant pills and smokes cigarettes. Research studies indeed indicate an association between weight-controlling behaviors, in particular the use of diet pills or purging, and engagement in smoking, as well as the consumption of other substances such as alcohol and marijuana (e.g., Neumark-Sztainer, Story, Dixon, & Murray, 1998). Further, hunger-related food restriction can in turn lead to heavier alcohol consumption (e.g., Piran & Robinson, 2006).

Sexual desire is as corseted as appetite among older adolescents. It is important to highlight that girls' descriptions of their common engagement in sexual activities often include no explication of their own wishes or preferences. Rather, girls describe guys' desires, wishes for "action," and coercive pressures. Further, girls sometimes describe social reasons for sexual engagement, such as, getting attention and avoiding "being dumped." Jackie describes girls' sexual engagement as follows: "Guys are way more into that action. Like, I was more, like, I didn't care, like a lot of girls are like that. Like, not excited or looking forward to it at all. Things just happen." Bronwen concurs, "I think in general it's seen as the guy who makes more decision and his motivation is to get some action and sex is kind of cool." Nancy goes on to describe,

> Like if a guy wants to do something and I don't I would just be like actually, 'what do I have to lose' type thing. Yeah, he is just like, 'yeah, I would like to make out,' and I'm just like, just go with the flow you know. But my body is like 'oh damn.'

Learned values of a rape culture perpetuate girls' violations. Not in their own schools, social environments, the media, occupational sites, or even the political arena do girls in late adolescence witness contrasting values.

Social fears, within the context of gender inequity, further compel girls to comply with sexual acts initiated by boys or men. Jackie describes how girls who are "easy" get attention from guys, "I think 'cause, it's more of an attention thing. Where these girls are like, 'I get more attention from guys than you do.'" Bronwen details the fear of rejection that comes from refusing to engage sexually: "The motive is to be accepted. To say 'no,' you have to be pretty secure in yourself and in that the guy's not going to dump you. Because you could say 'yes' out of fear. The fear of being alone."

Heteronormative beliefs disrupt the connection to desire for girls who question their sexual orientation during late adolescence. They describe situations where friends who are boys have come out in school and publicly identified themselves as being gay. In contrast, older adolescent girls we interview do not describe experiencing the same openness in relation to girls' sexuality. As Sarah describes,

> I have so many gay friends. Everyone knows they are gay. I do have one friend who is a lesbian, but she's not a close friend. But if you know that I'm straight and you decide to hit on me, then I'm uncomfortable.

Both younger and older adult women that we interview, who describe their sexual orientation as "lesbian," "bi-sexual," or "slightly trans lesbian," identify late adolescence as a time of struggle for them, as is detailed in the next chapter on adult women.

It is important to highlight that we do hear of a few situations where girls describe experiencing a connection to desire. Brady, for example, who receives at home strong encouragement and education regarding how to stay safe in the dating scene, is involved in an ongoing relationship with a respectful partner who lets her guide the nature of acceptable sexual activities. At age 16, she mentions that, "girls and boys can have sexual feelings. It's about the same. It works both ways."

Connection to desire post-violation is particularly challenging. For Jackie, continued connection to the remembered bodily joy of kissing keeps her connected to desire even after her sexual assault: "Yeah, that's one thing, I always get butterflies. It doesn't matter like how long I've been dating a guy. It doesn't matter how many times I've kissed him. I always get butterflies." When Andrea, a middle-aged White woman, reflects on her experience of being raped at the age of 15, she highlights how following the rape she was determined to stay connected to her desire: "If I never trusted anyone again... he would have won, and I didn't want to let anyone take that away from me."

Indeed, Freedom of Desire, a key dimension of Physical Freedom, is centrally related to experiences of embodied comfort, joy, and agency in engaging with the world, as well as to enhanced internal attunement. Social experiences during late adolescence tightly corset both appetite and sexual desire, situating them as areas of struggle as girls transition into adulthood.

To summarize, physical corsets encountered by girls in late adolescence reflect the proximity of this phase to young adulthood. Facing accentuated barriers to joyful physical engagements, aiming to fit restrictive fashionable clothing, and trying to meet the expectation that they occupy small physical spaces as "young women," girls are struggling with their bodies. Further, owning "young women's" bodies and commonly engaging in sexual activities in cultural contexts that do not maintain a firm stance against violence against women, girls face ongoing breaches to their safety and well-being; these experiences also convey to girls their disenfranchised status in the culture at large.

ALTERED EMBODIMENT: THE GOAL OF FITTING MENTAL MOLDS

> My biggest, the love of my life is probably *body modification*. I am in love with it to the max... I dye my hair every three days. It takes about 20 minutes. I like my makeup shimmery, and I wear highlighter under my eyebrows and lots of mascara, foundation, and blush.

> The foundation is to cover up because I hate how my face is uneven. I put mascara on and then separate the eyelashes with a pin… It takes about 45 minutes. *I will not let people see me without makeup on*, at least I have to have mascara on or it looks pretty bad… But I love playing soccer with the guys and when you are thinking of your next move you're not thinking of the way you look, and that's where my *carelessness* started. I used to walk after the game with baggy jeans or sweat pants. I would have loved to play more but there were no more spots for me on the boys' team. I tackled boys and they were like, 'what a *bitch*.' And my coach was joking, 'Oh, yeah, she is probably a *lesbian*'… For a girl to be as open [about sexuality] as a guy, I don't know, it might just be, well, I wouldn't say '*rude*,' it'd just be really *weird*. I don't really give it much thought. If it happens, it happens. It's kinda something *for him*. I did get called a *slut*, just because [guy's name] was mad at me about something.

This collection of narratives by Sarah at age 16 reflects the impact of varied social discourses on her embodied experiences. Sarah is White and from a middle-class background. On the one hand, she describes inhabiting her body as an object, in line with the Body as an Object of Gaze discourse, and also mentions deficiencies in her appearance that require alterations, which is in line with the Female Body as Deficient discourse. Importantly, similar to most girls in late adolescence, she describes having a *dependence* on body alterations, such that she would not be seen in the public sphere without makeup—a new phenomenon in late adolescence. It is this set of Appearance-related Discourses, under the Body as a Deficient Object cluster (see Table 1.2), that informs her self-criticism of being "careless" and "lazy," rather than "carefree" or "comfortable," when she (rarely) appears in public unaltered.

On the other hand, Sarah has a temporary opportunity to play on a boys' soccer team. Her joyful immersion in playing soccer shifts her experience, temporarily, from that of a deficient object of gaze to that of a competent agent, acting powerfully in the world. Despite her love of body modifications, the subjective immersion in action that comes from playing soccer provides her with freedom from her objectified position and makes her "careless." At the same time, acting with agency and power contradicts specific femininity Comportment-related Discourses of the Woman as Docile cluster, specifically: Engagement in "Feminine" Activities, and Woman as Submissive/Demure (see Table 1.2). For these deviations from constraining social expectations, she receives the labels of bitch and lesbian—penalizing labels aimed at restoring the oppressive social status quo. Similarly, regarding the discourse of Woman as Desired but Desireless, which sanctions girls' (and women's) availability as sexual objects for boys (and men) yet expects them to deny and contain their own—often vilified—desire, Sarah, like many girls, receives the arbitrary slut label and feels that, for girls, it is "rude" to be as open about sexuality in the way that boys are. Sexual things just "happen" to girls in late adolescence.

During late adolescence, the Body as an Object of Gaze discourse continues to exert a powerful effect on shaping girls' embodied experiences. In particular, in late adolescence, the intense objectification of girls' bodies is *suffused with their sexualization*. Various teen magazines, music videos, and porn sites are just some of the media outlets that girls in late adolescence refer to when harshly critiquing their own bodies.

> I think that body image is affected a lot by the media, and so magazines, even music videos, lyrics in songs. That is a huge contribution to negative self-image. You're never really going to measure up to those ideal standards that are set out by the media, and so it can be a little bit discouraging at times. Well I think even for girls the magazines where they're showing all the models that are really, really thin and full-breasted, the makeup, and those types of things. The music videos are unbelievably sexist, calling girls sluts. (Ashley)

> All the pressure to look like the magazine models… You should see the subliminal message in the media. Like all the guys had boners. And then there was like women at their feet, and women in vulnerable positions. What is this? Like that new show by the Pussycat Dolls, *Girlicious*… How low of a self-image you have to have to actually try out for something like that? Burlesque dancers with some talent. (Hazel)

Fifteen-year-old Ashley, of African-Canadian heritage, and 16-year-old Hazel, of Middle Eastern heritage, are active social critics, here addressing both the objectification and sexualization of girls and women.

The sexualized objectification that takes place during late adolescence also impacts fear and discomfort about being seen during sexual activities. Bronwen explains, "I would be scared of being judged, first, by society, and second, about how good I was by the boy… and you need to feel comfortable with your own body, knowing that they'll see your *flaws*." Jackie describes being stunned when the boy who assaulted her also labeled her fat, both to her face and on social media: "I felt like he accepted me for me. But it turns out… he has called me fat after the fact." Sarah too describes this struggle, feeling that alcohol relieves some of the tension around appearance evaluation:

> The magazines portray like the perfect woman. Top heavy. Skinny. Have the perfect stomach, the perfect legs, stuff like that. I try not to let that get to me too much. I would be more comfortable if I lost 10

> pounds... If a guy were to say like, you're fat and ugly, it would get to me that much worse, because knowing that you're not getting it [approval] from whom you want to get it... When I drink [alcohol] I'm in a big comfort zone. I don't care about what I look like and how everything is. I just really don't care.

Kelly, similarly, relays her concerns about being with her boyfriend, saying, "I'm always nervous like, I don't want you to see my tummy... I always feel like I should be covering myself up. I like to be covered." Looking into the future, Hazel, expresses concern about being with her future husband: "I am kind of worried about my weight. Hopefully my husband has never seen another woman's body before mine. Hopefully I've lost weight before I get married."

As exposure to sexualized objectification in both the media and sexual relationships increases during late adolescence, so too does the enhanced scrutiny of the body, revealing more "deficiencies" in relation to media-generated perfect bodies, and enhancing the adverse impact of the Woman's Body as Deficient discourse. Kelly conveys her incessant preoccupation with what she deems to be flaws: "I will always find flaws. It doesn't matter if I lost 30 pounds, there would always be something. I think it is normal, I mean all my sisters are the exact same way." During late adolescence in particular, we hear about two trends in relation to the Woman's Body as Deficient discourse. First, girls show a growing *dependence* on body alterations, such that appearing in the public sphere can become acceptable only in their altered forms. Second, girls start to develop a lifelong perspective in relation to the perceived deficiencies of women's bodies, expressing significant worry not only about their current deficiencies but also about those that they expect will accrue throughout their body journeys.

First, as the incessant preoccupation with, and skillful alteration of, bodily deficiencies becomes the new norm in inhabiting one's body, appearing unaltered in public thus becomes a shameful, and even phobic experience to be avoided. Girls in late adolescence repeatedly share their fears of being found out as "ugly" if exposed unaltered in public. Bronwen's description about needing to appear only altered in public, just like Jackie and Sarah's narratives earlier in this chapter, is typical for girls in late adolescence:

> I put on makeup and having my hair look good and accessories. I feel like, if I don't have any makeup on I'm not pretty and I feel like other people will think that too. So it's kind of like I'm hiding something from people. Like, you know, I don't really want everyone to see me without makeup because they are going to realize that I'm not that pretty.

Girls view appearing unaltered in public not only as shameful and a great social risk but also as indicative of character flaws, such as "carelessness" or "laziness." The longer the disciplined performance of body alterations continues, the more aversive appearing unaltered in public may become. The critical role of time-consuming and, often, costly body alterations to women's participation in the public sphere does not escape the eyes of older adolescents.

Second, as girls in late adolescence engage in body modifications, they also consider the deficiencies they will accrue throughout their body journeys. Adult women in their lives, as well as the media, commonly refer to the "perfect body," or to appearance and looks that women held as older adolescents or young adults and "lost" due to pregnancies, aging, illness, or other reasons. Women and the media may also refer to body alterations (including plastic surgery procedures) that support a promised "unchanged" appearance throughout this journey. It is not unusual for adult women to tell their body stories to girls, cautioning them to make choices in their lives that will prevent adverse age-related changes. It is disconcerting to read the degree of concern girls in late adolescence convey regarding anticipated changes to their bodies:

> This woman who exercises in my club, you can see her muscles visually. But she has stretch marks all over her stomach and she was showing them to me, and then, she's like, 'Yeah, that's what having kids does to you.' I thought not all ladies got stretch marks. I don't want to get stretch marks. I imagine when the time comes I will have kids regardless, but right now I am just like I don't want to have kids because of that. I know it's horrible. I can handle being pregnant; it's just the after effects. I also don't want to gain weight. I have that fear of being past my prime. I feel like I am good in my body right now, despite the fact that I want to lose 15 pounds. I am scared of not being attractive anymore. (Bronwen)

> My family gets big veins in their legs like my mom and grandmother. So that has always been a fear my sister and I have. So [sister] with her pregnancy is the first to get them on her legs and they are not very nice looking. I cross my legs a lot and I am trying not to do that anymore but I notice I am getting one on my leg. So I am trying to do whatever I can do. Like apple vinegar oil you rub it in. This is one thing I am nervous about the future. Also, my mother used to be really tiny and having six children, she could not get the weight off. It just makes me nervous about having kids. She said don't do what I did, take care of yourself. (Kelly)

Girls in late adolescence inhabiting young women's bodies often fear that they are following a trajectory in their body journeys where they are bound to incur more losses than joyful and functional experiences. Strikingly, these body losses figure centrally in girls' responses to our inquiries regarding their thoughts about the future.

Yet, on a positive note, we also hear in late adolescence the beginnings of critical commentary targeting extreme body modifications—commentary not heard during early adolescence. Fifteen-year-old Jessica, a White girl from a working class family, articulates her criticism of media expectations:

> I think that girls think that they should be like really skinny, and have like figures, and big boobs that fit with the supermodel look, which I don't think is right. They have to be perfect, like Barbie. They have to have the big-volume hair and the sunglasses and look like they're superstars when they're not. It's like, we think that we have nothing else in life. Like I think they all look sick and disgusting. Like look at *America's Top Model*, and they're all like anorexic little freak people. Like, they're all like so skinny, they look like you can snap them in half. Wearing mini skirts and high heels. I mean when do you ever see a supermodel not wearing high heels. I saw a picture of Fergie the other day and she was running in high heels with a jogging suit on! And I was like, 'How's that supposed to work?? I hope you trip and break your neck!'

Jessica makes a similar critical commentary about the ideal girl while drawing her:

> She's going to have a stick for a body, because girls are generally like supposed to be really skinny and kind of plasticy. And I'm making her blonde. That's the stereotype. And like straight kinda fake hair. I get told I should straighten my hair so many times a day. Just 'cause it gets in people's way. She's going to have really big eyes, 'cause her head's so small, shrunken from all her dieting. She's wearing like a lot of makeup, like a mask. She's not wearing very much. She can wear like a coconut bra. And like a little grass skirt. She'd probably be like wearing high heels to make herself taller. Just changing everything natural about you. Make them something they are not. It's kind of a message from the media but like also from people in everyday life. Like, I don't get that message, it's good to know you have people who don't think that you should change everything about you because that message is kind of that girls are never good enough and that girls constantly have to change themselves. I also hardly watch TV anymore. I don't really want to be like that 'cause they aren't happy. 'Cause if you're changing everything about

yourself, it's probably hard to be happy, 'cause you've got really nothing to work with.

Jessica, like few other girls, problematizes living in 'beautified' bodies, suggesting the impossibility of happiness among individuals who "change everything" about themselves, leaving them "nothing to work with." Like Jessica's, other girls' critical voices typically remain silent and are not validated or amplified in their social environments. They can, however, provide a basis for critical dialogues among peers regarding restrictive Appearance-related Discourses, and for setting alternative appearance norms.

Beyond appearance, the four Comportment-related Discourses of femininity, grouped under The Woman as Docile discourse cluster (see Table 1.2), continue to exert a corseting impact on the embodied lives of girls in late adolescence. During this time, the first Comportment-related Discourse, Engagement in "Feminine" Activities, shapes not only girls' daily activities but also their vocational plans, and considerations of their roles at home. In terms of shaping daily activities, body alterations and shopping—both aimed at appearance enhancement—are time-consuming activities in the lives of many girls in late adolescence. Shopping is sometimes constructed even as a *skill*, as Brady describes, "you go shopping and you have all these clothes in the morning, and you got to decide which outfit you want to wear for that day. Like being like a model-type thing." Girls whose families struggle financially might spend some time in malls, including with friends, but do not engage in as much shopping. Several girls describe shopping as a mood enhancer, similar to adult women's "shopping therapy": "Me and my friends love shopping. Like when I have the money, I spend it, which is a problem. I'm so happy when I shop. I love shopping. Like, shopping is my hobby. It's my comfort zone" (Sarah). Shopping is also a social activity in late adolescence, even for girls who, like Bronwen, resisted it throughout early adolescence: "It's changed. Now I like shopping. I like shopping with my friends. It's just fun to hang out and stuff like that." Sometimes shopping also provides bonding time between mothers and daughters—"Me and my mom we like totally go nuts in [lingerie store]. We get like three [bras] for 30 and we go insane" (Sarah).

Among older adolescents, engagement in feminine activities extends beyond the choice of sedentary activities and shopping to decisions girls are starting to make about lifelong engagements in tasks culturally delegated to women, both vocationally and in the domestic sphere. For example, girls in late adolescence are called, at times, to perform household duties, such as taking care of siblings or cooking for others—especially when their mothers are unavailable to perform such tasks. Being the primary target of such requests, unlike male members of the family, raises questions for girls regarding household chores and their designation as "feminine activities." Sarah shares, "My father goes, 'Sarah, make dinner, make dinner.' I'm like, he sits, watches TV, and does his own thing"; similarly, Hazel says, "My mom has been so busy, so my father goes, 'Hazel, do the dishes.' God! I just did the dishes. My brothers are playing video games." This role assignment often sparks thoughts among girls in late adolescence regarding the choices they will make in their own adult relationships. They produce responses all the way from full acceptance of gender inequity in the distribution of household activities—"Being around my family and watching TV, it seems mostly women doing those roles and men are not. It fits because girls are actually good at cleaning and guys are more lazy and don't want to clean" (Brady)—to feeling clarity about resisting such distribution—"I feel more confident in myself, and I am not having anyone else's expectations on me, so I step out of the parenting and caretaking role at home. I make sure I am not weighed down by these expectations" (Bronwen).

By the same token, when we examine the vocational plans of older adolescents, they describe seeking careers in education (teachers, teaching assistants, day-care workers, early childhood educators), helping professions (nurses, counselors), or communication. None of the girls mention careers in the sciences, technology, engineering, or math—vocations where women tend to earn more than they earn in most other sectors of the workforce (Hill, Corbett, & St. Rose, 2010). Some girls are strongly encouraged by their parents to prioritize their education and postpone decisions about personal relationships until after completion of at least their undergraduate education. As Hazel describes, "My plan is to go to university and study communications. My parents do not want me to take a gap year. They want me to go directly to university, and have it done with before I do anything else." Others, like Kelly, are discouraged from pursuing extensive higher education and encouraged to prioritize starting a family:

> My mom says [boyfriend] is making enough money; you can stay home with the kids and forget about your job. I want to go to university or college. I wanted to be a teacher for the longest time, but [family members] are trying to push me away from it because they know that I want to have a family. So I have decided to study to be an assistant.

Altogether, in relation to engagement in feminine activities, girls describe, to different degrees, continued acculturation pressures perpetuating inequitable participation in activities in both the private and public spheres.

The greater restrictive power of the Woman as Submissive/Demure discourse, the second discourse of the Woman as Docile cluster, during late adolescence relates specifically to the proximity of this developmental phase to adulthood. Girls in late adolescence perceive that as young women they are granted less freedom to be "disruptive" toward social structures of power when compared with earlier phases of girlhood. Bronwen describes this poignantly:

> I think to a certain extent, girls aren't supposed to be, like, really, like, in control, and, really, like too great. I think it actually applies more to adults [adult women], like, for a woman to be the boss or whatever, or even a political figure or something like that, there's something that people don't like about it. And I think that does filter down to teenagers, it affects teenagers. Like, for me personally, like I think it's great when girls are, you know, able to do that kind of thing, but, but, it's hard.

Bronwen's observations are apt; this chapter is written following the 2016 US Presidential election, which saw the defeat of a highly qualified woman candidate. It is not only the case in the United States but also in other Western countries that a woman head-of-state has never been elected. In 150 years as an independent nation, Canada has had only one woman prime minister, and for a period of just over 4 months. In addition to this, research studies consistently describe the penalties women receive for acting in ways that deviate from gendered expectations of being nice, submissive, selfless, and nurturing of others. Assertive and competitive women are viewed as aggressive or "too masculine," and are not liked in terms of social ratings (Heilman & Okimoto, 2007; Rudman, Moss-Racusin, Phelan, & Nauts, 2012). Similar backlash exists in relation to countering racial stereotypes (Phelan & Rudman, 2010).

Bronwen highlights the adverse impact that the dislike of women in power has, as she prepares for her transition into womanhood. She similarly describes the negative effect of oppressive "feminine" expectations, such as: "niceness," "submissiveness," and "being demure."

> There is that kind of thing for girls to be really *nice*. It makes me feel *weak*. Like if you're *competitive* you are being *mean* to other people. I'm always aware of the fact that there is a possibility that I am *intruding* on other people, like by being, you know, more *intelligent* or whatever than other people, that I am being, not *mean* necessarily, but like I feel I am taking away from others, kind of thing. It's almost like you're being a *bitch* if you are really *competitive*. I think it's something that happens in our society. *It affects girls' achievement. I think it definitely is an inhibitor for girls.*

Lacking relational forums that invite dialogues about such oppressive gender stereotypes, as well as their impact on the roles girls feel they can hold with power, agency and assertiveness, older adolescent girls like Bronwen "tone down" their way of being in the world—and with that, their dreams, hopes, and ambitions. While we do not continue to interview Bronwen beyond late adolescence, she does share some of the ways in which she "tones down" her power in the world. Self-identified as a feminist in early adolescence, she shifts away from this identity in late adolescence, stating, "I support equalism because feminism is an excuse for men bashing, which I am 100% against. I do not condone that and I don't hate guys. This does put a bad rap on feminism." She further puts a heavy emphasis on daily adherence to a routine of body alterations, commenting that when she draws herself and the ideal girl, "the picture of myself and the picture of the ideal girl has gotten less and less different." While she shares that by conforming to these appearance characteristics "you lose part of your power," she is pleased her alteration practices have led to her becoming more popular, and that she is no longer the "loser" she used to be.

Such struggles around voice and assertiveness, in light of the constraining discourse of Woman as Submissive/Demure, are common among girls in late adolescence. When Sarah, 16, raises her voice at home, her father tells her to "shut up and wash the dishes." Sarah, whose passionate and powerful involvement in sports is stopped against her will during late adolescence, is penalized further for this athletic passion by being labeled a bitch and a lesbian. She identifies her silencing as being related to the onset of acting without care or agency toward her body: "Calling me lesbian and not letting me play anymore with the guys, and you lose respect for yourself, and so with the guys, it doesn't matter, you want it [sex], you do it." Concurrently, she sometimes gets depressed.

Jackie observes her father's concern regarding his partner's non-demure demeanor, saying, "yeah, my dad is always worried that [girlfriend] is going to turn feminist! She is a strong-willed woman and he is scared she'll turn lesbian on him." The bitch and lesbian labels, given for acting in a non-demure way, are prevalent in older girls' narratives and, as Bronwen describes, "all girls are bitchy." Both boys and girls negatively label girls who act with assertiveness and competitiveness.

An aspect of being submissive or demure is prioritizing the care of others over self-care. Andrea, a woman in her 50s, describes the ways such learned expectations affected her during her rape when 15 years old,

> One thing I'm remembering, and this relates to being female and how most girls are taught to take care of other people before themselves. I remember when the rape was happening his [boyfriend's] sister was home and I chose not to scream because I didn't want her to see her brother doing this to me. In that moment I was worried

> about how it would affect her. So for me, it was a lesson in how much girls, how much I, put others before myself.

Clearly, the discourse of Woman as Submissive/Demure constrains girls' power and agency, and involves ongoing penalization for even slight deviations. Girls in late adolescence describe no presence of relational opportunities to examine the impact of this adverse discourse on their embodied lives and well-being.

Concurrently, the Comportment-related Discourse, entitled Woman as Desired but Desire-less, continues to exert a corseting impact during late adolescence. All girls in late adolescence endorse containing and "watching" their appetite as an aspect of being feminine—small, contained, and on display, as Brady described earlier in the chapter, "I want to try and stay skinny as long as I possibly can. I don't eat much and I'm really picky." Few girls in late adolescence, from families that struggled financially, also describe observing their mothers contain their own appetite to feed their children. Seventeen-year-old Kelly, Latina, raised by a single mother in a working class background, describes,

> My mom used to be really tiny and then have six children and she couldn't get the weight off, and soon after, my father left. She struggled with money, so she would feed us and whatever was left over she would eat herself. She was just so busy and we would just order pizza. So she hasn't been able to shake it (weight).

Containment of sexual desire while, concurrently, being the object of desire is yet another social expectation of women, expressed through the discourse of Woman as Desired but Desire-less. The vilification of girls and women's desire is a pervasive social message encountered by girls in late adolescence (as well as early adolescence) as they engage in sexual activities, most often without connection to their own desires and under coercive pressures from boys or men. The prominence of the slut label, the degrading presentation of girls' sexuality in the media, and the penalizing of girls' ownership of desire are ways through which such deprecation is communicated.

> I learned to see sex as something that stereotypically is slutty... I think our society makes it into something that is devalued. It shouldn't be demeaning to girls to have sex all the time with different people. It could be me judging but I think there should be respect there. I think our society really doesn't see it this way. I think if a teenage boy's having sex, they view him as cool, but for a girl it is slutty, which is a demeaning term, promiscuous? I think I am scared of society, scared of being judged. (Bronwen)

In line with the demeaning construction of girls and women's desire, agency in desire is also viewed negatively:

> I'm not the type of person who would go up to someone and ask them if they wanted to go out with me. It could be just like leftover thing from, whatever, in the 1800s when the man asked the woman to marry him. (Bronwen)

Approaching a guy in public takes place only in exceptional circumstances, such as being under the influence of alcohol: "I can never initiate anything sober, but if I am drunk I could do it. I am just more open. It's the same with all my friends. Guys initiate, they definitely do" (Sarah).

Similar to other girls in late adolescence, Ashley, of African-Canadian heritage, problematizes the public ownership of sexual activities by girls. Yet, while she criticizes girls who are active sexually and who brag about it, she also explores the possible history of such a negative bias,

> If some girls brag about their activities, they will be called sluts. Like, if you're going to be doing that in the first place, don't go spreading it around to everyone. And so you're kind of putting that label upon yourself. I guess once you've done what you've done I guess it's pretty much there to stay, like you're not going to be able to change the fact. It's always going to be there. It probably goes back to like, maybe like actual prostitutes and how they were the ones being punished for it but the guys would say, 'oh it was just like okay,' or normalized, and it was like, 'well it's the girl's fault, and not the guy's.' It's normalized. I think it's beyond the school system I think it's a reflection towards girl and guy dynamics and that just reflects into us teenagers.

Not surprisingly, respectfully owning one's own desire is difficult, if not impossible. Ashley, like all girls in late adolescence we interviewed, is burdened by the social deprecation of women's desires: "There's always the fear of being called a slut. I think it's mostly moderating your own behavior so that you don't get labeled that way." Similarly, girls find the sexualized presentation and descriptions of girls in the media as demeaning of both girls and their desires. As Ashley states, "Music videos are unbelievably sexist. And it's expanding tremendously because a lot more people are interested in it. And it's hurting African-American women as well as guys. Calling girls sluts, it's just keeping the word out there."

Slut, whore, skank, hooker, and other similar labels are pervasive in the narratives of girls in late adolescence and are used commonly by both girls and boys—and sometimes by significant adults in their lives. Girls (only) might be labeled sluts for actual or imagined sexual activity,

"'Cause the things you do with guys" (Bronwen), or "If a girl does it with multiple guys" (Sarah). Girls might also be labeled sluts for the way they dress: "Guys calling girls sluts because of the way they dress. But we all wear the same kind of clothes so if one wears a skanky shirt then we're all skanky girls" (Brady); or "Like if I'm wearing something that doesn't cover enough skin my mom would be like, 'You look like a slut!'" (Sarah). However, boys and girls might also assign the slut label simply for purposes of revenge: "I was called a slut because he was mad at me" (Sarah); "It's normalized between girls saying it to each other. Like because of jealousy, or getting back at them and spreading rumors about them" (Ashley).

As varied as the reasons are for receiving the slut label, the shaming and associated stigma carries with it social and emotional costs, and, occasionally, irreversible social consequences. As Brady describes,

> Once you have a slut label, it's hard to get rid of it. And, so, people tend to move schools because of it. It gets really bad. Like my friend got labeled a slut, and people would go 'There's the slut.' But I didn't want to drop her because of a stupid label, but it was hard because I don't want to get a slut label and move a school because I want to graduate with all the girls. So it's hard.

In addition to disrupting girls and women's joyful, respectful, and safe ownership of sexual desire, rape culture beliefs also include the expectation that girls and women contain the desires of boys and men. Consequently, adolescent girls and women are handed the responsibility for sexual violations of which they are the victims. As girls in late adolescence receive such messages from their dates, parents, schools, work sites, religious and other organizations, as well as from the media and the legal system, their embodied experiences shift. In particular, their responsibility for boys and men's desires further disrupts attunement to their own desires, increasing experiences of embodied oppression, fear, and self-surveillance. Ashley describes this at age 16:

> The church leaders were asking girls to cover up more in order to respect they guys so that they can respect you. Because if they're having impure thoughts about you, it was kinda like blame shifting, I thought, it's like taking off the blame from the guys and saying that the girls are responsible for the guys' emotions. They were trying to bring in the physical thing, like physically guys are more horny about visual aspects than girls are. That's stupid, guys should have to deal with that themselves. It shouldn't be our problem. But the problem is that the responsibility is of the girls. Like my friend that moved to a Middle Eastern country and a girl was raped but she was

> wearing a mini skirt and the guy ended up not getting in trouble because the girl was dressed too provocatively. I struggled with this a lot, and I think there is a whole bunch of hypocrisy. But it's just like okay, out of respect for church leaders I'm going to follow those rules. But it was by force, too, because they brought sweaters if they thought you were dressed inappropriately so you'd have to wear a sweater overtop. So there was the fear aspect. This is stressful now, because you have to layer things, like layers and layers. So you can't dress normally, like going to school. You notice it more. We monitor each other more, but I think it's mostly self. When I'm putting on clothes, I'll think twice about what kinda message I'm putting on for other people.

The pervasive social discourse that assigns girls and women responsibility for their sexual violations serves to re-traumatize them, deepening the experience of relational abandonment and worsening the disruption of inhabiting the body. Andrea, a woman in her 50s, shares the adverse and long-term impact of this responsibility shift—a burden she has carried with her since her rape at age 15:

> Your boyfriend or husband couldn't rape you. Just boys being boys, they had needs, and for a long time I felt responsible because what did I expect after dating for a year but not having sex, of course he was going to have trouble controlling his urges. Girls were expected to be responsible for preventing sex. When I sat to tell my mother, I will never forget. She said, 'Are you sure you didn't lead him on?' I just burst into tears. She did hug me but the damage was done. Actually, I think the way people reacted to the rape was actually worse than the rape itself. She blamed me for it. And my father wouldn't look at me or hug me for weeks. Up until then we were really close—I just felt abandoned. Yeah, abandoned. I starved myself and later had problems with bingeing. I hated my body, and when I felt hungry, I would say in my head to my body that it should feed on my fat, that I had enough of it, that I didn't deserve food. I never thought I would get to this age and still worry about my body and hate looking in the mirror when I get dressed. I am tired of this. I also started scratching and cutting my skin.

Rape culture beliefs are still prevalent despite the 35-plus years that have elapsed since Andrea was 15 years. They still shape all social systems, from the family to the legal establishment. It is high time to consider the damage these beliefs cause to large segments of the population and counter them forcefully.

The fourth Comportment-related Discourse described by the Developmental Theory of Embodiment (DTE), the Patriarchal Shaping of Relational Patterns discourse, further aggravates the well-being of girls by disrupting the much-needed networks of peer support. In particular, as expected in a patriarchal culture, girls in late adolescence often abandon relational connections with other girls to form dating relationships with boys, prioritize social input and feedback from boys, and, at the same time, engage in multiple betrayals and fights with girls over dating relationships. Since dating relationships at this stage are often still unstable and commonly involve sexual coercion, the relational disruptions to long-term friendships between girls leave them feeling vulnerable. Relational patterns in a patriarchal culture during late adolescence, therefore, perpetuate a divide-and-conquer dynamic, leaving girls isolated and unsafe.

Girls in a dating relationship with a guy often abandon even long-term friendship relationships with girls once they start dating. Brady explains, "I try to see my boyfriend as much as I possibly can. And so it is harder to spend time with my girlfriends because it's hard to fit them in." Brady also feels compelled to distance her friends from her relationship with her boyfriend, since she is afraid they will purposefully disrupt this relationship out of jealousy. However, girls often report being left without support when the dating relationship ends. As Jackie describes,

> It was like, I was ditching my best friends to hang out with him. Like I would see what he was doing, and then I would make plans with other people if he couldn't hang out. I thought he loved me, I felt like he accepted me for me. And all of a sudden it was just like, my world was revolving around him, and then [after assault], my world had nothing to revolve around.

Prioritizing and idolizing attention from guys, girls often discard input from other girls, given within a more equitable relational context, as Ashley and Sarah explain:

> Well, I think that girls are in relationships a lot of the time to kinda complete themselves, and it's just kinda like they want to maybe not even be affirmed by guys, but they feel that they're more complete when they're around guys. While, I think for guys it's more physical, and I've never heard a guy feeling like, 'you complete me.' (Ashley)

> I think guys control most women's confidence. For sure, because I could be called 'fat' and 'ugly' by a girl, and it probably wouldn't get to me, like I'd be like, 'you want like my fist?' Like I'm not afraid

> to stand up to that. But like if a guy were to say like, 'you're fat and ugly,' I'd go home and think about it, and it would get to me that much worse. It's probably because of the attention thing. Knowing that you're not getting it from whom you want to get it. That really sucks. (Sarah)

Vying for a place of power in a social peer system shaped by patriarchal values, the norms of relatedness between girls commonly involve competition, jealously, and betrayals. There are many reports of "cat fights," wherein the slut label is a common weapon:

> Girls are trying to be all tough. They're like, 'shut up, you slut,' like they'll say that kind of stuff to one another. There's little catfights going on. There's actually a fair amount of girl fights going on in our school. Like, more than guy fights. Like you see guy fights maybe twice very three or four months. With girls you'll see every week. There's tons of girl fights. It's just the littlest things. Like, the last fight I saw, there was this girl who came out and was yelling at this other girl because apparently she kissed her boyfriend. So this girl beat up that girl and broke her wrist! (Jackie)

> But I think it's being normalized between girls and girls saying slut to each other and then it kind of makes the guys… well if the girls say it to each other why can't we? I've seen girls say it to each other and then it's just, that's the kind of dynamic I've seen that term being used in. Well, maybe because they were jealous of them or something like that. And so just a way of kind of getting back at them and spreading rumors about them and saying bad things about them. (Ashley)

Common betrayals and the consequent lack of safety are deeply disruptive to relational connections between girls (Brown, 2003). Brady and Jackie explain:

> I actually don't let my friends know who my boyfriend [is]. I had a best friend and she hung out with me like every single day, and then when I first met him, I told her how much I liked him and like how much I wanted to go out with him and everything and then she actually stole him off my chat list and started liking him and telling him how much she liked him and she was trying to ask him out so she was trying to steal him from me. And then just a couple of months ago, my friends were trying to make up all these lies and tell me that my boyfriend was cheating on me and everything. So, I don't trust them around my boyfriend just 'cause I don't want to lose him to a

> friend. And like because they may be mad at me so they'll make up stuff to me so I'll break up with him. (Brady)

> Actually, I had this one issue. There was this girl who used to be in our group but we don't talk to her anymore because she stole my boyfriend. She literally did. He cheated on me with her. She was one of my best friends and I was so mad. I won't talk to her anymore. (Jackie)

More often than not, girls describe how broken friendships with girls are hard to resolve through dialogue: "If it's fighting with girls, it's a lot more like you don't talk to them for a couple of months" (Jackie). Overall then, at a time of challenges to physical safety, intense sexual objectification, concerns about body deficiencies, and exposure to the deprecation of girls and women's desires, girls often lose vital relational peer support. They therefore often do not have a social peer system that can help counteract adverse social pressures.

Considering socially constructed dichotomies and labels, girls in late adolescence clarify that the tomboy/girly girl dichotomy is no longer relevant to their lives, as they commonly consider themselves to operate within the girly girl spectrum. The tomboy position is often not socially accepted and receives harsh labels such as: "Oh my God, that's a man, a guy" (Bronwen); "They're manly. We don't really use the term tomboy; it would be more like, 'oh wow, she's a beast.'" (Jackie) Girls no longer refer to the losses associated with the girly girl identification in terms of freedom of engagement in meaningful passions, or hiding parts of themselves. While the slut label is still used profusely, the prude label becomes less relevant.

Together with gender-related discourses, discourses associated with other dimensions of social location shape embodiment and intersect with femininity discourses. Ashley, for example, describes encountering discourses related to the oppressive Black/White dichotomy, operating, like the woman/man dichotomy by idealizing one pole and deprecating the other. Ashley problematizes the stereotyped labels of slut, "gangster," and "white-washed," which she encounters among peers in late adolescence, especially in her social environment, which is mainly White with very few people who share her heritage. Those who do not share her heritage express surprise at her not fitting the gangster or slut labels sometimes portrayed in hip hop music videos. Indeed, Ashley problematizes stereotypes disseminated through music videos, especially the sexualization of African-American women via the slut label:

> If we're sitting and watching a rap video and someone says the word 'nigger.' Okay, what are you going to do about it? We know that this is a problem, where people say that on TV. It's a reality we live

> with... But working against stereotypes. I am not really 'gangster,' you know. So everyone's like, 'oh, yeah, you're not the stereotypical Black person. You're the whitest Black person I know. It's like you're not gangster at all. You're not like the girls in the music videos. Oh, wow, *you talk like you're blonde,*' and things like that. And I don't know if that's a compliment or whether you're dissing me 'cause I'm dumb. But it's just like they're *really surprised at like who I am.* 'Cause what you see on TV sometimes can be a really inadequate reflection on society. And, within one culture, there are people with many different interests. It would be like assuming all White people are farmers, like, if you're from Texas.

African-American scholars have criticized the sexualized representations of African-American women by Whites seeking to "justify" the violation, denigration, and commodification of Black women's bodies (see Simms, 2001). Indeed, Ashley is concerned about the sexualization and deprecation of African-American women in music videos, labeling them sluts. It is possible that Ashley's careful surveillance of her clothing—"When I'm putting on clothes, I'll think twice about what kinda message I'm putting on for other people"—and her behavior with peers, whereby she avoids the dating scene altogether—"There's always the fear of being called a slut. I think it's mostly moderating your own behavior so that you don't get labeled that way"—relate to her "working against stereotypes." In her astute commentary about new peers using the "blonde" label to describe her, Ashley highlights that the use of the label can reflect the racist idealization of "White" characteristics or, alternatively, the use of the sexist devaluation of the "dumb blonde" to devalue her.

Girls in late adolescence engage in critical reflections about the social constructions that shape their lives, such as Ashley's critique of sexualized representations of African-American women and the shifting of responsibility for sexual violations, or Bronwen's commentary about prohibitions of sexual agency among women. Such critical commentary provides a basis for generating liberating constructions, establishing them as new discourses to guide social interactions among peers. However, we do not often hear about relational forums where these social constructions are discussed critically. The rare examples of said critical forums, shared by girls, clarify their impact. Hazel, for example, finds enlightenment in a media class that focuses on the sexualized presentations of girls and boys in the media. However, to nurture an ongoing critical stance toward adverse social constructions and, in particular, to shift peer group norms, such consciousness-raising forums need to be ongoing.

To summarize experiences in the mental domain, girls in late adolescence experience the tightening of Mental Corsets related to femininity. These tightened Mental Corsets further intersect with discourses related to other aspects of social location. Regarding appearance, during late adolescence objectifying pressures become sexualized and, in addition, girls often become dependent on appearance alterations to be seen in public. Further, girls' relegation to "feminine" activities starts to determine their long-term participation in the public domain. Moreover, girls are penalized for not complying with "demure" expectations and for agency in desire. As girls prioritize relationships with boys, girls' relationships are marred by competition, fighting, and betrayals, depriving girls of much-needed support networks.

EMBODIED SURRENDER? ELUSIVE PATHS TO SOCIAL POWER

> I think in our society it's pretty important to be attractive, more for a girl… My pictures of myself and of the ideal girl are less different now so I don't need to draw two pictures. I used to be a loser. Now, I like making myself look pretty: I wear skirts and tighter clothes and I wear makeup most of the time. I use eyeliner, mascara, blush, and concealer. I have my hair down and accessories. I go on diets. I love American Apparel fair trade. I feel like if I don't have any makeup on, I'm not pretty… I don't want to get wrinkles or stretch marks; that's weird 'cause I am 15 and I'm worried about when I'm 60. I've heard from different people that women gain weight when they have kids. I don't want to be one of those old ladies who is really like past their prime and is not attractive any more.
>
> I would name the pressure to conform [in appearance] as *fear*. I think girls are afraid of *not being accepted* and not being loved and *not being able to be who they are*. By conforming it makes us feel that we are *part of a group*, so that must mean that *we're validated*. But in doing that you *lose part of who you are. You lose your individuality and part of your power.* Girls don't realize that, really, we are all beautiful and we are all powerful and we don't have to be the same. In order for a girl not to conform, she would need to be accepted as she is without the conformity, that's what gives you your power. If I was less attractive I would feel that *I don't have the right to be who I am anymore*. I would *be quiet*. Not as *big personality*. People who are not attractive are marginalized and it's easier for society to say, well their opinions don't matter. That happens in the media because you won't see an unattractive woman in the media, but you will occasionally see unattractive men.

In late adolescence, age 15, the search for social power takes a turn for Bronwen, a White girl of a low-to-middle class and rural background. In early adolescence (age 13), she derives a sense of personal power from her feminist convictions, and her resistant and critical stance toward what she views as a sexist way of accessing power—through a focus on appearance. However, at the age of 15, while continuing to criticize both institutional (e.g., politics, religion) and embodied (e.g., weight, clothing, and ownership of desire) sexism, she reveals her immersion in body modifications, which has led her to approximate the appearance of the ideal girl (blonde with hair down, thin, made up, tighter clothing). Distinguishing between different forms of power, Bronwen makes it clear that conforming to appearance expectations leads to having enhanced social power (in terms of popularity), though it takes away "your individuality and part of your power." In her experience, observing the media and interactions among her peer group, only attractive women can have a voice that is not marginalized. Indeed, at 13, when holding a critical, non-conforming perspective toward girls' self-sexualization, she lacks a validating community—an accepting community that supports her position—and, consequently, feels unsafe in her peer group.

At the cost of losing part of her individuality and power, Bronwen, at age 15, colludes with appearance-based peer norms. Concurrently, she disassociates herself from the feminist label—a common phenomenon among young women (Borowski, Eisenberg, Bucchianeri, Piran, & Neumark-Sztainer, 2015) citing a repeated stereotypic criticism of feminism: that of engagement in man bashing. While she strongly believes that only the acceptance of women, without conformity, will lead to uncompromised power, she also suggests that to feel comfortable in their bodies, girls and women have to hear such messages of acceptance from boys and/or men: "It shouldn't be that way, but because I think that girls want to look good to impress guys, the message [of unconditional acceptance] will have to come from boys and men." While Bronwen labels herself "a hypocrite" for holding both a critical and a conforming stance, she generously shares here the common dilemma of how to achieve social power from a place of disenfranchisement, combining collusion and resistance.

In relation to the Social Power and Relational Connections domain of the DTE, Bronwen addresses its first dimension, Exposure to Prejudice and Harassment, by criticizing the adverse impact of sexism (as well as weightism, heterosexism, and classism) on varied social institutions, and on the embodied lives of girls. The second dimension, Appearance-based Social Power, is a central aspect of Bronwen's commentary. She makes it clear that she has achieved popularity through compliance with the image of the ideal girl, and that girls and women need to be attractive to have a voice and not become marginalized. Accordingly, she also harbors fears about possible changes to her appearance in her future body journey. Two protective dimensions of the Social Power and Relational Connections domain, specified by the DTE, that could provide her with support for being unique without the need for conformity, are still not available to Bronwen, especially in her peer group and school environment. These dimensions are Empowering Relationships and Membership in Equitable Communities (see Table 1.2).

Beginning with the dimension of Exposure to Prejudice and Harassment, girls in late adolescence share examples and reflections regarding both aspects of this dimension: Access to Resources and Freedom from Body-based Prejudice and Harassment. These girls describe the existence of barriers related to education, health, and physical sites of safety and of meaningful activities related to their gender, race and ethnicity, social class, and sexual orientation. The discriminatory allocation of resources is grounded in prejudicial systems: privileging some bodies and disenfranchising others.

Several girls in late adolescence share barriers to their educational paths. Gender segregation in education and, later, occupation are in part maintained through prejudicial gatekeeping processes. Education and related occupational choices are important social resources correlated with material living conditions and embodied well-being. At the intersection of gender and (gender-biased) religion, the guidance counselor at Bronwen's religiously affiliated school steers her away from enrolling in all the science courses she wishes to take, leading to her decision to pursue correspondence science courses outside of her high school: "I am planning to take correspondence courses… I am really interested in science, but I was talking to the guidance councilor who said, 'You should only do two out of the three,' I really should talk to someone else." Her experience resembles that of Jane, a young White adult woman from a working class and rural background, whose guidance counselor tried to dissuade her from taking honors science courses: "I'm sitting with the guidance counselor and he's making comments like, 'You're taking all these honors. Are you sure you can handle honors chemistry?'" Research indeed indicates that multiple gatekeeping processes discourage girls from pursuing education in the sciences, technology, engineering, and math (STEM) (Hill et al., 2010). Due to the existence of yet another barrier at the intersection of gender and social class, Kelly needs to compromise her dream of pursuing the longer and more costly path of a university undergraduate degree and instead embark on a shorter college education, leading to fewer qualifications and a less-remunerated job: "My mother says that [boyfriend] is making enough money. [Family members] are trying to push me away from it because they know that I want to have a family."

Access to health services and proper nutrition is central to well-being. Considering health services, girls that we interview are particularly challenged in the area of reproductive health. Among our group of teenage girls interviewed, one has an unwanted pregnancy. Having no access to a health professional empathetic to the complexity of her situation, but instead seeing a physician who is likely covertly opposed to abortions, she does not have prompt access to an abortion—a situation that significantly challenges her life. In contrast, Nancy's access to health services at a hospital located in a major urban center is vital to her continued educational path and emotional health. In that hospital, Nancy receives the "morning after" pill, having been denied access to contraceptive pills by her significant adults. While writing this chapter, funding for Planned Parenthood in the United States is threatened should the organization continue to provide abortion services. Since this organization is centered on supporting women in making decisions about their health and lives, Planned Parenthood cannot accept such a condition. Excluding Planned Parenthood from public health programs will severely cut women's access to health care services (Planned Parenthood Health Centers, 2017). The adverse impact on teens' lives, should this happen, will be immense.

Healthy nutrition also contributes to well-being, as often stated by girls in late adolescence. However, several girls in the study living in financially strained homes highlight challenges to accessing healthy foods:

> There is too much fat and crap in the food, and then sometimes you see more kids and they're getting fatter. And I wouldn't blame them because healthy food costs more than the junk food! And they want us to be healthier, then lower down the cost of healthy food! It's like I could get this juice that's like three dollars or I could get the pop that's like 50 cents and you're like I could get six things of pop versus this one thing of juice, I think I'm going to get the pop! (Roxas)

Girls living in financially strained homes, who are trying to control their weight, sometimes resort to intake restrictions, though without being able to replace skipped foods with healthy alternatives.

Geographical sites of meaningful action—physical, cultural, spiritual, or social—are an additional social resource. Being barred from such sites clarifies to individuals their disenfranchised social status, depriving them from equitable participation and compromising their embodied self-worth. Access to sites of physical safety is central to well-being and embodied agency in the world. Girls in late adolescence experience a narrowing number of physical sites that are free from sexual harassment and other violations—disrupting their experiences of worth and agency in the world, even in their own schools and neighborhoods. As Brady describes, "it scares me if I'm walking home alone and I think of that, it's actually scary." Similarly, girls in late adolescence repeatedly detail the existence of barriers to participation in sites of physical activity available to boys, such as community centers and schools: "We can't play boys' hockey and there weren't enough girls for a team" (Brady); "There weren't enough girls and we couldn't play with the guys" (Sarah); "It was sad, our school didn't have enough girls to make a team" (Lauren); "Only one team for girls and I was cut; hurt like a burn" (Shannon). It is vital that girls in late adolescence have access to physical sites available to boys their age. As a reminder, women were only allowed to officially participate in a street running event, the Boston Marathon, in 1972; this followed the insistence of one woman, Kathrine Switzer, to run the marathon in 1967, whereby an official tried to bar her from running, reflecting a common view that women were "too fragile" to run a marathon.

Barriers to sites of physical action can relate to race and ethnicity. Ashley, an African-Canadian woman, describes being barred from participating in sporting events at a public park in an urban US center, and how it was related to her racial heritage: "They asked my (White) friend to play, but they didn't ask me. There is a lot of segregation in the US. Black people don't play with White people." Hazel, of Middle Eastern heritage, cannot swim in a public pool since she can only swim without her hijab at a women-only facility. Jackie, of Aboriginal heritage, brings forth the importance of embodied connection to meaningful territories:

> Aboriginals trying to gain rights back to their lands, like they tried to build a golf course on one of the Aboriginal graveyards and an Aboriginal man got shot because he had a stick in his hand and they thought it was a gun, so they shot him. But after that, when he died, they made a memorial for him there and they didn't turn it into a golf course. That's really sad. I want to do something about it. I get emotional about it. Like not a crying emotional, but determined. Like when I'm older, I'm definitely going to do something for my culture. We definitely need to get some land back; I don't want my relatives living [on] reserves forever.

Yet, she protests not being able to partake in a ceremony available thus far only to boys: "When they turn 16, they go on a dream hunt… by themselves in the wild for five days and you learn about yourself. And girls aren't allowed to do that."

Sarah gives an example of experiencing barred access, this one related to sexual orientation, which was later reversed:

> A guy that I know who is gay wanted to bring a guy who was his friend to the prom and our school wouldn't let him. So it was this big huge thing with the school and they just wouldn't let him and I don't remember if he won or who he went with or anything but now you're allowed to bring… the same sex. Like my friend [girl's name] she's not a lesbian or anything but like she brought her friend that's a girl… so I guess now you're allowed. It's a shame he could not do it.

Thus, the component of Access to Resources, in the lives of girls in late adolescence, conveys systemic social prejudices, affecting their embodied experiences of equity and worth at the intersection of gender, race and ethnicity, social class, and sexual orientation.

In addition to barriers to accessing varied resources, girls in late adolescence, living in young women's bodies, describe a greater exposure to body-based prejudicial treatment relative to early adolescents. In particular, they describe a compromised quality of embodied lives compared with boys and disruptive patterns of learned gendered relationships. Moreover, unlike during early adolescence, girls in late adolescence often link their daily body-based experiences to societal values, structures of power, and to social histories. Nonetheless, despite these expanded social and critical perspectives, they, like Bronwen, most often feel the pressure to collude with social norms, accentuating their experiences of body-anchored vulnerability and helplessness.

Comparing their quality of embodied lives with those of boys, girls in late adolescence highlight differences related to two main areas: appearance and sexuality. Starting with appearance, engagement in the public sphere at this phase requires, from girls, extensive, time-consuming, and often costly body alterations that further serve to reinforce their inherent flaws, and that leave them with "nothing natural to work with." Such alterations are not required of boys. Jackie, of Aboriginal heritage and working-class background, summarizes,

> Guys don't have to look as good. A lot of the guys they don't really care. You know, guys don't spend *an hour and half in front of the mirror every morning*, but they don't get judged as hard as girls do, either. There are guys you see and they're wearing the same clothes every day and nobody care! You're like, 'nice shirt, I thought I saw you wear that yesterday!' If a girl did that, they'd be like, 'ew, do you shower? Do you change your clothes? Do you wash your clothes?'

Of additional relevance here is social class—the daily availability of clean and different clothes—a stronger expectation from girls.

Girls also highlight being forced into much tighter and more restrictive physical spaces than boys, which in turn compromises their quality of life. For example, Roxas, of Caribbean-Canadian and working-class background, describes the pressure that family members place, specifically, on their daughters:

> My friend, her mom or dad bought her this bathing suit. It was smaller than she was. She had a little bit of fat here and there but not a lot. But they basically forced her to lose weight so that it would fit her. They put her on a diet and she was all sad. She looks really good now. She did before, but still. It's just the fact that they did that.

Further, the normative sexualized clothing and forced exposure in late adolescence are disruptive to girls, causing embodied struggles that boys do not have to deal with. Bronwen explains,

> Boys have more of their body covered. Hot girls show more skin. If you stop and analyze it, I guess clothes are kinda sexist. It's acceptable for guys to, you know, wear baggy clothes, and, you know, for girls to wear tight clothes. But I don't normally stop to analyze that. I don't wear the slutty look, like mini mini tube tops, revealing way too much skin, but I mean I do wear tank tops, I'm not saying that I always cover up. In our society it's pretty important for girls to be attractive.

Appearance expectations targeted specifically at girls, involving body alterations, size restrictions, and sexualization, convey to them their disenfranchised position when compared with boys.

Sexuality also informs girls about their disadvantaged position. Girls highlight the comfort, joy, and even cockiness of boys' expression of sexuality, contrasting it with the discomfort inherent in their sexual lives. As described earlier in this chapter, girls are burdened by the deprecation of ownership and agency of desire, expressed through the pervasive slut label. Sarah, a White girl of middle-class background, summarizes it in the following way:

> Guys in my school are so open about sexuality. For example, when I get to class one day and my friend has his biggest smile on his face. And I am, like, 'Why are you so happy?' And he's like, 'I got laid last night.' They are just open like that. But girls don't talk about it. They're probably just not too open with it. I don't know. That's kind of weird. I don't know. It's hard for girls…

Further aggravating this experience of powerlessness is the social expectation that girls carry the responsibility for pregnancy, even in the case of rape, as Sarah, who studies in a religious school, describes:

> Like I'm really, really extremely against what the Catholic religion [believes] because I'm pro-choice. Like I believe… well, my main beliefs are that like if, if you are a rape victim, it is your choice, like you shouldn't have to go through something you do not want to go through that you didn't plan.

Yet, Sarah is part of a school system that does not support a pro-choice stance. Girls, in reflecting about their experiences in the area of sexuality, compare their embodied experiences to those of boys and men, highlighting their disadvantaged social position.

Living in young women's bodies and engaging in the sexual dating scene, girls in late adolescence receive firsthand experience with respect to their vulnerability within heterosexual gender relations, shaped by patriarchy. An example of this is the rampant betrayals girls encounter, in particular from boyfriends, whose sexual betrayals are described earlier in this chapter. Girls also observe betrayals in the adult relationships around them, and witness older partnered men preying on adolescent girls. This breeds fear; as Bronwen describes, "I am afraid for the future. One of my hugest fears in life is either get a divorce or have my spouse cheat on me. I want to get married, but I'm like it's scary." Girls, therefore, stay vigilant about other girls' access to their boyfriends—for example, Brady bars her girlfriends from meeting her boyfriend. Accentuating this vulnerability is the clarity that girls' self-esteem is in the hands of boys and men:

> Husbands can help their wives to accept their bodies, rather than women themselves learn to accept their bodies. It shouldn't be that way, but I kinda think it is because girls wanna look good to impress guys. I'd rather look good for a guy. (Bronwen)

This evaluative gaze grants boys and men enhanced power over girls. Despite learning firsthand about their vulnerable position in relationships and institutions shaped by patriarchy and other oppressive ideologies, girls at this phase are often embedded within such systems (families, schools, varied community-based organizations). It is therefore not surprising that, without opportunities to engage differently with the social world, girls, even when holding a critical lens, often strive to achieve access to power through "conforming," targeting their bodies and appearances for alteration rather than the social environment.

Appearance-based Social Power is the second dimension of the Social Power and Relational Connections dimension of the DTE. Embodying idealized appearance characteristics comprises the most direct avenue by which a girl can become popular. As they draw and describe appearance characteristics of the ideal girl, girls of varied backgrounds (in terms of race/ethnicity, social class, and rural vs. urban sites of residence) produce striking similarities in their illustrations, reflecting the homogenizing influence of the media and widely disseminated social messages. When Ashley, African-Canadian and of a working-class background, draws herself and the ideal girl, her drawing of the ideal girl is about half the height and one-third the width of her drawing of herself—about one-sixth (about 17%) of the surface area of the self-drawing. The following is a common narrative among the girls,

> Well, obviously really, really skinny. More beautiful, like pretty type of thing. But you have to be thin, never, like, a chubby person. Blonde hair, nice sparkly blue eyes. Full breasted but not too much hips, just

> really feminine. Long hair and makeup. Like it would have to be really nice expensive makeup so that's kind of not even an option for me. She is wearing a skirt; she's showing off her nice long legs. She's wearing high heels. I think the media has a huge role in the way they're portraying what people expect girls to look like and what we expect for ourselves to look like. (Ashley)

This drawing and the associated narrative condense information about the embodiment of privilege in girls' peer groups. Ideal girls follow the expected spatially constricted, sexualized, made-up, and exposed appearance standards for girls; are never chubby; appear "White"; are materially endowed; and are feminine, in line with heteronormative expectations. The visual perfection also excludes disability or other visible differences. This privileged representation underlies girls' engagement in body alterations, including dieting and disordered eating patterns, hair bleaching and straightening, makeup applications, skin-lightening creams, lenses that changes eye color, shopping (at times even when financially strained), and plastic interventions. Jackie describes the effort taken to approximate the ideal "Barbie" look, from her perspective as a woman of color:

> Having to look perfect, like Barbie. The big-volume hair and sunglasses, looking like superstars when you're not. Like we have nothing else in life. Skin color matters and eye color. I wear cover up, eye shadow, and eyeliner. I feel terrible about myself when I'm not. A lot of girls try to have greener eyes. They get those colored contacts. I noticed that they look so dumb, but girls always do it. We have so many girls in our school that have green or blue color contacts.

Adhering to idealized feminine appearance standards might, however, prove an elusive path to social power. Approximating the ideal appearance is often associated with the fear of losing it. Commonly, girls, like Jackie, describe feeling "terrible" without their body alterations, hence living continuously with body discomfort. Ashley shares her reflection about the dependence on strict appearance standards for social acceptability:

> It's almost like the people who are really thin, like anorexic, or have to wear makeup every single day are addicted and they don't feel confident going outside their homes not looking up to the standards that are set out by the world. So I think that it's really interesting that studies like this are being done so hopefully those people can have hope.

Here is the paradox Bronwen and other girls refer to in relation to social power—while approximating the idealized feminine appearance can buy social popularity, being unable to engage with the world without such alterations can be deeply disempowering.

Heightening girls' concerns about the fickle nature of appearance-based social power is their growing awareness—through direct observations, media messages, and cautionary notes by older women in their lives—that appearance-based social power may in fact be a "shooting star." As indicated by Bronwen's narratives at the beginning of this chapter, girls commonly describe concerns that they may be at the pinnacle of their social power as far as their appearance is concerned, predicting, forebodingly, weight gain, wrinkles, and stretch marks rather than foreseeing the power and richness inherent in a full life. Therefore, while they commonly hold on to appearance as a source of social power, they also fear losing this special privilege.

Further clarifying the inferior status of women in a patriarchal society is the demotion of the socially idealized and marketed feminine appearance. This demotion is perpetuated by the prevalent devaluation, by both genders, of women or girls who embody the idealized appearance, using such deprecating terms as "dumb blonde" and "ditzy." It is problematic, for example, that Brady, who looks like the ideal girl, internalizes this negative stereotype: "One of my idols is [known celebrity] because she's so tall and she's blonde and stupid. Like I'm totally just like her pretty much." During late adolescence, within the context of heightened disempowerment, incessant appearance comparisons, and competition over accessing desirable guys for the purposes of dating, the hostility toward such popular girls is palpable. Hazel states,

> She's a whore, wearing low-cut jeans, like the whole Britney style, like thong showing and stuff like that. She has no brain. They are mean, preppy girls. If you're not the pretty girl you're the smart girl. I don't understand how it could be one and not the other. Can't you be pretty and smart? Can't you, like, flip your hair and be all like: 'So, E equals MC square,' you know? If boys, like men, are vocal, they are called strong, cool, calm leaders, but women are screechy, whiny. Women aren't given as much respect, I don't think.

This commentary reflects a common trend among girls in late adolescence, of concurrent collusion with dominant social forces and critical reflections. While Hazel is hostile and devaluing toward girls in the peer group who resemble the ideal girl, she also criticizes disempowering societal prejudices of women: women cannot be pretty and smart, they cannot be in power, and they are not treated with respect. Ashley's narratives reflect the same challenge of collusion via the social demotion of girls attempting to achieve idealized appearance standards—"they look like clowns"—yet she holds a critical stance not only toward the social forces that demote women but also toward her own participation in said adverse social forces, by being a (paying) consumer of media. She highlights her concern for African-American women and the hip hop culture:

> What about the roles that I play, which I know, if I see a music video and I watch it, I'm supporting that. So, it's really interesting that I can kind of share the blame for it. As well as calling other girls sluts, it's just keeping the word out there.

The oppressive idealized appearance standard counters both social justice and the well-being of all members of a social group. The allure of this image in the peer group relates to its embodied representation of social privilege with respect to key aspects of social location. As very few girls may approximate the idealized appearance image, most girls in the social groups of older adolescents are excluded and delegated to the category of "other." Such exclusion relates most often to social location and is often associated with varied forms of body-based prejudicial treatment and harassment. Girls who are considered "not White" may experience social exclusion or racist harassment, "We were competing for attention from my friend, and she was like, 'I don't want to hang out with the half breed anymore'" (Jackie).

Girls who live in financially strained circumstances are often excluded and face varied forms of body-based harassment. They may face teasing related to hygiene ["People make comments about like general uncleanliness and smell" (Bronwen)], not wearing "in" clothing or having material gadgets ["I go shopping and I like how it fits and it looks good, even though I don't buy the shirt… I know I am not one of the fashionable girls." (Kelly)], or to costly body alteration procedures ["It would have to be nice expensive makeup because I have allergies… so it's not even an option. So it's like do I want a bike or mascara? I'd rather spend the money elsewhere" (Ashley)]. Heavier girls are also commonly not included in the popular group ["But you have to be thin, never, like, a chubby person" (Ashley)], and face weight prejudice ["People have almost a fear of someone who's obese. Like, you know, 'stay away'" (Bronwen)].

Girls in our study from financially strained families describe constraints in being able to afford even low-cost school or community-based sports programs ["I didn't register to the body conditioning class at school because it cost an extra 15 dollars" (Roxas)], and the challenge of accessing healthier food choices. These constraints can lead to heavier weights (Ogden, Carroll, Kit, & Flegal, 2012). Kelly, for example, describes how, "in the winter I sleep more, and I like to wear pants and bulky sweaters, and I know I look chunky and I don't like that, but in the summer I can bike and I lose weight." Weightism, therefore, partly reflects social class prejudice.

Girls are marginalized and teased for not following heteronormative expectations: "But if they wouldn't shave their legs and wear shorts people would be like, 'ew that's gross... she is a lesbian'" (Kelly). Regarding sexual orientation, girls who do not identify as heterosexual are marginalized by some students: "There are a lot of students at our school now who are either bi or gay or something like that. Some people will make fun of them. Other people don't care, and some people can relate even though they're not" (Sarah). Margaret, a woman in her 60s, who has had a physical deformity since infancy, says in her interview that, "My teenage years were pretty difficult because of my physical deformity... I was rejecting boys before they could reject me."

The idealized appearance image for women comprises a major challenge to social justice. It condenses societal prejudices on multiple aspects of social location: gender, race and ethnicity, social class, sexual orientation, and physical ability/differences. This image serves to exclude most women, and does not provide safety or sustained power even to those who approximate it. Girls in late adolescence reflect critically about issues of power in relation to their social location; however, often within their oppressive social systems they may not be able to find paths to social power apart from striving to approximate this concrete image of intersecting privileges. Ashley highlights the possibilities in extricating oneself from such collusion:

> By looking at yourself and how you contribute, it gives you an element of like, I have some control in changing things. I can be a part of that power, a part of that movement, right, and so it makes you feel empowered.

This comment leads into the third dimension of the Social Power and Relational Connection domain: Empowering Relationships. Pressures on the body and appearance are so intense in late adolescence that having access to empowering relationships that counter these pressures and support girls in engaging with dialogues about their strengths, passions, beliefs, and values can nurture the transition into young adulthood. Supporting a critical stance toward body-related pressures can further help prevent challenges to well-being caused by negative embodiment.

As girls in late adolescence contemplate about their own transitions into adulthood, a few find inspiration in their mothers' journeys, especially once they understand that their mothers have dealt with social barriers with strength and integrity. A mother's resilience, based on cherished values shared with their daughters, can deepen the connection between them, especially when the relationships include love, acceptance, support, and guidance. In these situations, mother–daughter dialogues that focus on strengths, values, and relational connections, provide a buffer from social pressures in the body domain. Ashley's relationship with her mother is a good example of an empowering relationship. Ashley, who has faced social exclusion and prejudicial treatment related to racism, sexism, and classism, has a strong resistant stance toward appearance pressures, which she attributes to her relationship with her mother, a strong and inspiring role model. The following narrative reflects Ashley's respect for her mother, and their shared focus on cherished values, the maintenance of well-being, and the countering of adverse pressures related to appearance:

> My mother, she came from Africa and she really wanted an education and all odds were against her and she fought them and she was just able to be really successful and she's really happy with her life. And so I just want to be like her. I want to be really strong and supportive and caring. I listen to Oprah's programs. I really like the real life story of Oprah, like rags to riches type of thing, like how she started off with like nothing and she's so successful and happy with her life. Those are the kind of people that I want to be. I always go back to my values, so I always try and stay in touch with my beliefs. I attribute this strength definitely to my home. I think home has been a really positive environment for me. And I think also the people who I surround myself with, they're always people that are encouraging me to do the right thing and to strive to be the good person that I want to be. And I always try to give back the same way. I think for girls the magazines where they're showing all the models that are really thin, and the makeup, and all those types of things. So it can be a bit discouraging for me at times. I can only wear expensive makeup because of my allergies and we talked about it and do I want my mom to spend so much money on mascara? I'd rather spend it elsewhere. So with body image, I like to keep active. My mom explained to me that people have different body types and you can only compare yourself to what is healthy for you. She wants me to stay active, so I play sports; it's a positive thing and I make friends. I guess the social pressure just kind of always been there, so you kind of get used to it and cope with yourself. I try to focus on the things that will benefit me more than say boost the way people look at me. I'd like to think that I have a pretty good self-image. Like I know who I am and my identity is really strong. So even though there are things that are trying to tell you who you are, stereotypes, I always find it a challenge to break those stereotypes and just stand out and be myself.

Ashley's mother, who raises her daughter as a single parent, fosters resistance toward pursuing idealized appearance standards and assists Ashley in body and self-acceptance, and in making choices that enhance her sense of identity, power, and well-being.

Several girls find that their mothers empower them by focusing on their relational strengths, suggesting ways and values of being in the world that differ from the appearance-focused values prevalent in their peer groups. For example, having faced racism, sexism, and classism, Jackie has received support from her mother, who guides her in constructing a meaningful life, outside of a focus on appearance:

> My mom helps me with my attitude about body image. She's a good person to talk to. It doesn't matter who you are on the outside, it should matter who you are on the inside. If you're pretty, but you're rude and don't care about anybody but yourself, that's not going to help you in life. But if you're bigger or you don't like how your nose looks, but you're kind and help everyone, then you're going to get far.

Similarly Kelly, Latino and of a working-class background, having faced sexism and classism, is inspired by her mother's strength, prioritizing the care of others and disregarding external appearance:

> Like my mom's always been a very giving person, like she's always put us first before herself. Like when my dad first left she'd go for years wearing rags so that we could have stuff that we wanted and stuff like that. I learned to take care of people.

Jessica, White and from a working-class background, specifically addresses the strength she derives from receiving acceptance at home, unrelated to her appearance: "The message to change everything natural about you, I don't get that from anyone except from TV, and I don't watch much TV. It's good to know you have people who don't think that you should change everything about you."

Focusing on athletic abilities and the functionality of the body, without any focus on appearance or stereotypes of girls in sports, can be both a source of strength and buffer against the demotion of girls' bodies. Shannon's mother and father have empowered her by focusing on her athletic abilities. From a young age, Shannon, White and of a middle-class background, has, along with her two brothers, felt empowered to engage in sports: "I just always had a lot of fun, I'm not sure maybe it's because my dad brought me into sports. I have always felt really good at sports." Often coached by her father, her athletic experiences have been respectful and equitable, on co-ed and all-girls' teams; she has not experienced being given demeaning labels, such as bitch or lesbian. Her parents, both involved in team sports, have also modeled equity in different domains of life. Her father has modeled social power by opening up opportunities for Shannon to play sports even when facing barriers common to girls; however, these opportunities close for Shannon during her last year of high school. Regardless, her pride in the functionality of her body is clear:

> I feel proud about my body, being good in sports. I'm glad I am interested in sports because it keeps me fit. Part of my identity is being athletic. I like the picture of myself better than the ideal girl. I really like my curly hair. I'm just relaxed. The ideal girl picture looks awkward. Like there's this thing, the Dove for Real Beauty Campaign, and they show average, normal women. I love that. Not the airbrushed photos. Like, there are some times when I don't wanna look bad, but it's like I don't do anything crazy, like, I don't straighten my hair constantly, I like the way it is naturally. Like, everyone has straight hair these days, but I won't fall for that. It's too much work and it damages your hair. It's not like you have to please everybody, like just be yourself. Like for a boyfriend I don't want to be fully made up. I just need to be comfortable.

The experience of body competence and comfort is much more important to Shannon than having an objectified and sexualized appearance. Recognizing the personal power involvement in sports has given her, Shannon is also aware of the financial privilege she has that has made it possible—"Hockey is more like an elitist sport, because it costs so much. Everyone around the world plays soccer, all you need is a ball and some shoes."

During late adolescence we hear of only a few close friendships that provide girls with an empowering base from which to act in the world. In addition to imparting full acceptance and even cherishing of one another's unique qualities, these friendships specifically counter adverse body-related experiences. Bronwen, for example, develops a non-sexual friendship with an adolescent boy her age, and they share their love for cross-country running. This relationship involves mutual respect; it is the only relational space where Bronwen is comfortable being in the world without makeup, and where she experiences no demotion related to her gender or her body: "I don't have makeup on, I look like crap and I'm just like—I'm here. And that brings you *freedom*. With the popular guys, it's almost like they like you for your looks and I have to be pretty." This respectful friendship provides Bronwen with the power and freedom, for the first time in 2 years, to stop wearing makeup at all times.

Hazel, who has been the target of body-based teasing related to weight, clothing, and wearing a hijab, finds her first friend in high school—a girl who connects with her unique qualities of story writing and other creative pursuits. This relationship shifts Hazel's body, self, and social experience, as no other peer in her social environment has bothered to get to know her beyond her embodied presentation. "We draw and write stories, and she likes my ideas and tells me how cute I am… I am not as shy anymore."

Empowering relationships in the lives of girls in late adolescence can have a powerful effect in buffering prevalent experiences of embodied demotion, body-based harassment and violations, and appearance-based pressures, especially when countering adverse social pressures, in addition to providing safety, acceptance, and inspiration.

Like Empowering Relationships, Membership in Equitable Communities, the fourth dimension of the Social Power and Relational Connections domain of the DTE, can also help buffer experiences of embodied inequity. However, such communities are far and few between for girls in late adolescence, with forces perpetuating the social status quo creating rifts between and within communities along varied aspects of social location. For example, the network of friendships between girls at this phase is marred by betrayals. Racial, ethnic, and religious stereotypes serve to demote particular groups and, when internalized, may create rifts within them. Despite a growing awareness of the link between social power and embodied pressures, girls in older adolescence continue to operate in systems that perpetuate social inequities and rifts (e.g., schools, clubs, other community-based organizations), necessitating a level of compliance for survival. Consequently, it is hard to find, or help form, alternative communities.

We hear at this phase about a few opportunities to access such alternative communities. Large high schools sometimes allow for a number of alternative social groups to form. Such alternative social groups sometimes resist prevalent norms and hold a critical lens toward them. Hazel's friendship group in high school is diverse in terms of gender, race/ethnicity/religion, sexual orientation, and class. This group cherishes their diversity, loyalty, alternative behavioral rules (being loud and different), and their production of alternative media:

> Most of the preppy girls didn't really talk to me, too snooty. We call them fashion freaks. We have a fun group, the loudest group. We have our own place in the cafeteria. This group made me less averse to touching because our group is very physical. I have also become just more accepting of myself because I have nice friends. They're like, 'you're so cute' all the time. We are preparing for [alternative] art production. Somebody's got to break those gender stereotypes.

> So we can do it through fantasy stories. Have strong female characters... And one of my friends in the group, he's gay, and it is okay with us! But because of the sheltered environment they say, 'that's unnatural,' and I'm like, 'don't say that.' We don't dis about each other's body. If one of us is dissed we form an attack team until we are satisfied.

As Hazel mentions, the inclusiveness in her peer group breaks social barriers in relation to gender and sexual orientation. In terms of her body- and self-acceptance, Hazel's embodied experience has shifted significantly since finding membership in this alternative high school group.

Exposure to alternative communities that counter oppressive social pressures in the body domain can take place outside of schools and the dominant school-based peer environment. Regarding gender, for example, Bronwen visits a Scandinavian country where she finds a greater acceptance of girls' sexual desire and their access to contraceptives without relying on medical prescriptions. This allows for a shift toward a greater acceptance of her own desires:

> In [Scandinavian country] sex is definitely more talked about. It's not a stigma. It's not a bad thing. I thought it was a very good thing actually. It's just more present. That takes away, you know, the badness about it. They talk about it more and most of them had had sex. Sometimes they'd have conversations about it. At first I was totally freaked out. I was like, 'Oh my God.' You know? But I got used to it. I realized I don't have to be scared about that. I thought it was actually pretty healthy. Also, they don't need prescriptions for birth control. It's a trust thing and it's more accepted. I think it made me more comfortable with it... I am more confident with myself.

Additionally, girls indicate that athletic communities, more often co-ed communities involved in leisure sports activities, can provide them with an empowering body experience:

> I pretty much only have guy friends and only one friend who is a girl. I go to lunch with them and hang around. Catch up. Like guys aren't all having to be like potential boyfriends. Like, I don't have to put on an act. When I am with people who are athletes, also girls, they are in sweatpants. So I am not the only one who doesn't need to wear revealing and tight clothing. (Shannon)

Ashley has a similar group she connects with around community sports. Both Shannon and Ashley have experienced social exclusion. In the leisure co-ed social athletic groups, girls appreciate not only the emphasis on their athletic performance (rather than on their objectification) but also being invited to join in with what they perceive as greater norms of acceptance and loyalty.

Being embraced by one's ethnocultural community is a powerful embodying experience. In late adolescence, as girls examine issues of identity, they sometimes start to explore their connection to their heritage. This journey is particularly meaningful for girls whose heritage has been devalued by the dominant culture. Jackie, a member of the Aboriginal community, lives in an urban center with a White majority and a significant percentage of "visible minorities" (over 40%), yet an overwhelming minority of members of the Aboriginal community. For Jackie, taking part in ceremonies within her community is an important embodying experience:

> Well, every year, my mom brings us to a Pow Wow, which is a Native get-together from all the tribes that live in Canada, like people come from British Columbia. It's actually held in [city]. I remember the first time I ever went to one and my mom got me this little wishing stone, it was a hand-painted stone, and I thought it was the most amazing thing ever... Soon, when I turn 16, I am going through a girls' ceremony, which is to go to a Shaman and get a package, a leather bag with items that they put in the bag for you. My mother has her own bag and in it things for her journey.

Jackie feels "proud of my heritage, I've got a very proud heritage. It gives me more self-esteem than other people." Her connection to her heritage through collective ceremonies and shared rituals with members of her family is important in withstanding racism. In late adolescence, she makes a commitment to become an activist for Aboriginal Peoples, saying, "I want to do something about it... determined... to do something for my culture."

Ashley also notes, in particular in late adolescence, her wish to learn and be connected to the richness of her African heritage:

> When my cousins moved here, they are speaking with my mom in her language. So that's when I had the opportunity to hear my own language. This gives me the opportunity to get immersed in my culture, when I'm with my family. My mom tried to teach me the language when I was growing up, but I was stubborn. But now I'm a little bit more passionate. Like whenever they're speaking something, I'm like, 'Oh what are you saying?' I feel not included. Because having conversations, telling this wonderful story and they're all laughing around the dinner table, 'Tell me please what are you saying?' So they're just like, 'learn the language.' So just little motivational things like that. But that's when I get really involved in my culture, when my family's over.

Living "isolated" from any close-knit community until the arrival of extended family members, both Ashley and her mother have been exposed to, and affected by, widespread body-shape pressures. Nonetheless, Ashley holds a broader, alternative, lens toward weight and aging, informed by her mother's heritage, making her more respectful of the natural diversity of bodies and of the grace of aging:

> When she [mother] was younger, if you were overweight because you have so much money and you have so much food to eat then it's like a positive thing, because many people starved all the time, so it wasn't uncommon to see people who were skinny... For real in Africa if you get gray hair, it's a positive thing, because you're getting older, you've lived that long, you have a lot of wisdom, and it gives you respect, whereas here it's a negative thing to have gray hair and people are trying to fight ageing, whereas there people are embracing aging. So my mom doesn't think it's a big deal to be getting older and I don't think it's a big deal either. So I try to embrace it. I try to retain some things from my culture.

To summarize experiences in the domain of Social Power and Relational Connections, girls in late adolescence learn firsthand about their vulnerable position in relationships and institutions related to patriarchy and other oppressive ideologies. Yet, by partaking in such institutions, they sometimes find that their only way to access power is to conform to said ideologies and alter their own bodies and embodied practices, rather than target the social environment for change—even when holding a critical lens toward oppressive ideologies and structures. Girls in late adolescence describe the existence of barriers in accessing resources related to education, sexual health, and geographical sites of safety and of meaningful activities. Further, they highlight a compromised quality of embodied lives when compared with boys, especially with respect to appearance and sexuality. Concurrently, pressures mount to achieve social power by embodying idealized appearance characteristics that condense societal prejudices on multiple aspects of social location. While pressures on the body and its appearance are intense, having access to empowering relationships and to equitable communities can enhance girls' experiences of embodiment.

CHAPTER SUMMARY

During older adolescence the body is commonly a site of heightened struggle. Girls in older adolescence often engage in body practices aimed at the constriction of body size, self-sexualization, and approximating an idealized image of women. Concerns about body appearance extend beyond late adolescence to possible future changes related to pregnancy or age. Examining the social experiences of girls in late adolescence in the physical, mental, and social power domains can help clarify girls' embodied experiences during this phase. In the physical domain, girls aim to comply with restrictive constraints regarding size and appearance; they also face growing risks of sexual violation as they become more regularly engaged in sexual activities within a culture that does not sanction women's agency, nor their well being, in desires. In the mental domain, girls face greater sexualized objectification and greater pressures to comply with "feminine" expectations regarding comportment and relational patterns. In the social power domain, girls sometimes find that their only way to access power is to try and approximate idealized appearance characteristics, even when holding a critical lens toward oppressive ideologies. Nonetheless, empowering relationships and membership in equitable communities can provide girls with some relief from adverse pressures.

References

Borowski, H., Eisenberg, M., Bucchianeri, M. M., Piran, N., & Neumark-Sztainer, D. (2015). Feminist identity, body image, and disordered eating. *Eating Disorders: The Journal of Treatment and Prevention, 22*, 1–15.

Brown, L. M. (2003). *Girlfighting: Betrayal and rejection among girls*. New York, NY: New York University Press.

Desruelles, F., Cunningham, S. A., & Dubois, D. (2013). Pubic hair removal: A risk factor for 'minor' STI such as molluscum contagiosum? *Sexually Transmitted Infections, 89*(3), 216.

Heilman, M. E., & Okimoto, T. G. (2007). Why are women penalized for success at male tasks? The implied communality deficit. *Journal of Applied Psychology, 92*, 81–92.

Hill, C., Corbett, C., & St Rose, A. (2010). *Why so few? Women in sciences, technology, engineering, and mathematics*. American Association of University Women. Retrieved from: https://www.aauw.org/files/2013/02/Why-So-Few-Women-in-Science-Technology-Engineering-and-Mathematics.pdf.

Neumark-Sztainer, D., Story, M., Dixon, L. B., & Murray, D. M. (1998). Adolescents engaging in unhealthy weight control behaviors: Are they at risk for other health-compromising behaviors? *American Journal of Public Health, 88*(6), 952–955.

Ogden, C. L., Carroll, M. D., Kit, B. K., & Flegal, K. M. (2012). *Prevalence of obesity in the states, 2009–2010 United States, 2009–2010. NCHS Data Brief No. 82*. Retrieved from: www.cdc.gov/nchs/data/databriefs/db82.pdf.

Phelan, J. E., & Rudman, L. A. (2010). Reactions to ethnic deviance: The role of backlash in racial stereotype maintenance. *Journal of Personality and Social Psychology, 99*, 265–281.

Piran, N. (1999). The reduction of preoccupation with body weight and shape in schools: A feminist approach. In N. Piran, M. P. Levine, & C. Steiner-Adair (Eds.), *Preventing eating disorders: A handbook of interventions and special challenges* (pp. 148–150). Philadelphia: Brunner/Mazel (Taylor & Francis Group).

Piran, N. (2001). Re-inhabiting the body from the inside out: Girls transform their school environment. In D. L. Tolman, & M. Brydon-Miller (Eds.), *From subjects to subjectivities: A handbook of interpretive and participatory methods* (pp. 218–238). New York: New York University Press.

Piran, N. (2010). A feminist perspective on risk factor research and on the prevention ofeating disorders. *Eating Disorders: The Journal of Treatment and Prevention, 18*(3), 183–198.

Piran, N. (2015). New possibilities in the prevention of eating disorders: The introduction of positive body image measures. *Body Image, 14*, 146–157.

Piran, N., & Robinson, S. (2006). The association between disordered eating and substance use and abuse in women: A community-based investigation. *Women and Health, 44*, 1–20.

Planned Parenthood Health Centers. (2017). *American Public Health Association*. Retrieved from: https://www.apha.org/~/media/files/pdf/advocacy/letters/2017/170203_plannedparenthood.ashx.

Rudman, L. A., Moss-Racusin, C. A., Phelan, J. E., & Nauts, S. (2012). Status incongruity and backlash effects: Defending the gender hierarchy motivates prejudice toward female leaders. *Journal of Experimental Social Psychology, 48*, 165–179.

Simms, R. (2001). Controlling images and the gender construction of enslaved African women. *Gender and Society, 15*(6), 879–897.

CHAPTER

6

Re-capturing Qualified Freedom: Possibilities in Adult Women's Journeys

> I think of my body as the temple that holds my soul. So I have to take care of it and treat it with respect and if I mean just on the physical level if you want to be able to do the active stuff then I have to keep it in good shape you know... I'm at home in my body, I'm at peace in my body you know and I'm comfortable and it's not perfect but that's okay... I worked for these wrinkles. [Marie]

> I have transcended this awful negative self-concept, feeling ugly, to be completely happy with myself at this age in my life. I am happy in my body... My voice blossomed... I am a sexual, sensual person... I take care of myself and I think I will be able to work for a while... I can wear a lumber jacket if I want, I can still feel sexual, I can still feel good about myself. [Gwen]

> I've gained weight in, on my abdomen, a belly, and it's just not going, I can't take it off. I can't lose that belly fat. I can't get the muscle back in my arms and legs and so you see the little loose skin you know, arm flab. It's an obsession... I have to use weights now. I need it for self-image... I was always inhibited a lot because of my body. You feel bad about yourself and inhibited out in public. [Reni]

These narratives by Marie, Gwen, and Reni, all women in their 60s, reflect different ways of inhabiting one's body at this stage of older adulthood. Marie, a White woman of middle class and rural background, has cherished her body, considering it a comfortable site to inhabit throughout most of her life journey. Enjoying a similarly positive Experience of Embodiment (EE) in her 60s, Gwen, a White woman of a working

Journeys of Embodiment at the Intersection of Body and Culture
http://dx.doi.org/10.1016/B978-0-12-805410-9.00006-2

class and rural background, alludes in her narrative to a very different body journey—transforming the experience of her body from that of a deficient and constrained site to one of embodied agency and passion. On the other hand, Reni, a Asian-Canadian woman from a working (in childhood) to a middle class (in adulthood) and urban background, describes a lifelong struggle with her body, which she has consistently experienced as a burdensome and disruptive site. Women's body journeys throughout adulthood, reflect both the continued hold social structures have on women's bodies and new possibilities of freedom from oppressive forces.

The range of experiences of embodiment during adulthood, resembling the tweens phase in its breadth, relates to renewed processes of dismantling corsets, which take place throughout adulthood. Most women engage in body journeys that aim to shift, and even counteract, adverse body-anchored experiences in the physical, mental, and social power domains. Processes that are constructive to women's ownership of their bodies are complex, involve the interaction of women's agency with alternative social experiences and structures, and lead to important shifts in women's embodied agency, connection, and well-being. For example, Alex, a Latina woman in her early 20s who endured poverty, sexual abuse, immigration, date rape, and a physically and emotionally abusive relationship with her adult male partner, describes the following EE at the point of deciding to leave her abusive partner:

> *I am more with my body*, more connected, and I respect my body more. But when I pay attention to him [boyfriend] I am back to the same place of being self-conscious and very uncomfortable… Like I haven't gone to school, because this guy's in my life and I can't make that decision for myself. So I feel trapped at this moment, but I am in a process of trying to make decisions for myself… I begin to come to terms with my own desires. I have to learn again about what I want, what makes me feel good, what I need, what I liked in bed, and that I like music and romance and stuff like that… It's not like now after sex I would be curious, 'how is he looking at me,' very self-conscious. I accept my body more now.

Sam, a White woman in her mid-20s starting to address neglect in the context of poverty, a breach of her sexual boundaries, and exploitation of her physical labor—all during her childhood—similarly describes initial shifts in her EE. These shifts relate to her ability to reflect critically about herself in relation to her social context and to forming a supportive relationship with an older woman who becomes her role model. Yet her narratives also reflect continued social oppressions related to sexual harassment by male colleagues, the impact of limited access to education resulting in lower paying and possibly riskier jobs, and the lack of validation of female desire.

> I do feel that *'waking up'* is mostly about bringing my needs to the surface, being aware of them, and acting on satisfying them. I believe in trying to return to an awareness of my own needs and desires, and standing up for them, learning about myself and others in that process… I don't usually comment to other people on how I see my body. I rarely say anything like 'I feel fat.' I am trying to maintain an inner focus… Exploring my own body sexually has always been a challenge. I am still quite self-conscious, not of my own physical body, but the exploration of it, even with a partner… [At work, with male colleagues] I have felt that I had to give in to any request, that I was not clear. So I ended up in situations that I had no control, that I didn't feel safe. But now I can say, 'no thank you.' I can take care of myself better… Often women's positive connections to their bodies occur within the context of relationships with others and with themselves. Those that are confused have to find that inner self and other people give important lessons that help find that.

These narratives depicting important shifts in Alex and Sam's embodied agency and attuned self-care reflect the continued social hold on their bodies, maintained by oppressive social conditions as varied as: physical violations and sexual harassment in the domestic and work spheres, restricted access to resources (e.g., education), and lack of validation of female sexual desire. At the same time, particular social processes in adulthood, such as validating and empowering relational connections, support their movement toward positive embodiment. Our research suggests theoretical continuity between corseting during adolescence or childhood and the unhooking of corsets by some women during adulthood. The same corsets imposed on girls' bodies, latest by adolescence, to create docile "feminine" bodies, get dismantled by some women during adulthood. Processes associated with dismantling corsets therefore deepen the understanding of the relationship between body and culture. Further, dismantling corsets leads to embodied agency and attunement to passions and self-care. This chapter focuses on these processes of dismantling corsets in the physical, mental, and social power and relational connections domains. However, this chapter also reflects the complexity of making changes within existing social structures of power, validating both barriers and shifts.

YES, I CAN! PATHS TO PHYSICAL FREEDOM

> I think one of the most amazing things was that I got to see the weaknesses of the men that I always thought were so physically powerful and strong. Like a guy who was running, a big guy. By the time we ran 7.5 K he was bawling, crying. So I mean I was sensitive to his feelings but at the same time I thought, 'How do you men just brag about how tough you are and here you are with little tears coming out of your eyes.' And I was in just as much pain as he was, except that, you know, I just did it!

Alex, who joined the army immediately after high school to contest gender-based constraints transmitted by her father, describes her delight in discovering her physical prowess in early adulthood, after years of not engaging in any physical activities. During second grade, while living in Central America, Alex was summoned away from the playing fields, as well as from school, and placed into the restricted domestic sphere to take care of her younger siblings. Like other girls and women, her joyful, immersed engagement in intense physical activities stopped then, arresting experiences of physical competence, agency, and related joy. The unexpected discovery of her physical prowess in young adulthood shifts, for the first time in a long time, Alex's sense of her body, away from being merely a constrained sexualized object. Her narrative also suggests the value of systemic changes that provide girls and women with access to sites of physical activities in the public sphere.

Freedom in Physical Engagement and Movement is one of the four dimensions of Physical Freedom (see Table 1.2). Restrictions to physical engagement, free movement, and taking physical space remain active throughout adulthood during most women's lives and are "efficient" in reducing their agency in the world. Multiple barriers to physical engagement, introduced throughout girlhood, continue in adulthood. Most women reach adulthood having ceased immersion in joyful physical activities, feeling removed from the passion associated with such immersion, and, not surprisingly, noting their underutilized and underdeveloped physical skills (e.g., Roth & Basow, 2004). Exposure to uncommon opportunities of physical engagement, such as those described by Alex who is "allowed" into male territory—the army—frees physical prowess. However, there are still many more opportunities for men, compared with women, to participate in sports and related activities. Many professional and leisure sports organizations are led by men, continuing men's hold on territories of action and agency. Similarly, the social construction of the field of sports as a "masculine" domain still persists (Connell, 1987; Messner, 2002).

Media images that represent the functional strength of women, rather than their sexualized "fit" bodies, are disruptive to the social status quo. For example, a 2015 article in the *New York Times* (Rothenberg, 2015) described Serena Williams' "large biceps and a mold-breaking muscular frame... Her rivals could try to emulate her physique, but most of them choose not to." The article continued with a quote from Tomasz Wiktorowski, coach of Agnieszka Radwanska, who is listed as 5′8″ and only 123 pounds (a BMI = 18.7, which is at the lower end of normal weight): "It's our decision to keep her as the smallest player in the top 10. Because, first of all she is a woman, and she wants to be a woman." While Radwanska is a world-class tennis player, requiring muscular strength, she is also kept "small!" The need to be physically small in body size, observed in our studies among early and postpubescent girls, remains important and an area of struggle for many women in adulthood. These findings are in line with other studies that have examined adult women's weight preoccupation (Maine & Kelly, 2016; Tiggemann, 2004) and their restrictive physical comportment in public (Bartky, 1988).

Hand in hand with the restrictions on taking physical space are restrictions on women's free movement in the public sphere. Such restrictions are common among adult women in many parts of the world. Yet, differences in the freedom of movement between women and men exist in North America as well. Violence against women is an important factor that restricts women's movement in the public sphere, as discussed earlier in the chapter on late adolescence. In addition, values held by different groups are unfavorable to women's free movement. Several women in the older women's study had been directly instructed, during different times in their lives, to restrict their movement outside of the house. Reni, early 60s and of Asian-Canadian heritage, was discouraged from driving since it was seen as being not "traditional enough for a wife;" and Louise—early 50s, White and of a working class and rural background—was not only discouraged from driving but also penalized for moving away at the age of 17 to pursue her education. Her narratives illustrate the intertwining of different forms of restrictions, as well as directives to stay confined to the domestic sphere:

> I feel like a black sheep of the family, maybe because I have seen the world, I have traveled. [Family members] make some inappropriate comment about, you know, I go where it's greener. I was reprimanded for leaving. Man goes to work, the woman stays home. The man does the earning, the woman has no education and just

> takes care of the children. Just to give you an example. I wanted to get my driver's license. My dad said no way although my mom drove and my brothers got a license. I wanted to go to school. No way, you don't go to school like after high school. Yeah you don't do that. I did go to school. I left [place] and came here [urban center] so I could pursue my study. My family was not happy. My mom told me 'Oh your dad is not happy'... My brothers say, 'you move out, you're on your own,' penalizing me and [woman relative] for moving.

Women like Sarah, White and in her early 50s, of a middle class and a rural background, similarly describe how giving up Physical Freedom as a young adult derailed their professional pursuits:

> Leaving to [urban center] at 18 was freedom. It was embracing change. I had a job with a large corporation... I came back to [rural site] to marry as my parents wanted. I think that the pain I am living today, that some people will live a lifetime without having discovered their passion, links to that decision. I feel in my body today that I should have stayed over there.

For most women, physical confinement either relates to or is compounded by being inequitably delegated a range of domestic chores, including the care of others. Jean, a White woman in her 50s from a middle-class background describes staying home in a rural area with her daughter "because my husband had the car so I was stuck in the home and it was the loneliest time." Louise, a White woman in her early 50s from a working-class background, waited for her children to grow so she "could have the freedom to go and do yoga." And as Reni describes, "I wanted to get back to school, I got in, I put my children in daycare, but because they got sick, he [husband] said, 'You quit.'" For several women, being restricted to the domestic domain continues into old age. According to Guinness, White and from a middle-class background, "I spend eleven-hour days in my daughter's house taking care of my grandchildren... I had more time to myself when I worked full-time and taught courses." For others, like Sonia, an immigrant to Canada of Asian-African heritage, making a living at old age involves working in domestic sites—"I take food orders from neighbors."

Lack of freedom of movement in the physical sphere also involves a woman moving, often repeatedly and against her will, to sites that fit her male partner's wishes. This precludes engagement in valued domains of life, such as: sustaining deep relational connections during child-rearing ("And my ex-husband had a penchant for quitting jobs so we kept moving, and I had my children away from my mother who was my biggest helper" [Gwen]), pursuing education ("Actually I had finished high school and I had been saving my money to go to university, and then I met the man that I married, and... we moved again and again so it wasn't possible to continue..." [Nina]), and work opportunities ("There were no more opportunities where we lived" [Sarah]). Having no choice or equitable dialogues regarding freedom of movement and physical location in the world compromises individuals' freedom, agency, and fulfillment.

The dismantling of corsets restricting Freedom of Physical Engagement and Movement takes place throughout adulthood and has an immediate positive impact on embodied experiences—verifying the power and importance of such freedom in women's lives. Meaningfully, Freedom of Physical Engagement evokes powerful childhood memories of competence, passion, and body connection. The journey, therefore, is often easier and sometimes only possible for women who have experienced such freedom in childhood. In addition to the emergence of childhood embodied memories of freedom, adult women's narratives regarding re-engagement in physical activities often include critical commentaries about restrictive factors that they have faced, as well as their strong support for enhancing such opportunities among girls and other women. For example, Laya, a White woman in her mid-20s of middle-class standing, who had been a strong skier from childhood to early adolescence, describes living the following decade of her life disconnected from her body: "Well I know I wasn't in touch with it (body) at all." However, once she re-engages in physical activities as a young adult, she also reconnects with her body:

> We went on a mountain bike ride, and my body was relaxed. I was just in the zone. And to me this is the most amazing feeling of being in your body. It's so liberating and I really feel sorry for women that can't get that. And the further I am from that physical part of me, the less strong I feel in my body, the more distant and disconnected I am to myself and what I need. I think there is a stigma for some men that women aren't supposed to be as athletic. I think that is threatening for some men. What they don't realize is that they will have a healthier, more balanced, strong woman. But I think if we teach women that they can be free, that they should get to know their bodies in a healthy way, we'd have a lot healthier women and [fewer] women with depression. That is actually a positive thing to pass on to girls, 'you will be on the soccer team!' So it helps having these spaces for girls and young women, like actually having the teams available whether it's community teams or school teams.

This transition from inactivity to activity can take place at any time during adulthood. It is not surprising, though, that for adult women such re-engagement occurs sometimes only in later adulthood, when constrictive ties related to the care of children, domestic chores, and work are loosened. Further, changes in health status during older adulthood may compel some women to attend to such needs, including engagement in attuned physical activities. A shift toward attuned physical activities incites not only renewed experiences of embodied pride, agency, and well-being but also often childhood memories of such engagements among older women as well. For example, Louise, White, in her early 50s, from a rural and working-class background describes the continuity between her engagement in yoga and running in her early 50s to childhood freedoms:

> The sense of freedom never changed, to be honest. It's still there. Maybe that's why I don't like to be tied down to anything. So when I had my kids I had to stay in one place, I couldn't do as much. And then when the children got older and I didn't need a babysitter I started to look after myself a little bit and started taking yoga. And then I got diagnosed with [health condition], and I investigated it, lost a ton of weight, changed my diet, started running, and continued with the yoga... I find that my body is much better than where I was maybe when [I] was married... When I was a girl there were no restrictions. We were so free. We were outside almost 24-seven. I had a lot of freedom and I was very active. It felt good, it felt right. I guess I could compare to those *wild horses that live outside*.

Similarly, other women, free to roam as children, highlight the surfacing of childhood memories of Physical Freedom on re-engaging in physical activities during older adulthood. Jean, White and in her 60s, from a middle-class background, describes the surfacing of these body memories when she starts practicing yoga as an adult:

> I think when I was a small child I remember being at the beach with my cousins and I think we were very, very small; two or three, and just total freedom running up and down the beach and just sitting in the sand, and I could reflect inside myself and I was aware then and I never really re-captured that feeling until I started yoga [during her 60s]. You almost get back to a child-like state.

The journey back to physical engagement is more arduous for women whose access was barred throughout most of their lives. Gwen, a White woman in her 60s from a rural and working-class background, details this internalized message: "I was a girl and I bought into the stereotype of no sports for girls. My brothers were all in hockey and my father was involved with them." The family's limited financial resources were thus channeled to her brothers' physical activities. Consequently, she learned to fear the ball—a fear she still holds: "I saw the ball coming and I just covered my head and ducked; I still do." Gwen has returned to physical activities only after developing health issues in her late 50s, a time she associates with other practices of attuned self-care, including leaving a constrictive heterosexual marriage. She was both surprised and proud to find herself physically competent during her 60s. "My trainer at the gym bashes my body around. I can run, I can jump, more than in my 40s." Getting university training in her late 40s and, consequently, gaining employment in the health field, Gwen was able to access a trainer's help.

Our research suggests that re-engagement in physical activities during adulthood is facilitated by: having experienced passionate immersion in such activities during childhood and adolescence and being involved in relational connections and larger social contexts that support such freedom. Participation in different community-based programs can be costly, and hence, inaccessible to some women. Nonetheless, as long as the public sphere is safe, women living with financial constraints can sometimes find ways to engage in physical activities. According to Alice, a White woman in her late 60s who lives on old-age government pension, "I walk and I bike in the summertime and down into the ravines and if you bike off rush hours it's no so bad." However, we find that, at the intersection of limited past exposure to physical activities and freedom of movement, social norms (or laws) prohibiting freedom of physical engagement and movement in the public territory, and financial constraints, the likelihood of engagement in physical activities during adulthood is reduced.

Safety for the Body Territory, another dimension of Physical Freedom, is encroached upon in two main ways: violations against the body, and coercive body alterations and practices. National surveys in North America indicate no decline in the rates of police-reported violence against women during the past decade (Sinha, 2013; Sexual violence: Facts at a glance, 2012). In Canada (Sinha, 2013), rates of police-reported cases of violence against women that pass the "threshold" of the criminal code was around 1.2%, higher than the rates for men. Men perpetrated 87% of crimes against women, with intimate partners (45%) committing most of these crimes. Police-reported violent assaults against women included both physical (around 75%) and sexual assaults (around 35%). Clearly, the domestic sphere is not safe for many women. About 60% of homicide victims had a prior history of family violence inflicted by the same male perpetrator, yet these women were not protected. In Canada, women members of the Aboriginal community have suffered from the highest prevalence of violence. Among women in the United States (Sexual violence: Facts at a glance, 2012), highest rates of reported rape were among American Indian/Alaska Natives (26.9%) and African-American women

(22%)—this compared with Whites (18.8%) and Hispanics (14.6%). Overall, about one in five women (18.3%) (compared with one in 71 men (1.4%)) reported rape at some time in their lives, with 37.4% of women victims raped between the ages of 18–24. This pattern is continuous with the youth data: 42.2% of girl rape victims were first raped before age 18, 29.9% were raped between the ages of 11–17, and 12.3% were first raped when they were age 10 or younger. Among female rape victims, perpetrators were reported to be intimate partners (51.1%) and family members (12.5%). History of violence is associated with significant morbidity. Most rapes, especially those perpetrated by intimate partners, go unreported due to women's low belief that the police will help and fear of reprisal, among other reasons (Langton, Berzofsky, Krebs, & Smiley-McDonald, 2012).

In our studies, 7 out of 11 young women (64%) and 17 out of 31 older women (56%) detail a history of physical or sexual violations of a range of severities, including sexual harassment. Most women reached adulthood with a history of such violations. However, one young woman and two older women describe having been involved as adults with abusive partners; one older woman describes forced sexual intercourse with her husband, which she did not label as rape; and four women (two younger and two older) describe sexual harassment involving physical coercion in the workplace. Further, women, either as girls or adults, have experienced limited or no support around their experiences of violations, often believing themselves culpable in such violations. Women and girls (including very young girls) commonly internalize dominant values of a rape culture, such as: they "asked for it" or it was "their fault" (Buchwald, Fletcher, & Roth, 1993). Alex, early 20s and of Latina heritage, for example, shares her thoughts about being molested as a nine-year-old girl by an older family member in the following way: "I felt completely responsible for it. I thought maybe I was doing something wrong, so I wouldn't tell anybody. Absolutely no one." Alex carried this sense of isolation around trauma to adulthood. As Judy Herman (1992) described in her groundbreaking book *Trauma and Recovery*, the experience of trauma involves disrupted connection to one's relational and social communities.

Violations disrupt women's experiences of well-being and agency, and challenge their comfort and connection to their bodies. The impact of violations depended on age of the woman, the severity, length, and number of violation, and availability of other relational connections and support. Despite continued systemic factors that perpetuate violence against women, generally, with greater violence toward girls and women in specific social contexts, the adult women in the study sometimes engaged in processes of healing, facilitated by their own courage and determination, as well as access to social and relational contexts that provided support, such as therapy.

The tasks of healing from trauma in early adulthood complicate the normative challenges of that phase, in particular identity explorations and relational connections involving intimacy (Arnette, 2000). Claire, early 20s, of Caribbean-Canadian heritage and a working-class background, was raped during her tweens and was the victim of pervasive sexual harassment during adolescence. She relied on forming several safe relational adult connections and a gradual shedding the layers of baggy clothes she had worn for a decade, to become more present in her body: "I've always had problems with the perception of my own body. I didn't wear like shorts or skirts or fitting shirts since the rape." She also risked relationships that involved intimacy with both genders, saying, "I want to get out there and meet people. Not that I didn't meet people but just to really not be afraid, I mean life traumatic things." For Sam, who experienced sexual violation and neglect as a child, and sexual harassment at work, establishing boundaries as a young adult was a new experience, "I'd never established boundaries for certain situations even basic social situations."

Similarly, Ashley, early 20s and from a middle-class background, was sexually abused as a young child by a family relative and then raped as a tween by an older peer. She works in and outside of therapy to deal with intense anxiety and panic, overcome her disconnection from her body, and tackle both education and forming intimate relationships:

> The past comes back and haunts you. You spend your whole life trying to deal with it. I started cutting myself, anorexia and stuff, I was detaching myself... I had flashbacks. I was attacking myself. For me my body, I'm not attached to my body. So if I damaged my body, it was because I had no control in my life. My social abilities got severely affected... I am on [antidepressant]. I can't go past some places anymore...

In order to move on from her burdensome past, it was important for Ashley to hear from a health professional that her emotional and behavioral experiences are related to being sexually abused and assaulted.

> Like I had to do a lot of work with a psychologist to find out, okay this is why I'm doing it... Now I'm in the post. You know, trying to run a career and be, you know, an adult, and I hopefully want to start a family but... I don't want to raise another girl like me.

Striving to own one's body with agency, comfort, and joy following trauma is often a lifelong process, as reflected in the narratives of older women. An adult partner who perpetuates the experience of trauma can prolong the process of recovery. For example, Jordan, who was sexually abused as a girl, married young to an abusive older man who was later discovered as sexually abusing children. "I married a molester, and I did not realize it until later." Not until she started therapy, following the dissolution of her marriage, did she realize the scope of her abuse history. As her trauma-related memories emerged and were processed in therapy, she was able for the first time to connect to her own desire and express it within the context of an intimate relationship.

Sometimes trauma can only be addressed later on in life, once a woman has experienced sufficient emotional and physical safety from earlier violations. Orchid, a Caribbean-Canadian woman in her late 50s, remembers her sexual trauma only in older adulthood, after witnessing the impact of trauma on a younger female relative abused by the same perpetrator. For Orchid, addressing trauma is associated with improved boundaries and self-care, "Not until [name] came up with her memories that I dealt with that in therapy for years. And I am only learning now [late 50s] to take care of myself." Other life events can facilitate processes of healing, as Gwen notes in reference to her experience of fear associated with threats and physical abuse by a relative: "It kept me from exploring the world… feeling not as capable. When he died, it allowed me to open up and expand." Further, women use their own healing to support the healing processes of others. For example, Jane, a White woman of a middle-class background in her late 50s who experienced severe physical and sexual abuse during childhood, and has faced multiple mental and behavioral disruptions including disordered eating and substance abuse describes being dedicated to using her knowledge to help others in similar situations: "I do peer support and I'm able to help in my community with women. Every day I deal with lots of feelings and pain about everything I witness, but it also fills me with deep compassion."

Whether or not women have been free of body violations through childhood and adolescence, they still encounter sexual harassment at work and in other public spaces, again disrupting their experiences of power, agency, and body comfort. Marie, a White woman of middle-class background who grew up with a sense of safety and healthy boundaries, faced harassment by her instructor during training in the educational field: "He pulled me into a room and touched my breasts… I did not even think about reporting him… He was too high up there." Again, she experienced harassment and threats of serious violation while traveling, both abroad and at home, concluding that, as a woman, "I always thought you you're different, so you always have to be aware, to be careful."

Times of war and forced geographical dislocation severely challenge the safety of women, who become targets of rape (Hargreaves, 2001). Vivian and May, women in their late 50s of Asian heritage, and who resided in refugee camps while fleeing war, were aware of the greater risks for women.

As Vivian describes, "I always feel that women tend to be victims of many things. Women tend to be much more vulnerable and more at risk."

Violence against women is a serious phenomenon that, despite greater national and international awareness, and recognition as a human rights issue, has not been addressed systemically in a way that assures women's well-being. Even in the few countries in the world that specifically address gender equity in their constitution, social processes, educational institutions, the legal system, and the police have not adequately addressed this important human rights issue, with great cost to women, children, and society. This challenge is more severe among specific groups of women, such as women of color and members of indigenous communities in North America (Daniel & Dale, 2013).

Care of the Body is another key dimension of Physical Freedom. For adult women, Care of the Body is centrally related to structural and social inequities that privilege some bodies and disenfranchise others. It is well established, for example, that socioeconomic status is strongly related to health outcomes and mortality (Lantz et al., 1998). In the United States, poverty rates are consistently higher for women than for men (Who is Poor?, 2016). The differences in the financial conditions between women and men are particularly revealing when the rates of poverty are compared between families headed by women and families headed by men: in 2014, 30.6% versus 15.7%, respectively. Rates of poverty are also affected by additional social factors such as race, age, immigration status, and disability. In the United States, rates of poverty are highest among African Americans (26.2%) and Hispanics/Latinos (23.6%), as compared with Whites (10.1%). The higher rates of poverty among women are related to multiple factors, including: the gender gap in salary (women working full time in the United States made 79% of men's salaries in 2014, with gaps existing even when factors such as college major, occupation, hours worked, age, and other factors are controlled), job segregation (wherein "female" jobs pay less than "male" jobs while similar level of skills are required), and the inequitable share in domestic duties, especially childcare (employers are less likely to hire mothers and offer them a lower salary) (The Simple Truth, 2016). While White women make 78% of White men's earnings, African-American women make 63% of White men's salaries.

Thus, women are systemically disadvantaged in their ability to care for their bodies. Single women, single mothers, older women, immigrant women, and women of specific heritages face greater challenges still. In our studies, we found that divorce, for example, represented a marked lowering of women's financial well-being and, with it, challenges of body care were paramount. Louisa, a White woman in her early 50s, had to resort to food banks after her husband left her without a divorce settlement; meanwhile, he continued to work as a professional, making above average income: "Eating right will help with the depression. I have food insecurity, well because I can't go and buy whatever I need. Luckily I happen to live in a catchment area for a good food bank." Grace, in her early 50s and of African-Canadian heritage, describes the challenge of living healthily following her immigration to Canada with her daughter:

> I came here pretty slender... and then I was getting bigger. I was cutting back on nutritious food because of affordability, so I was buying cheaper things—filling but not nutritious. No vegetables. I was also stressed out so I was eating cheap cookies. I had to count my pennies.

May, a woman in her late 50s who immigrated to North America from an Asian country as a young adult, without knowledge of the English language, has health problems related to needing to hold three jobs simultaneously for a total of "eighty hours for a week, not two weeks, one week" to support her daughters and herself. Louise, a White woman in her early 50s, similarly holds multiple part-time jobs to support herself: "I try to make the best for my income. That's why I'm taking contracts and I have like I say 18 jobs all over the city." Women in the study with mental health challenges requiring repeated hospitalizations also faced multiple challenges in caring for their bodies.

Social ideologies both reflect and maintain social structures of inequity. A key social ideology related to Care of the Body involves the care of others. As Tronto (1993) suggests, the care of others, especially the physical care of others, is often delegated to less privileged members of society. It is important to examine how this ideology affects women's care of their own bodies. Most girls, and younger and older women in our studies, from all walks of life, reached adulthood having learned and internalized their particular role in the complex task of caring for others. This task requires ongoing emotional attunement and physical labor. Already acculturated from early girlhood to take care of others in the domestic sphere, adult women face accentuated challenges during the child bearing and rearing phase in homes organized around the ideology of gender inequity. As adulthood progresses, women often continue with this care taking role, including of aging parents.

What is so striking about this ideology is that no counter ideology exists that aims to protect women from the eroding impact of such engagement. The lack of such an ideology reflects the disregard for women's health and well-being, and women's inequitable status in society. Additionally, women's labor in the domestic sphere is neither valued nor financially remunerated. Nina, a White woman in her late 60s, describes this eroding process, commenting on how helpful an alternative ideology could have been for her:

> I was expected to be this perfect wife and mother. And it's not a comfortable place to be when you know someone is criticizing you

> and at the same time is expecting so much of you. And I actually felt that it was a kind of abuse... Everything in place and neat, so that he could go to work and he didn't have to work at home. It isn't as though I didn't work. I couldn't keep up, and it was raising the children as a single parent because he was working a lot of the time. Cooking had to be exceptional... I was getting tired. It got harder to keep up. I could not keep up with everything. It's too much. I'm tired. He was draining me, chiseling into me, taking out what was sustaining me. That's sometimes the early teachings that we have as children, have sort of attached themselves to us in ways that we don't realize and so behavior continues, that you, when you should have said no, I shouldn't have that happen but I would definitely say, 'listen, listen to your body you know, and if you're tired rest, if you are feeling worn out then nurture yourself in some way' and I wish that I had known how to do it back then. I wish someone I respected would say to me, 'you know just enjoy your life, too.'

Being of a middle-class background, Nina was able to delegate a few tasks or get help at home—though the multiplicity of tasks continued to take a toll. Other women could not get help, either because gender ideologies in their social environments precluded their "release" of household duties or, importantly, because they could not afford such help. Reni, Asian-Canadian and from a middle-class background, says that she was never allowed to loosen the tight noose of the care for others ideology:

> You're sick and, you know, we just still have to get up and do what we have to do normally. They [male partners] are not going to feel that they need to help us. I have learned to play my role what is expected of me... If I was a boy, my mother would have overprotected me, nourished me over a girl. If there was food left, she would have given me more than my sister. The boys are usually not expected to do too much. Girls are expected to do cooking... everything. I didn't have the chance to go out with friends or to watch movies... I basically went to school and came home to help my mom. I still have that engraved in my mind. So yeah growing up I continued that way. And then my husband also expects me to do all the housework and cooking. Yeah it's like when I'm busy or when I'm tired or when I'm depressed then I don't want to do it but I do.

Reni's moving words clarify her wish for protection, which she believed she could have had as a boy and, later, a man. For Orchid, a

Caribbean-Canadian woman in her late 50s, the idea of self-protection came only at a later age:

> Yeah because we're not taught to value ourselves as much as we value our products like our children and our man, we polish and shine them and don't really look at ourselves too much. But I am learning the airplane rule: put my emergency mask on first and then put on theirs. I used to be the opposite. This is just in my late 50s. Lately I have just started to focus more on myself.

As these narratives suggest, several women problematized the way they lived in their bodies and took active steps to incorporate care of themselves into their lives. At times, this was accomplished by leaving traditionally organized marriages. If they then decided to construct new relationships with female or male partners, they consciously considered their well-being and the care they could receive in said relationships. Andrea, a White woman in her 50s from a middle-class background, states:

> I actually think he [husband] resented having to take care of me [when sick]. I really felt very lonely… It made me think about getting older and what if I became sick later on. Part of me knew that I couldn't depend on him to really take care of me, not in the way I would take care of him. It made me look at my marriage differently.

The road to Freedom of Desire, the fourth dimension of Physical Freedom, can be challenging; yet, owning and embracing one's desire is associated with embodied joy, agency, and well-being. Social conditions can be so constraining and prohibitive as to bar some women from ever connecting with their desires. Other women, however, go through a challenging and sometimes lengthy process to owning their desire, sometimes achieved only in older adulthood. These reconnection journeys involve countering key adverse social processes to owning desire, in particular: body violations, the lack of social validation and sanctioning of women's desires, and heterosexism.

The aggregated history of body violations in the different domains of women's lives—at home and at public sites—comprises an ongoing challenge to owning sexual desire. Alex, early 20s and Latina, exemplifies the struggle to connect to desire within the context of repeated violations in a rape culture:

> [Childhood] I was sexually molested when I was a child [for a few years, by a family member]. While it happened I was completely terrified. I thought the world was going to end. I knew that there was

> something being done that wasn't supposed to be done. I felt completely responsible for it. I thought maybe I was doing something wrong. So I kept it to myself.

Nonetheless, during early adolescence, while already in North America, she reconnected with desire despite her fear, shame, and worries about not being "normal." In reconnecting positively with desire, she utilized childhood images that equated her mother's adult sexuality with power and made the decision to relinquish her belief in God—a belief that, during childhood, caused her to view herself as a "sinner:"

> I wanted to feel in love, infatuated. I was trying to experiment with my body. I was curious about my body. I didn't know what's going on in my body or sexuality. Am I normal or abnormal? And at the same time, I felt guilty, I felt scared. I felt very ashamed. Sometimes I thought, is this like death? But after three years I decided to stop being constantly scared, maybe because nothing bad happened to me, maybe I am normal. I just kind of decided to accept myself… I thought if I looked like my mother, it meant power. She was cocky. I thought either I go mental and see psychologists or try to deal with it on my own.

However, at mid-adolescence, after one positive sexual experience, a date rape shattered the positive connection to desire Alex had succeeded to attain. After the rape, she engaged in sexual activity without the experience of desire and without protection, along with other potentially harmful behaviors, searching for psychological relief:

> That year I was raped and that's a big difference. He started kissing me and then he forced himself on me… I specifically said, 'No.' I said, 'I'm a virgin,' and he said 'So what?' I thought, 'I don't think I can deal with another thing. Like one was enough. Like two things now.' After that, I did not care anymore. I would sleep with guys just to do it. There were times I didn't use protection. I felt bad, cheap, dirty. I was skipping school. I wasn't eating right. I was smoking and drinking. I would let myself go hungry for a while. I was so angry with everything and everyone at this time. Maybe I had given up on sex being a special thing. I wanted that feeling of heaven and candles and music, but I was fooling myself.

Following these experiences, in early adulthood Alex embarked on a relationship with a man who was emotionally and physically abusive to her, which further disrupted her healing and reconnection to desire. In particular, he blamed her for her sexual history and for not being a virgin: "I did get one boyfriend. But out of my past, he affected me the most. He made me feel wrong about my past, criticized me. It hurt a lot. Obviously, I wasn't at peace with everything that had gone in my past." Supported by her family and friends, and even by the individual "integrated report" written for her as a participant in the embodiment study (Piran, 2006, 2016), she left the relationship and started processes of self and body reconnection, including reconnection with desire: "I begin to come to terms with my own desires. I have to learn again about what I want, what makes me feel good, what I need, what I liked in bed, and that I like music and romance and stuff like that." What stands out in Alex's story, and in the stories of other women striving to reconnect with desire following body violations, is the determination and courage it involves.

Following a violation, the journey during adulthood to reconnect positively with desire can be a lengthy one. Andrea, White and in her mid-50s, from a middle-class background, made the following decision in early adulthood, after a date rape in her mid-teens where her life was threatened:

> I told myself that if because of what my ex-boyfriend had done [rape with a death threat] I never trusted anyone or let someone else in, then really he would have won, I would have been a victim forever, and I didn't want to let anyone take that away from me… take my power away, so, when I was ready I started letting people in again.

After the rape, Andrea developed an eating disorder and a range of self-harm behaviors. While she found that it was difficult for her to trust men for a long time, feeling safer around women, she sought partners of both genders who were "sweet," and where she "took control over sexual situations." While she has had positive experiences in desire throughout her adult years, it was only in her late 40s that she found complete comfort and safety in desire:

> At this point in my life I find it much more erotic to be with a woman than a man. It's more exciting. There is complete closeness and physically there's a lot of passion between us. She is very thoughtful, and that makes me feel close to her. It's hard to describe, I just love her and when we are together I just feel more myself. She also has a little extra weight and a tummy, and I think that connection and closeness makes my weight not matter.

Finding desire within the contexts of safety, thoughtfulness, and closeness helped Andrea's acceptance of, and connection to, her own body—aspects of experience that were disrupted for many years. Like Andrea, several

other women who experienced violations could only reconnect to their desire in older adulthood. Others, exposed to repeated violations, were never able to reconnect with their desire, and thus were barred from it as a source of a joy and power.

Lack of validation (Fine, 1988; Tolman, 2002) and concurrent vilification of women's sexual desire is yet another barrier several women were able to cross during their adult journeys, subsequently owning their desires with joy and agency. In our studies, girls and younger and older women similarly (!) describe a lack of knowledge about the physiological bases of their desires, and of safe and supportive relationships that could validate their processes of desire and guide or support them in negotiating joy, comfort, and agency in desire. For example, descriptions of health education classes in school were too similar across the age span of our participants: sexually transmitted diseases, protection from pregnancy—often through abstinence—and, commonly, a discussion of male desire. While older women had less access to sexual content in the media, younger women and girls were inundated with representations of sexuality and pornography constructed through the lens of men.

Jane, a young White woman from a working-class background, describes this aptly:

> You have naked women on the magazine covers, on TV, movies, everywhere! And there's very few naked men, and women are often put in sexually suggestive situations. And so women are very sexualized... This made me realize at the age of 10 that women's bodies are to be looked at.

This pervasive objectification and sexualization disrupts girls and women's subjective immersion in the experience of desire (Smolak & Murnen, 2011). Further, all girls and women in our studies fear the impact of the negative construction of women's desire—while older women want to avoid the label of bad girl/woman, younger women fear the slut label.

Most commonly, the narratives of younger and older women who engage in journeys aimed at re-owning sexual desire allude to the different expressions of the socially prohibitive stance toward women's desire. For example, with respect to her own journey, Louise, a White woman in her early 50s of a working class and rural background, describes the adverse impact of: her lack of sexual knowledge, centrality of men's desire over women's, the objectification of women's bodies, and the vilification of women's desire:

> I was very, very naïve when I moved out. I didn't know about sex to be honest... I had dreams about it [desire] because like you watch

> TV where it is all very rosy. I didn't know what to do or what to ask. And, having intercourse I still felt ashamed because I did not know what I was doing. I was worried about my flaws like I have a flat butt. I didn't have any breasts. The people I went out with they seemed to know more than me so I felt intimidated. I did not know how to satisfy a man or what to do with a man… My husband wasn't experimental. It was like, doing it while we were watching TV. With [long-term date following her divorce] I was learning, like learning a new language. He opened my eyes, showed me books, and very open-minded, and I learned a lot more about my body. The approach was slowly, really courting me, really getting into sharing. He did respect that. He never pushed. When I was with him, my body felt great. I felt sexual in sweat pants. And I felt very passionate and natural in my body. I wish I had gained that experience much younger. But I don't know if it was good or not. I don't want to be called like a slut or whatever. The way I was brought up: bad girls do that.

While most younger women and girls in our studies started their sexual activity at an earlier age than the older women, often in early or late adolescence, their early experiences reflect the operation of the same adverse social forces; there is little that guided them in desire at a young age. As Beth, a White woman in her mid-20s from a middle-class background, describes:

> I started having sex when I [was] 13. I don't know what the hell I was doing. It was terrible. It hurt, it was boring. Everybody would get drunk. There was definitely pressure to do it. The girls hated it. I kept doing it. Once I did it guys expected that of me.

Assigned the label of slut, Beth's body was thus the target of increased social violence. As such, she has not been able to connect positively with her desire.

Healing from this adverse stance toward women's bodies and desires can take place within an equitable relationship, where dialogue, experimentation, safety, and mutual interest in and respect for embodied passions exist between both partners. In other words, healing is possible in relational conditions that counteract prohibitive social structures and values. Further, this healing can occur at any phase of life, from early to late adulthood, though it is not uncommon for it to occur only in older adulthood.

For most women in the older women study, the institution of marriage, especially first marriages that followed patriarchal and heterosexist values, served more often to curtail, rather than nurture, passions. Reni, an Asian-Canadian woman in her early 60s from a middle-class background

details how her early experience of desire, in mid-adolescence, was rapidly squashed by a forced arranged marriage:

> He [husband] did not love me; I didn't care for him to touch me. I didn't do anything, but you know men you know they want what they want [sexually]. He did what he wanted. It was terrible. I had a child.

Pressures to engage in early marriages and to abstain from pre-marital intercourse shaped the desire journey of most participants in the older women study:

> The way we were brought up is wrong! I'm mad of how religion controlled sexuality because it is an important component of a couple's life. To have brainwashed people into believing that you had to be a virgin before you got married, I'm so mad at that! [Sarah]

Despite being a passionate adolescent, Sarah, White and from a middle-class background, disavows passion in her own marriage, saying, "My husband and I are sexually active… it's more to give him pleasure than me. It's a choice I am making, accepting his limitations. Perhaps I don't value sex." For the few older women in the study who have reconnected with desire, such reconnection occurred in re-marriages and partnerships outside of marriage, whether heterosexual or lesbian.

The crucial role of healing relational connections in women's repossession of sexual desire cannot be overestimated. Jane's journey in her early 20s toward owning her desire, despite exposure to the disruptive sexualized objectification of women, relates to her mother and her familial environment. During adolescence, Jane's mother guided her in the experience and practice of sexuality, defined sexuality broadly (rather than limiting it to intercourse), and emphasized the quality of relational connections that would enhance intercourse when Jane felt ready for it. Jane's mother also accepted Jane's questioning of her sexual orientation ("Okay, if you're going to be a lesbian that's fine") and conveyed her support for having sexual experiences before marriage ("'You should try two men before you marry.' She [mother] married a virgin and she didn't recommend that"). Consequently, as a young adult, Jane's experiences of desire within the context of dating a man, and in her heterosexual marriage, have been joyful and a source of embodied agency. In her dialogues with her husband and female friends, she openly addresses issues of desire:

> I do feel sex was a very good thing for my body. I was 18 before I had my first intercourse. I felt it was important to be in a comfortable relationship. Being loved by somebody, it's very good because

> he likes my body… I stumbled on a sex personality quiz and I did it, and lo and behold I have healthy attitudes about sex. We [husband and Jane] did a sex pop quiz together and we chatted about it for a while. I have been trying to bring up masturbation with my husband. It is something I feel comfortable with… I have taken some people [women friends] who had recently broken up to the sex shop because, you know, you have to feel comfortable with it. I am realizing I'm more comfortable with saying, yes, I have one at home because my husband is sometimes away.

Partnership-based healing conditions also exist. Amber, an Asian-Canadian woman in her mid-20s who suffered rape during mid-adolescence by an adult man, experiences healing in early adulthood with a man her age, where friendship and open dialogue existed within the context of power equity: "Just fooling around for hours to kind of feel each other. I was attracted to him, and he made sure I was turned on, so we ended up sleeping together a lot and I totally enjoyed it. I trusted him totally. Like, he was my best friend, I could talk to him about anything." Gwen experienced reconnection to desire in adulthood. Like a few other women in older adulthood, she found desire in a lesbian relationship following a heterosexual marriage:

> I always felt like I was kind of asexual 'cause I didn't have that sexual feeling toward my husband. My husband was the only man I'd ever had sex with. I knew I wasn't happy in my marriage for a long time. The way he had sex with me was the old traditional chore like lie there and count the dots. But I knew I was sexual so I would fantasize about a porn movie that we had seen—take me to another place… [In new relationship] I was falling in love and that was a new learning experience. I was learning and reading about sex… When you are with a body that knows instinctively your own body, you're with bodies that are more understanding each other. I could not have predicted that it was just more fun, lovely, and more enjoyable. With her I didn't have to run my own attention away. I stayed present. Before I was not comfortable in my body all the time and now I feel acceptance of my body. It's free. I know she loves me. My ex-husband loved my body when it was right, not pregnant. He couldn't walk with me into becoming more open minded. It doesn't scare [partner]: we can stretch our minds separately or together, and whoever we are, the other person loves, and appreciates.

Such relational connections counteract adverse social factors by providing safety, information, and the sanctioning and cherishing of a range of women's desires.

In summary, women enter adulthood having experienced the toll of aggregating Physical Corsets on their experiences of embodied agency, comfort, and joy in engaging with the world. Yet, whenever possible, women engage in processes that restore Physical Freedom. This involves restoring physical activities and movement in the public sphere, addressing the impact of violations on well-being and seeking alternative relational forums of safety, critically examining barriers to the practice of self-care and resuming attuned self-care activities, and seeking reconnection to desires. We find that older adulthood sometimes provides enhanced opportunities for such positive transformations. Alternatively, adulthood can involve continued journeys of restrictions. Relational forums, such as new partnerships, sisterhood, therapeutic relationships, or community and educational organizations, that counteract adverse social factors, are important facilitators of such constructive shifts.

BREAKING LEARNED MOLDS: PATHS TO MENTAL FREEDOM IN ADULTHOOD

> My mom was the little woman... she would let my dad be the boss and so what we were exposed to was that traditional patriarchal, heterosexist couplehood, and that's what was normal. The traditional expectation of a girl that we'd get married and look after our husband, I bought that. I wanted that... When I first got married I was still in that very kind of heterosexual sense of self that wanted to be attractive to my husband and there was no sense that I could choose not to be. I used to wear makeup all the time. I had to wear clothes a certain way. I was not comfortable all the time in what I wore... Our lives were managed in that heterosexist kind of patriarchal way of like he's the dad and father.
>
> Over time it made me very angry and it worked into my expanded awareness of feminism and patriarchy... I remember having a conversation with ex-husband about it, 'You knew that I was under your patriarchal hand and I'm going to come out from under it. These old roles never really fit me perfectly anyway'... There is this strong belief in justice that [partner] and I have... There is acceptance of the body, being happy with what I have... Whereas in heterosexual womanhood there is media patrolled expectations, there is more freedom in the lesbian community. I had a lot of inner prohibitions against homosexuality until my feminist consciousness was raised to the point where I could see that it was okay for people to be lesbian, heterosexual, bisexual.

In this narrative, Gwen, a White woman in her late 60s of a working (childhood) to middle (older adulthood) background describes learned molds related to gender and sexual orientation that have shaped not only her girlhood and adolescence but also a significant portion of her adulthood. Within her constraining, patriarchal marriage, she inhabited her body as an object requiring ongoing beautifying and acted demure: "I needed to feel pretty... I wasn't respected as a person unless I toed the party line." Further, her learned heterosexist mold constricted the possibility of finding passion with another woman. She was also intermittently depressed. Her growing attunement to her emotions, needs, "rebellious" voice, and social justice values, as well their validation within sites of education and meaningful work, mobilized her to critically examine these learned molds and break free. And as she freed herself, she started inhabiting her body with a sense of subjective connection and comfort, free from the objectifying gaze: "I can wear a lumber jacket if I want, I can still feel sexual, and feel good about myself." Increasingly, her life in older adulthood involves embodied agency and power, acting with voice and meaningful passion in the world—"I love my job, it's exactly what I've always dreamt." She also feels free to develop an equitable and mutual relationship with a woman partner, as well as "lusty" and open to staying present with sexual desire for the first time.

In her narratives, Gwen addresses both types of gender-related discourses delineated by the Developmental Theory of Embodiment (DTE): the Appearance-related Discourses categorized under the Body as a Deficient Object cluster and the Comportment-related Discourses categorized under the Woman as Docile cluster. The Appearance-related cluster of Body as a Deficient Object includes both the prevalent social discourse of the Female body as an Object of Gaze, described also by Objectification Theory (Fredrickson & Roberts, 1997; McKinley & Hyde, 1996), and the Female Body as Deficient. These femininity discourses remain adverse and active factors throughout adulthood. Among younger and older women, some continue to abide by these adverse discourses, even feeling a heightened sense of deficiency with bodily changes associated with pregnancy and aging; others, meanwhile, go through processes that free them from self-objectification and from inhabiting their bodies as deficient objects. Among the latter group, there are often explicit references to a resistant stance toward these discourses.

An intensely objectifying social environment surrounds young women in peer and dating social forums, social media, and other media outlets. Further, the youth fashion industry is geared toward smaller bodies. Crystal, early 20s, White and from a working-class background, describes media-related pressures:

> Girls are skinny, so I feel huge. Growing up in a woman's body, you get the idea that your body is wrong. Just like the pressure on women to be thin and have the model look. The whole media messages, your body is not good. It makes us feel powerless and disconnected.

Similarly, Joanne, an Asian-Canadian woman in her early 20s, states the impact of peer-related pressures, saying, "I have a weight complex. Like at work, working with thin girls wearing small things… I am physically insecure with my date, I wish I was more toned." It is therefore instructive to examine the varied processes in which young women engage that facilitate a resistant stance toward these adverse Appearance-related Discourses.

For Claire, a woman in her early 20s of Caribbean-Canadian heritage and from a working-class background, an academic focus on social justice enhanced her critical stance toward objectification:

> There is a privilege of gaze because the presumption is that the spectator is a White male, so it is masculine and patriarchal, and ethnic as well. And we are in the 2000s and there is no progress. The project I am doing on male gaze is also for myself so I could work through all these norms and wanting to know how it has taken a toll as you get older.

For Jane, a White woman in her mid-20s of a working-class background, it has become essential to prioritize health in the short term—"I decided I need to be healthy, be prepared for child birthing. So like, a strong back and I don't need to look a certain way. I have a big frame so I don't need to look like a model"—and longer term as well:

> In terms of the whole long-term aspect. Seeing women in my family. [Health condition] is a problem. So it's a very different focus on being fit and being active and being healthy. What I am doing to my body now will impact when I'm 50.

For Laya, a White woman in her mid-20s from a middle-class family, the struggle with objectification has taken a different form. Having disconnected from her body during adolescence in response to objectifying experiences and ending her passionate engagement in physical activities, Laya's challenge has been to find a way of re-inhabiting her body, in adulthood, with attuned care and without self-objectification:

> I think that my exposure in high school to self care was negative because these women would spend a lot of time on primping and

> priming. I rejected everything related to caring for the body because of that. I realized I do have my own style and femininity I'm comfortable with, elegant and serious.

Discourses of objectification and the woman's body as inherently deficient are active forces in women's lives as they journey toward older adulthood. In these journeys, women either collude or resist these discourses, or both. For some, like Reni, early 60s and of Asian-Canadian heritage, the oppressive power of these internalized discourses continued, becoming more pronounced in response to changes in body shape related to pregnancies and aging: "I always tried not to gain too much weight in pregnancy, to stay slim. After they were born, it was all about losing all the weight again. I tried everything, diet, walk, exercise, important for self-image." This harsh scrutinizing lens has continued into older age: "Now my body is sagging… I've lost muscle in my arms and legs and I can't lose the belly fat and arm flab and I am walking and exercising."

Other women have lived in their bodies, moving between collusion and resistance to objectification, between "watching" and "repairing" their bodies, and appreciating other aspects of their bodies such as: health, pregnancies, physical abilities, running a home, and sexuality. Yet, within the context of ubiquitous objectification, particular life events or social experiences may activate the internalized objectification and deficiency discourses. For example, Nina, a White woman in her 60s from a middle-class background, encountered pressure from her husband, during her early 50s, that she "work hard to lose a bit of weight." At that time, she already felt she was "slender," and was intensely involved in keeping a "perfect" home and raising her children. Nina's initial self-critical response that she "let her husband down" suggests the activation of the discourses of objectification and deficiency. It took her several years to move from shame and guilt to anger about being objectified, and from accentuated self-objectification to a critical understanding of the ways in which appearance discourses reinforced gender inequity. These shifts led to her decision to leave her husband.

> I felt self-critical like why am I letting him down… I went out and bought new clothes that were more modern than what I would normally wear, but I couldn't starve myself… I wondered about how he saw me. Am I an accessory? Someone relating my body to a certain look? I don't want to fit your body image of what a woman should look like! What I understood was what a power someone can have over you in your relationship when they start criticizing what you look like and it is a form of abuse. I still get angry about it. These men

> are not thinking about women the way they deserve to be thought about.

Consequently, she developed new ways of inhabiting her body, including an inward connection with her body and resisting objectification:

> I love going to yoga and not to the gym. I like being at peace with myself and being in the moment. It's an embrace; it is soothing. I want to be who I am: a woman in her 60s, grow old gracefully without [Botox] injections. I don't need people to admire me.

As Nina's narratives indicate, arriving at a place of resistance to appearance-based discourses is associated with enhanced well-being, body connection and comfort, and embodied agency and power. Gwen, as described at the beginning of this chapter, similarly experiences more positive embodied experiences as she abandons her pursuit of "being pretty" by altering aspects of her appearance and instead attends to her health, comfort, and desires.

Such journeys are easier for women (like Marie or Maggie) who stay engaged in physical activities, for pleasure, throughout their lives, or return to such activities in early adulthood (like Jane, Laya, or Louise). They are also easier for women who are not involved in partnerships organized around gender inequity, in cases of heterosexual partnerships. Reduced objectification pressures at older age and the growing presence of health issues may further alleviate the power of self-objectification. Women's objectification enhances inequity, as "being perfectly pretty"—which commonly involves inhabiting 'White', able-bodied young bodies, buying pricy cosmetic products and procedures, and acquiring fashionable heterosexualizing clothing—reinforces not only sexism but also classism, racism, heterosexism, ageism, and able-bodied-ism.

To function in the world with embodied agency and power, women need to resist not only Appearance-related Discourses but also Comportment-related Discourses, labeled by the DTE under the gender mold of Woman as Docile, aimed at maintaining patriarchal social organizations. This mold involves a number of social discourses or expectations that influence adult women journeys, including: be demure and submissive by restricting one's voice, needs, wishes, and passionate pursuits, and prioritizing others' needs and wishes (Jack, 1991); engage in feminine activities in the domestic (e.g., shopping, household chores) and work spheres (e.g., pursue feminine vocations, accept lower pay); contain bodily and other desires (sexuality, appetite, and other passions) while being a perfect object of desire; and prioritize social relations that reinforce patriarchy, even at the cost of friendships or loyalty between women. Sustaining and amplifying these discourses are related linguistic labels that adult women learn about as girls and continue to be exposed to. For example, labels that aim to discipline women include aggressive, bitch, castrating, selfish, and hysterical. Similarly, labels that aim to make women docile by confining them to chosen feminine activities include butch and lesbian (while these are labels people may choose to adopt later as part of their own sexual identity, they often hear them first as derogatory terms for women who contest constrictive feminine molds). Disciplining labels of desire include whore, slut, bad, miss piggy, and fat. Finally, women learn to label other women with negative terms such as cunt, whore, and ditsy when competing for resources within patriarchal organizations. Linguistic terms also aim to discipline women of color, poor women, or women disenfranchised in other ways.

Women start their adult journeys in different places on the collusion to resistance continuum, in relation to the social discourses grouped under the Woman as Docile cluster. Among younger women in the study, adult women who, with clarity and comfort, held a resistant stance toward these discourses found it easier to act in the world with embodied agency and power. Regarding the discourse of submission, Jane, a White woman in her early 20s of a working-class background, is clear about the connection between voice, anger expression, and power:

> I am a competitive person. I was never withdrawn. I was always fairly aggressive-assertive. I would state my ground. I never really backed away. Being called a *bitch* when angry. I'm very proud about being a bitch sometimes, too. And bitch again is one of those comments that has a fairly negative connotation, but women need to take ownership of it. And I think it is a very empowering thing. To be a bitch you can get so much further in defining an injustice or trying to have your opinion heard, especially in a room fully of men. So anger is just another emotion and we just have to identify with it, and men are allowed to feel angry and women tend not to be. Just like men have to be able to experience sadness.

Considering the discourse of expected engagement in "feminine-gendered" activities, Jane has a clear stance of resistance toward being pressured to stay home when she has children: "You don't have to take five years off when you have a kid. I know I can do it my way and it will still be all right." Jane is also clearly resistant to discourses that problematize women's connection to desire:

> Why shouldn't women sit around and talk about sex and about masturbation? Because I find that a lot of women have issues with sex

> and don't feel comfortable to talk about it. But if you don't talk about it, then you can't help yourself figure out where your issues lie.

After years of feeling different from other women, often related to this resistant stance, Jane cherishes how in young adulthood she has the special opportunity to join a sisterhood circle: "A lot of my ideas have resurfaced because this peer group now of women, a sisterhood, that I can talk with." Resisting all aspects of the Woman as Docile mold, Jane acts in the world with a strong sense of power and agency, while also maintaining equitable relational connections with her husband, family members, and friends.

Amber, in her late 20s, who grew up in South Asia in a middle-class family and immigrated to Canada as an adult, holds a similar critical stance toward these discourses. Despite growing up in a different cultural context, Amber counters the same aspects of the Woman as Docile mold:

> I have moved from trying to be feminine according to someone else's definition of gender expectations to a more comfortable thing. I was never classified as feminine. I have the freedom to express a critical view about it. I don't have to do things just because I am a woman. In the community where I grew up, women are treated as equals and are not subjugated like, a woman's place is at home and with kids. My mom is a [health practitioner], but at home she gets taken advantage of because she is a *nice* caring person. She bends over backward for the people she cares about, she just helps out anyone and everyone and I can't be like that. I can't be that nice. I'm too much of a *bitch* to do that. I don't wish to do that. I admire that she can be so selfless, but there's no way in hell that I'm going to do it because I'm too *selfish* for that.

Amber studied and now works in the sciences, in an area strongly male dominated. It is important to note that even though both Jane and Amber operate in the world with power and agency, resisting confining gender roles, they are still adversely affected by the nice/bitch and selfless/selfish dichotomies used to describe women, with positive (nice and selfless) versus negative (bitch and selfish) poles. By resisting the nice and selfless poles, which imply a good and "feminine" woman, their experience is that they, in fact, embody the bitch and selfish poles, characteristics attacked and devalued in women (unlike men). In these socially constructed dichotomies, there is no place for strong and powerful women, only selfish and bitchy ones. This is exactly how culturally constructed dichotomies serve to maintain the social status quo.

Young adult women who start their adult journey constricted by the Woman as Docile mold find it harder to act in the world with power agency in the public and private spheres. Crystal, a White woman in her mid-20s of a working-class background, describes the following challenge in starting her own business:

> It wasn't only in my family or in the stories that we read, the way females are supposed to be, there were no strong female models, like opening businesses or doing something original, but only a sidekick to some male. I have this business idea, but because I can't say no to people, I'm not able to do it. Yeah, I don't wanna offend anybody, people consider you selfish if you say you wanna do that. I do feel like society makes us feel like we are being selfish if we try to assert ourselves or take care of ourselves. It's because we've been taught, take care of other people, or put other people first. Give, give you know! I don't think a guy who is trying to assert himself, like start his own business. I don't think he will be criticized or called selfish for it. Like I think that would seem kind of natural.

Similarly, Eva, a woman in her mid-20s of Asian-Canadian heritage, describes struggling with the Woman as Docile mold, not only in the professional sphere but also while dating: "We've known each other for little while, and I realized, 'hey I don't have a lot of my personal input in this relationship.' Which is why I'm feeling insecure because we're only talking about his stuff." The Woman as Docile mold burdens the adult journey of women like Crystal and Eva, and complicates their journey toward empowerment.

Examining older women's journeys, the Woman as Docile mold has been a central constraining force in most of their lives, yet it has been challenged by several women, sometimes only at an older age. Several of these women's stories appeared earlier in this chapter, like Gwen's journey from "deference" to "rebelliousness" as she came "out from under the patriarchal hand" to become an accomplished professional; or Nina, who depleted herself in the role of the perfect wife and only found meaningful employment after leaving her marriage. Orchid, similarly, started to engage in attuned self-care only at an older age, no longer "polishing the shoes" of men in her life.

At times, women's efforts in releasing themselves from the hold of the Woman as Docile mold have taken the form of secret subversive acts. Sonia, of Asian-African heritage and in her late 60s, who immigrated to North America as an adult, has single-handedly supported her addicted husband and other unwell adult members of her family while holding a secretarial position. She chose to have an abortion, unbeknownst to her family, due to extreme fatigue, despite her religious beliefs. Nonetheless, when a family relative discovers it later, Sonia is labeled "a murderer." Similarly, Sarah, early 50s and from a middle class and White background, who is a mother of two children, resisted being forced into the domestic sphere from the work life that she cherished. She carefully planned ways to avoid getting pregnant again, "You kind of avoid sex and make sure you don't get pregnant again. I tried to tell him that, but it was no use."

Common linguistic labels that aim to dis-validate and penalize women, their passions, achievements, worth, and well-being confirm the centrality of the Woman as Docile discourse cluster as described by the DTE. They also clarify the role of this discourse cluster in keeping women of all ages "in their place," subjugated to the world of men. Women who do not act demure by putting aside their own needs receive a range of labels: selfish, narcissistic, and worse. Crystal, in her 20s, is labeled selfish for focusing on developing her own business: "We are being selfish if we try to assert ourselves or take care of ourselves." The terms bitch and aggressive are common when both younger and older women act assertively. Reni, a woman of Asian-Canadian heritage in her early 60s, describes,

> He [husband] calls me 'aggressive' because I tell everyone at home what to do, let's do this first and the other thing later, but if I was a man it wouldn't be an issue at all, but because I'm a woman it is a big issue.

Reni's husband, supported by broader values in their community, restricts her from working outside of the house.

The labels hysterical, PMS (premenstrual syndrome), and emotional were common in response to expressions of strong passions regarding issues of social justice or other cherished social values. Gwen's ex-husband, for example, called her hysterical in front of her children: "When I had an opinion about injustices, his line was, 'Oh there she goes again, that's just your mom, boys, women are hysterical.'" Writing this chapter during the 2016 US Presidential Election, the relevance of these labels for ambitious women is reflected clearly. The common use of these labels needs to be contested in all social domains.

While the mental molds described so far addressed gender, such molds exist and shape embodied experience in relation to all aspects of social location. Patricia Hill Collins (2000), a leading African-American sociologist, coined the term "controlling images" to describe images of subordinate groups developed by dominant groups to suppress and control subordinate group members' hopes, actions, and possibilities. Hill Collins and other writers (Simms, 2001) problematized controlling images of African-American women, such as "mammies" and "Jezebels." Indeed, the narratives of adult women in the study reflect the disruptive impact of race-related mental molds on embodiment. Claire, a woman in her early 20s of Caribbean-Canadian heritage, describes how the constructed "animalistic" and "primitive" molds assigned to individuals of African heritage paralyzed her from protesting racial prejudice. When a White woman fell in the street, Claire rushed to help her. The woman rejected Claire's help but was open to receiving the help of a White woman. As she did with respect to earlier violations, Claire felt she had to suppress her embodied reaction of anger, fearing that an angry response by a person of Caribbean or African heritage would confirm the animalistic mold, a prejudice she did not want to reinforce:

> You cannot stoop to the stereotype that they're [White people] expecting, that doesn't further anything... Those are the kinds of things that will cause Black people to get aggressive, or violent, or rude. That's exactly what they're looking for to reaffirm that we are animals or primitive or Indigenous or whatever.

Rather than express her strongly felt embodied protest toward such racist behavior, Claire constrained herself and acted in a docile and silent manner. Similarly, a mold of Asian women as "subservient" seemed to "justify" an expectation by an older White man, while on a date with Vivian, late 50s and of Asian heritage, that she would clean his apartment: "I ended up cleaning his bathroom for him."

Older women face a number of constraining molds that privilege younger individuals. For example, the "you are what you do" mold of a capitalistic society privileges young professional people, and deprecates and dehumanizes people of lower socioeconomic and professional standing, including older people and people with disabilities. Marie, a White woman in her 60s and a retired health professional, struggles with this mold as she attempts to feel comfortable as a retiree in her embodied daily life on a farm:

> I have to figure out myself and if I'm not happy doing what I'm doing then I should be doing something else. But I mean a big part of society says *you are what you do* and I'm cleaning the barn so what am I? You know so this has been a big thing: coming to the realization that I'm not what I do. It's *what I am* and trying to keep working on that.

To summarize adult women's experiences in relation to learned mental molds that define and shape what women of different social locations could or should be like, women's embodied journeys reflect both collusion with, and resistance toward, such molds. Over time, and sometimes only in older adulthood, women challenge these constraining molds, at the domestic and public spheres, seeking greater Mental Freedom and positive embodiment. Dismantling Appearance-related corsets enhances women's self- and body-attunement and body comfort in engaging with the world. Developing a critical stance toward Comportment-related constraints, often mobilizes women to take steps to alter (sometimes in secret) or leave social systems that reinforce such tight molds, and, instead, seek alternative social systems of validation. Challenging mental molds threatens the social status quo and, therefore, may be associated with social penalties; one expression of such negative response involves negative linguistic labeling. Yet, freedom from constraining molds is associated with body acceptance and comfort and opens new possibilities for engagement in the world. In addition to gender, adult women confront mental molds associated with all aspects of social locations. The disruptive effect of mental molds requires an active stance of resistance on an ongoing basis as different social experiences may activate them. Women who enter the adult phase with a strong resistant stance toward constraining discourses find it easier to act in the world with embodied agency and power, while for others the journey toward embodied agency is more complex.

SOCIAL POWER: RECAPTURING SOCIAL POWER WITH OTHERS

> My family was well off in [country in Asia]. But my father said, 'Women don't need to have higher education because eventually they get married, they give birth to the kids. They should be submissive and not outdo men.' I was really angry about his attitude about women. But I think he grew up in that kind of environment. I got only up to Grade 6. But I decided to learn more. I was interested in writing so I kept a journal, and even though I was not given more education, I read a lot of newspapers and I copied the special idioms that they used. So I enjoyed writing a lot. I was eager to learn new things. I was interested in the English language so I signed myself [up] for a correspondence class through [cultural association]... We then had to flee [country] and we were in different refugee camps in [a second country]... It was hard. Finally, we got an interview in the Canadian Embassy. I was happy the Canadian government wanted knowledge of English, so I went for the interview and that's why I got accepted as an immigrant. We were flown to Canada... I often feel very strongly about women. You know, the equality and all these things. And my argument is that you know a lot of time men do say, 'oh women are not good drivers or not good at this and that,' and I always think it's a matter of nurture. And, if you give that girl the equal opportunity, she

could be a doctor or be a scientist, you know. When I see women, successful women in the news and they have children, I always admire them because to me being a successful woman is a huge challenge and this woman, whoever she is, has overcome that. Given the environment that I grew up with, I didn't get a chance to finish high school. Some people say like, 'oh with your ability you deserve like a higher job than being a filing clerk.' But I didn't think about it. I had a job…

In the above, Vivian, a woman in her late 50s living with her husband in a working-class context, describes her experiences with education and her thoughts about gender equity and access to education. Vivian also addresses other aspects of social power and prejudicial treatment related to gender, immigration, ethnicity/race, and age in the domains of marriage, immigration, employment, and body shape:

[re: voice and power] I know that I have to keep my mouth shut not to irritate my husband too much. You are liked if you are not too bossy… My dad was always very concerned about a woman not married at this late age you know. At the time, I was very happy with my life. I had my job. I owned a house with my cousin, and we really didn't miss anything. I was too old to have sparks or anything, but [husband] was educated and I just said, 'Okay,' you know. He is not very affectionate but he is a good person… I'm aware of being an immigrant and I make sure I don't break any rules or do things that people would easily stereotype me in a negative way. My husband and I are very conscious about this because of our exposure to the Western culture. I don't speak [native language] in public because it's very rude for other people not to understand you… The feeling of being equal never came. I have a strong sense of justice and it's not fair that I was laid off; it was sexist and racist. The other [still employed] person knew how to talk to the supervisor more appropriately, and made her feel good…

[re: body shape] I tend to look at people and some people are so slim, but I am talking about women my age. I've always had the right figure, not too skinny not too fat, and when I hit my middle age you know there is this excess pouch here and there. Yeah, and my family doctor, she's ultra skinny and at any check-up she turns around and says, 'Can you lose some pounds?' Every time I go there I feel so much under pressure. I think I should not feel bad about this because people who know me know that I eat very healthy stuff and I don't eat junk food and I don't drink any pop, and I'm very concerned if I put on an extra pound. Yeah in terms of image I am just being unrealistic. And in my culture, if you get plump it means you've had a good life. And we are immigrants, lived in refugee camps, and we've had probably much tougher life.

Vivian grew up in an affluent family in an Asian country, from which she fled as a young adult due to war. She resided for a year in different refugee camps in another country, under conditions of starvation and physical duress (accentuated by the particular challenges of being a woman in a refugee camp), until her immigration to North America. Being barred from education beyond Grade 6 was but one expression of exposure to gender-related prejudicial treatment. It was her persistent study in the private sphere that enabled her to gain admission to North America by passing an English proficiency test—a requirement from the Canadian immigration agency. Her English skills also helped her get a job as a filing clerk in Canada. Yet, Vivian experienced another barrier to accessing social resources when she was laid off from her job while a non-immigrant was retained, despite her seniority and good job performance.

Prejudicial treatment related to her gender and immigration status taught Vivian to be guarded about expressing her voice with agency. In her life, there was little modeling of empowering relationships either in her nuclear family, her marriage, her job, or the medical system; she was always cognizant of her disadvantaged status. Nevertheless, there were sources of social power in her life. Her higher social class as a youth afforded her access to a correspondence course, reading materials, and time to read. Though her mother was silenced at home, it was important to Vivian that her mother was literate and interested in books, got to play sports, and used a contraceptive method after having a number of children. Further, Vivian felt safe to contest to her father his treatment of her by writing him a letter—though she received an intense, angry response. Later in life, she initiated different political actions to try and reverse being laid off.

While a refugee, Vivian received help when moving between refugee camps and, sometimes, money through her familial contacts. Her most equitable experiences were with her cousin, with whom she owned a house before getting married, and with several women friends: "Women are resourceful and they are very good at caring for others." Importantly, Vivian's keen critical analysis of social structures of power provided her with some protection from internalizing experiences of disempowerment in relation to being a woman and an immigrant. Her story exemplifies how access to social power in relation to varied aspects of social location strongly shapes embodied lives, from material and physical living conditions to agency in voice and action, comfort in inhabiting the body while engaging with the world, and experiencing a sense of fulfillment in life.

Freedom from Prejudice and Harassment, involving both equitable Access to Resources and Freedom from Body-Based Harassment, is the first dimension of the Social Power and Relational Connection domain of the DTE (see Table 1.2). Inhabiting diverse bodies in terms of social location is associated with differential access to resources (Bourdieu, 1984). Education is a key social resource related to projected earnings, affecting living conditions and well-being. In our research program, we found that higher education was more accessible to the younger women. Most younger women pursued higher education at the community college or university levels; this is an important step toward social equity, though pursuing such education was more difficult for women of lower financial means. Further, in line with recent large-scale surveys that found that higher education in the sciences, technology, engineering, and math is pursued mainly by young men (Hill, Corbett, & St. Rose, 2010), we found that only two young adult participants pursued education in these fields, while the other nine participants pursued careers in teaching, social work, media, art, fashion design, and human resources. Gender segregation in education is one contributor to the gender gap in pay. While over the past 50 years women have made large gains in historically male-dominated fields such as business, law, and medicine, progress in the physical sciences—engineering, technology, and math—has been slow. Research indicates that multiple environmental influences in families, schools, and communities shape educational gender segregation, including, among others, negative stereotypes about women's capacity in these subjects, differential environmental patterns of encouragement and support, and employment opportunities. While these environmental influences are powerful, they can also be subtle and therefore may not be consciously observed by either young women or other members of their social environment.

Jane's narratives exemplify the powerful yet subtle impact of environmental influences that shape educational choices toward higher education and future occupation. Jane is a White woman in her early 20s from a rural, working-class background. Earlier affirmation she received in middle school regarding her talent in math helped her to withstand barriers erected by her high school guidance counselor and mitigated concerns about peer acceptance. Considering her working-class background and intermittent parental unemployment, barriers to academic excellence could have sabotaged her access to scholarships and bursaries in higher education:

> In school, the fact that I would answer some of the teacher's questions, some students don't like it, especially the sciences. And I had

to fail a project in science to be accepted [by peers]. With the girls it was more that I wasn't much the girly girl. By the time I reached high school, I realized just how important school was. You could get a scholarship or you can go on to university, get out of [small town].

In junior high, a student teacher who was helping out with the class said, 'you know, you're doing math well and you're a girl and there are not enough women in math. You might want to consider pursuing a career.' He didn't announce it to the entire class, so I wasn't being pointed out to the group as being *outside the norm*. That positive comment stayed with me all this time. He was Native Canadian and I don't know if he was more sensitive to the issues of minority groups. It stuck with me. When girls are put down because they are girls, I always say, 'There was this one teacher in the history of the schools that I went to who did say I was good in math, and it may have been one of those things that helped build my self confidence.' So by the time I reached high school and I'm sitting down with the guidance counselor and he is making these comments like, 'You're taking all these honors? Are you sure you can handle honors chemistry?' 'Yes, I can handle honors chemistry. Thank you for your comments. Let me.' In the honors chemistry class in Grade 12 in my high school there were fewer women, and we tended to outperform. By that point I'd developed self-confidence. I was feeling more okay being *outside the norm*, that, you know, it's not normal to want to pursue honors chemistry. That's all right. I'll try it anyway. So that gave me freedom: 'Thanks for the advice. I choose not to take it.'

These narratives reflect subtle prejudicial processes related to gender and, possibly, social class. The increased percentage of young women who pursue higher education in a larger range of fields is important; however, at the same time many girls and young women still encounter significant challenges in pursuing education, in relation to economic barriers and prejudicial treatment related to gender, race/ethnicity, social class, ability/disability, and other social factors.

Unlike young women, who most often pursued higher education at the college or university levels in North America—accessible to those from working-class backgrounds only through scholarships, loans and employment while in school—the older women, despite residing in North America, commonly described the existence of significant barriers to pursuing higher education. Like Vivian, other women were outright prohibited, often by men in their social environments (fathers, brothers, husbands), from pursuing such education, as it was considered contradictory to women's role in society as wives and mothers. Other women could not access education as limited familial resources were channeled exclusively to their brothers' education:

> I am a low income senior. I always remember my father saying that it was more important for boys to go to university because I was going to get married and someone would come, and would look after me. It made me feel not as smart as my brother, less special. I took a community college course and I worked as an educational assistant. It bothered me so much so in my 50s I actually took the Mensa test, and I am now a Mensa member. I got my undergraduate only in my senior years. I did not get to do much with it… I live on government pension. [Alice]

Several women in the study who did not have access to education as young women, and who were not partnered, lived in relative poverty, working at times in multiple part-time, low-paying jobs and, at times, relying on food banks.

Older women who had access to higher education as young women were commonly directed to pursue education in teaching, nursing, or secretarial training (typing, in particular). Of the 31 older women we interviewed, 12 out of 18 who completed university or college degrees were trained as teachers, nurses, or librarians. According to Jean, a White woman in her mid-60s from a middle-class background:

> That was the norm like girls grew up and once they hit 18, 19 you married them off or they became a teacher or a nurse. That was the end of the line for you. I worked [as secretary] when I was married. When I got pregnant I hid it quite well because once you were pregnant you were let go from a job. So my boss called me in and said, 'Is there something you're not telling me?' And I said, 'Maybe.' By that time I was seven months… When I went to [teachers' college] my stepfather thought that women were wives and mothers. His daughter was a beautician and his sons were lawyers. For him, women were less. He said, you don't need any of that education; you're married. It made me very angry. I figured him out. I used to argue with him and I think I gained more strength from that. I stood up for myself more and more. It was good. It made me feel kind of proud.

Jean's description resonates with the experiences of most women who wished to pursue education, but faced barriers in doing so, and clarifies the link between access to social resources and individuals' experiences of embodiment. Not only do such barriers constrain material conditions, they also squash agency, voice, and experience of worth. For Jean and the other women, being critical of prejudices related to gender and race/ethnicity, and contesting such biases, was essential in re-capturing embodied freedom.

The gradual broadening of educational options for women may be reflected in that only women who were in their 50s during the time of the study, compared with women who were in their 60s, pursued education in fields other than secretarial, nursing, teaching, or library sciences. Within the context of educational barriers, it is important to highlight the power of social and systemic interventions aimed at occupational skill enhancement for women of diverse backgrounds. Gwen, for example, did not have access to higher education as a young woman of a working-class background, but connected during adulthood with a community-based program that started her immersion in education:

> The government had this wonderful course for stay-at-home moms who were wanting to go back into the workforce. I got some testing done and I found out what I had an aptitude for. Raising kids was not enough. That developed my little seed for education.

Following this community course with university education has changed Gwen's embodied life in multiple favorable ways:

> My life is around maintaining a healthy balance between the work that I love to do, exactly what I've always dreamt, and maintaining a good enough relationships with my family, socializing, time off work, and having money to travel. It's a good life. I mean, it's the best time of my life.

Similar to access to education, occupational paths are shaped by structures of privilege related to gender, ethnicity/race, and all other aspects of social location. The young women in the study were all at initial phases of their career paths. Nonetheless, it is important to note that, in addition to the occupational gender segregation we observed among younger (and older) women, other gender-related factors adversely affected their occupational experiences. In particular, several young women experienced varied forms of body-based harassment. Sam, Laya, Alex, three women of diverse social locations and sites of employment, experienced sexual harassment at work. Sam, a single White woman who grew up in poverty, was sexually harassed at her low-paying evening job that she had taken, in addition to her day job in sales, to finance part-time college education. Laya, a White, married, professional woman with a university education and from a middle-class background, experienced sexual harassment at her agency. Alex, a single Latina woman of a working-class background who joined the army at age 18, partly to protest gender bias and restrictions at home, left the army within a year due to sexual- and gender-based harassment. Experiencing another type of body-based harassment, Eva, a single woman of Asian-Canadian heritage working in the fashion industry, felt criticized for her appearance related to her ethnicity and weight.

Social expectations regarding gender roles introduced additional pressures to pursuing occupational careers. Jane, who was excited about completing her advanced university training and launching her upcoming career, was pressured by her mother to "take a few years off" while raising her planned child:

> I am going to have a career, but my mother still assumes that I will take five years off when I have that baby because it's the woman thing to do. I don't think she understands how much I enjoy my career.

Jane's concerns about pursuing a career as a mother are justified. Research suggests that employers are less likely to hire mothers than childless women, and, if they do hire mothers, they tend to offer them lower salaries; fathers suffer no such penalties (The Simple Truth, 2016).

The two young women who pursued careers in the fields of science and technology also faced particular gender-related barriers. Crystal, a White woman of a working-class background who planned to develop her own start-up company, was discouraged from taking on such a project; studies suggest that raising capitals for projects is harder for women (Eswaran, 2014). Amber was encouraged by her family to move from South Asia to North America, as they suspected she would face less prejudice in her science career in North America: "Career wise I can get a job in [sciences] more easily out here than in [South Asian country] because they won't accept females in this male-dominated field. In Canada, being a female is not that much against you." These and other employment challenges highlight that, within the context of progress, there still is a long road ahead toward achieving equity in education and employment across gender and other diverse social locations.

At times, young women with access to higher education and satisfying employment options may dis-identify with challenges faced by diverse women with respect to pursuing educational and occupational equity, believing feminist goals in this regard to have been achieved. However, even in developed countries, multiple challenges remain. The ongoing pay gap is one such challenge. At every level of education, women's median earnings are lower than men's median earnings, and the same applies in relation to other aspects of social location, such as race/ethnicity (The Simple Truth, 2016). Similarly, while more families are currently dual earner in structure, women's burden regarding housework is not reduced in proportion to their increased work hours outside of the house, maintaining traditional gender ideologies. Further, only a few developed countries provide parents with subsidized, quality-controlled daycare centers, and even fewer require both partners to take parental leave (Legerski & Cornwall, 2010).

Not surprisingly, older women tackled many barriers to gainful employment. The few with the longest occupational careers were those who were not married or partnered during most of their adult lives, or those who single-handedly carried the burden of supporting their families, including single mothers. Others with longer-term employment were teachers, librarians, and nurses. Several married women were strictly barred from pursuing work outside of the house, most often by their husbands. Almost all marriages followed traditional gender ideologies, prioritizing the husbands' employment and relying mainly on women to care for children, parents, and household tasks. Consequently, women's employment was often sporadic, even when they made a concerted effort to pursue education and gain employment. Several of these women found themselves severely compromised, financially and personally, following divorce.

In addition to gender prejudice and sexual harassment, the women described the impact of prejudices related to race/ethnicity, immigration status, and age. The experience of Jan, a woman of Asian heritage in her mid-50s and an immigrant to North America who pursued a career in technology, reflects the challenges of pursuing a male-dominated career within the context of inequity, along different aspects of social location:

> I think boys should go to [technological profession]. It's very hard for a woman. You do all the training. Yeah, I did it, I was always a good student, but I'm unemployed. You work hard and you need to raise family, you take care of husband, you care for your parents, your children, you don't have energy to concentrate on your work. I also followed my husband so I lost my job [in another city], but men many times have their wives support them… I also did not intermingle with the young men at work in my new job. My manager was a White man so I left… But right now I want a job. I want to be independent. I want to live alone. My husband has a bad temper. I want to support my mother and he does not want to… When I live alone, I feel internally strong, I feel free. But with him, I am almost defeated. Before, when I worked, I loved my work. My body felt accomplished.

Rather than bear the fruits of intensive education—in which she excelled—and unique work opportunities, Jan is unemployed, and facing both financial challenges and being deprived of fulfillment from the work that she loves.

When women's passion for fulfillment in acting meaningfully in the world is blocked, their embodied well-being is deeply affected. Sarah, a White woman in her early 50s who grew up in a working-class context, describes this poignantly. Within the context of constraints, she believed that her drive to hold meaningful employment indicated that she was *not normal*:

> For me education was not an option. My parents being uneducated and isolated prevented me from the possibility. They didn't approach it the same way with my brothers. You know my brothers went away to school; my parents saved a little money for them. It was nothing big, but you know, it stands out to me now. I was not jealous, don't get me wrong… I left to [larger city] and got a job in an international company. I loved the city and felt such freedom. But I returned to [small town of origin] to get married. How I feel in my body today is that I should have stayed over there and maybe the pain that I am feeling today links to that decision… I took a job in a small local company. My father said to me, 'Now you're married, your place now is in the home,' but I said to him that work was important to me. But we went for opportunities for my husband… *I don't think I'm a normal woman*. I have this deep need. I am purposely driven. I am trying hard to find my talent and I can't find my place. I wanted to do something better with my life… If I cannot use my talents, then I am not worthy of them. It hurts. It's sad, it's painful. Maybe I should just minimize my dreams?

The second dimension of the Social Power and Relational Connections domain, Freedom from Appearance-based Social Power, links back to the first dimension. As opportunities for women to engage powerfully in the world are blocked, work on the body as a site of power may take on a central focus. Reflecting her highly developed critical stance toward social pressures on women, Sarah contrasts "work on the body" with "work on the mind." She further clarifies that she resists diverting her wishes to act meaningfully in the world to acting on her body:

> I don't want to work out my body. I have a need to work out my mind. I want to develop my mind; that's my focus. I have not much interest in making my body look good. I'm not fat but I'm a little bit fat. But I have no need to exercise to look better, even though I would love to look better. Our society is too focused on body shape. I have never been controlled by it. I recognize my friends have a better body than I have. It bugs me, but I don't let that intimidate me! When I turned 30, I looked at my body and I said, 'it's not quite the body I had 10 years ago, but that was okay.' When I turned 40,

> I realized that I did not have again the same body, but I did appreciate who I became as an individual in my mind. So I was ready to give up how the body looks for that level of intellectual, that level of wisdom that I had acquired in my mind. At 50, with my friends, I said the wisdom that I have acquired in my last 10 years, I love the way I think, see life, and become as an individual and a woman. It's worth it.

Diverting women from acting powerfully in the world to altering their bodies, especially when in the public sphere, helps maintain dominant systems of power and privilege. The same prejudicial systems that constrict women's access to social resources, such as education and occupation, also reinforce women's preoccupation with body deficiencies and their ongoing repair. For Reni, of Asian-Canadian heritage, who was barred throughout her adult life from pursuing both education and gainful employment, her self-esteem is strongly tied to body shape and weight: "I was always inhibited a lot because of my body. You feel bad about yourself and inhibited out in public." Appearance might stay a central aspect of experience in other disempowering situations, in addition to gender. For example, Grace, a woman in her early 50s who immigrated to North America from Africa as an adult, experienced prejudicial treatment at her work from both women and men:

> Heritage has probably been an issue at the workplace. There are times, for example, you will say good morning to somebody continuously every morning, but if the person sees you first they will never say good morning to you. So it puts you in a sort of subservient position and I don't like this position. So I take myself out of it; if when you see me you look me straight in the face and you don't say morning, you will never get another morning from me. It's a common thing… I think I feel differently about myself when I am not with my own people. One of the things I think about is, am I speaking clearly enough for them to understand me? Also, am I in perfect order? Are my fingers manicured properly? Am I well put together? I'm pretty conscious about that. I always want the affirmation that I am looking my best and doing my best at presenting myself. I have this feeling that I want to be perfect… It takes longer to get ready to prepare myself for work in terms of my physical appearance there. I am doing everything to stay in shape. I make sure that when I am preparing myself for work I am wearing the right bra so it is not showing any back fat… I see how my body is changing and I am fighting for my appearance until I die! Sometimes I exercise too long and may end up hurting myself, and I need to listen to my body.

Grace, an accomplished woman, underpaid in her technical field, has already witnessed body-based weight and social class prejudice in her home country. Facing racism in addition to sexism in her workplace in North America, she aims to address this prejudicial treatment by presenting perfectly, above fault, and acting in ways that are not subservient while also performing well at work. She recognizes that this focus on appearance, aimed at counteracting social prejudices, might challenge her well-being.

It is common for women to shift from a focus on appearance as a source of social power during adolescence and early adulthood, to experiencing the body as a cherished site that enables being and acting fully in the world. This can happen at any time along the adult journey, not infrequently in an accelerated way during older adulthood. Leaving oppressive systems that maintain the focus on appearance as a central source of social power and, concurrently, finding alternative sources of social power is one avenue toward positive embodiment. Alex, a Latina woman in her mid-20s who left an emotionally and physically abusive relationship where she felt objectified and self-conscious about her body, describes the shift in her embodied experiences that took place as she drew on alternative sources of power and validation:

> I am more with my body, more connected… My relationships with my family and girlfriends are stronger. My brother said, you have some very strong qualities. You always managed to get what you want and you are still like that. And this year I started [university] and I'm doing pretty good.

Similarly, upon pursuing her education and career, Gwen shifted from feeling that she "needed to feel pretty" during a constraining marriage where she was discouraged from seeking education or employment and took on all childcare and household tasks, to "feeling good about myself… even if I am dressed in a lumbar jacket… I'm doing exactly what I've always dreamt." Nina's experience as a woman in her 50s of "letting [her] husband down" by not being "more slender" shifted when she became aware of the "power someone can have over you in your relationship when they start criticizing what you look like." Nina left the marriage to work in a clerical capacity, in a setting where she derives a strong sense of meaning and a critical stance toward women's issues, "It is so sad to know that there are women who have given up so much to be what other people wanted them to be or to fit that image. I don't want that. It freed me to develop." In turn, she feels "Strong, something I omitted for many years," and accepting of her body: "I'd never have plastic surgery. I just want to grow old gracefully. I want to be who I am, a woman in her 60s."

Both the third and fourth dimensions of the Social Power and Relational Connections domain focus on how relational factors shape embodied possibilities of engaging with the world with agency and power. The third dimension, Empowering Relationships, highlights the unique impact of such relationships on adult women's embodied journeys. Empowering relationships typically include elements of: a positive connection, the modeling of living in the world with power and agency, and, at times, guidance about ways to achieve such agency. Women who have had empowering relationships during girlhood and adulthood often discovered ways to engage with the world with strength despite the existence of systemic obstacles. Most often women highlighted the power of relationships with others who shared important characteristics with them, such as gender or ethnocultural heritage. Empowering relationships can take place with nuclear or extended family members, or others (e.g., teachers or coaches).

Both younger and older women describe how empowering relationships have shaped and enhanced their acting in the world with agency while surpassing constraints related to gender, race/ethnicity, social class, disability, and other oppressive structures. Younger women detail a number of such relationships. Jane's aunt routinely took her to the library and taught her to love books—inspiring her academic pursuits beyond those of her parents, who have only had the opportunity to complete elementary school. Alex's North American step-mother modeled self-care, behaviors her mother in Central America could not practice. Crystal's teacher modeled how to live in the world as a strong woman, which stood in stark contrast to the way her mother could act at home. However, the lifelong impact of empowering relationships becomes even more pronounced when longer adult journeys are considered. Jean, a White woman in her 50s who grew up in a middle-class background, experienced her body in childhood and parts of adulthood as a "prison"—the physical space her body took, her movements in public spaces, and even her control over her own embodied practices were all constricted. Her mother and grandmother were obsessed with thinness and with a dainty "feminine" appearance and comportment. As a result, she was guided to halt athletic engagements, and her clothing and hair style were chosen for her. She was given the forced choice of being either nurse or a teacher (or a housewife). Meanwhile, pursuing higher education was ridiculed. Fortunately, her great-aunt—her role model—embodied how to engage with the world differently: by taking space through physical size, voice, and actions, including pursuing an academic career and seeking varied sources of pleasure:

> I knew that wasn't right and that women were capable of much more and I had my great aunt as an example of that. She was a [health professional]. She had gone far and I think she almost had a

> Ph.D. She taught in [city in the United States]. I admired her spirit. She was a real character. My mother didn't like her. She didn't fit into her little niche. When I was with her, I felt more relaxed in my body than with my mother. My aunt was a very large woman. She was very strong. She was very outspoken. She had a loud voice. She was also very wealthy so all the things that women weren't at that time period. She was married, but only lived with husband in [small rural town where they met] sometimes. She didn't have children. She influenced me. She encouraged me to be healthy. She encouraged the arts and took me to see theatre and a lot of other things. It was great. I would have never experienced all of that without her.

For Jean, her journey has involved achieving gradual freedom from being a "prisoner in the body" through enhanced agency and voice, engagement in attuned body practices, and pursuing passions in academia and the arts.

Gwen, a White woman in her 60s, similarly feels that her role model—her grandmother—modeled how to act in the world as an adult, with a core of rebelliousness. In turn, this rebelliousness has facilitated Gwen's acting with agency during adulthood to promote justice, even when it defies power structures:

> My favorite person in the world, my grandmother… She was sent overseas from a poor family in [a country in Europe] to work as a nanny as a girl. Her mother died shortly after she was born and she was raised by foster parents and she had a brutal life… The thing about her that was so special was everyone was loved unconditionally. It reminded me that I can love myself… I would say that I'm somebody who, like my grandmother, is a late bloomer… I had a strong core of rebelliousness. It flourished, it blossomed. This rebelliousness comes from Grammy. She told a story about how she was living alone in [urban center] and she was young before she married and there was a big noise outside one night and she went outside and saw a woman being attacked by several men, and she started yelling and chased them and she brought the woman in and called the police and took care of her. And the police came and told her what kind of craziness is that? You never, ever go and put yourself out in danger. You should have just called us first, and, of course, my grandmother wouldn't do that. She rebelled against what the police told her was the right thing for her to do because she knew what the really right thing to do was. She listened to herself. She had an incredibly strong character. I believe that's part of what drives me. I have this. I have struggled with the medical establishment. I also had a situation that happened to me that was very

> similar to my grandmother. I answered the door to a man who was running outside in the middle of the night and needed help. I called the police to help him. The police said, 'you never let somebody in your house,' but it was like of course you do, you save the other person. There were other times too. The rightness of doing justice to disempowered people, trying to right wrongs, a belief in justice, I share that with my grandmother.

Gwen's agency around issues of feminism and social justice blossomed during her adult journey, inspired by her grandmother.

The impact of empowering relationships on surpassing constraints relates to all aspects of social location. For Margaret, a White woman of a working-to-middle-class background who grew up with a visible physical disability, her mother modeled how to defy medical and other institutions of power, and act with care against all odds:

> I would have died in the hospital. They said, 'well why don't you leave her here to die,' and my mom said, 'She might as well die at home, she is my daughter and I'm going to look after her.' At that time you would put your kid into institutions because there were no services in the community. When the hospital agreed for my mother to take me home they thought she was a nurse. They didn't realize she was just an ordinary woman who couldn't let her daughter go. I came out in a plaster bed, flat on my back never to be walking or to die. And my mother was a strong, leadership, decision-making woman much loved by everybody in her environment, well respected, full of integrity… She took me to a specialist who said I'll never walk. I had body supports made of metal and leather and, even though I was going to yell and scream and my mother went through the agony of forcing me to do the exercises, I started to walk. My mother grew up in the '20s and was most ambitious, but she was a woman, and was taken out of school at 14, and she resented her brothers who stayed in school. She vowed if she had daughters, she was going to get them an education so that they could choose what they wanted to be. So she moved us near a school. She wasn't going to get the money from him [husband] so she went and set up a business… After I left home, she saw the lack of service [for] children with disabilities in the community, so she sat up a charitable organization. Learning from her experience and skills, this is one reason I knew when my friend got sick that I could do it, I could look after her. My mother was my role model. What's the big deal [looking after a person]? It's just so natural. I think that's the way my mother used to think… I chose [profession in health services] because I wanted to help people.

Grace, a woman in her early 50s and an immigrant from a country in Africa, describes how her aunt inspired her:

> As I become older I cherish my mother [who lived in a rural site in a country in Africa] for what she did for us, and the sacrifices that she made. She was a very strong woman, but, at that time, I yearned for her to be a professional in something. I never considered the housewife being with much status to it. My aunt [who lived in a higher social class in an urban center in the same country] wanted me to behave, speak, and dress a certain way. But it worked out well in the end. I think it refined me to some extent because I was exposed to their social conditions and I think perhaps I aspire to achieve more.

Inspired by her aunt, Grace pursued academic degrees, gained high-level employment in her country of origin, and was hired for a professional job in Canada following her immigration.

The fourth and last dimension of the Social Power and Relational Connections domain of the DTE, Membership in Equitable Communities, reflects the contribution of participating as an equitable member in at least one desired or valued community at some phase during girlhood and adulthood. This community provides an important function—a place in which members can dialogue equitably about their experiences, from their unique social locations. Such dialogues validate members' experiences and nurture the development of critical knowledge regarding social context, so that members are empowered to act in the world guided by said critical knowledge (Hill Collins, 2000; Weedon, 1997). Membership in a desired community, where one experiences equity and acceptance, also provides a respite from repeated exposure to oppression and the cherishing of one's embodied location and knowledge.

As I am writing this chapter, I think about opposing experiences two colleagues have shared with me about membership in communities of equity and acceptance. A South African academic related to me the way her embodied experience of herself, as a Black girl in South Africa during apartheid, shifted after living for a while in Europe. Returning to continued apartheid in South Africa, she retained the embodied experience of equity, an experience that propelled her toward social action and empowered her to surpass racial barriers. In contrast, another colleague, who self-identify as queer and of mixed Indigenous and Jewish heritage, described the acute pain of having never found a community of acceptance, validation, and equity.

The inequitable and often dichotomous construction of different variables of social location, may disrupt relationships not only across differences but also within communities, as dominant ideologies are incorporated, to differing degrees, among community members, leading to rifts within groups. Such rifts may weaken possibilities for personal, social, and political changes. Creating bridges of understanding across differences, on the other hand, can deepen the experience of safety among group members and help them act in the world with enhanced social understanding and greater freedom. Jane, a White woman in her early 20s, was often rejected by girl groups for not dating, declining parties at bars, excelling in the sciences and, overall, her lack of compliance with girly expectations. Not until university, was she able to find, for the first time, a community of women where she felt validated and supported. Within norms of acceptance across differences in this group of women, topics often silenced by the culture at large could be openly discussed.

> For me the whole sisterhood concept, the whole being able to be more open, being able to talk more freely with people here and get deeper in conversations. I actually found people who had the same values, similar ideals. And I could have some conversations here that I couldn't have in my previous degree or high school. Yes, and you have a *sounding board* when you can say something and feel comfortable saying something and have somebody who's from a very different cultural background, ask you questions that you've never explicitly considered. So tell me about this culture, growing up in [town]. And then you have to *stop and do some processing* and it makes things clearer for you, and how things can be different between different cultural backgrounds. So it's also very *educational*... And for the first time I am with a peer group who is actually comfortable discussing sexuality, and we talk about relationships. We can talk about the continuum of sexuality from straight to purely homosexuality. When you share experiences they understand, and if they don't, they'll still accept it and they will question you to explain more about it and they show interest in what you're saying, even though it may not fit with their reality. This kind of female friendship I didn't have until I came to this program.

While Jane had the fortune of partaking in multiple critical discussions within her equitably organized family, an experience she also found in university, most women did not have such experiences until later adulthood, if at all. Gwen, for example, had experienced the oppressive impact of living in rigid patriarchal systems, both with her family of origin and in her early marriage. It was not until attending a community course for women and obtaining a university education in her late 40s that she found relational communities, where critical dialogues took place within the context of equity. It is there that she felt mobilized to nurture her rebellious side and act in the world with agency and power:

> People were talking and debating and, being able to watch it, witnessing, and shifting ideas. It allowed me to open up my mind and

> challenge myself. With them I was able to move aside shame and be more critical of my own thinking. I was gaining a voice and gaining a conceptual understanding.

Exposed to such dialogues, Gwen was no longer interested in a relationship where she was "under the thumb of the patriarchal hand," and left her marriage.

It is also important to highlight the role of equitable communities in breaking professional barriers for women. Amber, a woman in her mid-20s of South Asian heritage who immigrated to North America, pursued a career in the sciences. It is of note that she describes gender equity in her learning environment not only in relation to professional pursuits, but also in the way body issues were handled. Unlike other professional, educational, or athletic settings, the body domain was not used to make women feel out of place.

> Always in school, also in university, we were a bunch of us, like girls and guys in a group and there was never any kind of consciousness, none of us ever treated the other person as someone of the opposite sex. It was just a friend kind of thing. For all of us, studies were something you were serious about and most of us had some idea of what we wanted to do. It wasn't for fun. Most of us were pretty frank with each other about anything. Like some guys asked us, 'what is it like to get your periods,' and things like that. It was just natural curiosity. It was no hassle. I mean you could describe anything to them and it wasn't any kind of sexual interest. It was just genuine interest in something that was alien to them. And most of the guys, if you've got your period and you've got bad cramps, they'll get you coffee or some medicine, even if you run out of pads they'll go and buy them for you. I was lucky. Most guys aren't like that I think. It was during undergrad that I became comfortable saying, 'I do not have to do things [like house cleaning] because I am a woman.' I was never treated unequally at school. At home, my mother catered to my dad, and I never accepted that reasoning. Don't give me this weak statement that because you're a girl then therefore it should be like this.

Similarly, experiencing equity at work in a technology lab while young encouraged Jan, a woman in her 50s of Asian heritage who immigrated to North America as an adult, to pursue an advanced academic degree in technology:

> I worked in a tech plant when I was 18. So it made it easy in school because I already had work experience. I did everything. We were

just like boys and girls that worked and studied together. Girls didn't feel differently from boys.

Anu, a woman in her early 50s who emigrated from South Asia to North America as a young adult, was embraced in early adulthood by her university-educated husband and her husband's extended family, who supported her in owning a business outside of the house. These extended family members took on many household and child-raising chores, empowering her to succeed in her business: "They helped me open the business, and they raised the kids. I feel very comfortable with myself and my body."

Support is another vital element provided in equitable communities. At times, women need to overcome learned and experienced rifts between women to seek and benefit from such relational support, which enhances their adult journeys. Alex, a Latina woman in her early 20s, experienced painful ethnicity- and weight-related body-based teasing by girls in her high school, which turned her off such friendships. After experiencing sexual and gender harassment in the army, and physical abuse by her boyfriend, she turned, for the first time, to women friends for support, especially during the difficult process of leaving the abusive relationship.

> And that was really hard for me to finally accept that that might be part of the whole process of overcoming an abusive relationship. I did not want to do what I always do to feel good about myself by reaching out to other guys and getting some sort of feedback from them. And my girlfriends, I let them do their thing. Like one time I really broke down and I said, 'I don't know if I'm doing the right thing.' And that's when, when I felt really, really vulnerable on my own, I looked just for reassurance from my girlfriends and they said, 'You did the right thing. You're doing fine. Just take each day at a time.' I have to say that relationships with my girlfriends are stronger. Relationships with my family are stronger. So, yeah, I think that in my life journey, connections to other people have been really important. I don't know how my situation would have been without my girlfriends. I am not confident enough to think that I would have left him, or it might have taken a longer time.

Communities of equity are important in relation to all aspects of social location. For Grace, early 50s and of African heritage, who experienced racism in her professional place of work, finding a community of women who'd also emigrated from her country of origin and spoke her indigenous language was important for her experiences of embodied identity, comfort, and pleasure. It's from this place of cherishing her embodied identity in equity that she hopes to become an activist, inviting others to share her heritage. In contrast, as she illustrates, racism prompted self-scrutiny and immobilization:

> People from the rural area spoke [local, indigenous language], but we are educated in English. It's almost as if you're substandard if you spoke that language. But today people believe it identifies with your culture, and future generations should not lose it. It is a *pleasure* for me when I meet with my friends and we speak the local language and you feel that sense of identity, and that's what I like about it… One of the things that I really want to do is to try and see if I can get into a group where I can share more of my culture. I'd like people to know about our culture, history, the different races that make up that region, the food we eat, the plants, trees, everything that is unique to that place. I know that I can do more and that's something I'm going to focus on this year. I need to participate more. Life is more fulfilling when you actively participate in life. It makes life's journey more pleasant… I think I feel differently about myself when I spend time with people of different cultures, not with my own. I am extremely self-conscious.

Similarly, Margaret, who grew up with a physical disability and visible difference, silenced her attraction to other women, fearing she would lose her community of friends if she presented them with another "minority status." However, being welcomed to a new community, while preserving her older one, has enabled her to live comfortably in the world in a way that aligns with her embodied desires.

> When you are living in a heterosexual world and you were brought up in a heterosexual world and, and maybe I wasn't secure enough in myself as an accomplished human being to go back into another minority status. I mean you come out of this minority, deformed body-status individual and then, do you want to walk into another one? But you have to feel stronger, whole, in the first one before your subconscious can let you acknowledge you got to go and do it again. I have to now go around my whole circle of straight friends and say, 'Well I got something to tell you, I'm lesbian. I want you to stay in my life, but I'll understand if you can't but I hope you will,' and nobody rejected me. That was a beautiful thing. But again, I was secure. My friend and her partner introduced me to the community and it was an absolutely wonderful experience. So that was how I was able to come out after all these years.

To summarize, breaking barriers in the Social Power and Relational Connections domain during adulthood is central to the embodied well-being of women. Yet, the inequitable allocation of resources in relation to gender, race, or other aspects of social location persists across generations, with only limited progress. Nonetheless, adult journeys convey that diverse women commonly seize opportunities to claim a broad range of educational and occupational paths, and to act in the world with passionate immersion, even at older age, whenever such shifts are possible. Body-based inequities and harassment continue to encumber such progress. An important avenue toward positive embodiment involves leaving oppressive systems that maintain the focus on appearance as a source of social power and finding alternative sources of power. Relational factors are also important to acting in the world with agency. The presence of empowering relationships in women's lives facilitates engaging in the world with embodied agency, even when encountering obstacles related to gender, race, ethnicity, social class, disability, and other social factors. In particular, women highlight the role of strong women in their lives. Further, membership in equitable communities provides important respite and validation and facilitates the development of critical knowledge and of a support network that empower individuals to act in the world.

CHAPTER SUMMARY

Women's body journeys throughout adulthood reflect both the continued hold of social structures on women's bodies and, conversely, new possibilities of freedom from oppressive forces that facilitate acting in the world with embodied agency, comfort, and attuned self-care. Understandably, women who start their adult journeys having experienced significant disruptions to their embodied experiences during childhood and adolescence—such as physical violations—face more complex and sometimes longer journey toward embodied comfort and agency. Women's common engagement in dismantling oppressive corsets in the physical, mental, and social power domains, processes that take place throughout adulthood, is indeed inspiring! Confirming the theoretical structure of the DTE, our research suggests that the same corsets imposed on girls to create docile, feminine bodies get partly dismantled by some women during adulthood, with a positive impact on the restoration of embodied agency, passion, and attuned self-care.

As described in this chapter, re-capturing Physical Freedom involves enhancing joyful and attuned engagement with physical movement, physical safety, care of the body, and ownership of physical desire. Positive experiences in any of these four dimensions of Physical Freedom establish the body as a territory that entails physical power, rights, and passion.

With respect to Mental Freedom, this chapter describes ways in which developing a critical lens and a resistant stance toward widely disseminated constraining social molds, aimed at maintaining the social status quo of privilege, can work to liberate and expand embodied possibilities of engaging more fully with the world. For example, women who learn to resist the expected feminine molds of self-objectification and body deficiency, acting demure and selfless, and inhibiting bodily desires can act in the world with greater power. Socially constructed molds exist in relation to all dimensions of social location, and aim to discipline women of color, poor women, and those disenfranchised in other ways. The journey toward resistance is therefore important to all women's well-being, younger, older, and of diverse social locations.

Further, addressing the domain of Social Power and Relational Connections, this chapter examines adult women's embodied journeys as they confront barriers to accessing social resources and prejudicial treatment. Both barriers and prejudicial treatment relate to the social location embodied by the women. Diverse women tackle educational and occupational segregation and body-based harassment. As some women access resources (such as desired education or occupation) entailing social power, sometimes only during older adulthood, they commonly rely less on obtaining social power through adhering to particular standards of appearance. Relational factors can reinforce an adult woman's embodied agency in the world. One such factor involves experiencing the empowering and inspiring impact of a person with whom the women share important aspects of social location. A second factor is equitable membership in a validating, accepting, and supportive desired community where, often, the development of critical knowledge regarding the social context is nurtured.

Women can achieve greater Physical Freedom, Mental Freedom, and Social Power with Others at different points in their adult journeys. Such changes always involve greater embodied agency, attuned connection to the body and self-care, and well-being. Conversely, lack of change or further disruptions in the three domains of social experiences during the adult journey relate to body disconnection and embodied powerlessness, engagement in potentially harmful behaviors, and physical and/or mental challenges. Processes that are constructive to obtaining greater freedoms are complex, and involve the interaction of women's agency and critical reflections with alternative social experiences, social structures, and relational communities. At times we find that changes are only possible at older adulthood, when social roles and structures, as well as priorities, tend to shift.

References

Arnette, J. J. (2000). Emerging adulthood: A theory of development from the late teens through the twenties. *American Psychologist*, *55*(5), 469–480.

Bartky, S. (1988). Foucault, femininity, and the modernization of Patriarchal power. In I. Diamond, & L. Quinby (Eds.), *Feminism & foucault: Reflections on resistance*. Boston, MA: Northeastern University Press.

Bourdieu, P. (1984). *Distinction: A social critique of the judgment of taste*. Cambridge, MA: Harvard University Press.

Buchwald, E., Fletcher, P. R., & Roth, M. (1993). *Transforming a rape culture*. Minneapolis, MN: Milkweed Editions.

Connell, R. W. (1987). *Gender and power*. Stanford, CA: Stanford University Press.

Daniel, J. H., & Dale, S. K. (2013). Women of color: Violence and trauma. In B. Greene, & L. Comas-Diaz (Eds.), *Psychological health of women of color* (pp. 133–146). Santa Barbara, CA: Praeger.

Eswaran, M. (2014). *Why gender matters in economics*. Princeton, NJ: Princeton University Press.

Fine, M. (1988). Sexuality, schooling, and adolescent females: The missing discourse of desire. *Harvard Educational Review, 58*, 29–53.

Fredrickson, B. L., & Roberts, T. (1997). Objectification theory: Toward understanding women's lived experiences and mental health risks. *Psychology of Women Quarterly, 21*, 173–206.

Hargreaves, S. (2001). Rape as a war crime: Putting policy into practice. *Lancet, 357*, 737.

Herman, J. (1992). *Trauma and recovery*. New York, NY: Basic Books.

Hill Collins, P. (2000). *Black feminist thought: Knowledge, consciousness, and the politics of empowerment* (2nd ed.). New York, NY: Routledge.

Hill, C., Corbett, C., & St. Rose, A. (2010). *Why so few? Women in sciences, technology, engineering, and mathematics*. American Association of University Women. Retrieved from: https://www.aauw.org/files/2013/02/Why-So-Few-Women-in-Science-Technology-Engineering-and-Mathematics.pdf.

Jack, D. C. (1991). *Silencing the self: Women and depression*. New York, NY: Harper Perennial.

Langton, L., Berzofsky, M., Krebs, C., & Smiley-McDonald, H. (2012). *Victimizations not reported to the police, 2006–2010. Special Report: National crime victimization survey*. US Department of Justice. Retrieved from: https://www.bjs.gov/content/pub/pdf/vnrp0610.pdf.

Lantz, P. M., House, J. S., Lepkowski, J. M., Williams, D. R., Mero, R. P., & Chen, J. (1998). Socioeconomic factors, health behaviors, and mortality: Results from a nationally representative prospective study of US adults. *Journal of the American Medical Association, 279*(21), 1703–1708.

Legerski, E. M., & Cornwall, M. (2010). Working-class job loss, gender, and the negotiation of household labor. *Gender and Society, 24*(4), 447–474.

Maine, M., & Kelly, J. (2016). *Pursuing perfection: Eating disorders, body myths, and women at midlife and beyond*. New York, NY: Routledge.

McKinley, N. M., & Hyde, J. S. (1996). The objectified body consciousness scale: Development and validation. *Psychology of Women Quarterly, 20*, 181–215.

Messner, M. A. (2002). *Taking the field: Women, men, and sports*. Minneapolis, MN: University of Minnesota Press.

Piran, N. (April 2006). The end point: Maximizing participants' verification of emergent understanding in a feminist-informed qualitative study. In *Paper presented at the Annual Conference of the Association for Women in Psychology. Ann Arbor*.

Piran, N. (2016). Embodied possibilities and disruptions: The emergence of the experience of embodiment construct from qualitative studies with girls and women. *Body Image, 18*, 43–60.

Roth, A., & Basow, S. (2004). Feminity, sports, and feminism. *Journal of Sports and Social Issues, 28*(3), 245–265.

Rothenberg, B. (2015). Tennis's top women balance body image with ambition. *The New York Times*. New York. Retrieved from: https://www.nytimes.com/2015/07/11/sports/tennis/tenniss-top-women-balance-body-image-with-quest-for-success.html?_r=1.

Sexual violence: Facts at a glance. (2012). US: Division of Violence Prevention, National Center for Injury Prevention and Control, Center for Disease Control. Retrieved from:https://www.cdc.gov/ViolencePrevention/pdf/SV-DataSheet-a.pdf.

Simms, R. (2001). Controlling images and the gender construction of enslaved African women. *Gender and Society, 15*(6), 879–897.

Sinha, M. (2013). *Measuring violence against women: Statistical trends*. Canada: Canadian Centre for Justice Statistics: Statistics. Retrieved from: http://www.statcan.gc.ca/pub/85-002-x/2013001/article/11766-eng.pdf.

Smolak, L., & Murnen, S. K. (2011). The sexualization of girls and women as a primary antecedent of self-objectification. In R. M. Calogero, S. Tantleff-Dunn, & J. K. Thompson (Eds.), *Self-objectification in women: Causes, consequences, and counteractions* (pp. 53–75). Washington, DC: American Psychological Association.

The simple truth about the gender gap pay. (2016). American Association of University Women. Retrieved from: http://www.aauw.org/files/2016/02/SimpleTruth_Spring2016.pdf.

Tiggemann, M. (2004). Body image across the life span: Stability and change. *Body Image*, *1*(1), 29–41.

Tolman, D. L. (2002). *Dilemmas of desire: Teenage girls talk about sexuality*. Cambridge, MA: Harvard University Press.

Tronto, J. C. (1993). *Moral boundaries: A political argument for an ethic of care*. New York, NY: Routledge.

Weedon, C. (1997). *Feminist practice & poststructuralist theory*. Oxford, UK: Blackwell Publishers.

Who is poor?. (2016). Institute for Research on Poverty: University of Wisconsin-Madison. Retrieved from: http://www.irp.wisc.edu/faqs/faq3.htm.

CHAPTER

7

Charting a Different Future: Embodied Possibilities

PART I: THEORETICAL PERSPECTIVES

THE "HEART" OF THE BOOK: CONSCIOUSNESS RAISING REGARDING THE WELL-BEING OF GIRLS AND WOMEN

At the heart of this book is the well-being of diverse girls and women. Blanket statements or beliefs about gender equity, or even about progress made toward gender equity, stand in stark contrast to the quality of embodied lives of girls and women, as has been reflected in the preceding chapters. Multiple social measures indicate there being little consistent progress toward equity made in the past decade in terms of salary gaps, rates of violence against women, women's access to a range of health services, or percentage of women in corporate boardrooms. These measures reflect a more problematic picture for women of color, immigrant women, and other groups. Similarly, rates of disruption to girls and women's well-being, as indicated by a higher prevalence of eating disorders and/or depression among post-pubertal girls and women when compared with boys and men, also suggest there being little to no change. It is sometimes forgotten how central women's health is to the well-being of society as a whole (Kawachi, Kennedy, Gupta, & Prothrow-Stith, 1999).

This book is a call to action. It is grounded in, and inspired by, girls and women's accounts of their embodied experiences. It engages in a bottom-up process, starting with research narratives that capture the experiential journeys of girls and women through different life stages, arriving at a theoretical understanding of the quality of embodied lives and the social processes that shape them. It raises awareness regarding major losses to the experience of embodiment, which intensify during the tweens phase and throughout adolescence. These losses alter the way girls engage with the

Journeys of Embodiment at the Intersection of Body and Culture
http://dx.doi.org/10.1016/B978-0-12-805410-9.00007-4

world around them, and go on to encumber the lives of adult women. In line with the qualitative research program, our quantitative studies suggest the existence of a strong link between the quality of experiences of embodiment and a range of measures of well-being (e.g., Teall & Piran, 2015).

The critical examination of the social forces that maintain the social status quo, and that disrupt embodied ways of engaging with the world for diverse girls and women, addresses body politics, namely: the regulation of the body by structures of power. Recall that the focus on body politics was central to the powerful social transformations that took place during second-wave feminism in North America, in the late 1960s and early 1970s. Then, as described in Chapter 1, social activism focused on transforming the quality of embodied lives through addressing pay inequity, violence against women and children, and other challenges (e.g., Fonow & Cook, 1991; hooks, 2000). At that time, consciousness raising was important in problematizing women's embodied lives (MacKinnon, 1989).

Raising consciousness regarding the experiences of diverse girls and women at different ages is one of the main goals of this book. The hope is that this knowledge will propel readers—including scholars, practitioners, educators, and parents—to take transformative action. Ample opportunities exist for such initiatives, addressing physical conditions, social discourses, and access to sources of social power. While this chapter includes implications of the Developmental Theory of Embodiment to therapy and health promotion initiatives, it is not written with a prescriptive intent. On the contrary, we believe that the book, as a whole, is an invitation for readers to become invested in their own creative processes of action. Such creative processes will be enriched by each reader's unique social location and experiences.

THE "CORE" OF THE BOOK: A DISCUSSION OF THEORETICAL PERSPECTIVES

By virtue of being born female and socially labeled girls, the lives of diverse girls and women are shaped by different constrictions and privileges along various dimensions of social location: gender, race/ethnicity, immigration status, social class, health/physical abilities/appearance differences, sexual orientation, gender identity—all shape one's engagement with the world. This book is an exploration of embodied journeys through the lens of gender as it intersects with other aspects of social location. New theoretical perspectives emerged in this research that can expand the understanding of embodied distress and the social forces that shape it.

Anchoring the inquiry in the construct of embodiment provided a productive conceptual basis for engaging in research located at the intersection of psychology and sociology: studying individuals' experiences of their bodies as regulated by social structures and ideologies. The construct of embodiment, as conceived by Maurice Merleau-Ponty (1962), sets mind and body as inseparable, and the body as a site of subjectivity. Further, dialectical relationships exist between body and culture such that the body both performs and shapes culturally informed practices, and boundaries between body and culture, and inner and outer, are blurred (Crossley, 1995). The embodiment construct therefore allows us to focus on participants' internal experiences of embodiment while also holding a mirror to culture via descriptions of embodied practices and their cultural context.

The Experience of Embodiment (EE) construct captures the *quality* of embodied experiences along five dimensions: body connection and comfort, agency and functionality, experience and expression of desire, attuned self-care, and subjective immersion in inhabiting the body/resisting objectification. This conceptualization of the quality of embodied life is unique in being anchored in *girls and women's* narratives, spanning the age range of 9–70. The range of experiences captured by the EE, all the way from "positive body connection and comfort, embodied agency and passion, and attuned self-care" to "disrupted body connection and discomfort, restricted agency and passion, and self-neglect or harm" (see Chapter 1) is broader than those captured by other constructs, such as body esteem, alexithymia, objectification, or positive body image. The different age-related chapters of the book reveal the advantage of the breadth of experiences captured by the EE as we follow, prospectively, the embodied transitions of girls from childhood to womanhood, and, similarly, as we study adult women's retrospective recall of their embodied journeys. Importantly, we find that the EE captures the shift from inhabiting the body with agency, power, and freedom, to inhabiting 'docile' bodies.

The multidimensional nature of the EE is important as well for a number of reasons. First, the construct integrates domains of experience that have, thus far, been conceptualized and studied as separate phenomena; hence, the EE implies that considering these dimensions concurrently offers a deeper understanding of embodied lives. Second, the construct delineates a research-based *positive* way of inhabiting the body that is anchored in girls and women's lives. Indeed, girls and women's embodied lives are commonly disrupted, and psychological research has tended to focus on their disruptions; however, a positive delineation sets positive possibilities for girls and women of diverse backgrounds as a social agenda, informing activism towards social transformations and health promotion. Third, by the same token, the construct describes the problematic losses to body connection, agency, self-attunement, desires, and freedom from self-objectification, that take place during adolescence, changing the way girls and women engage in the world; these changes are greater than the commonly reported drop in body esteem and need to be considered in examining girls and women's lives. Fourth, the linking of behavioral expressions of disruption on the different domains of the EE, commonly studied as separate phenomena – such as the pursuit of thinness or self-harm behaviors – may counter tendencies to either 'pathologize' specific behaviors or to devise behavior-specific social theories; Rather, it highlights the impact of power inequities on a range of embodied disruptions. Fifth, the articulation of the five key domains of the EE suggests that feminist theories need to examine the *targeting of all five domains by social forces* in producing 'docile' bodies.

The research-based Developmental Theory of Embodiment (DTE) is a new social theory that examines the shaping of the quality of embodied lives over a broad range of social experiences subsumed under three domains physical, mental, and social power and relational connections. In turn, each of these domains includes a number of factors that either enhance embodiment or disrupt it (corsets). The DTE is contributory in specific ways: being anchored in lived experiences, the concurrent consideration of experiences in three social domains, the inclusion of both protective and risk factors, the delineation of changes in girls' social environment throughout their development, and the application of the same theoretical constructs over time. Most importantly, however, is that the theory holds a mirror to culture, looking critically at the myriad factors that operate concurrently to shift the experiences of girls, moving from embodied agency, functionality, and passion during early childhood, through restriction, shame, and self-neglect or harm in puberty, to the challenges of re-capturing agency during adulthood.

At the intersection of gender and other aspects of social location, the DTE problematizes Physical Corsets that: restrict access to free movement and engagement in physical activities, breach safety of the body territory, challenge care of the body, and disrupt the expression of desires. The theory similarly problematizes Mental Corsets that involve constraining messages regarding femininity and their intersection with discourses related to other aspects of social location. The DTE also problematizes the privileging of some bodies over others in terms of access to resources, exposure to prejudice, and barriers faced with respect to relational resources such as validating communities and role models. While most research has to date focused on the impact of single social factors on body esteem, such as engagement in physical activities or images of idealized appearance, the DTE suggests that to promote the embodied lives of girls and women, multiple social factors need to be addressed concurrently toward equity and social justice.

Further, the DTE offers a critical perspective on age-related shifts in the social environment of girls. Social processes differ between girls, such that a girl's physical environment, her exposure to social expectations and labeling, as well as to embodied social power will be affected by her social location. Nonetheless, a brief summary of the social processes that take place during puberty can highlight some key points in the changed environment of girls. Already in early childhood, girls learn that access to physical territories of action is mostly controlled by boys—hence, they can immerse in such actions as "tomboys," rather than as "powerful girls." As girls go through puberty, their growing physical body becomes not only a site of "deficits" but also a target of size restriction (frequently disrupting connection to appetite). Next, just as girls start to experience sexual desire in their pubertal bodies, this desire becomes the target of negative characterization (e.g., slut label). Moreover, they experience a marked reduction in their physical safety related to sexual harassment and dating violations. At the same time, social expectations shift from those associated with being a "girl" in early childhood to being "girly" during puberty—denoting sexualization, physical daintiness, and a demure, submissive, or other-attuned comportment. To complicate things further, with puberty, girls' social power becomes connected to embodying culturally idealized images of privilege, accentuating rifts within their peer groups. Overall, then, within a period of 5 years or so (ages 8–13 years), associated with puberty, the social environment of girls changes, such that they become acculturated to inhabit their bodies with diminished agency, disrupted connection to desire, reduced self-attunement, and greater self-objectification. These compounded losses undermine girls' ability to act in the world with power.

An integrated feminist model of social factors that affects the EE, such as the DTE, has a range of applications toward social justice and equity. Below we consider three examples of the use of an integrated theory: the first discusses gender gap indices, the second relates to STEM education (science, technology, engineering, and math), and the third to the clinical phenomena of eating disorders.

Gender gap indices rely primarily on financial, educational, and political information. For example, the Gender Gap Index (The Global Gender Gap, 2015; Top 10, 2016) derives its data from the following dimensions: economic participation and opportunity (e.g., labor force participation, wage equality), educational attainment (e.g., literacy rate, level of education), political empowerment (e.g., women in parliament), and health and survival (sex ratio at birth and life expectancy). While these dimensions provide a useful understanding of the gender gap, from the perspective of the DTE they correspond only with the *social power domain* of the theory. When viewed from the wider lens of an integrated feminist model (the DTE in this case), the Gender Gap Index includes very limited information from the *physical domain* and lacks input from the mental domain.

Considering the physical domain, the lack of information regarding violence against women is particularly glaring. Violence against women is a powerful social factor that oppresses women, encumbers their social progress, and affects their well-being. Such data are also widely available for most countries. While Iceland, for example, ranked first as the country with the smallest gender gap and the Philippines ranked seventh, surveys conducted in these countries indicate no differential rates in violence against women (Male violence, 2012; Violence against women, 2008, respectively). Including information regarding violence against women in the Gender Gap Index would clarify *the centrality of this issue* as relating to the welfare of women, and also as a human rights issue. Other important information that could be added to the Gender Gap Index related to the physical domain includes, for example, the ratio of funding for women's sports compared with men's, a scale documenting different gender-related levels of restrictions to the freedom of movement in the public sphere, and rates of access to health services (in particular, sexual and reproductive health).

The Gender Gap Index can further be informed by including information from the *mental domain*, such as a critical view of the media's portrayal of women and men of diverse backgrounds. For example, the use of sexist labels in dominant media outlets regarding women and men in power in the public sphere has garnered attention internationally (e.g., Frazer, 2016; Wonder Women and Macho Men, 2015). Women politicians themselves have spoken about sexist media presentations and cyberbullying, highlighting that sexist language is often infused with violent overtones (e.g., Tremonti, 2017). As Tremonti describes, labels and descriptions of women politicians have included, for example, "bitch," "dumb broad," "bimbo," or "belong in the kitchen." A recent example includes the labeling of California Senator Kamala Harris' incisive questioning of Attorney General Jeff Sessions during the Senate Intelligence Committee hearing as "hysterical" (Riotta, 2017). The concern regarding this type of media relates to its sanctioning of sexism and targeting of women who occupy leadership positions around the globe. Similarly, women politicians have expressed concern that the perpetuation of a sexist construction of women in media will deter young women and girls from seeking roles in leadership. Progress toward gender equity should reflect the implementation of clear policies and enforced legislation regarding the use of sexist, racist, and other prejudiced presentation in the media. Other measures of adverse social constructions of women in the media can focus on their visual presentations as sexual objects compared with the presentation of men. While current measures used to describe the gender gap are limited mostly to the social power domain, an expanded view, informed by integrated feminist perspectives, can assure the visibility of problematic domains in women's lives toward social justice.

Another example of the application of the DTE in examining social phenomena relates to STEM education. It is well established that fewer young women pursue education in the sciences, technology, engineering, and mathematics (Hill, Corbett, & St. Rose, 2010). This occupational gender segregation may contribute to the gender income gap. Spatial skills, especially measures of mental rotation, seem related to success in specific STEM careers, such as engineering, and to predicting entry into the STEM field (Baker & Cornelson, 2016). Yet, boys outperform girls on measures of visual–spatial abilities (Halpern et al., 2007; Hyde, 2014). Halpern emphasizes the complex influences of biological and social/environmental variables on cognitive abilities. In particular, she cites studies that suggest that boys' greater engagement in activities that improve spatial skills, such as playing organized sports or roaming their neighborhoods (creating "mental maps" of their environment), could enhance the development of spatial skills. The development of spatial skills relies on extracurricular activities, as they are not commonly part of school curricula.

The research cited above highlights the importance of examining girls' embodied lives using an integrated lens. Returning to the DTE, the theory problematizes social forces that constrict girls' engagement in physical activities and in free movement in the public sphere. Further, the theory highlights the importance of equitable access to social resources, such as a range of occupations. An integrated lens involves the *concurrent* consideration of a range of social factors. Therefore, as we aim to work toward social equity, the DTE suggests the importance of social transformations in all three domains of social experiences.

The third example relates to the clinical phenomena of eating disorders. The DTE emphasizes the importance of examining multiple pathways to understanding embodied distress. Unlike the dominant pressures-for-thinness social theory of eating disorders, the DTE suggests that, to understand eating disorders, both risk and protective experiences in the physical, mental, and social power and relational connections domains have to be explored. The next section on Implication to Therapy describes and discusses the development of disordered eating patterns related to adverse experiences in the physical domain, specifically, the withdrawal of joyful engagement in physical activities and exposure to sexual harassment and other forms of violations. Similarly, the Implication to Therapy section describes the development of disordered eating in response to pressures to appear "demure." It further describes the development of an eating disorder in relation to exposure to racism, classism, sexism, and weightism. Katzman and Lee (1997) who advocated for a transcultural perspective to eating disorders have similarly criticized the singular emphasis on the pressures-for-thinness theory, "In case studies of rural Chinese women… feelings of powerlessness, oppression, and experience of sexual abuse are reported, but fat phobia is not" (p. 390). Both therapy and health promotion programs, therefore, need to be informed by the complexity of social factors that contribute to embodied distress.

The DTE puts at the center of inquiry the loaded intersection of body and culture, with the goal of contributing to feminist, social, critical, and psychological theory; to social transformations; and to the well-being of girls and women of different social locations. Girls and women who participated in the 171 interviews, as well as research team members, were from a range of ages, ethnocultural and racial heritages, social classes, and sexual orientations. Nonetheless, the emergent theoretical constructs and their mirroring of social processes aimed at preserving the social status quo, and ideas for systemic and individual interventions included in this book, are presented as bases for dialogue, recognizing the situated and partial nature of all constructed knowledge (Hill Collins, 2000). Beyond methodological rigor, further validation lies with readers—with the way experiences and constructs addressed in this book resonate with their own.

In particular, the embodiment program examined the experiences of girls and women as they intersected with other aspects of social location. All girls and women who volunteered to participate in the studies were cisgender, save for one participant who identified as a "lesbian woman slightly transgender". While younger and older adult women who participated in the study described different sexual orientations, girls who joined the study at the ages of 9 to 14, and were interviewed prospectively during the following 5 years, described only heterosexual sexual orientations. It is of interest to examine whether studies that center on social class, race/ethnicity, sexual orientation, gender identities, or physical ability/disability will also find that disciplining social factors take place in the physical domain (e.g., safety), the mental domain of constraining and disciplining discourses (e.g., demeaning labels), and the domain of social power and relational connections (e.g., access to resources, isolation). In addition, different social factors described by the DTE may take different forms in varied societies or countries. For example, the Physical Corset described as Blocked Physical Engagement and Movement, or the Social Power Corset entitled Exposure to Prejudice and Harassment, might relate to social norms in one country while being enshrined in laws in others.

PART II: IMPLICATIONS TO THERAPY

The DTE can inform therapy for girls and women in relation to three main areas: goals and conceptualizations of challenges in the body domain, body journey inquiries, and interventions toward healing and re-capturing embodied well-being in the physical, mental, and social power and relational connections domains.

GOALS AND CONCEPTUALIZATION

Starting with the EE, this construct, anchored in the narratives of girls and women, outlines a positive way of inhabiting the body while engaging with the world. Positing "positive body connection and comfort, embodied agency and passion, and attuned self-care" (see Chapter 1 and Piran, 2016a) as goals of therapy for girls and women is in line with conceptualizations of health as a state of well-being, and not merely the absence of disease (WHO, 2005). To date, most treatment (and prevention) approaches for the widespread embodied distress of "negative body image" identify the reduction of body dissatisfaction as the goal of intervention, with focused interventions aimed at addressing coping—cognitively or emotionally—with appearance-related pressures. Therapeutic goals, therefore, have not been informed by a research-based delineation of positive ways of inhabiting the body. Positive formulations of embodied well-being may work to enrich current approaches to the treatment of embodied distress. In particular, looking beyond the reduction of body dissatisfaction, the EE construct suggests broadening the goals of treatment to enhance positive ways of inhabiting the body, including establishing a positive connection to the body and to desires, physical agency and/or agency through voice, and attuned physical, emotional, and relational self-care. Engagement in meaningful pursuits and interventions that enhance body attunement will also support the resistance to objectifying pressures.

Outlining the multidimensional aspects of positive EE can also guide therapists in addressing sometimes-silent disruptions in girls and women's embodiment. For example, it is common for post-pubertal girls and women to experience discomfort with having an assertive voice, suppress their ownership of desire, or live their lives without the experience of physical agency. Consequently, these domains of experience may not be invited into the therapy process. The "omissions" related to the EE can be further accentuated at the intersection with other aspects of social location. For example, ageism among therapists may leave the domains of sensuality, desire, or physical agency (attuned to one's abilities) out of the therapy room. Similarly, stereotypes related to ethnicity may silence the exploration of assertiveness.

Looking at the negative pole of the EE, the construct suggests a general state of disruption best summarized as "disrupted body connection and discomfort, restricted agency and passion, and self-neglect or harm" (see Chapter 1, and Piran, 2016a). Interviewing girls longitudinally clarifies that disrupted embodiment is common among girls at and post-puberty and that adverse social conditions affect *all* of the following five domains: body connection, agency, desire, self-attunement, and inhabiting the body as a subjective site (resisting objectification). Indeed, women often start their adult journeys with such a broad embodied disruption. Informed by this broad state of disconnection, therapy can proceed with ongoing monitoring of this disruption and its expression in all these domains. Further, therapists should be mindful of, and deliberately enhance, the way progress in one of these five domains can facilitate changes on other domains of the EE.

Disrupted embodiment is also associated with a range of behavioral disruptions, such as: disordered eating patterns, the consumption of substances aimed at weight control (e.g., smoking, diet pills, amphetamines, cocaine), self-harm or neglect, sexual activities with no desire or protection, or the avoidance of public exposure without body alterations aimed at approximating 'beauty ideals', as found in this research program among cisgender girls and women. Rather than recognizing the shared state of embodied disruption, both assessment procedures and treatment approaches have tended to focus on just one behavioral disruption or another, without recognizing or addressing the shared state of body disconnection and disruption. The EE construct suggests employing therapy approaches that target the underlying experiences of body disconnection, rather than focusing exclusively on specific behavioral disruptions.

Describing shared embodied developmental disruptions in the lives of girls and women, in relation to adverse social conditions should caution therapists against conceptualizing behavioral expressions of embodied disruption—such as eating disorders—as related exclusively to intra-individual difficulties. For example, due to the dominance of the pressures-for-thinness social theory of eating disorders, and the recognition that such pressures are ubiquitous, the tendency among therapists has been to "look elsewhere" for the causation of clinical eating disorders; this may involve a focus on personal difficulties, often without a thorough exploration of the complex social environment, as would be suggested by the DTE. Experiences such as loss of physical functionality, exposure to a continuum of violations, expectations to fit constraining social molds, challenges to owning sexual desire, encountering sexism, racism, weightism, heterosexism, and other prejudices that leave one powerless, to name a few, may not comprise part of the clinical formulations of eating disorders or other behavioral expressions of disrupted embodiment.

The focus on intra-individual conceptualizations risks silencing and dis-validating girls and women's embodied experiences in a complex social environment; in particular, the dis-validation of adverse social experiences in the therapy relationship can have a devastating impact on the welfare of clients and disallow their healing. For example, not exploring the impact of early sexualization or of sexual harassment, as well as violations in peer and dating relationships, and associated fears and body discomfort, is highly problematic. A psychiatrist interviewed Claire, a young woman research participant raped twice during her tweens by a peer, about her "behavioral problems" at school following the rape; however, the psychiatrist did not ask about experiences of violence outside of inquiring about sexual abuse, hence never finding out about her rapes (see also the description of a case of sexual harassment by Legge, 2009 in Chapter 4 on early adolescence). Furthermore, experiences of body-based harassment—not only in relation to weight but also gender, gender identity, ethnicity/race, sexual orientation, or social class—are often not explored in detail.

In a similar vein, clinical conceptualizations of embodied disruptions, such as disordered eating, should consider the withdrawal of protective social factors as contributing to disrupted embodiment. For example, we find that girls' joyful engagement in physical activities (not related to body alterations), and that involve a strong sense of physical agency and functionality, comprise a protective factor against the objectifying gaze. Similarly, the presence of an accepting, validating, and empowering relational community relates to body comfort. Yet, losing both protective factors can lead to embodied disruption. Chapter 6 on adulthood described how Laya, at age 14, stopped engaging in athletic activities and, concurrently, lost membership in a validating, gender-equitable community. From skiing competently and equitably with boys, her social experiences became confined to the highly objectifying gaze of her peers at the private school she attended, a gaze accentuated during co-ed parties she attended. Finding this environment adverse to her self- and body experience, "You don't have as much contact with the opposite sex in a friendly, healthy way, so it ends up being very sexualized," she withdrew from inhabiting her body with care and agency and began a pattern of self-neglect. Mental health conceptualizations and related treatment recommendations she received for her disrupted embodiment focused exclusively on intra-individual factors, such as anxiety. However, she has since learned, with considerable psychological insight, that in order to feel well she needs to re-capture experiences of body attunement, which she had during her childhood athletic pursuits:

> It's so liberating… and the further I am from that physical part of me, the less strong I feel in my body, the more distant and disconnected I am to myself and what I need… But I think if we teach women that they can be free, that they should get to know their bodies in a healthy way, we'd have a lot healthier women and fewer women with depression.

Laya now knows the role of having such a body connection to her well-being. Diverse girls and women live in a complex social environment that challenges their body connection and embodied agency. The goals and conceptualization of disrupted embodiment should be anchored in a comprehensive look at the complex social environment inhabited by diverse girls and women. Such a scrutinizing look at the social environment is in line with feminist perspectives on therapy.

THE BODY JOURNEY

In the explorations of body journeys, we invited girls and women to describe the way they felt in their bodies, all the way from their earliest memories to the present, and to describe their social environment at each point in time. Participants found their own chronological accounts of their body journeys to be productive in identifying points of transition in the way they have lived in their bodies, and in connecting to a range of embodied experiences, often including positive memories of agency and joy.

Girls, for example, found opportunities in the interviews to uncover and share stories that had been silenced in their social environment. Alice, from an Aboriginal and middle-class background, shared her persistent exposure to sexual harassment, and her consequent experience of fear and food refusal—a story otherwise buried within an unchanged social environment. Jackie, a girl from an Aboriginal and working-class background, shared for the first time during the interview, at age 11, her profound experience of social alienation at the intersection of sexism, racism, weightism, and classism, leading to her self-starvation and rapid weight loss. Bronwen, a 16-year-old White girl of low-to-middle class background, only understood her behavior of wearing makeup at all times, even at home, after being reminded of her interview at age 12; at that time, she highlighted the adverse impact of her father pressuring her to wear makeup because of her pale complexion, leaving her feeling "not pretty" at home. Ashley, of African-Canadian heritage, only noted during her interview at age 16 how her church's expectations that girls cover up to help boys control their own sexual desires, shaped her own careful surveillance of her clothing: "Well like, just so like when I'm putting on clothes or I'm buying things at the mall I'll think twice about what kinda message I'm putting out." Interviewers, keen on inviting girls' reflections about their social environments, provided validating relational connections, which girls often described as being helpful.

Women, similarly, found their own body journeys to be revealing, sometimes reinforcing embodied paths they may want to pursue as they chart their future journeys. For Alex, a woman in her 20s of Latina heritage and a working-class background, the body journey interviews were an opportunity to examine, among other factors, the aggregated impact of a range of body violations leading to disconnection from her body, herself, and others. Clarifying this state of disconnection mobilized her to initiate significant shifts in her life informed by self- and body connection, and restoring significant relationships in her life:

> I realized (after first two interviews) that I was growing up kind of disconnected, neglecting myself, and now I begin to re-connect with myself. So I begin to find who I am as an individual. I had a difficult time feeling genuinely good about myself with other people. I was thinking about as a child what happened to me, and the rape, as another thing of why I was disconnected. I never really analyzed my life. It was something new for me to look at, and it will help me in the future, because I'm aware. I'm aware now that there is a point in my life where I may feel disconnected from myself, and I need to be connected to myself. I just feel that it's a process. And I don't think for a moment that I'm going to be connected to myself for the rest of my life. It took me a long time, but I found out what I need to do. I am more selective about friendships in my life and the bonds are more genuine. I just need to stay connected with myself.

For Jane, a White woman of a working class and rural background in her early 20s at the time of the study, telling her story highlighted the marked shift in her body experience after being exposed for the first time at the age of 10 to *Playboy* magazines, as well as the effort it took to reverse the impact of sexualized objectification, even within the context of an overall positive body journey: "I started wondering about me personally as a sexual object" (see Chapter 1). During her interviews, Jane also started to question the "natural" transition away from sports during puberty:

> It [interview] makes me question some of the decisions that I've made over the years. I wonder was I pushed or maybe I just didn't think consciously enough about it. I was very active until I hit puberty and then became very docile. I want to go back to that 11-year-old me and say, "smarten up" [laugh]. It didn't feel like pressure. It felt "natural." So, yeah, there could definitely be something there and it's making me curious. It's making me want to go back and figure it out myself. It made me re-define what does activity mean to me and where do I fit back into it.

With older women, the body journey explorations provided the opportunity to consider social experiences that have shaped their embodied lives for many years, all the way from "mundane" to traumatic experiences. For example, Alice's father's comment that she had a "broad bottom," affected her body experience all the way into her 60s. Another research participant disclosed, for the first time, sexual abuse by a priest, an experience that led to body disconnection, shame, and appearance preoccupation for years to come. At other times, body journey inquiries with older women, provided an opportunity to support and validate women's self-care strategies. The interview with Sonia, a woman in her 60s of African and Asian heritage, honored the care she took of multiple ill family members while working as a secretary and a cook, and validated her new choices of pursuing self-care and joy. For Marie, the interview reinforced the positive role of physical activities in her life. For Orchid, the interview validated the "airplane rule" of self-care before the care of others.

Considering the contribution of body journey inquiries to identifying points of embodied transitions, un-silencing social stories, and guiding girls and women toward healing, we have started to use body journey inquiries in different clinical situations. Legge (2009), who published an example of using the body journey inquiry in a clinical setting, was one of the research interviewers in the girls' prospective study. She conducted a body journey inquiry with an adolescent girl, hospitalized repeatedly over a number of years for anorexia nervosa with no consistent progress, being prescribed antidepressant medication. The body journey interview led to a new etiological understanding and positive treatment outcome. Specifically, the chronological body journey inquiry led to the discovery of ongoing severe sexual harassment at the girl's school, causing her wish to "disappear" by becoming anorexic. While the routine clinical interview at the hospital included an inquiry about sexual abuse, the occurrence and relevance of the pervasive sexual harassment only surfaced in the body journey inquiry. In turn, this discovery facilitated her progress in treatment, as well as guided changes in her social environment. A chronological body journey inquiry can therefore be a valuable tool for clinicians.

Another benefit of body journey inquiries relates to the power of connecting experientially to embodied experiences of body comfort and agency. Commonly, post-pubertal adolescent girls and women recall positive body experiences from early childhood, prior to the introduction of corsets in the physical, mental, or social power and relational connections domains. For example, Jean, a White woman in her 60s from a middle-class background, described how body memories from around the age of three surfaced when practicing yoga as an older adult: "I remember being at the beach… two or three, and just total freedom running up and down the beach… and I never really re-captured that feeling until I started yoga" (see Chapter 6). Identifying and re-living such memories as an aspect of the body journey inquiry propels girls and women of all ages to seek paths in their current lives that help re-capture such embodied experiences. These embodied memories can also be returned to as a place of body connection when challenges to embodiment present themselves, either in or out of the therapy process.

THE PHYSICAL DOMAIN

The DTE emphasizes the importance of the physical domain to positive body connection and comfort, embodied agency and passion, and attuned self-care throughout one's life span; hence, in line with the DTE, the body should be integrated into therapy, and experiences of Physical Corseting and Freedom validated and processed during sessions. However, there is a risk that the physical domain might be de-emphasized in therapy. First, irrespective of gender, the Cartesian division between mind and body that dominates Western thinking has informed many schools of therapy that focus exclusively on the treatment of the mind. Second, disruptions in the physical domain might be "normalized," and therefore omitted in therapy with girls and women. For example, the loss of physical agency and functionality, related to the cessation of engagement in physical activities, may not seem relevant to their well-being. Similarly, the vigilance and fear with which diverse girls and women inhabit their bodies, reacting to the range of sexual violations in their lives (both experienced and witnessed), or to common exposure to racist events, might not be problematized in therapy unless these violations fit with therapists' own criteria of what comprises a traumatic experience (e.g., sexual abuse or rape).

In line with the DTE and, ideally, informed by body journey interviews, it is recommended that therapists address all aspects of Physical

Corseting and Freedom with girls and women, including both current and past experiences. Encouraging engagement in activities that restore physical agency and functionality in ways that resonate with clients' positive embodied memories, history, wishes, and abilities can contribute to renewed body connection and embodied well-being. Engagement in such physical activities can also help counter experiences of physical restraint and entrapment and associated emotions of helplessness and fear that may be brought on by a range of physical restraints and violations. Therapy can then, concurrently, invite girls' and women's mindful awareness to their embodied experiences as they engage in physical activities, with the goal of a gradual increase, at a pace determined by clients, in activities that enhance embodied body connection and agency.

The recommendation to integrate the body in therapy, anchored in the DTE, is in line with different approaches to therapy advocated for the treatment of trauma. For example, the sensorimotor approach to therapy (Ogden, Minton, & Pain, 2006; Rothschild, 2000) involves work with the body without the use of hands-on intervention and can be integrated with other approaches. It enhances non-judgmental awareness to learned body reactions. The sensorimotor approach can therefore be particularly useful in enhancing mindful awareness of internal body sensations and movements related to a range of physical constrictions, such as: constriction of movement, of taking space, or of voice. Engaged in processes of somatic re-learning about inhabiting the body with agency, comfort, and attunement, clients are encouraged to perform in therapy movements of resistance or escape that were arrested during the physical entrapment of violations. Similarly, Laura Brown (2013), a leading feminist therapist, described how mindful engagement in movement informed by the martial art of aikido, can help empower clients of feminist therapy to re-connect with their bodies. Yoga has also been found to contribute to the treatment of individuals with eating disorders (Carie, Fyfe-Johnson, Breuner, & Marshall, 2010).

In a similar vein, the incorporation of a physical component to intensive treatment programs for girls and women is in line with the DTE. For example, D'Andrea, Bergholz, Fortunato, and Spinazzola (2013) found that adding a trauma-informed sports component to their treatment protocol with a diverse sample of adolescent girls, exposed to trauma in their family environments and treated in residential settings, had a significant positive impact on behavior and mental health:

> Perhaps the more embodied, physiologically regulating nature of trauma-informed sports, in the context of a supportive community of peers, may be functioning as a more rapid catalyst of behavioral change than traditional psychotherapeutic with this population. Engaging in a shared shift in collaborative behavioral practices through guided and contained opportunities for repetition and mastery may further solidify these gains (van der Kolk, 2006). ***D'Andrea et al. (2013, p. 747).***

Indeed, a recent meta-analysis of 57 studies (Spruit, Assink, van Vugt, van der Put, & Stams, 2016) found significant positive effects related to interventions involving physical activity on different measures of well-being among adolescents treated in different mental health centers. In particular, this meta-analysis found there to be larger positive effects on depression and anxiety in studies with more girls and more severe clinical cases. D'Andrea et al. (2013) suggest that greater restrictions in the daily activities of girls compared with boys could relate to the higher effectiveness of group-based engagement in exercise.

There are relatively limited data regarding the impact of physical activities on adults with mental health difficulties, though there is some support for incorporating exercise as an aspect of care (Zschucke, Gaudlitz, & Ströhle, 2013). However, it is worth noting a debate that transpired regarding the treatment of hospitalized girls and women with eating disorders. For several decades, the treatment regimens of girls and women hospitalized with severe forms of eating disorders involved not only bed rest but also the restriction of engagement in all physical activities. Such restrictions aimed to facilitate weight gain and control intense engagement in physical exercise. However, imposing such restrictions should be reconsidered in light of research findings showing that, as a group, girls and women with severe eating disorders have endured trauma at higher rates compared with non-clinical control groups (e.g., Tagay, Schlottbohm, Reyes-Rodriguez, Repic, & Senf, 2014). Considering the histories of trauma of girls and women, as well as exposure to a range of violations and widespread physical restrictions, such confinement risks re-traumatizing them or replicating their physical constriction. Instead, our research supports a comprehensive treatment plan that involves girls and women re-learning how to engage in safe, attuned, mindful, and joyful physical activities. Rachel Calogero and Kelly Pedrotty (2004, 2007) described the implementation of such an exercise program within an inpatient eating disorder program. A pilot study of this program with adolescent girls and women diagnosed with anorexia nervosa (who were medically cleared to participate in the exercises) revealed that they gained about 30% more weight and shifted in their thoughts about compulsive exercise regimens when compared with a (non-random) control group of girls and women also hospitalized for anorexia nervosa.

While our research is in line with the range of proposed approaches that incorporate working with the body in therapy within the context of trauma, this research suggests that such approaches may be relevant to all girls and women presenting to therapy, related to their common exposure to physical constraints and a range of violations. In the body journey interviews, all post-pubertal girls and women responded in visceral and emotional ways to body restrictions and violations, even when they never sought therapy or received a trauma diagnosis. Alice, a 13-year-old girl of Aboriginal heritage, for example, likened the emotional response to pervasive sexual harassment in the school corridor to that of being a victim in a war:

> Oh my God, find a place to hide. Find a teacher. Nervous breakdown… Sad, unhappy, scared. Maybe she should have worn pants. Maybe that wouldn't happen when I'm a woman. Hope I forget who he is when I grow up. Oh no, if I forget who he is, he may become my future husband. Oh, no, no! It makes a girl nervous, kind of sad, sometimes scared if they'll do it again. When she grows up she may be afraid to go outside. Stay in her house. Like this guy, when he was 15 was hiding from the Nazis. And he stayed there fore 75 years.

Working with the body in therapy includes also the area of desires. Girls and women described embodied challenges they faced in owning desires comfortably and joyfully. For Sarah, a White woman in her 50s, the re-living of the embodied memory of adolescent desire and its longstanding corseting was a way to re-connect with body desires and consider, possibly, reintroducing such desire in her life. For Andrea, also a White woman in her 50s, memories of her tween years, involved a lived experience of parental prohibition of same-sex desire. Even for Reni, an Asian-Canadian woman in an arranged, passionless marriage, an awakening memory—fleeting experiences of prohibited adolescent desire—shifted her embodied self-experience.

In addition to supporting mindful body attunement, the DTE aims to enhance therapists' awareness of varied Physical Corsets and their presence in different life phases. In turn, that can facilitate the validation of such (often silenced) experiences, and through such validation, mobilize girls and women to engage in the world with greater embodied agency and freedom. This validation of girls' and women's experiences was central to the interview processes. At times, especially in the third and fourth interviews, once rapport deepened, interviewers sometimes focused on addressing such Physical Corsets directly, often by reframing girls' perceptions of such corsets. For example, when Jackie, age 15, described her weight preoccupation, the interviewer addressed the constriction in space:

> Jackie: Like I said today to [boy] 'I weigh more than you,' but boys are supposed to be all muscle-y and he's like 'no way!' But, we checked and I weigh more than him.
> Interviewer: Interesting how we have this notion that we're supposed to weigh less than men, but you have just as much right to take up space too, right?
> Jackie: It's actually funny when you put it that way. I'm going to use that line! 'Take up space!' Yeah!

It is meaningful that Jackie continued this dialogue about taking up physical space with a discussion about the struggle over Aboriginal territories and about land-related ceremonies in the Aboriginal community. "Aboriginals trying to gain rights back to their lands… I am determined [to help]." She also problematized being unable to go through a land ritual at the age of 16, unlike boys who share her heritage. So for her, taking up physical space became linked with territorial rights, connecting Jackie to activism.

Another example of reframing experience—this time of the restriction on free movement—took place with Melissa, a White 13-year-old girl from a middle class and rural background. Melissa described and contested her mother's expectations that she engage in constricting girls' activities, rather than roam the fields and collect bugs:

> Melissa: That's what's expected and accepted. Like: 'You're a girl, this is what you do.' You're taught that from like 1 year old. 'You're a girl, go play with Barbies.' Like they set that up.
> Interviewer: It makes me wonder if girls are really connected with their actual interests, or if it's just that they've been pushed to that.
> Melissa: Yeah, they have just been programmed to do.
> Interviewer: And I think it takes a very strong person to be able to say, 'No, like, I'm going to dig up bugs.'
> Melissa: Or a *weird* person.
> Interviewer: No, not at all. I would reframe that and say that you're *strong* and you're assertive
> Melissa: (Laughing) I will tell my mom that… 'I'm strong.'

These excerpts are described to exemplify the way in which corsets can be addressed and girls mobilized to examine new possibilities of action.

THE MENTAL DOMAIN

The DTE clarifies links between the embodied lives of diverse girls and women and constraining social discourses. In particular, constraining social discourses about members of disenfranchised social groups disrupt their embodied attunement, as well as their acting powerfully and passionately in the world. Mental Corsets related to gender intersect with those related to ethnicity/race, social class, sexual orientation, and other social dimensions. As diverse girls and women internalize these constraining social discourses and labels, and inhabit their bodies in line with them, their docility assures no disruption of the social status quo.

The process of developing resistance to these internalized, widely enforced social constructions is both demanding and, yet, empowering. Anti-oppressive- and feminist-informed approaches to therapy aim to support diverse girls and women in this empowering process. Making Mental Corsets explicit in therapy is an important step in reinforcing diverse girls and women's search for shifts in their embodied engagement with the world. Moreover, naming these corsets validates the experiences of constraint for diverse girls and women and further clarifies the broad exposure of other girls and women to the same adverse social constructions.

As described in the chapters on tweens, early, and late adolescence, the enforcement of femininity-related Mental Corsets intensifies during and following puberty. While the research interviews with girls focused on the exploration and validation of their experiences, at times, during the final interviews with girls, the interviewers engaged in the explication of some of the Mental Corsets. These processes can be used to inform interventions with girls.

The following excerpt—a dialogue with 13-year-old Alice, who is a member of the Aboriginal community—relates to two discourses of femininity: the Body as an Object of Gaze and the Woman as Submissive/Demur. Alice struggled to juggle her athletic passions with her wish for peer acceptance as a feminine girl:

> Alice: Like when you play sports, you get more competitive, but when you're, like, not, you're just like, 'Oh my God! Like totally!' and stuff like that. Most girls are like, 'Oh my God! Your shoes don't match. Is my hair growing curly? Oh, my God!'
> Interviewer: [laughs] So, you kinda leave the sports on the field? Is that what you mean?
> Alice: Yeah.
> Interviewer: And then you act *more girly* when you're with your friends?
> Alice: Yeah.

While the interviewer referred only to girly discourses, the process of analyzing discourses in therapy with older adolescent girls and women can also involve addressing discourses at the intersection of several dimensions of social location. The strength, size, and functionality of Alice's body countered not only docile femininity but also social constructions aimed at silencing and disciplining members of the Aboriginal community. Alice's peers at her school, located in a White-majority middle-class neighborhood, tell her that she takes up "too much space. Leave some space for me"; they also make her feel scary: "When I stand, they'll back away and they'll run away from me like I'm a giant and they're afraid of me. I don't like that." These two constructions, related to taking space and being a scary enemy, resonate with tensions between the White political majority and Aboriginal Peoples across the country, including in the place where Alice resides. Further, Alice's friends tell her that she could join their planned trip as a "luggage carrier," reflecting a racist construction similar to what Patricia Hill Collins (1990) described as the "mule"—a discourse justifying the exploitation of African-American labor.

Another example from the study with girls involves explicating and challenging the Woman's Body as Deficient discourse. It also reflects possibilities of shifts toward greater freedom in engaging with the world inherent in analyzing and countering constraining discourses. Thirteen-year-old Erica, a White girl from a working-class background who loved sports, viewed sweating as a body deficiency, saying that "pretty girls don't sweat." Consequently, she restrained her passionate immersion in physical activities:

Interviewer: Has your body ever stopped you from playing sports?
Erica: A lot of times in gym when we're doing running, I worry about sweating, 'cause I think it's gross for girls because like boys are meant to sweat... I sweat but I try to avoid it. Like, I try not to run and move that much... Usually if you don't work as hard, then your grades will drop, so you have to find a balance between trying not to sweat too much and run so your grades don't go down... I love sports. If I didn't sweat, I'd be playing sports, like, every day!
Interviewer: What's another way of looking at sweating? Like, we've talked about it in terms of being a negative thing. What's positive about sweating?
Erica: That everybody does it, so it doesn't matter. Like, it's a normal thing.
Interviewer: Yeah. It is also neat if you think about it in terms of strength, that you are working hard.
Erica: Like I'm trying so hard, super hard.
Interviewer: And you are not doing it for other people, you are doing it...
Erica: For yourself.

This exchange was significant for Erica. At the end of that interview—her fourth and final in the study—when asked about her experience as a study participant, she highlighted the exchange about sweating:

Interviewer: So, how's it been for you being part of the study?
Erica: I like it. It makes me feel important.

Interviewer: Has it changed how you've thought about being a girl?
Erica: More secure.
Interviewer: Can you give me an example?
Erica: About the sweating thing. (laughs) It's like I used to think, 'oh, it's gross.' It still is but I can feel better now about it because you're like working really hard to do it and stuff.
Interviewer: Yeah, and it's kind of more for you than for whoever is looking at you. Like, 'I don't care what you see. I just had a lot of fun playing soccer.'
Erica: No kidding!

A third example, reflecting the explication of discourses and the possibilities of shifts in embodiment in relation to challenging said discourses, involves the Woman as Desired but Desireless discourse and the use of the slut label. Fifteen-year-old Ashley, of African-Canadian heritage and a working-class background, contended concurrently with discourses related to gender, race, and class. In the following excerpt, Ashley shifted from being critical of girls who engaged in sexual activities to problematizing the use of the slut label in relation to women, and African-American women in particular. She even concluded with a resistant stance of no further collusion with the perpetuation of this label.

Ashley: It's [slut label] being normalized. There is no distinct boundary between girls saying it to each other and guys saying it… If you're going to be doing that in the first place… it's your business… but don't go spreading it around. So you're kind of *putting that label upon yourself.*
Interviewer: If a guy kisses and tells, does he get called a slut?
Ashley: No, which is really dumb, like he might just be almost celebrated, like, 'oh, yeah, you're such a player, you're like a pimp. I think it probably goes back to like actual prostitutes and they were the ones being punished for it. It's a reflection on the society's reaction towards girl and guy dynamics and that just reflects into us teenagers… Music videos are unbelievably sexist, and the Hip Hop community is embracing it. And it's hurting African American women as well as guys. Calling girls sluts. That's when I started thinking about the roles that we play, even myself. What about the roles that I play, which I know, if I see a music video and I watch it, *I'm supporting that.* So it's really interesting that I can kind of share the blame for it. As well as calling other girls sluts and something. It's just keeping the word out there. Yeah, it's just like my part in it. I think the best thing is to fix yourself before you can start trying to fix other people.

Girls sometimes present to therapy due to peer taunting with corseting labels. Once girls start to inhabit women's bodies, these labels serve as penalties aimed at coercing them to comply with dominant social discourses. Girls who do not engage in self-objectification and beautification aimed at resembling idealized appearance standards might be labeled manly, butch, jock, or dyke. Girls who do not act demure and, instead, exhibit physical and social power or competitiveness, might also be labeled bitch, butch, or mean. Girls who take care of their needs are labeled mean or selfish. Problematizing these labels in therapy and clarifying their corseting roles is important. Therapy, similarly, needs to highlight girls' strengths and acts of freedom in resisting constrictive labels.

For example, a 14-year-old girl was referred for treatment regarding her rapid weight loss, which was triggered by peers who labeled her butch (Piran, 2001). The girl described having had multiple previous positive experiences in her body, including pride in her agency and joyful immersion in athletic pursuits. Her weight loss related to hoping to put a stop to her peers' teasing by looking demure and less muscular. The short therapy process problematized the butch label and encouraged the girl to stay connected to her sense of pride in her body and the joy she took in athletic activities—activities she could no longer perform while starved. Concurrently, the therapist, in her role as a school consultant, met with the group of girls in her class who teased her, as they themselves contacted the school consultant to request a group session because they had teased a girl and noticed that she was losing weight. The group process sought to uncover the learned meaning of the butch label and its disciplinary use:

> [Facilitator]: What is the butch label about?
> [Girls in group]:
> -She has strong muscles, she can lift a guy.
> -So what if she is strong?
> -A girl is not supposed to be stronger than guys; she is supposed to be smaller.
> [Facilitator]: Is it only in physical strength?
> -Everything. Guys don't like it when you are too strong, like too opinionated or something.
> -Girls can't have too much power.
> -I can't believe what we did. We wanted to take her power away. Remember how [staff] said I am too loud… [More examples of girls' silencing]. ***Piran (2001, p. 225).***

This group became aware of their learned prejudice regarding "girl power," and of their actions colluding with the disciplining of girls. They approached the girl they had labeled butch and apologized for their teasing and lack of awareness in taking away her power—taking power from girls made *all of them* feel unsafe. While the opportunity does not often present itself to work with the social system of girls, it can be a very powerful intervention.

Social discourses are entrenched in diverse women's lives, and penalties for deviations are readily present. Counteracting constraining Mental Corsets is a difficult process, and if it takes place, as described in Chapter 6 on the adulthood phase, it may be a long and demanding process, sometimes possible only at older adulthood (see also Piran, 2016b). Therapists cherish women's journeys toward liberation from constraining social constructions and validate the challenges of introducing even small movements toward such changes, especially in unfavorable, unsupportive circumstances. Enhancing self-compassion during processes of change is also important.

There are particular pivotal moments that women in the study highlighted as significant points of shift in relation to constraining social expectations and labels; their experiences could inform therapists. First, the realization of losses accrued while living in docile bodies can mobilize women toward change. As described by Gwen, a White woman in her 60s of a working-class background who had had a "patriarchal and heterosexist" marriage, "I was deferent… I wanted to be attractive to my husband… I think I suffered from depression."

Nina, a White woman in her 60s of a middle-class background, described her breaking point as one of extreme fatigue:

> I think that I always wanted to be a perfect wife where I did everything well… everything was orderly and neat and taken care of… I was getting tired. It was harder to keep up with that. And he could pick up on the slightest thing not done. It was impossible. The first thought was, 'I'm not good enough, I'm not meeting your expectations, I'm not trying hard enough. *It was 20 years ago and I do remember it clearly*, and I thought I can't do it. *I can't do it anymore. I'm tired.*

A second important transition point involved women's realization of the role of constraining discourses in maintaining social structures of power and privilege. Nina, for example, started to realize over time that her husband's objectification and devaluing of her body, and his demands for perfection in conducting household chores and in catering to his needs, were reinforcing a power imbalance in which her sense of self was eroding. This insight mobilized her shift from depression and fatigue to taking action and leaving her marriage:

> What I understood was what a power someone can have over you in your relationship when they start criticizing what you look like and it is a form of abuse. … with his little [critical] remarks he was

> chiseling into me and taking out what was sustaining me. It took me a while to realize there's nothing here for me and move on.

Gwen similarly assessed the issue of power when she decided to leave her docile existence, telling her husband, "I was under your patriarchal hand and am going to come out from under it. These old roles never really fit me perfectly anyway." For Reni, an Asian-Canadian woman in her early 60s of a middle-class background, who could not leave her arranged marriage as her education and professional development were forcibly stunted, her gender analysis of her husband's use of the term "aggressive" to describe her ("if I was a man it would be not be a problem") allowed her to maintain clarity of voice. Shifts in relation to constraining social discourses can take place first within the self, explicating and naming them; individual and social action may follow (see also Hill Collins, 2000).

Another transition point women described related to an acute realization that compliance with social expectations afforded them no care or protection. Indeed, women's narratives regarding the social forces that shaped their lives revealed a glaring absence of social messages toward women's well-being or safety. Having excelled as a caretaker of many family members and friends, Reni has little expectation of reciprocity; even her "dream situation" of being taken care of, involves minimal expectations,

> You're sick and, you know, we just still have to get up and do what we have to do normally. They [male partners] are not going to feel that they need to help us... If I was a boy, my mother would have overprotected me, nourished me over a girl. If there was food left, she would have given me more than my sister... A dream care would be someone to make me lunch once in a while. I don't expect big things. If I'm sick and I have told him and two days later he'll phone and say, 'Are you feeling better?' Just little things.

The realization that "there is nothing here for me," as relayed by Nina, often came at a time of being unwell or needing support. Nina had arrived at a place of depletion and depression when she mobilized herself to search for a better quality of life outside of her marriage. Importantly, as she reflected about her life, she highlighted the absence of social messages supporting self-attunement, and embodied care and joy, stressing that such messages would have changed her life journey:

> I think that's sometimes the early teaching that we have as girls that sort of attached themselves to us in ways that we don't realize and so behavior continues, when you should have said no, I shouldn't

> have that happen. I would definitely say listen, *listen to your body*, and if you're tired rest, and if you're feeling worn then nurture yourself in some way and I think those are the things that I did not do, and I wish that I had known how to do it back then or that someone I respected would say to me just *enjoy your life too*. I know you're making it good for other people but enjoy your life too. Slow down and take the time. Also, prepare yourself for things. I think that's something that I didn't really do in lots of ways. I wasn't prepared for things not going the way that I thought they would. I wish I addressed things as they arose.

For Andrea, a White woman in her 50s of a middle-class background, confronting illness has similarly clarified her rights and needs for attuned care and where she might find it. "I can't depend on my husband to really take care of me... I need to have other arrangements... support from my friends."

Transmitting in therapy the value of inhabiting the body with attuned self-care and meaningful passions can occur alongside problematizing the glaring absence of social messages regarding women's well-being while living in docile bodies. At times, mobilizing imagery and metaphors can be useful. For Orchid, a Caribbean-Canadian woman in her 50s, the "*airplane rule*" is her guide for self-care in older adulthood:

> Yeah because we're not taught to value ourselves as much as we value our products like our children and our man, we polish and shine them and don't really look at ourselves too much. But I am learning the airplane rule: put my emergency mask on first and then put on theirs. I used to be the opposite. This is just in my late 50s. Lately I have just started to focus more on myself.

Some women inhabit their bodies with caring attunement for the first time in older adulthood, raising new hopes regarding embodied paths. For Sonia, a woman of Asian and African heritage in her late 60s and a retired secretary who dedicated her life to supporting unwell family members, older age represented the first respite she could recall: "Before I couldn't do anything for me, now I'm alone by myself and I can do whatever I want." Therapist's modeling of engaging with the world in ways that challenge constraining socially sanctioned molds and inhabiting the body as a site of care provides an important component of therapy.

The invitation by therapists to examine linguistic labels that reinforce constraining social discourses opens up domains of experience in the lives of clients that otherwise may not be problematized. For example, labels such as selfish or hysterical (or PMS) can, respectively, restrain women from attuned self-care, or from expressing anger or assertive views. As expressed by Crystal, a White woman in her early 20s from a working-class background, "If I take care of myself, my dreams, people consider you selfish… society makes us feel like we are being selfish if we try to assert ourselves or take care of ourselves." Gwen heard the label hysterical repeatedly in her marriage, in response to her strong social justice convictions: "When I had an opinion about injustices, his line was, 'Oh there she goes again, that's just your mom, boys, women are hysterical.'"

Even women who resist social constraints, and operate in the world with power and agency, might utilize problematic labels to describe themselves. For example, two women in their 20s assigned the bitch label to themselves in describing their assertive style: Jane, White and from a working-class background, and Amber, Asian and from a middle-class background. Working with women therefore necessitates the ongoing challenge of contesting linguistic labels and imagining new ways of describing and engaging with the world. For example, the term "powerful woman" can be used as a replacement for the bitch label; "self-attuned" can replace selfish. As terminology is questioned and changed, so too are one's embodied experiences, resulting in the opening of new possibilities of acting in the world.

Cherishing women's strengths in breaking long-held constraining molds of engagement is important in empowering women. Memories of acting in the social environment with embodied agency, assertiveness, clarity, and desire prior to the intensification of pressures in one's social environment are additional facilitators in breaking constraining molds. Reni, for example, during her interviews, was able to re-connect with her passion for academic pursuits and her experiences of desire from before her arranged marriage. Sarah was able to remember her experiences of adolescent desire and her agency in the business world before frequent physical moves, related to her husband's employment, deprived her of the career she sought. These embodied memories mobilize women to seek new possibilities for engaging with agency and passion in the world.

THE SOCIAL POWER AND RELATIONAL CONNECTIONS DOMAIN

The DTE highlights the importance of embodied equity to experiences of positive body connection and comfort, embodied agency and passion, and attuned self-care. Anti-oppressive, social justice, and feminist approaches to therapy emphasize client empowerment as a key element in therapy (Brown, 2010; Oakley et al., 2013). The exploration of embodied journeys highlight particular equity-related issues that could inform therapy.

One issue the DTE underscores is the living conditions of diverse girls and women, and their impact on well-being, both physical and mental. Inequitable access to resources and exposure to prejudicial treatment and harassment lead to adverse living conditions. Girls and women of all ages described such challenges—in particular, girls living in single-parent households with their mothers shared challenges related to financial distress. Fifteen-year-old Roxas, of Caribbean-Canadian heritage, contested that, "Healthy food costs more than the junk food! Idiots! And they want us to be healthier, then lower down the [price of] healthy food!" Indeed, in the United States, the poverty rate for single mothers is 39.8% (Older Women and Poverty, 2016). Sam, a White young woman, reflected about growing up in poverty and its impact on her job situation in early adulthood; having had no opportunity to pursue university education, she has tried to make a living by holding more than one job at a time, including being a night security guard, where she does not feel safe from harassment.

However, the *aggregated impact* of inequitable access to resources became particularly clear in the stories of older women, of whom several were subsisting on small governmental pensions, food banks, or by holding multiple low-paying jobs, such as cooking or babysitting, that stood in stark contrast to their abilities. For example Alice, a white single woman in her 60s who lived on government pension, did not have an opportunity to pursue university education until older age, when she also joined the Mensa organization; however, it was too late for her to benefit financially from her education. Recent US statistics suggest that during the past 5 years, poverty rates have increased significantly among older women (Older Women and Poverty, 2016), so much that among Americans older than 65, twice as many women as men live in poverty, with women comprising 68.1% of the elderly poor. Additionally, poverty is highest among African-American women and lowest among White women. Such challenges to living conditions, related to inequity and maltreatment, suggest the importance of attending to the physical living conditions of women in therapy. This can include help in accessing different social and community resources and therapy centers that are free of charge or use sliding scales. In addition, poverty is associated with stress, depression, and embodied helplessness that need to be attended to in therapy.

A related issue, examined previously in the field of therapy (e.g., Brown, 2010; Jordan, 2010; Oakley et al., 2013), involves the internalization of inequitable and prejudicial treatment, adversely shaping self- and body concept, as well as interpersonal relational patterns and agency. Our research supports the importance of examining such internalizations in therapy, as girls and women often referred to them. Fifteen-year-old Ashley, of African-Canadian heritage, described her ongoing struggle with negative stereotypes: "So even though they are trying to tell you who you are, stereotypes, I find it like a challenge to break those stereotypes and just stand out and be myself." Alice, a White woman in her

60s living on government pension, shared how not receiving parental support for her education "made me feel not as smart as my brother, less special… It bothered me so much so at [middle age] I actually took the Mensa test, and I am now a Mensa member." Therapy can support women in examining their experiences through a critical lens by exploring the impact of inequity, prejudice, and maltreatment along the different dimensions of their social location on self- and body-experiences and on relational patterns. Becoming aware of these influences can support shifts to self-concept, opening new relational possibilities and enhanced agency.

Within the broader agenda of exploring the internalization of inequity and prejudicial treatment in therapy, related to self-concept and relational patterns, the DTE also suggests to maintain a critical focus on embodied patterns of engagement with the world. The internalization of inequitable treatment can be expressed through embodied practices. Such embodied internalizations, unless examined critically, can perpetuate adversity. For example Jackie, who experienced body-based teasing and social alienation in relation to her Aboriginal heritage, social class, and weight, and who described wanting to access White privilege, was susceptible to sexual exploitation during her teens by a White boy she falsely hoped cared for her. Sarah, a White girl of a middle-class background, mentioned how the disrespect she experienced toward her girl's body was perpetuated through her engagement in sexual activities without caring about her own experience:

> Losing respect kind of started with… putting me on a diet and then the [critical] comments… and calling me a 'lesbian' on the hockey team with guys… And then, like with the guy, what does it matter, you want it [sexual activity], you do it.

The impact of internalized inequity on embodied patterns of engagement with the world is as relevant for therapy with women. Grace, a woman in her 50s of African-Canadian heritage, detailed how racism at work motivated her to look impeccable, leading her to be at medical risk: "I am fighting for my appearance until I die! Sometimes I exercise too long and may end up hurting myself, and I need to listen to my body." Fern, a White woman in her 60s diagnosed at a young age with a genetic disposition to cancer, felt that, by virtue of this "deficit," she was not entitled to a family of her own. Sam, a White woman in her 20s, whose labor as a young girl was exploited toward maintaining two different households, described how this history made it difficult for her to stop others' exploitation of her. The exploration of embodied practices as expressions of internalized inequitable treatment can help diverse girls and women to re-inhabit their bodies positively.

The focus on embodied lives can help uncover creative strategies and insights employed by girls and women in dealing with inequities and prejudicial treatment. Such an emphasis on strengths is in line with feminist and anti-oppressive treatment approaches (Brown, 2010; Jordan, 2010; Oakley et al., 2013). For example, the successes of Madison, a girl of Aboriginal heritage and a working class background, in initiating activism projects at her school continued to empower and inspire her, despite facing ongoing racism, classism, and weightism. While living in an Asian country, Vivian, at age 12, barred from continuing her education, registered herself in an online English course, thereby acquiring a skill that facilitated her immigration to North America; her early embodied agency inspired her while in her 60s to try and contest being fired from her job through contacting different political figures in her region. Similarly, Jean, a White woman in her 60s, stood up to her stepfather, making a case for her wish to pursue education; this inspired her to address prejudice in her life: "my stepfather thought that women... were less. He said, 'You don't need any of that education; you're married.' It made me very angry. I used to argue with him and I think I gained more strength from that." These actions reflect strengths to draw upon in engaging in the world with agency.

The body, as a site from which to engage with the world, can become a focus of therapy. One task of therapy is to examine the way in which social ideologies of power and privilege become encoded onto widely disseminated visual images. In our studies, girls' drawings of ideal girls reflected the consistent internalization of heteronormative images of idealized femininity: thin and small, blond and blue eyed, perfectly made up, clad in tight, and exposing clothing, and static as objects on display, like "porcelain dolls" [Jackie]. Presenting a challenge to social justice, these images perpetuate the social status quo of privilege. Girls and women are affected by these internalized images, criticizing their "deficiencies" and engaging in multiple appearance alterations.

In therapy, girls and women can examine the impact of these oppressive idealized images on their self- and body experiences in the different domains of their lives: social relationships, work, sexuality, and identity. Clarifying the function of these visually encoded ideologies in maintaining the social status quo of privilege, oppressing girls and women of diverse backgrounds, is important in starting to build a position of resistance. It can be useful, as well, to identify times, situations, and relationships where girls and women feel relatively free from these oppressive ideologies. Such freedom is associated with greater well-being and greater opportunities to engage with the world unencumbered:

> At [sport], I show up at 5:30, I don't have make-up on, I look like crap, and I'm just like—I'm here. And that kind of brings you freedom. It's almost like everywhere else I have to be pretty. Like, I don't want

> [them] to see me without makeup, which is bad. So when people see you when you are just like not up to anything [without makeup] and who can still love me for it, it's kind of important to me. [Bronwen, 16 years old]

Even though for Bronwen, at age 16, athletics is her only place of freedom, it provides her with an opportunity to be powerful in the world and develop friendships with boys, unencumbered by appearance alterations. Gwen clarifies the relief from "media patrolled expectations" she experiences in the lesbian community,

> Before I had to feel pretty. I don't have to feel pretty now. And a part of that is aging and acceptance of some kind of change in my body and being happy with what I have. There isn't the same expectation in the lesbian community to be hot by wearing high heels and putting makeup and looking a certain way. And even body size. I mean you see a lot more bigger women in the lesbian community than you do in the heterosexual community. Yeah, it seems that women are more comfortable in their bodies. It might just be that there's more freedom to be different. Whereas in heterosexual womanhood there are media patrolled expectations. Norms are pretty tight on what's feminine. I can wear a lumber jacket if I want, I can still feel sexual. I can still feel good about myself. I can still be happy if I'm wearing sweatpants and no makeup, and still feel good about myself. I like to sometimes look at myself with makeup on but I don't need to and I don't feel less good about myself when I'm not wearing makeup. And it's better because it's free, and it's free. You don't have to, it doesn't matter. [Gwen, 60s]

Therapy can encourage girls and women to develop relational connections that resist the messages transmitted via idealized images, and cherish, instead, the richness embedded in the uniqueness of group members and their contributions. Finding alternative ways to experience social power is another important task of therapy.

Examining another social ideology, the binary division of gender, can cause significant distress. In our studies, only one woman, in her 50s, described herself as "lesbian/slightly trans because I have some penis envy, but I don't want to live this life as a man, and when I realized I was lesbian and I could date women, I became happy with being a woman." Her social environment accepted her engagement in shared activities with boys, and later with men, when she became an adult; however, her lesbian social orientation was not accepted. The available relevant-yet-limited research in this important area indicates the social stigmatization, discrimination, marginalization, and disenfranchisement of transgender people (e.g., Grossman & D'Augelli, 2006). In all social contexts—not just therapy—people should be encouraged to live in their bodies in ways that fit their gender identity. The overall goal of this work is social transformations: combating oppressive ideologies that privilege some bodies and disenfranchise others.

As a central component of therapy, empowerment should be practiced in the therapy relationship, respecting clients' goals, choices, and evaluations of the process. As clients examine power in the therapy relationship, they can address such issues in other relationships in their lives and choose to engage in relational communities that validate their strengths, values, contributions, histories, and heritages. The hierarchical oppression of certain communities can cause rifts within them, which leads to further disempowerment of said community members; this emphasizes the role of continued dialogue across established differences (e.g., Hill Collins, 2000). To this end, finding relational forums of equity and power among the girls and women in our studies—in schools, at work, in partnerships, and in their friendship circles—has been central to achieving experiences of positive embodiment. Relational forums of equity and power can further mobilize social activism and shared resistance toward adverse social conditions.

PART III: IMPLICATIONS TO HEALTH PROMOTION AND PREVENTION

The DTE delineates a positive way of inhabiting the body with respect to the quality of embodied lives. Toward that goal, health promotion and prevention activities can take place in the three domains of social experiences: physical, mental, and social power and relational connections. In particular, the DTE emphasizes systemic interventions that concurrently address all these domains.

PHYSICAL FREEDOM DOMAIN

Toward health promotion, the DTE emphasizes focusing on several protective factors in the physical domain: joyful engagement in physical activities, safety from violations and from forced compliance with harsh appearance standards, experiences of attuned self-care, and a pleasurable connection to desires.

Regarding joyful engagement in physical activities, health promotion interventions need to increase access to physical activities that involve immersion and pleasure (Paxton, Estabrooks, & Dzewaltowsky, 2004), enhance the experience of physical agency and functioning, and support a positive connection to the body. Azzarito and Solomon (2005) recommend seeking students' own choices regarding physical activities and related clothing. Physical activities could include: team sports that are non-competitive and that involve no weight criteria or disruptive clothing, wilderness trips, hiking, freestyle dance, or yoga. The importance of experiencing comfort in one's body during physical activities cannot be overstated. In our prospective study, girls often described skipping physical activities, such as swimming, if they were not comfortable in their bodies or with the associated dress code. Chapter 1 described how following the introduction of Lycra bodysuits, instead of using shorts and t-shirts as the uniforms for netball, 35,000 fewer girls and women across Australia participated in the sport (Dubecki, 2007). Both girls and women complained about experiencing bodily discomfort while playing in the Lycra bodysuits. In a prevention program I implemented in a dance school (Piran, 1999a, 1999b), students—both girls and boys—asked to have at least one class a week where they could choose what to wear, enhancing their body comfort and immersion in movement and dance.

Inherently, systemic changes need to take place in sports organizations, schools, community centers, families, and multiple other social organizations to successfully enhance girls and women's participation in pleasurable physical activities. The most important systemic intervention to date that has contributed to girls and young women's participation in sports in the United States has been Title IX, the Education Amendment Act, which ensures there is no gender discrimination in educational institutions receiving federal funding (Koller, 2010); in turn, Title IX was used toward the cause of equalizing opportunities for girls and women in sports. While Title IX increased participation in sports among girls and women, inequities are still common (Senne, 2016), and women remain poorly represented in positions of leadership within sports organizations (Burton, 2015). In particular, 2016 participation rates for high school girls involved in athletic activities have not yet reached that of boys in 1972 (Senne, 2016). Furthermore, during the past decade, participation rates for boys and men in high school and university sports have increased at a rate higher than girls and women (Brown, 2012). There are still many more opportunities for boys and men to participate in sports and related activities, and, similarly, inequitable funding. Additionally, girls are socialized to pursue feminine activities rather than sports, which are still commonly constructed as "masculine"; female athletes also face sexualization as well as prejudicial treatment and negative labeling (Senne, 2016). Continued systemic interventions are needed in order to establish and implement institutional policies that encourage equitable participation, as well as changed norms related to the masculinization of sports—from sports media coverage, to school- and peer-based norms.

At the school level, for example, systemic changes could target the allocation of equitable resources (funding, sites of engagement within school yard territory, intramural sports) across genders, as well as staff education aimed at changing oppressive norms regarding diverse bodies and physical action. In turn, such changes can coincide with critical dialogues among students regarding gender norms and sports, such that new constructive norms could be established.

A health initiative geared toward engagement in pleasurable physical activities (yoga, freestyle dance, nature walks, or team sports), can be incorporated into a school-based prevention program aimed at preventing negative body image and eating disorders. In such a program, participants can be invited to discuss their positive body experiences with their peers and write about them in their journals. Discussion and validation of girls' needs for immersed physical movement, comfort in performing physical activities, pleasure in action, and physical strength can help in establishing positive group norms about engagement in physical activities. A related empowering component can involve asking girls to describe how their experiences might help younger girls engage in pleasurable physical activities. Enlisting older girls' help in planning ways to support younger girls has been a component in different eating disorder prevention programs (e.g., Becker, Bull, Schaumberg, Cauble, & Franco, 2008; Stice, Marti, Spoor, Presnell, & Shaw, 2008; Wilksch et al., 2014).

Another protective factor in the physical domain is the presence of environments that are physically safe and free of harsh, externally enforced appearance standards. Physical violations of the body, especially sexual harassment and sexual violations, are common in adolescence (Tjaden & Thoennes, 2000; Young, Grey, & Boyd, 2009) and disrupt body connection, agency, and attunement while at the same time engendering a range of negative feelings (van der Kolk, 1996). Such violations may lead to a range of behavioral disruptions such as self-harm, self-neglect, eating disorders, or a lack of protection used during sexual activities (Harned & Fitzgerald, 2002; Piran, 2010; Piran & Thompson, 2008). It is indeed during puberty that we started to hear about self-harm activities and prevalent engagement in disordered eating patterns among girls. Furthermore, women are susceptible to such violations throughout their lives. Addressing safety as a *general protective factor* to a range of embodied disruptions, including the prevention of specific behavioral expressions of such disruptions (e.g., self-harm and eating disorders), is therefore central to the well-being of girls and women (Piran, 2010). It is vital that institutional policies regarding sexual harassment and violations are adopted in schools, then disseminated, implemented, and enforced. Education and a clear stance regarding sexual harassment and violations are vital for the well-being of all students as such violations are related to widely accepted beliefs and to existing structures of power (Senn, Gee, & Thake, 2011). The end goal is institute-wide change—in addition to implementing specific programs for young women geared at lowering the risk of sexual violation (Senn et al., 2015).

It is important to reinforce, as well, that socially oppressive pressures to comply with harsh, externally enforced appearance standards (e.g., regarding weight, tight and exposing clothing, and hair removal) also compromise the experience of inhabiting one's body as a respected site of ownership. Girls in the study described pressures regarding body alterations: "My dad got me a razor and put it in my stocking"; "My dad told me that I should wear makeup because my skin is fair"; or "My friend's mom and dad… forced her to lose weight so that it [bathing suit] would fit her. They put her on a diet and she was all sad." These dictates had a clear adverse impact on the embodied lives of these girls. Health initiatives should therefore include educational programs with school and health personnel, as well as with parents, about reasons to avoid criticizing a child's appearance characteristics (Rodgers & Chabrol, 2009; Hart, Damiano, Chittleborough, Paxton, & Jorm, 2014). For example, despite a very small number of controlled outcome evaluation studies of programs aimed at the prevention of body dissatisfaction and eating disorders that also include a planned parental component, a review by Hart, Cornell, Damiano, and Paxton (2015) suggested that children who perceived a reduction in thinness-related pressures from their parents, showed a subsequent reduction on measures of risk of body dissatisfaction and disordered eating. Similarly, establishing peer norms of no mutual appearance evaluation among peers can be a valuable component of a prevention program for eating disorders (Piran, 1999a, 2001, 2010).

A third protective factor in the physical domain of the DTE involves the development of attuned self-care, including attunement to internal cues and acting in line with them (Cook-Cottone, 2006; Piran, 2016a, 2016b). While self-attunement and affect regulation are learned within a child's primary relationships (Shore, 1994), social variables also have a hand in shaping their development. For example, social expectations of girls and women include the care of others while silencing their own needs—socialization with long-term implications to women's embodied well-being (Ussher & Perz, 2010). Similar to other disenfranchised groups, the social environment is not attuned to the well-being of women, as revealed, for example, by the lack of equity in domestic chores in heterosexual households where both partners work outside of the house, and the lack of physical safety for girls and women (see also Kawachi et al., 1999). Girls, and younger and older women described experiencing such inequities, which led them to regularly override or disavow their own needs. Reni, for example, felt that had she been a boy, she would have been fed differently and not held responsible for household chores; the overriding of her needs continued all the way to her current age, in her 50s: "…when I'm tired or when I'm depressed or something then I don't want to do it [housework] but I do." Bronwen, in her tweens, similarly described overriding her wish to play sports during recess, doing homework instead, so she could help with household chores—unlike her brother. Girls and women often described such misattunement by their social environment.

Toward health promotion, girls and women need to re-learn attunement to their physical, emotional, and relational needs, as well as to engaging in meaningful pursuits. Such re-attunement during the body journeys of girls and women had immediate impact on their well-being. For example, as 15-year-old Bronwen described, "I feel more confident in myself and I know who I am more because not having anyone else's expectations [of others' care] on you, you really define who you are rather than allowing others to define that; it's great." Sam said, "I believe in trying to return to an awareness of my own needs and desires." Nina, in her 60s, stated "I would definitely say listen, listen to your body... wish someone I respected would say to me just enjoy your life too." And Orchid, in her 50s, described the "airplane rule" of taking care of herself before assisting others. Health-promoting situations among our research participants that contributed to the re-learning of attunement involved therapy, role modeling, a supportive and validating community, and physically centering activities such as yoga. Scime, Cook-Cottone, Kane, and Watson (2006) reported on a positive outcome of a yoga-informed prevention program for children with eating disorders that also focused on self-attunement. Similarly, Atkinson and Wade (2015) found positive results with their mindfulness-based prevention program for eating disorders among school-aged children.

Parents can help adolescent girls stay attuned to their changing bodies as they go through puberty and face intensified pressures to engage in body alterations or negotiate their sexuality. For example, Amber's mother helped her to remain physically active while menstruating, and Alice's mom bought her a sports bra when she started to feel awkward about engaging in sports without one. Lauren's mother understood her daughter's refusal to wear tight and "very short shorts" and, instead, took older pairs of pants and cut them long enough so Lauren felt "really comfortable" in them. During Jane's adolescence, her mother helped guide her in negotiating sexual activities, which enhanced Jane's engagement in such activities—but only once she felt ready and comfortable: "I was always very much in touch with the sexual feelings that my body had." Ashley's mother supported her daughter in learning how to accept the changing shape of her body by educating her about weight diversity: "Some people have different types of bodies... You can only compare yourself to what's healthy for you." Significant adults can therefore enhance self-attunement among adolescents by modeling such attunement for their daughters.

Attunement to caring for the body should be the goal of health promotion programs in schools. In a health-promoting school model, such attunement takes place through consultation with all stakeholders, including students. In the prevention program for eating disorders that I developed and implemented at the residential competitive ballet school (Piran, 1999a, 1999b, 1999c, 2001), a key guiding question in focus groups with students was: How do you feel about your body in the school, and what would you like to change or see changed? Enhanced attunement to students' body-anchored experiences led to changes to many aspects of the school environment, including the curriculum, staff, physical spaces, cafeteria foods, peer norms, and school policies. It also conveyed to students the importance of attuned self-care and respect toward their bodies while at the school. This program was associated with positive outcome on measures of body image and disordered eating patterns. Such attunement to students' needs may have long term effects towards health promotion; an initial 15-year follow up evaluation of this program suggests the maintenance of gains in the prevention of disordered eating patterns (Bar, Chassin, & Dionne, in press).

In different schools where I worked as a body image consultant, pubertal girls often wanted greater comfort in dealing with their menstrual cycles, such as having tampons or sanitary pads available for purchase in washrooms, or having the freedom to leave class to take care of menstrual needs discretely—desires often not respected. Additionally, discomfort with the lack of privacy in change rooms deterred pubertal girls' participation in sports. Health promotion interventions that create relational spaces where youth can express their body-based concerns, and have their concerns attended to, enhance embodied comfort at schools. Such forums could be part of a health-promotion program, or simply take place in physical education or health classes. Educational activities with significant adults—parents, teachers, coaches, and health professionals—can help toward achieving this goal (McVey, Gusella, Tweed, & Ferrari, 2009; Piran, 2004). Attunement to the nutritional needs of youth should also be part of a school's health promotion and social justice agendas, providing and modeling the consumption of nutritional foods.

Inquiries with stakeholders in designing health promotion initiatives aimed at care of the body, including at the policy level, can also take place in research. For example, Rodgers, Ziff, Lowy, Yu Ba, and Austin (2017) conducted a strategic science study with professional fashion models that was aimed at assessing the potential impact and feasibility of seven policy proposals that could support their health. Fashion models experience strong pressures for thinness and have high rates of unhealthy weight control behaviors. While imposing restrictions on minimum BMI has been a policy proposal aimed at reducing pressures on models to be thin, the fashion models in Rodgers et al.'s study did not support said policy, rating it as unlikely to have a positive impact and difficult to implement. Instead, they more favorably rated policy proposals that suggested providing models with more employment protections and better working conditions, such as breaks and meals during their workdays. This research emphasizes the importance of attunement to stakeholders when designing health promotion initiatives.

The fourth protective factor in the physical domain details a positive connection to bodily desires, both appetite and sexual. Positive connections to appetite and eating, including the multiple functions of eating (e.g., nutrition, pleasure, comfort, social, and other), are learned throughout childhood. Prospective, cross-sectional, and retrospective quantitative research as well as qualitative research with girls suggests the protective role of regular family meals during adolescence, particularly in relation to lowering the prevalence of engagement in extreme weight control behaviors (Neumark-Sztainer, Eisenberg, Fulkerson, Story, & Larson, 2008). Regular family meals are also associated with reduced use of tobacco, alcohol, and marijuana, as well as reduced rates of depressive symptoms and suicide attempts among girls (Eisenberg, Olson, Neumark-Sztainer, Story, & Bearinger, 2004). Neumark-Sztainer et al.'s (2008) research also highlights the importance of the role of positive atmosphere during family meals. Family meals associated with a positive atmosphere provide a good opportunity for the modeling of the role of appetite in guiding eating, the savoring of food, and the social functions of eating with others. Ideally, such meals provide protection from the (approximately) $60 billion diet industry that presents food dichotomously as "good" and "bad," advocates for the restriction of intake for the sake of weight loss, and disrupts connection to appetite and eating.

In this regard, it is important to highlight the Health at Every Size (HAES) approach to living positively in one's body (Bacon & Aphramor, 2011). As these authors describe, this approach focuses on body acceptance (vs. weight loss or maintenance), attunement to internal regulation of hunger and satiety, and active embodiment. Indeed, in a study of the HAES approach, women who took part in a 4-month HAES group treatment, as compared with women who participated in social support groups and those still on the waiting list, showed a greater connection to their experiences of appetite and satiety (Provencher et al., 2007). This highlights the value of an approach that de-emphasizes weight and, instead, heightens awareness to internal cues such as appetite and satiety, bodily responses to food, and the varied positive functions of food. The HAES paradigm can be utilized at home and in school settings as a way to counteract the multiple disruptions to appetite and eating presented by the culture at large.

Our embodiment research program also indicated a clear disruption to girls' connection to sexual desire, in line with other researchers (Fine, 1988; Tolman, 2002); yet the research program also clarified the important contributions of connection to desire to embodied agency, positive body connection, subjective immersion in the body, and attuned self-care. Within the context of sexual violations and adverse social discourses that validate and present boys and men's sexual desires as intense and elevating of their social status, the sexual desires of girls and women are often deprecated and stigmatized, with little opportunity for them to connect positively with their own sexual desires. Furthermore, there exists a glaring lack of relational forums that give girls and women the opportunity to address their own desires: sexual education classes are significantly lacking and parents/mothers rarely engage in such discussions, leaving girls to draw upon the experiences of their peers or pornography for such information.

Toward the goal of health promotion, and tailoring content to participants' ages, important aspects of such relational forums are: providing pubertal girls and women with opportunities to examine their own sexual desires, the spectrum of ways they can engage sexually (vs. an exclusive emphasis on intercourse), their sexual boundaries and rights, and communicating these preferences assertively (Senn et al., 2011). Our embodiment research program suggested the value of counteracting adverse social discourses regarding sexual desire in such relational forums. Senn integrated a unit on Sexuality and Relationship to her Assess, Acknowledge, Act (AAA) sexual assault resistance program (Senn et al., 2015), which she implemented among first-year students at several university campuses. Senn's stated rationale for including such a unit was that adverse social discourses and norms make it impossible for girls and women to identify rape, and that clarity about one's own desires, boundaries, and safety helps women assess and resist rape; our research findings confirm Senn's rationale in that girls often did not identify their violations as rape. Senn's AAA program was successful in decreasing the occurrence of rape, attempted rape, and other forms of victimization among first-year university students (Senn et al., 2015). Helping girls and women connect with their sexual desires can improve their embodied well-being in varied ways.

MENTAL DOMAIN

With respect to health promotion in the mental domain, the DTE emphasizes processes that counter and liberate diverse youth and adults from constraining social discourses; these discourses reproduce existing power structures and disrupt embodiment by sanctioning some bodies and disenfranchising others. Such liberating processes involve looking critically at intersecting social discourses in relation to all aspects of social location, naming and problematizing them, and guiding social transformations.

According to the DTE, a broad spectrum of discourses and associated social labels affect embodied agency and body comfort. Related to femininity alone, girls and women describe both Appearance-related and Comportment-related Discourses. The two Appearance-related discourses, the Body as an Object of Gaze—transmitted and internalized in early childhood and becoming more sexualized over time—and Women's Body as Deficient—expressed during and following the tweens phase—can be targets of varied initiatives at all levels of the social environment. Similarly, the Comportment-related Discourses of Woman as Submissive/Demure, Engagement in "Feminine" Activities, Woman as Desired but Desireless, and the Patriarchal Shaping of Relational Patterns all need to be addressed with respect to enhancing girls and women's embodied agency to act powerfully and comfortably in the world. Girls suffer a barrage of penalizing labels, both for failing to comply with femininity discourses (e.g., manly, butch, bitch) or for complying with them (ditsy, dumb, slut). In relation to ethnicity and race, girls and women in our studies of Aboriginal and African or Caribbean heritage faced being labeled primitive, scary, or sluts, as well as white-washed (or, similarly, blonde). The range of discourses is larger and needs to be contextualized in relation to the experiences of particular communities.

The multiplicity of discourses that shape embodiment need to be attended to in health promotion initiatives. If we examine toys, for example, research suggests that dolls and action figures (a disturbing yet meaningful binary classification in and of itself) transmit a complexity of discourses. For example, Boyd and Murnen (2017) coded Internet depictions of popular female dolls and male action figures, and found that more dolls had thin bodies and more action figures had muscular bodies. Furthermore, the thinner dolls, compared with the less-thin dolls, were also portrayed in a more sexualized and objectified way (e.g., revealing and tight clothing, high-heeled shoes), as well as in less assertive positions (e.g., a curved spine, bent knee, and head cant). The facial expression of the thinner dolls was more sexually appealing. In contrast, the more muscular male action figures, compared with the less muscular ones, were portrayed as dominant, with their hands in fists with angry emotional expressions. The findings of this study resemble girls' drawings of the ideal girl and the ideal boy in the embodiment research program. Importantly, Boyd and Murnen's research confirms the multiplicity of discourses that operate concurrently to socialize girls into inequity according to the DTE. Several studies with girls, for example, suggest that playing with Barbie is associated with lower body esteem (Dittmar, Halliwell, & Ives, 2006) and the internalization of thinness (Rice, Prichard, Tiggeemann, & Slate, 2016), as well as with the number of career options girls imagined for themselves (Sherman & Zurbriggen, 2014). These toys therefore embody both Appearance- and Comportment-related Discourses, and girls' exposure to them, in turn, adversely affects their own embodied experiences.

Countering the multiple constraining stereotypes that disrupt girls' embodiment, according to the DTE, would therefore require more than focusing exclusively on the discourse of thinness (Piran, 2015). However, even youth programs that focus specifically on counteracting media-generated pressures for thinness and other appearance-related pressures might include additional components that address Comportment-related Discourses. At times, Comportment-related Discourses are addressed through the process of prevention programs, rather than their content. For example, the Cognitive Dissonance (CD) prevention program (Stice et al., 2008), aimed at reducing the internalization of thinness, body dissatisfaction, and disordered eating among weight-preoccupied adolescent girls and women, might also include other components that empower participants and counteract Comportment-related Discourses (e.g., speaking in front of others, problematizing large corporations rather than the body, and constructing ideas to help younger girls). This hypothesis can be studied further by including only specific components of the CD intervention in an outcome evaluation design or by incorporating measures that aim to tap changes in empowerment or agency among participants as mediating variables.

The Media Smart program (Wilksch & Wade, 2009) is an eight-lesson media literacy program developed for mixed-gender, universal audiences in Grades 7 and 8. The program starts with a critical discussion of social stereotypes portrayed in advertisements and continues with a discussion of image-altering devices used by the media. It further includes discussions among peers regarding social pressures and encourages students to put pressure on the media through email campaigns. Therefore, just like the CD program, the Media Smart program empowers participants in multiple ways and possibly helps create more cohesive peer relationships as children work through critical explorations of cultural stereotypes. While the Media Smart program does reduce media internalization (Wilksch et al., 2014), it could be enriching and informative in terms of further theoretical and practical developments in the field, to conduct intensive, qualitative case studies of specific Media Smart processes with children. For example, such studies could reveal the wealth of stereotypes or social discourses students bring forward in relation to media images and the ways these discourses relate to different aspects of their social locations.

Tebes, Kaufman, and Connell (2003), as well as Fishman (1999), suggested that intensive case study analyses of community-based prevention programs could advance health promotion programs. The intensive case study of the prevention program implemented in the residential dance school (Piran, 2001) enriched the theoretical understanding of disrupted embodiment and mobilized the initiation of the embodiment research program. Furthermore, the intensive case study highlighted key processes in the prevention of eating disorders, in particular the importance of dialogical and participatory processes, and of systemic and ecological approaches to prevention at a time when most programs relied on didactic paradigms (Piran, 1995). While time consuming, such intensive case studies could enrich the practice of prevention.

Beyond school-based programs that equip youth with a critical perspective toward stereotyped, media-transmitted messages, other research critically examined media portrayals of women with the goal of larger-scale social transformations. Not only are women and girls marginalized in US media in terms of their presence in films and TV programs (Smith, Choueiti, Prescott, & Pieper, 2012), but they are depicted in stereotypical ways: sexualized, subordinate, and pursuing feminine activities (Collins, 2011). Women are rarely depicted in the media as athletes (Daniels, 2009a), and the majority of the photographs of women athletes in *Sports Illustrated* were taken in non-athletic settings (Fink & Kensicki, 2002). Researchers have also problematized the intersection of racism and sexism in the portrayal of women athletes (Schultz, 2005).

Elizabeth Daniels (2016) followed a research program aimed at examining the impact of different presentations of female athletes on girls and women. In one study, Daniels (2009b) found that participants who looked at images of women athletes in action tended to make physical statements about themselves (e.g., I am strong), and viewed the athletes as transgressing traditional gender stereotypes (e.g., she is fierce). In contrast, participants who looked at images of sexualized women athletes tended to make more negative appearance-related statements about themselves and viewed the athletes in stereotyped and objectified ways. In a follow-up study, Daniels and Sherman (2016) found that girls in their teens responded to images of women holding non-appearance–focused occupations (e.g., CEO, military pilot) by describing these women as good role models. In contrast, girls considered the women portrayed as holding gender-congruent appearance-focused occupations (e.g., model, actor) to be more competent, likeable, and more similar to themselves.

Daniels (2016) recommended that academic researchers get involved in transforming the stereotyped and limited depictions of women in media and, through such transformation, change the embodied experiences of girls and women. In particular, she highlighted the work of the Geena Davis Institute on Gender in Media and the non-profit organization LeanIn.Org, in presenting less-stereotyped images of women in the media. Daniels also described activism projects led by girls and women athletes, challenging corporations and the media in their stereotypical presentations of girls and women.

Parent education is another important initiative toward the health promotion of children. There is consensus among prevention scholars that parents should focus on children's positive qualities, interests, and values rather than their appearance, encouraging them to accept their child's weight, size, and body shape (see Hart et al., 2014). Findings from the embodiment research program suggest possible expansions to educational programs for parents. For example, parents of young children need to model body acceptance and avoid describing their body deficiencies and actions of "appearance repair." Similarly, parents should avoid communicating to children that the way they are comfortable in inhabiting their bodies should be altered for special scrutinizing events, such as "picture day"; girls in the embodiment study protested needing to wear dresses or straighten their hair for special occasions. Further, it is advisable for parents to support children in prioritizing the experience of *comfort* in choosing shoes and clothing—clothing that will also give them the freedom to pursue the activities they like (e.g., climbing on play sets, running); under the pressures of objectification and sexualization, girls sometimes choose clothes they are uncomfortable wearing.

Parental education also relates to the Woman as Docile cluster. It is important that parents are conscious of treating children of both genders similarly, encouraging their strengths, assertiveness, voice, and "taking space," all within relationships of respectful dialogues and positive relational connections; often girls and women described the expectation that they act nice and demure, and serve others in the household. In a similar vein, children of both genders should be encouraged to follow their interests, rather than classify activities as being for either girls or boys. In particular, it is important for their well-being that girls play sports and play with toys that enhance the development of spatial skills; these activities can help maximize their future career options, including in the fields of technology and engineering. Similarly, it is best for parents to avoid using labels commonly assigned to girls (e.g., PMS, hysterical, emotional, bitch, slut) and the common tomboy/girly girl dichotomy. Parents also need to be aware that their children may be teased not only about their appearance but also about their comportment—for example, among girls, assertiveness, being opinionated, physical strength, a passion for sports, and prioritizing self-interests, might all be penalized by one's peer group.

Overall, broadening the domains of discussion with youth regarding the impact of social stereotypes beyond thinness, or appearance, invites a deeper understanding of the social context related to femininity and masculinity, social class, race/ethnicity, and other social factors. The impact of critical inquiry of social stereotypes and labels with youth is more likely to be maintained if this critical lens becomes normative at home, in the media, at school, and among peers.

SOCIAL POWER AND RELATIONAL CONNECTION DOMAIN

The DTE highlights the privileging of particular bodies and the disenfranchising of others at the intersection of different aspects of social location. With the body being a site of social capital (Bourdieu, 1984), individuals inhabiting particular bodies have differential access to resources, are exposed to varied prejudicial treatments, gain differential entry to communities of validation and support, and benefit differently from guidance given by inspiring role models. Girls' drawings of the ideal girl provided a clear picture—literally—of intersecting dimensions of privilege (and disenfranchisement related to gender). Drawings of the ideal girl by all 27 participating girls, throughout their three to four interviews over a 5-year period, were consistent: ideal girls were thin and small in size, blue eyed, blonde and straight haired, objectified and hetero-sexualized (in revealing and tight clothing, with big breasts in relation to hips), perfect and physically abled, made up, and clad in brand-name clothing and material gadgets. Other research similarly indicates that prejudicial treatment and harassment tend to co-occur in relation to intersecting dimensions of social locations (e.g., Bucchianeri, Eisenberg, Wall, Piran, & Neumark-Sztainer, 2014) with adverse disruptions to self and body experiences. Therefore, health promotion initiatives, in line with the DTE, need to proceed from a *social justice* perspective.

Weight-based stigma, prejudicial treatment, discrimination, and harassment in different domains (e.g., home, education, work, accommodation, health settings, and social) have been important topics of research. Weight-based harassment is common among adults—more so among women (Puhl, Andreyeva, & Bronwell, 2008)—leading to disrupted ways of living in the body, poor self-esteem, and depression. A meta-analysis conducted to assess the outcome of different approaches to changing weight-based prejudices yielded small-to-medium effect sizes, suggesting some, yet limited, impact (Lee, Ata, & Brannick, 2014). Consequently, scholars studying these challenges highlight the role of anti-discriminatory policies and related legislation in protecting individuals living with obesity (Pomeranz, 2008; Puhl, Himmelstein, Gorin, & Suh, 2017). Furthermore, a public health perspective also advocates for the implementation of food policy supporting improved school nutrition (Pomeranz, 2008).

Stakeholders should have a say about strategies chosen to address weight stigma. Toward that goal, Puhl et al. (2017) conducted a study inviting overweight and obese women, most of whom experienced weight stigma, to rank the importance of 35 stigma-reduction strategies. The women ranked highest school-based interventions—in particular, providing training for staff regarding strategies to address weight-based bullying and advocating for the implementation of weight-related anti-bullying policies; raising awareness about weight-related bullying or including content in the curriculum about weight-related bullying were important but did not rank as high. Interventions in the health care domain were highly ranked as well, particularly education about obesity in medical schools and training professionals in providing respectful and compassionate care to patients with obesity. Interventions in the home domain related to educating parents about ways to support a child facing weight-based bullying. Also ranked important, though slightly less commonly, was changing the portrayal of individuals with obesity in both the media and anti-discriminatory legislation. Clearly, these stakeholders were favorable toward multiple systemic changes in their environment.

Examining gender inequity and disrupted embodiment, girls and women of diverse social locations described limited access to social resources, exposure to discrimination and prejudicial treatment, exploitation of their labor, and gender harassment and violations. Girls and women's embodied realities stood in stark contrast to prevalent ideologies regarding gender equity; clearly, health promotion strategies toward social justice need to be informed by the embodied lives of girls and women, and not by ideologies of equity. Girls' drawings alone, even without considering the rich interview narratives, provided striking embodied representations of inequity; unlike drawings of ideal boys, ideal girls were much smaller (in height and thinness); clad in restrictive, tight, and exposing clothing and high heels that constricted movement; and inhabited altered and made-up bodies. The common labeling of ideal girls with demeaning terms (e.g., ditzy, dumb, cow, mean, slut) clarified that ultimately *any* position on the girl spectrum is devalued, even when a girl or woman tries to embody said ideal characteristics. Examining older women's experiences, all women, even those who found facilitative factors that helped them re-capture embodied agency and well-being, experienced the aggregated impact of inequity on their well-being for at least a segment of their adult journeys; and some were fatigued and living in poverty. We can therefore not hide behind ideologies any longer; we need to return to the body politic of second-wave feminism and convey this need to the younger generation of women—however, with a greater emphasis on diversity. The presence of pay inequity in institutions is unacceptable; these exist even in institutions thought to be progressive, such as universities. The lack of quality, subsidized day care for children, and legislated *shared* parental leave, such as Sweden has, hurts women, children, and families. At the intersections of gender with ethnicity/race, social class, sexual orientation, gender identity, disability, immigration, and other social locations, women face greater challenges that need to be addressed through changes to policy and legislation.

The embodiment research program confirms the strong interest girls and women have in examining their lives critically. Social power figures centrally in diverse girls and women's lives; however, without the presence of relational forums that validate this critical lens, critical perspectives remain silenced. In the embodiment study with girls, for example,

Bronwen, a White girl of low-to-middle class financial standing and a rural site of residence, clarified:

> By conforming [to appearance and comportment standards] it makes us feel that we are *part of a group*, so that must mean that *we're validated*. But in doing that you *lose part of who you are. You lose your individuality and part of your power.* In order for a girl not to conform, she would need to be accepted as she is without the conformity, that's what gives you your power.

Claire, a participant in the young women's study in her early 20s, of Caribbean-Canadian heritage and working-class background, described her intention to create media with an alternative gaze:

> There is a privilege of gaze because the presumption is that the spectator is a White male, so it is masculine, and patriarchal. This takes a toll. These sexualized images of women on screen all the time on TV, magazines. So it's the privilege of the gaze. Here we are in the 2000s and there is no progress!

Both Vivian, a woman of Asian-Canadian heritage in her late 50s, and Gwen, a White woman in her early 60s, highlighted the centrality of power in their embodied journeys. For Vivian, rebelling, as a tween, against being barred from education due to her gender by registering herself in a correspondence course, mobilized her to protest her firing from her clerical job in Canada by contacting different political figures. Gwen emphasized that her life transformations involved "coming out from under the patriarchal hand."

Similarly, schoolgirls are keenly interested in discussing issues of power. For example, I described elsewhere (Piran, 2001) a group process whereby two girls who participated in a prevention program for eating disorders, Sarah and Mary, both 12 years old, compared their body experiences. Sarah felt hate toward her "fat" body and was scared that, "she will look like [her] mother," while Mary felt comfortable in her body and did not fear the same. Both girls reported that their fathers regularly put their mothers down for their body weight. The group then engaged in comparisons of these mothers' social situations in terms of their ages, weights, other appearance characteristics, education, immigration, and employment. While Sarah's mother was an immigrant (from Eastern Europe) and had no employment outside of the home, Mary reported that, "When my father puts my mother down she could not care less. She has a really good job and she loves it so she just does not care… She likes going out with her girlfriends." The group's conclusion was clear: "It is power… Mary's mother has power so she can feel good about herself the way she is, and that makes Mary feel good about herself… You need power to feel okay about yourself… Girls need power" (Piran, 2001, p. 225).

Recognizing the centrality of critical analyses of social power in the narratives of diverse girls and women, and the aggregating impact of inequity on their lives, the role relational forums play—whereby diverse girls and women engage in dialogues about their embodied experiences within the context of equity, support, and community validation—cannot be overstated. Lyn Mikel Brown (2016) emphasized the possibilities inherent in girls and adults working together in coalitions to transform culture. Such collective work necessitates self-reflection on the parts of adults (and girls) regarding their roles in sanctioning adverse social structures. Oppressed by hierarchical structures, girls and women (Brown, 2003), people of African-American heritage (Hill Collins, 2000), and members of other social groups might experience social rifts within their communities. Deepening the understanding of these social rifts can enhance cohesiveness, and through that, social power.

The link between embodied equity and well-being can inform programs aimed at parental education. Girls and women frequently described the adverse impact of gender inequity in their families and, more rarely, the constructive impact of equity. Parents should be invited to examine such differential treatment of gender in the home environment, in terms of allocation of family resources (e.g., time and money spent on gendered sports), differential assignment of household chores, and other expressions of prejudicial treatment. Such scrutiny also includes the use of demeaning gender-related labels (e.g., hysterical, PMS, bitch). Parents also need to avoid inequitable treatment related to skin color, weight, and other appearance characteristics. The equating of appearance with social worth and power among girls, and children in general, is a problematic practice, diverting children from the power inherent in their unique qualities, values, talents, aspirations, and creative pursuits. Further, parents need to learn strategies to support children through body-based harassment related to gender, weight, social class, disability, sexual orientation, or gender identity. Awareness of body-based cyberbullying (Slonje, Smith, & Frisén, 2013) is important for parents as well—they should be encouraged to reach out to health and mental health resources should they be concerned about their child's well-being in relation to teasing or harassment.

Schools comprise important sites of intervention toward social justice and health promotion. Just like families, schools can reinforce embodied inequity, or, alternatively, counter inequity by viewing embodied disruptions as sources of information about the need for systemic changes along all dimensions of social location. Laws prohibit discrimination in educational institutions on the basis of gender, sex, race, and physical ability (e.g., Titles VII and IX, and the Americans with Disabilities Act in the United States); however, no such protection regarding weight discrimination is available, though this should not prohibit schools from establishing such policies. In addition to establishing anti-harassment policies, schools need to educate students about these policies, their role in promoting social justice, and implications for those who deviate from said policies.

However, the occurrence of harassment often reflects not only socially prevalent inequities but also expressions of such inequities within the school organization (e.g., is the senior administration comprised mainly of White, able-bodied men?). As a school consultant, for example, I was invited to conduct body image groups in a private all-girls school, where all senior administration members were strikingly thin, White women. Several teachers confidentially shared that they had being exposed to weightist prejudice; indeed, many students could not feel safe in that school. Schools therefore need to examine organization-level challenges to social justice (e.g., differential allocation of school resources, equitable representation of diversity among senior staff).

By inviting input from all stakeholders of a school community, the health-promoting school model (Langford et al., 2014) can inform organizational changes toward enhanced social justice and embodied well-being. In particular, providing relational forums for students to critically examine their embodied experiences at school and, further, inviting their input about systemic changes that will improve their well-being can be a powerful step toward embodied equity, should the school administration be supportive of such a process. In a prevention program for eating disorders, Haines, Neumark-Sztainer, Perry, Hannan, and Levine (2006) invited students to identify an issue central to their body experiences at their school. Following up on the students' choice of targeting weight-based teasing, the program focused on a range of environmental-level strategies—such as school-wide training, a no-teasing campaign, and a theater production to which parents were invited—aimed at changing social norms regarding teasing. The program resulted in reduced weight- and appearance-related teasing. As mentioned earlier in this chapter, in the participatory program I implemented in a dance school (Piran, 1999a, 1999b, 2001), I invited students to reflect critically about the impact of their school environment on their body experiences and to use these reflections to guide school-wide transformations. A cohort-based comparison suggested that this program was associated with reductions in negative body image and disordered eating. Other authors emphasized students' own collective critical examination of systemic oppression and their engagement in collective action, with adults as allies (Cammarota & Fine, 2008).

Embodied equity is related to well-being. In turn, health promotion activities should aim at enhancing social justice. Rather than leading to rifts and social vulnerability, embodied experiences can inform relational dialogues toward social equity and, hence, deepen relational connections.

References

Atkinson, M., & Wade, T. (2015). Mindfulness-based prevention for eating disorders: A school-based cluster randomised controlled study. *International Journal of Eating Disorders, 48*(7), 1024–1037.

Azzarito, L., & Solomon, M. A. (2005). A reconceptualization of physical education: The intersection of gender/race/social class. *Sport Education and Society, 10*, 25–47.

Bacon, L., & Aphramor, L. (2011). Weight science: Evaluating the evidence for a paradigm shift (online publication) *Nutrition Journal, 10*(9). Retrieved from: https://nutritionj.biomedcentral.com/articles/10.1186/1475-2891-10-9.

Baker, M., & Cornelson, K. (2016). *Gender based occupational segregation and sex differences in sensory, motor and spatial aptitudes*. National Bureau of Economic Research. Working Paper 22248.

Bar, R. J., Chassin, S. E., Dionne, M. M. (in press). The long-term impact of an eating disorder prevention program for professional ballet school students: A 15-year follow-up study. *Eating Disorders: The Journal of Treatment and Prevention.*

Becker, C. B., Bull, S., Schaumberg, K., Cauble, A., & Franco, A. (2008). Effectiveness of peer-led eating disorders prevention: A replication trial. *Journal of Consulting and Clinical Psychology, 76*, 347–354.

Bourdieu, P. (1984). *Distinction: A social critique of the judgment of taste*. Cambridge, MA: Harvard University Press.

Boyd, H., & Murnen, S. K. (2017). Thin and sexy vs. muscular and dominant: Prevalence of gendered body ideals in popular dolls and action figures. *Body Image, 21*, 90–96.

Brown, C. (June 27, 2012). *Forty years after title IX, men still get better sports opportunities*. Washington DC, USA: US News. Retrieved from: https://www.usnews.com/opinion/articles/2012/06/27/40-years-after-title-ix-men-still-get-better-sports-opportunities.

Brown, L. M. (2003). *Girlfighting: Betrayal and rejection among girls*. New York, NY: New York University Press.

Brown, L. M. (2016). *Powered by girl: A field guide for supporting youth activists*. Boston, MA: Beacon Press.

Brown, L. S. (2010). Feminist therapy. In *Theories of psychotherapy series*. Washington DC: American Psychological Association.

Brown, L. S. (August 2013). Breathing in power: Bringing the body back in feminist practice. In *Paper presented at the American psychological association annual convention, Honolulu.*

Bucchianeri, M. M., Eisenberg, M. E., Wall, M. M., Piran, N., & Neumark-Sztainer, D. (2014). Multiple types of Harassment: Associations with emotional well-being and unhealthy behaviors in adolescents. *Journal of Adolescent Health, 54*(6), 724–729.

Burton, L. J. (2015). Underrepresentation of women in sport leadership: A review of research. *Sport Management Review, 18*(2), 155–165.

Calogero, R., & Pedrotty, K. (2004). The practice and process of healthy exercise: An investigation of the treatment of exercise abuse in women with eating disorders. *Eating Disorders: The Journal of Treatment and Prevention, 12*, 273–291.

Calogero, R., & Pedrotty, K. (2007). Daily practice for mindful exercise. In L. L'Abate (Ed.), *Low cost approach to promote physical and mental health: Theory, research, and practice* (pp. 141–160). NY: Springer.

Cammarota, J., & Fine, M. (2008). Youth participatory action research: A pedagogy for transformational resistance. In J. Cammarota, & M. Fine (Eds.), *Revolutionizing education: Youth participatory action research in motion*. New York, NY: Routledge.

Carie, T. R., Fyfe-Johnson, A. L., Breuner, C. C., & Marshall, M. A. (2010). Randomized clinicaltrial of yoga in the treatment of eating disorders. *Journal of Adolescent Health, 46*(4), 346–351.

Collins, R. L. (2011). Content analysis of gender roles in media: Where are we now and where should we go? *Sex Roles, 64*, 290–298.

Cook-Cottone, C. (2006). The attuned representation model for the primary prevention of eating disorders: An overview for school psychologists. *Psychology in the Schools, 43*, 223–230.

Crossley, N. (1995). Merleau-Ponty, the elusive body and carnal sociology. *Body and Society, 1*, 43–63.

D'Andrea, W., Bergholz, L., Fortunato, A., & Spinazzola, J. (2013). Play to the whistle: A pilot investigation of a sports-based intervention for traumatized girls in residential treatment. *Journal of Family Violence, 28*(7), 739–749.

Daniels, E. A. (2009a). The invisibility of women athletes in magazines for teen girls. *Women in Sport and Physical Activity Journal, 18*, 14–24.

Daniels, E. A. (2009b). Sex objects, athletes, and sexy athletes: How media representations of women athletes can impact adolescent girls and young women. *Journal of Adolescent Research, 24*, 399–422.

Daniels, E. A. (2016). Replacing sexy and skinny with strong and powerful: How feminis-tresearch on media depictions of women can effect change. In T.-A. Roberts, N. Curtin, L. Cortina, & L. E. Duncan (Eds.), *Best perspectives on building a better psychological science of gender* (pp. 257–274). Switzerland: Springer.

Daniels, E. A., & Sherman, A. M. (2016). Model vs. military pilot: A mixed methods study of adolescents' attitudes toward women in varied occupations. *Journal of Adolescent Research, 31*(2), 176–201.

Dittmar, H., Halliwell, E., & Ives, S. (2006). Does Barbie make girls want to be thin? The effect of experimental exposure to images of dolls on the body image of 5-to 8-year old girls. *Developmental Psychology, 42*, 283–292.

Dubecki, L. (February 08, 2007). *Skimpy dress code deals a body blow to netball numbers*. Melbourne, Australia: The Age. Retrieved from: http://www.theage.com.au/news/national/skimpy-dress-code-deals-a-body-blow-to-netball-numbers/2007/02/07/1170524164114.html.

Eisenberg, M. E., Olson, R. E., Neumark-Sztainer, D., Story, M., & Bearinger, L. H. (2004). Correlations between family meals and psychosocial well-being among adolescents. *Archives of Pediatrics and Adolescence, 158*(8), 792–796.

Fine, M. (1988). Sexuality, schooling, and adolescent females: The missing discourse of desire. *Harvard Educational Review, 58*, 29–53.

Fink, J. S., & Kensicki, L. J. (2002). An imperceptible difference: Visual and textual constructions of femininity in sports illustrated and sports illustrated for women. *Mass Communication and Society, 5*, 317–339.

Fishman, D. B. (1999). *The case for pragmatic psychology*. New York: New York University Press.

Fonow, M. M., & Cook, J. (1991). *Beyond methodology: Feminist scholarship as lived research*. Bloomington, IN: Indiana University Press.

Frazer, R. (June 16, 2016). *Sexism in politics 2016: What can we learn so far from media portrayals of Hillary Clinton and Latin American female leaders? Council on Hemispheric Affairs*. Retrieved from: http://www.coha.org/sexism-in-politics-2016-what-can-we-learn-so-far-from-media-portrayals-of-hillary-clinton-and-latin-american-female-leaders/.

Grossman, A. H., & D'Augelli, A. R. (2006). Transgender youth: Invisible and vulnerable. *Journal of Homosexuality, 51*(1), 111–128.

Haines, J., Neumark-Sztainer, D., Perry, C. L., Hannan, P. J., & Levine, M. P. (2006). V.I.K. (Very important kids): A school-based program designed to reduce teasing and unhealthy weight-control behaviors. *Health Education Research: Theory and Practice, 21*, 884–895.

Halpern, D. F., Benbow, C. P., Geary, D. C., Gur, R. C., Hyde, J. S., & Morton, A. G. (2007). The science of sex differences in science and mathematics. *Psychological Science in the Public Interest, 8*(1), 1–51.

Harned, M. S., & Fitzgerald, L. F. (2002). Understanding a link between sexual harassment and eating disorder symptoms: A mediational analysis. *Journal of Consulting and Clinical Psychology, 70*, 1170–1181.

Hart, L. M., Damiano, S. R., Chittleborough, P., Paxton, S. J., & Jorm, A. F. (2014). Parenting to prevent body dissatisfaction and unhealthy eating patterns in preschool children: A Delphi consensus study. *Body Image, 11*, 418–425.

Hart, L. M., Cornell, C., Damiano, S. R., & Paxton, S. J. (2015). Parents and prevention: A systematic review of interventions involving parents that aim to prevent body dissatisfaction or eating disorders. *International Journal of Eating Disorders, 48*, 157–169.

Hill Collins, P. (2000). *Black feminist thought: Knowledge, consciousness, and the politics of empowerment* (2nd ed.). New York, NY: Routledge.

Hill, C., Corbett, C., & St Rose, A. (2010). *Why so few? Women in sciences, technology, engineering, and mathematics*. American Association of University Women. Retrieved from: https://www.aauw.org/files/2013/02/Why-So-Few-Women-in-Science-Technology-Engineering-and-Mathematics.pdf.

hooks, b (2000). *Feminism is for everybody: Passionate politics*. London: Pluto Press.

Hyde, J. S. (2014). Gender similarities and differences. *Annual Review of Psychology, 65*(3), 373–398.

Jordan, J. V. (2010). Relational-cultural therapy. In *Theories of psychotherapy series*. Washington DC: American Psychological Association.

Katzman, M. A., & Lee, S. (1997). Beyond body image: The integration of feminist and transcultural theories in the understanding of self starvation. *International Journal of Eating Disorders, 22*, 385–394.

Kawachi, I., Kennedy, B. P., Gupta, V., & Prothrow-Stith, D. (1999). Women's status and the health of women and men: A view from the states. *Social Sciences and Medicine, 48*(1), 21–32.

Koller, D. L. (2010). Not just one of the boys: A post-feminist critique of title IX's vision for gender equity in sports. *Connecticut Law Review, 43*(2), 401–456.

Langford, R., Bonell, C. P., Jones, H. E., Pouliou, T., Murphy, S. M., Waters, E., & Campbell, R., et al. (2014). The WHO health promoting school framework for improving the health and well-being of students and their academic achievement. *Cochrane Database of Systematic Reviews, 4*:CD008958 (published online). Retrieved from: http://onlinelibrary.wiley.com/doi/10.1002/14651858.CD008958.pub2/pdf.

Lee, M., Ata, R. N., & Brannick, M. T. (2014). Malleability of weight-biased attitudes and beliefs: A meta-analysis of weight bias reduction interventions. *Body Image, 11*, 251–259.

Legge, R. (2009). If I am thin, I am safe: Speaking through the body following trauma. In O. Oulanova, I. Stein, A. Rai, M. Hammer, & P. Poulin (Eds.), *Within and beyond borders: Critical multicultural counselling in practice (pp. 84–92). Critical multicultural series*. Toronto, ON: University of Toronto, OISE. Retrieved from: http://www.oise.utoronto.ca/cdcp/.

MacKinnon, C. A. (1989). *Towards a feminist theory of the state*. Cambridge MA: Harvard University Press.

Male violence against women in intimate relationships in Iceland. (2012). Iceland: Ministry of Welfare. Retrieved from: https://eng.velferdarraduneyti.is/media/rit-og-skyrslur2012/Ofbeldi_gegn_konum_enska_feb_2012.pdf.

McVey, G. L., Gusella, J., Tweed, S., & Ferrari, M. (2009). A controlled evaluation of web-based training for teachers and public health practitioners on the prevention of eating disorders. *Eating Disorders: Journal of Treatment and Prevention, 17*, 1–26.

Merleau-Ponty, M. (1962). *Phenomenology of perception* (C. Smith, Trans.). New York: Humanities.

Neumark-Sztainer, D., Eisenberg, M. E., Fulkerson, J. A., Story, M., & Larson, N. I. (2008). Family meals and disordered eating in adolescents: Longitudinal findings from project EAT. *Archives of Pediatrics and Adolescent Medicine, 162*(1), 17–22.

Oakley, M. A., Addison, S. C., Piran, N., Johnston, G. J., Damianakis, M., Curry, J., et al. (2013). Outcome study of brief relational-cultural therapy in a women's mental health and body strategies. *International Journal of Eating Disorders, 41*, 134–142.

Ogden, P., Minton, K., & Pain, C. (2006). *Trauma and the body: A sensorimotor approach to psychotherapy*. New York: W.W. Norton.

Older women and poverty. *Woman View, 19*(9), (March 30, 2016) Sargent Shriver National center on poverty law. Retrieved from: http://www.ncdsv.org/SSNCPL_Woman-View-Older-Women-and-Poverty_3-30-2016.pdf.

Paxton, R., Estabrooks, P., & Dzewaltowsky, D. (2004). Attraction to physical activity mediates the relationship between perceived competence and physical activity in youth. *Research Quarterly for Exercise and Sport, 75*, 107–111.

Piran, N. (1995). Prevention: Can early lessons lead to a delineation of an alternative model? A critical look at prevention with school children. *Eating Disorders: The Journal of Treatment and Prevention, 3*(1), 28–36.

Piran, N. (1999a). Eating disorders: A trial of prevention in a high risk school setting. *Journal of Primary Prevention, 20*(1), 75–90.

Piran, N. (1999b). The reduction of preoccupation with body weight and shape in schools: A feminist approach. In N. Piran, M. P. Levine, & C. Steiner-Adair (Eds.), *Preventing eating disorders: A handbook of interventions and special challenges* (pp. 148–150). Philadelphia: Brunner/Mazel (Taylor & Francis Group).

Piran, N. (1999c). On the move from tertiary to secondary and primary prevention: Working with an elite dance school. In N. Piran, M. P. Levine, & C. Steiner-Adair (Eds.), *Preventing eating disorders: A handbook of interventions and special challenges* (pp. 256–269). Philadelphia: Brunner/Mazel (Taylor & Francis Group).

Piran, N. (2001). Re-inhabiting the body from the inside out: Girls transform their school environment. In D. L. Tolman, & M. Brydon-Miller (Eds.), *From subjects to subjectivities: A handbook of interpretive and participatory methods* (pp. 218–238). New York: New York University Press.

Piran, N. (2004). Teachers: On 'being' prevention. *Eating Disorders: The Journal of Treatment and Prevention, 12*, 1–9.

Piran, N. (2010). A feminist perspective on risk factor research and on the prevention of eating disorders. *Eating Disorders, 18*, 183–198.

Piran, N. (2015). New possibilities in the prevention of eating disorders: The introduction of positive body image measures. *Body Image, 14*, 146–157.

Piran, N. (2016a). Embodied possibilities and disruptions: The emergence of the experience of embodiment construct from qualitative studies with girls and women. *Body Image, 18*, 43–60.

Piran, N. (2016b). Embodied paths in aging: Body journeys towards enhanced agency and self-attunement. *Women and Therapy, 39*, 186–201.

Piran, N., & Thompson, S. (2008). A study of the Adverse Social Experiences model to the development of eating disorders. *International Journal of Health Promotion and Education, 46*(2), 65–71.

Pomeranz, J. L. (2008). A historical analysis of public health, the law, and stigmatized social groups: The need for both obesity and weight bias legislation. *Obesity: A Research Journal, 16*(S2), S93–S103.

Provencher, V., Begin, C., Temblay, A., Mengeau, L., Boivin, S., & Lenieux, S. (2007). Short-term effects of a "health-at-every-size" approach on eating behaviors and appetite ratings. *Obesity, 15*(4), 957–966.

Puhl, R. M., Andreyeva, T., & Bronwell, K. D. (2008). Perceptions of weight discrimination: Prevalence and comparison to race and gender discrimination in America. *International Journal of Obesity, 32*, 992–1000.

Puhl, R. M., Himmelstein, M. S., Gorin, A. A., & Suh, Y. J. (2017). Missing the target: Including perspectives of women with overweight and obesity to inform stigma-reduction strategies. *Obesity Science and Practice, 3*(1), 25–35.

Rice, K., Prichard, I., Tiggeemann, M., & Slate, A. (2016). Exposure to Barbie: Effects on thin-ideal internalization, body esteem, and body dissatisfaction among young girls. *Body Image, 19*, 142–149.

Riotta, C. (2017, June 14). Jeff Sessions knocked 'Hysteria' out of Kamala Harris, former Trump adviser says. Retrieved from: http://www.newsweek.com/kamala-harris-jeff-sessions-russia-probe-questions-donald-trump-putin-625679.

Rodgers, R. F., & Chabrol, H. (2009). Parental attitudes, body image disturbance and disordered eating amongst adolescents and young adults: A review. *European Eating Disorders Review*, *17*, 137–151.

Rodgers, R. F., Ziff, S., Lowy, A. S., Yu Ba, K., & Austin, S. B. (2017). Results of a strategic science study to inform policies targeting extreme thinness standards in the fashion industry. *International Journal of Eating Disorders*, *50*(3), 284–292.

Rothschild, B. (2000). *The body remembers: The psychophysiology of trauma and trauma treatment*. New York: W.W. Norton.

Schultz, J. (2005). Reading the catsuit: Serena Williams and the production of blackness at the 2002 U.S. Open. *Journal of Sport and Social Issues*, *29*, 338–357.

Scime, M., Cook-Cottone, C., Kane, L., & Watson, T. (2006). Group prevention of eating disorders with fifth-grade females: Impact on body dissatisfaction, drive for thinness, and media influence. *Eating Disorders: The Journal of Treatment and Prevention*, *14*, 143–155.

Senn, C. Y., Gee, S. S., & Thake, J. (2011). Emancipatory sexuality education and sexual assault resistance: Does the former enhance the latter? *Psychology of Women Quarterly*, *35*, 72–91.

Senn, C. Y., Eliasziw, M., Barata, P. C., Thurston, W. E., Newby-Clark, I. R., Radtke, H. L., et al. (2015). Efficacy of a sexual assault resistance program for university women. *New England Journal of Medicine*, *372*, 2326–2335.

Senne, J. (2016). Examination of gender equity and female participation in sport. *The Sport Journal*, *19*, 1–10.

Sherman, A. M., & Zurbriggen, E. L. (2014). Boys can be anything: Effect of Barbie play on girls' career cognitions. *Sex Roles*, *70*, 195–208.

Shore, A. (1994). *Affect regulation and the origin of the self: The neurobiology of emotional development*. Hillsdale, NJ: Lawrence Erlbaum Press.

Slonje, R., Smith, P. K., & Frisén, A. (2013). The nature of cyberbullying, and strategies for prevention. *Computers in Human Behavior*, *29*(1), 26–32.

Smith, S. L., Choueiti, M., Prescott, A., & Pieper, K. (2012). *Gender roles & occupations: A look at character attributes and job-related aspirations in film and television*. Retrieved from: https://seejane.org/wp-content/uploads/full-study-gender-roles-and-occupations-v2.pdf.

Spruit, A., Assink, M., van Vugt, E., van der Put, C., & Stams, G. J. (2016). The effects of physical activity interventions on psychosocial outcomes in adolescents: A meta-analytic review. *Clinical Psychology Review*, *45*, 56–71.

Stice, E., Marti, N., Spoor, S., Presnell, K., & Shaw, H. (2008). Dissonance and healthy weight eating disorder prevention programs: Long-term effects from a randomized efficacy trial. *Journal of Consulting and Clinical Psychology*, *76*, 329–340.

Tagay, S., Schlottbohm, E., Reyes-Rodriguez, M. L., Repic, N., & Senf, W. (2014). Eating disorders, trauma, PTSD, and psychosocial resources. *Eating Disorders: The Journal of Treatment and Prevention*, *22*(1), 33–49.

Teall, T., & Piran, N. (August 2015). Embodiment scales for women: A psychometric study of the experience of embodiment scale. In *Poster presented at the American psychological association annual convention, Toronto*.

Tebes, J. K., Kaufman, J. S., & Connell, C. M. (2003). The evaluation of prevention and health promotion programs. In T. P. Gullotta, & M. Bloom (Eds.), *Encyclopedia of primary prevention and health promotion* (pp. 42–61). New York: Kluwer Academic/Plenum Publishers.

The Global Gender Gap Report. (2015). *World economic forum*. Retrieved from: http://reports.weforum.org/global-gender-gap-report-2015/.

Tjaden, P., & Thoennes, N. (November 2000). *Full report of the prevalence, incidence, and consequences of violence against women*. Washington, D.C.: U.S. Department of Justice, Office of Justice Programs, National Institute of Justice. Retrieved from: https://www.ncjrs.gov/pdffiles1/nij/183781.pdf.

Tolman, D. L. (2002). *Dilemmas of desire: Teenage girls talk about sexuality*. Cambridge, MA: Harvard University Press.

Top 10 Most gender equal countries in the world. (2016). University Women of Europe. Retrieved from: https://uweboard.wordpress.com/2016/02/28/top-10-most-gender-equal-countries-in-the-world/.

Tremonti, A. M. (February 14, 2017). *Female politicians speak out about sexist, violent cyberbullying*. *The Current, Canadian Broadcasting Corporation*. Retrieved from: http://www.cbc.ca/radio/thecurrent/the-current-for-february-14-2017-1.3981592/female-politicians-speak-out-about-sexist-violent-cyberbullying-1.3981651.

Ussher, J. M., & Perz, J. (2010). Gender differences in self-silencing and psychological distress in informal cancer carers. *Psychology of Women Quarterly*, *34*, 228–242.

van der Kolk, B. A. (1996). The complexity of adaptation to trauma: Self-regulation, stimulus discrimination, and characterological development. In B. A. van der Kolk, A. C. McFarlane, & L. Weisaeth (Eds.), *Traumatic stress: The effects of overwhelming experience on mind, body, and society* (pp. 182–213). New York, NY: Guilford Press.

Violence against women (VAW). (2008). *Philippines commission on women*. Retrieved from: http://www.pcw.gov.ph/focus-areas/violence-against-women.

Wilksch, S. M., & Wade, T. D. (2009). Reduction of shape and weight concern in young adolescents: A 30-month controlled evaluation of a media literacy program. *Journal of the American Academy of Child and Adolescent Psychiatry*, *48*, 652–661.

Wilksch, S., Paxton, S. J., Byrne, S., Austin, S. B., McLean, S., Thompson, K., et al. (2014). Prevention across the spectrum: A randomized controlled trial of three programs to reduce risk factors for both eating disorders and obesity. *Psychological Medicine*, *45*(9), 1–13.

Wonder Women, & Macho Men. (August 22, 2015). *The Economist*. Retrieved from: *http://www.economist.com/news/americas/21661800-latin-american-women-are-making- great-strides-culture-not-keeping-up-wonder-women-and*.

Young, A. M., Grey, M., & Boyd, C. J. (2009). Adolescents' experiences of sexual assault by peers: Prevalence and nature of victimization occurring within and outside of school. *Journal of Youth and Adolescence*, *38*, 1072–1083.

Zschucke, E., Gaudlitz, K., & Ströhle, A. (2013). Exercise and physical activity in mental disorders: Clinical and experimental evidence. *Journal of Preventive Medicine and Public Health*, *46*(Suppl. 1), S12–S21.

Appendix 1: Demographic Summaries of Participants in the Three Interview Studies

GIRLS STUDY

This study included 87 interviews with 27 girls, who were interviewed 3–4 times over a 5-year period (years 1, 2, 4, 5): 11 girls were 9–11 years old, and 16 girls were 13–14 years old during the first phase of the study. Girls were interviewed in years 1, 2, 4, and 5 of the study. Of these girls, 14 were from working, and 13 from middle-class background. 11 girls resided in rural settings and 16 in urban centers. In terms of ethnicity: 4 were of Aboriginal, 1 of African, 1 of Caribbean, 1 of Roma, 2 of Hispanic, 4 of white East European heritage, and 14 of white West European heritage. All girls described heterosexual interests and were cisgender. All girls resided in Canada during the time of the study. 2 girls were immigrants from two East European countries, and 6 additional girls had parents who immigrated to Canada from the Caribbean (1), Europe—Hispanic heritage (2), Middle East (2), and another Western country (1). In terms of family composition, 3 were living with mother and lesbian partner, 6 were with single parents (5 with mothers), 4 with mother and stepfather, 12 with biological mother and father, and 2 with adoptive parents.

YOUNG WOMEN STUDY

This study involved 30 interviews with 11 women, ages 20–27. Of those, 9 took part in three interviews, 1 in two interviews, and 1 in one interview. All women resided in Canada during the time of the study. Most (8) women grew up in urban settings, and most (7) described their background as working class while the rest as middle class. Regarding ethnic heritage, 2 were of Asian, 2 of Caribbean, 1 of Hispanic, and 6 of white European heritage. 7 women described their sexual orientation as heterosexual, 3 as bisexual, and 1 as lesbian. All young women were cisgender. 5 women had high school diplomas, 4 an undergraduate degree, and 2 a graduate degree. 3 women were working full time, 2 were full-time students, 5 were working part time, and 1 was on a disability allowance.

OLDER WOMEN STUDY

This study included 54 interviews with 31 women, ages 50–68 who resided in Canada during the time of the study. Of these women, 23 were interviewed two times and 8 one time. Of these women, 8 were from a working-class background, 16 from a middle-class background, and 7 from a middle–upper-class background. 10 were residing in rural and 21 in urban sites. In terms of ethnic heritage, 5 were of Asian, 1 of African, 2 of Caribbean, and 23 were of white European heritage. About half (18) of these women were born in Canada. Most women (26) described themselves as heterosexual (1 with same-sex experiences), 3 as lesbian, 1 as bisexual, and 1 as bi/lesbian. In terms of gender identity, all were cisgender with 1 participant describing herself as a "lesbian woman/slightly transsexual." In terms of the highest educational degree attained: 3 completed elementary school, 4 high school, 6 college, 8 a university undergraduate degree, 9 a master's degree, and 1 a doctoral degree. 13 women were working full time, 2 were working part time, 2 were unemployed, 11 were retired, 2 were on disability allowance, and 1 described herself as a "homemaker." In terms of relationship status, 18 were married/partnered/common law, 11 divorced/separated, and 2 were widowed. Most (24) had children. About half had physical challenges, and 4 had mental health challenges requiring treatment.

Index

'*Note*: Page numbers followed by "t" indicate tables.'

G

H

I

L

M

CPI Antony Rowe
Eastbourne, UK
April 06, 2021